BLOOD
AND
THUNDER

BLOOD AND THUNDER

THE BOYS OF ETON COLLEGE AND THE FIRST WORLD WAR

ALEXANDRA CHURCHILL

For my Grandad, who would have loved sharing this
experience with me: December 1929–December 1995

And for 'Mummy', who is so many miles away but is always
in my heart and never far from my thoughts.

First published 2014

The History Press
The Mill, Brimscombe Port
Stroud, Gloucestershire, GL5 2QG
www.thehistorypress.co.uk

© Alexandra Churchill, 2014

The right of Alexandra Churchill to be identified as the Author
of this work has been asserted in accordance with the
Copyright, Designs and Patents Act 1988.

British Library Cataloguing in Publication Data.
A catalogue record for this book is available from the British Library.

ISBN 978 0 7524 9003 8

Typesetting and origination by The History Press
Printed in Great Britain

Contents

Acknowledgements

First and foremost thanks is due to the Provost and Fellows of Eton College. I would also like to thank, for tireless efforts that now span a number of years and without which this project would have been impossible, Penny Hatfield, former College Archivist, Jackie Tarrant-Barton of the Old Etonian Association, Roddy Fisher in the Eton College Photographic Archive and Mrs Christine Vickers, latterly of the same, and the staff of College Library.

The enthusiasm for commemorating their school's contribution to the Great War has been overwhelming amongst Old Etonians and the families of those that fell. In particular I would like to extend special thanks to Sir Andrew Leggatt, proud nephew of Logie, for his persistent encouragement and kindness in ensuring that this remarkable young man's story and that of his friends was given the platform that it so richly deserved. Additionally I would like to thank David Napier for his support and an enthusiasm for the project that far exceeded his donation of material concerning his father. Also Benjamin Carey, great nephew of Henry Dundas, and his parents, the late Mr Simon and Mrs Renata Carey, for not only providing me with rich material but for giving me such freedom to write about a very special young man and to share his vibrant personality on a public stage.

My thanks also to the late Dr J.G.C. Blacker, Sam Cholmeley, Mike Dottridge, John Drummond, the Drake Family, the Fleming Family, Henry Gold, Jerôme Gonçalves, Antony Grant, Constance Hargreaves, Nick Kaplowich, Gordon Lee-Steere, Willie Manners, Katharine Meynell, Bruno Schröder and Debbie Mesquita, Simon Shaw, The late Mr J. Shaw-Stewart, Pamela Shearn, the Stockdale Family, Magnus Spence and Anthony Whitaker.

In addition I would like to thank the staff/archivists of the following organisations: the British Library, the Commonwealth War Graves Commission, the Royal Air Force Museum, the National Army Museum, the Imperial War Museum, 1st The Queen's Dragoon Guards Heritage Trust & 'Firing Line' The Museum of the Welsh Soldier, Cardiff Castle, Summer Fields School, Oxford, the Dragon School, Oxford, Oxford University, Balliol College, Oxford, Trinity College, Cambridge, Magdalen College, Oxford and Harvard University.

My sincerest thanks to Andy Pay and Jonathan Saunders for the many thousands of miles driven backwards and forwards across the Western Front in search of the final resting places of literally hundreds of Old Etonians. Additionally, both of them have regularly contributed their time, knowledge, research, moral support and possibly even their sanity in the pursuance of this project when they have no personal connection to Eton College.

I also owe a debt of gratitude for the unwavering support of Eric Sauder, Peter Devitt of the RAF Museum, John Hayes-Fisher, Paul Reed and Joshua Levine (particularly in respect of his assistance in sourcing Etonians involved in aerial warfare and the loan of his research material). Also to Sophie Bradshaw at The History Press for believing in this book before it existed, and Lauren Newby for the time and effort spent turning it into the finished article.

For advice and use of their own work/material as well as some outstanding research: Robin Schäfer, of the German Society for Military Research, Bastian Atzger, Katya Airapetiants, Tom Coghlan, Brian Curragh, Simon Ball, Andrew Birkin, Andrew Dally, Peter Doyle, Peter Hart, Allegra Jordan, Andy Lonergan, Jerry Murland and Geoff Whitfield.

I wish to thank Sam and John Sawyer, Garry Brown, Graham Bush, Andrew Holmes, Carol, Scott, Emma, Arnie, Liz and all the others that have encouraged me and pushed me to carry on working all over Europe; in particular Pete and Mark, the self-appointed phone police on the way to Leeds, without whom the Somme chapters would not exist. Win or lose up the Blues. Also Derek Lee, Lesley Castle, Chris Ford, Karen Perkins and the team at Lees Chartered Accountants; James Hall, Karl Houghton, Trudie Lonergan, Timothy McCracken, Conor Reeves, Inger Sheil, Nicholas Hellen and Adam Young.

Finally I wish to thank mother for all of her encouragement and for not batting an eyelid when her only daughter shunned romantic comedies and all girly pursuits for a life of military history and ftball.

Eton Glossary

4 June – George III was a notable patron of the school and his birthday is given over to festivities in his honour. Prior to the Great War the school would fill with invitees and relatives of the boys for a combination of speeches, cricket and impressive teas during the day. In the evening there would be a grand procession of boats and a fireworks display.

Fagging – A period of servitude that each boy would undertake at the beginning of his time at Eton. Broadly speaking a younger boy (a fag) would be allocated to an older boy (a fagmaster) and would undertake general tasks and errands for him (fagging). The practice was abolished in the 1970s.

King's Scholar / Colleger / Tug – At any one time, as dictated by the school's founder Henry VI in the fifteenth century, there is space for seventy Foundation Scholars at Eton College. They live off the main schoolyard and are nicknamed 'Collegers' or sometimes 'Tugs'. Entrance is by examination and these boys have the initials 'KS' after their name throughout their time at Eton. Rather than say they live in the house of a particular Master, it is termed that they are 'in College'.

Lord's – Since the turn of the nineteenth century the boys of Eton have traditionally taken on the boys of Harrow School in an annual game of cricket at Lord's. Prior to the Great War the match lasted for two days in July and attracted crowds in the region of 20,000. It was a social event to rival Ascot and Henley.

Newcastle Scholarship – The most prestigious academic contest at Eton, the scholarship was founded by the Duke of Newcastle in the 1820s. Prior to the Great War it comprised a set of competitive examinations on Classics and Divinity and was extremely stringent. The winner was titled the 'Newcastle Scholar' for that year and received a monetary award. The runner-up was the 'Medallist' and a list of boys who had performed well would be one of the 'Newcastle Select'.

Oppidan – An Oppidan is one of the 900 or so boys who are not King's Scholars. They live in the myriad of boarding houses across the road from the original school buildings.

'Pop' / The Eton Society – A debating society founded at the school in 1811. Traditionally Pop comprised about thirty members. Apart from a few ex-officio places, admission is by election and is highly coveted.

The Wall Game – A type offtball specific to Eton. Played up against a wall in College it is traditionally more associated with King's Scholars. On St Andrew's Day every year though, the Collegers play a match against the Oppidans.

Introduction

Why do the pupils of Eton College who served in the Great War matter more than anybody else? The answer is that they don't. But describing the war through the eyes of her old boys enables a unique, personal retelling of a conflict approaching its centenary. This war continues to capture interest despite the fact that it has all but slipped out of living memory.

That is not to say that one could not do just that using a group of combatants from any number of organisations, or indeed any other major British public school, but that will fall to someone else. This was my choice and for the purpose of this volume it just so happens that the soldiers, sailors, airmen, prisoners, politicians and civilians whose experiences fill its pages all happened to have had one thing in common. Their transformations from schoolboys to participants, whether direct, interrupted, reluctant or entirely involuntary, began on the banks of the Thames as they worked and played in the shadow of a grand medieval chapel and 450 years of history.

Eton's iconic chapel, its clock tower and its playing fields have seen their fair share of conflict in the past five-and-a-half centuries; whether it be Royalist cannons bombarding Windsor Castle from the grounds during the Civil War, or Luftwaffe bombs being run out of harm's way by brave masters. Her founder, Henry VI, was undone by his own wars; those between the houses of Lancaster and York in the mid-fifteenth century and defeat almost saw the end of his vision of a college. Eton survived and for half a millennia has, in military terms, supplied primarily the army with Old Etonians, or 'OEs'. One was unceremoniously beheaded during the Wars of the Roses and more met their end two centuries later when the New Model Army swept away the monarchy. An Etonian died at the Battle of Buda in 1686 as the Ottoman Empire was driven out of Hungary; at least one too during the American War of Independence. Nearly fifty OEs perished in the shambles that was the Crimean War, and at the end of the nineteenth century, old boys who had not taken up a military occupation volunteered in large numbers for the Boer Wars. In fact, 1,424 Old Etonians went to South Africa and 129 died in a conflict that was to become aftnote to the numbers who sacrificed their lives when King and country came calling a decade or so later. Neither was the Great War the end of the Etonian contribution to armed conflict. More than 700 former pupils would fall during the Second World War, followed in turn by those who perished in the Far East in the years following 1945. Old Etonians saw distinguished service in the Falklands and the cycle has sadly continued into the 21st century. On 22 April 2003 Lieutenant Alexander Tweedie died as a result of wounds received in Iraq.

It was the most famous of military Etonians, the Duke of Wellington no less, who (apparently) claimed that the Battle of Waterloo was won on the playing fields of Eton. That he meant this in terms of the spirit engendered by the public school emphasis on sporting achievement is more probable than the literal meaning. Whatever sentiment he was trying to convey as he passed by a cricket match at the school after his own sons had passed through her boarding houses, the response of Etonians a century after his own victory over Napoleon would not have disappointed him. In fact, his own great-grandson would be one of fifteen OEs to fall on 29 October 1914 alone.

Dense populations of Old Etonians, as they had pre-war, would populate the Guards' regiments, the Cavalry, the Rifle Brigade and the King's Royal Rifle Corps in particular. Many would embrace new aspects of industrialised warfare, flying above the battlefields and taking to them encased in tanks; but the truth is that the nearly 6,000 old boys involved in the Great War, not including those serving or forming part of the government, represented themselves and their school in a never ending spread. From Highland regiments to the Imperial Camel Corps, the Devonshire or Gloucestershire Yeomanry to, of course, the Royal Navy; hundreds of units found within their ranks at least one OE during the course of the Great War. The overwhelming majority were officers. Some enlisted as privates but most inevitably found a commission sooner or later. Only a tiny fraction of Old Etonians who fell did so serving in the ranks.

Whilst Eton College is iconically British, her doors were not closed to boys from abroad and it was not only home forces that were represented by former pupils. Whether by national allegiance or circumstance, armies from all corners of the Empire found Etonian representatives, be it Canada, Australia, New Zealand or India. Beyond the influence of the British flag, OEs wore the uniforms of the United States, Italy, and France as well as Serbia and Russia. Neither did every Etonian represent the same cause, for one solitary boy would serve with the Kaiser's army.

It stands to reason then, that the war experiences of Old Etonians were not limited to the trenches of the Western Front. As it was for the rest of the world, so it was in microcosm. The Etonian experience of the Great War was truly global. As well as France and Flanders, old boys fought and died at Gallipoli, in Africa as well as the Western Desert and Egypt; in Palestine, Mesopotamia and Persia, in the waters of the Atlantic and the Baltic and on fronts in the Balkans, the Alps, India, Siberia and Northern Russia.

The first Old Etonians to see action were professional soldiers, regulars and reservists who had made a choice to answer a call to arms. With these and close on their heels came the Territorials, the Yeomanry; part-time soldiers who volunteered to go abroad. Eton's old boys not only swelled the ranks of the armed services and Sandhurst on the outbreak of war, but with them the colleges of Oxford and Cambridge. Members of Officer Training Corps, they knew as little of life in the wider world as they did of the realities of war when they followed their elder brothers and former schoolmates to war. And then there were the schoolboys themselves. Washed into the army on a wave of patriotism when war was declared, by 1916 it was a very different story. The Military Service Act, not enthusiasm, dictated a boy's path into the forces whether he wished to serve or not. The Old Etonian of this generation sat dejectedly in his house library or at the dinner table with his friends as his departure loomed. They debated regiments, not professions and spoke of where their futures might lie only in terms of which cap badge would adorn their uniforms. These boys marched straight out of school, into the army and then on to the battlefields before they had left their teenage years behind.

Wellington's great-grandson may strike a chord, as would Charles Dickens' grandson or the father of Bond author Ian Fleming, but a total of 1,168 Old Etonians are now known to have given their lives as a result of the Great War and the sons of clergymen, bankers, peers and businessmen were as valuable to those that knew them as the notable names.

That the surroundings of their education were privileged is undoubted. But privilege does not follow a man, or indeed a boy, on to the field of battle. Life or death is dictated by sheer dumb luck. Littered amongst the Victoria Crosses and the famous names are the muted ends of people's fathers and the as yet undiscovered heroism of sons and brothers. For that reason, this book is dedicated to the hundreds of fallen Etonians who have no space dedicated to them within it.

1

'God Grant I May Be Old Enough'

Gareth Hamilton-Fletcher was interested in international politics even at Eton. In addition to being a top-notch cricketer he was a talented linguist, carrying off school prizes in French and German. In 1909, at the age of 15, he wrote home to his mother on the subject of Germany. He had been reading about the Royal Navy in the *Daily Graphic*. 'Why are we deceived into thinking that Germany really means well to us?' he fumed. 'We are not really deceived; we only say so because it is a good excuse and we would rather go and have a game of golf or have a day's hunting. What fools we are!' Gareth didn't doubt for a moment that war was imminent. 'God grant I may be old enough to fight for my country when the time comes. God help us!'

Spy fever was at its zenith. Paranoia about the might of Germany and her intentions sent a chill through vast numbers of Britons. The Secret Intelligence Service, the forerunner to MI6, came into existence that year. A large part of their remit became, naturally, German naval construction and the arms race. If it seemed at all likely that war was about to break out then information on naval mobilisation and troop movements, especially in the northern German ports, would become an overwhelming priority.

Britain's new intelligence agency was tested thoroughly during the Agadir Crisis of 1911 when the Germans felt the wrath of France for landing a gunboat at the Moroccan port. Europe was spiralling ever closer toward was. Interested British parties began to panic about the disposition of German warships, whether or not they planned to attack the Royal Navy. The SIS was called in and the chief of army intelligence sent a man to Brussels to undertake some intelligence gathering activity at German North Sea ports.

A few weeks later his man was seized by the German authorities and detained on charges of espionage. Some accounts say he was dragged from his bed in the middle of the night, others that he was taken into custody whilst trying to dispose of a code book that had been planted on him by a German double agent in a public toilet.

The arrested man was an Old Etonian. Bertrand Stewart came from an established Scottish family. He himself was born in London and went to Walter Durnford's house at Eton in 1886. After Oxford he joined Markby, Stewart & Co. as a solicitor in London until the outbreak of the Boer War, when he enlisted in the Imperial Yeomanry and left for Africa.

Bertrand was indicative of the enthusiastic amateur gentleman plying the espionage trade just prior to the Great War. Working directly under the chief of the Secret Intelligence Service he had that summer been firstly to Nijmegen to contact an agent working in Germany. Unwisely he crossed the border with him and he had been gathering information in Hamburg, Cuxhaven and Bremerhaven before the authorities caught up with him. It was plausible that the book had been planted. The chief of the SIS speculated that the agent he had travelled with had sold him out, having been a decoy all along. 'It is annoying,' stated his associate, the Director of Naval Intelligence, 'but we must expect drawbacks such as these in this kind of business.'

Bertrand Stewart's trial by the Supreme Court of Germany opened at Leipzig on 31 January 1912. Throughout he continuously proclaimed his innocence amidst a media storm; claiming that he barely spoke enough German to order meals and to talk to natives at train stations and hotels. The charges against him mainly related to naval defences that he had apparently never seen. The only specific evidence, it was claimed, was that of a penniless ex-criminal in the employment of the prosecutors. After a trial lasting four days, Captain Stewart was nonetheless found guilty, which for all of his bluster he was, and he was sentenced to detention for three and a half years.

Before leaving the court Captain Stewart proudly declared to his captors that if their distinguished nation was ever at war with Britain, he hoped he would be fighting against them. As he was dragged away to serve his sentence at the fortress of Glatz, Europe was less than three years away from a monstrous industrialised war the likes of which the world had never seen. Bertrand, Gareth Hamilton-Fletcher and nearly 6,000 fellow Old Etonians, whether they wanted to or not, would get just such an opportunity to participate. Over 1,200 of them would not return.

2

'The Faces of Souls in Hell'

'The sky was just beginning to light up: a pale yellow streak had appeared in the east. The clouds were tinged with pink. In a few moments the horizon was ablaze, yellow, gold, orange and blood.' It was 5 August 1914, the end of a Bank Holiday weekend at Ramsgate. The day before had been bright, sunny, 'glorious' with a clear blue sky. Scores of families had flocked to the seaside but there were unsettled tones running underneath their careless frivolity. For three or four days there had been one strange word whispered by everyone … War. 'It sounded terrible enough, and yet, to the uninitiated, it was a word of excitement, it almost sounded romantic.'

The young man watching the sun rise had had a troubled night's sleep after news arrived that Britain had declared war on Germany. That morning he looked down on the crowds from the pier. 'It did not seem to make much difference whether there was war or not.' On the sand was 'a seething mass of humanity, happy bright faces, huddled together in a great jumble. The children jumped over one another, burying their heads in the sand and laughing. Below, in the calm sea there were little groups of yelling persons, bobbing up and down, knee deep in warm water.' As he watched them he was already uneasily settling on the prospect of offering his services to his country for the duration of the conflict. This restless Old Etonian was 21 years old. He would not see 24.

In August 1914 enthusiasm for war ripped through the ranks of Old Etonians and they prepared to fight in their hundreds. Anti-war sentiment was not generally found amongst old boys who were getting ready to depart for

France with the British Expeditionary Force. One OE from a military family had a way with words and he encapsulated the sentiment that many displayed when they scribbled their last letters home. He declared that if Britain failed to intervene 'we are as chicken-hearted a lot as ever existed … Nobody will ever help us or trust us again.'

Born in April 1880, another, Aubrey Herbert, was an unlikely volunteer who would be amongst the first Old Etonians to depart for war. A Member of Parliament, he had seen his fellow politicians in London as they had stumbled towards oblivion. Ashen, they had 'the faces of souls in hell'. A son of the 4th Earl of Carnarvon, it would be Aubrey's elder half-brother who would open Tutankhamen's tomb with Howard Carter in 1922. Aubrey was the eldest son of the earl's second marriage and his father doted on him. Lord Carnarvon died when his son was 10 and Aubrey was still being privately educated at 13 when his aunt began advocating a public school education. He arrived at Benson's house at Eton in 1893 with no experience of school life and crippled by awful eyesight.

Aubrey was practically blind. His mother had to employ the services of a tutor to go through Eton in his company, reading aloud to him throughout his time at school, though he was already showing a remarkable aptitude for languages, speaking fluent Italian and French, and good German. Owing to his disability though, his performance at school was moderate. He also found it hard to adjust to life in the house and found solace in spending his pocket money too quickly and adopting any pet he could find, be it jackdaws, squirrels or mice. On one occasion he discovered some larks in the town being kept in a 'dreadfully' small cage and conspired with two schoolmates to buy them and set them free.

In 1897 Aubrey went to Germany to undergo radical eye surgery and it had a massive impact on his life. The operation was carried out cautiously on one eye and he found that he could read for himself, distinguish people from across the room, even shoot. He went up to Oxford the following year to read history but was famed more than anything else for his climbing. One acquaintance remembered Aubrey, 'finger holds alone' and 40ft off the ground swinging from ledge to ledge along the tall houses on King Edward Street. It was not unusual for him to tap on the outside of a window and wave to the people inside three floors up. He once managed to get from Christ Church to Balliol by nothing but rooftops, gutters, window sills and pipes. T.E. Lawrence, a near contemporary and future acquaintance in Egypt, reminded Aubrey during the war of how he had been traversing rooftops and singing Italian love songs when he fell into a bank and was held up at gunpoint as a robber.

After Oxford Aubrey began a career in diplomacy, firstly in Tokyo and then in Constantinople. He travelled greatly in the years before the outbreak of war, taking in the United States, Canada, the Balkans, Africa, the Far East, Spain, Italy, Greece and Turkey as well as the far reaches of the Sultan's empire. His career as a diplomat lasted until 1905 when at the age of 25 Aubrey left Constantinople. He soon decided to resurrect his travelling and toured extensively through the Mediterranean, Arabia, Palestine, the Caucasus, Mesopotamia and India. Compelled by an agreement with his mother that he would settle down to life in politics he returned glumly to England.

By 1912 Aubrey had married and been elected as MP for Yeovil. He proved enthusiastic in his political endeavours; but within a year he was off again, this time to the Balkans, travelling from Vienna to Sarajevo and then on to Albania. He would fall wholeheartedly in love with this last country. At the conclusion of the First Balkan War, Aubrey assisted an Albanian delegation visiting London for a peace conference. This rendered him a national hero to the extent that he would twice be offered the throne. He toured the country in 1913 triumphantly, but politely declined the opportunity to become King of Albania.

With his eyesight, Aubrey never would have been passed fit for military service. He was, however, determined to take care of unfinished business, having missed out on the Boer War. Having volunteered to go to Africa, concerns about what the dry climate might do to his eyes compelled him not to go and he had long felt it a stain upon his honour. In August 1914 he resorted to buying a khaki uniform and attaching himself to the 1st Irish Guards as they marched out of barracks and headed for France. The battalion's commander was complicit and his presence was only revealed after their transport had sailed, but by then it was too late. With his fluency in multiple languages he was to act as an interpreter.

Another of the first OEs to report for embarkation with the British Expeditionary Force (BEF) but again not one of the most likely, was Walter George Fletcher. As war was declared he was with a contingent of over 500 Etonian boys and masters at Mytchett Farm near Aldershot with the Eton College Officer Training Corps. Every year, in addition to field days and parades the OTC, which provided the boys with basic military training, would congregate under the supervision of regulars with contingents from other public schools and universities for a two-week camp. In 1914 the camp rapidly broke up as it became apparent that war was imminent and as the regulars were mobilised the boys were turned out and sent back to school early.

George Fletcher should have been in the Navy. That was his parents' plan when they decked their middle son out in a little sailor suit as a child. He duly

made such an awful mess of it that his father Charles saw it as a bad omen and
began having second thoughts. When his brother piped up and said that actually
he wouldn't mind going to sea instead, the plan changed. George had always
had an interest in soldiering, having been at Oxford a member of the cavalry
section of the University OTC and an extremely keen territorial; or 'Terrier'.

The middle child in a family of three sons, George's father was a noted
historian and all three boys, Alexander 'Leslie', George and the youngest,
Reginald William, or 'Regie', were born and raised in Oxford and sent to
the Dragon School as day boys. Nicknamed 'Dormouse' within the family,
George had been educated at Eton as a King's Scholar like his father before
him; rowed with the VIII and had gone up to Balliol College, Oxford in 1906
on the fringes of a set of great minds that included the likes of Raymond
Asquith and Monsignor Ronald Knox.

Now 26, George was stocky, 'slightly ungainly' but memorable for his 'gor-
geous laugh'. Bubbly, witty, always with a good story to tell, he was passionate about climbing, travelling and Italy in particular. George had spent two
recent years teaching English in Schleswig and in addition to German he
also spoke French and Italian. In 1911 he returned home and took up a post
at Shrewsbury School. Unable to continue rowing due to a weak heart, he
endeared himself to the boys by coaching them on the river and threw himself fully into school life.

He found a happy home at Shrewsbury. Another OE, Evelyn Southwell,
remembered one particular night at the end of a winter term. They had sat
up most of the night drinking tea and marking exam papers. George left
them at 3 a.m. and started off across the river on his way home shouting
Die Meistersinger. They all lived together in his last term at New House, a
rowdy establishment full of unmarried masters where every month the lift
sank to the basement and shattered the unwashed crockery. The garden was a
jungle that belonged to their pet cat and dinner was so loud and argumenta-
tive that one of them was forced to make himself heard by chalking on the
wall 'you owe me £2 2s 6d' to another. His demand remained there until they
all moved out. George had left Shrewsbury in 1913 when the headmaster of
Eton, Edward Lyttelton, came calling. George couldn't resist returning to his
old school and he had just concluded his first summer back on the river and
was thoroughly enjoying life at his old school when war came.

Although George was not versed in nearly as many foreign tongues as
Aubrey Herbert, he was hopeful that the Army might make use of him too.
While he was making his intentions to go to war known a summons arrived
at Eton via telegram asking for he and two other young masters with linguistic

skills and he didn't hesitate. After a late-night meeting at the War Office he returned to Eton to say a hasty goodbye to his father, who came over from Oxford with supplies, and began getting ready to leave.

Once in London George and his colleagues were sent to Kensington Gardens, one of several sites where commandeered commercial vehicles were being deposited. Here they were issued with a motorbike each, or a 'smell' as George would always call it. Quite devastated that he would not be riding off to war on horseback, he found himself instead riding – 'smelling' – through Piccadilly Circus, along Oxford Street and up to Holborn where the manufacturers attempted to give them a crash course in maintenance. A mere four days after war had been declared, these three young masters congregated outside the War Office shortly after dawn. They jumped on their smells and rode off on an elbow-jarring adventure; a miniature convoy of post-Edwardian hell's angels in khaki awkwardly rattling their way to Southampton. They arrived ahead of most of the regular soldiers, drenched with rain and with raging headaches after being shaken all the way from London to the coast. They were now part of the 'Intelligence Corps', which they would soon find was as vague in composition and organisation as it was in name.

George's whirlwind dispatch to the south coast was the exception, rather than the rule. His ad-hoc recruitment and vague job description was nothing like the regimented, precise and well-rehearsed mobilisation that got hundreds of other OEs to the front. Excitement was building. A great number of Etonians populated the Guards regiments. The 2nd Battalion of the Grenadier Guards was at Wellington Barracks on the doorstep of Buckingham Palace when war was declared. Having been mobilised they were out on a route march in London the day before their departure when they passed the gates of the palace on their way home. Quite by chance, the king and queen wandered down to watch them pass by. Leading his platoon was 'Jack' Pickersgill-Cunliffe. The only son of a gentleman from Huntingdonshire he was less than a year out of Sandhurst and only two out of Eton. Not yet 20, bright and with a permanent smile on his face, he saluted proudly and was captured by a photographer as the battalion marched past His Majesty in fours and found their salutes returned by their king and Commander-in-Chief.

Many of the Etonians who had left the school for a career in the army before the war had joined the cavalry. There were fifteen mounted regiments mobilised at the outbreak of war, almost ten thousand men on horseback. The 9th Lancers were at Tidworth near Salisbury and before they left for war a photograph of its officers was taken that literally overflowed with Etonians, including three sets of brothers. Eleven pictured would die, a great many of

them before 1914 drew to a close, and of those nine had been educated at
Eton College.

Francis and Riversdale, or 'Rivy', Grenfell were identical twins in their
mid 30s. They came from an enormous family that had seen six of their
brothers go up to Eton before them and the family knew what impact war
could have on a household. Three boys had already fallen violently in the
service of their country, including one murdered during the Matabele rising
and another participating in the charge of the 12th Lancers at Omdurman.
The twins were devoted to each other. Both were 'simple' in their countenance, not stupid, but measured and quite calm; there was little fussiness
about them. Neither liked to blow his own trumpet and both thought a
great deal more of others than they did of their own glory. Being awarded
a gallantry medal was all but mortifying for Francis, whilst Rivy, despite
the fact that the twins were suffering a great deal of financial misfortune
themselves, spent his spare time on a charity he had set up for impover-
ished children. Their closeness as brothers had not restricted them to the
same career. Rivy was in business whilst Francis had begun army life in the
infantry. He never had any disdain for it but his heart was with the cavalry
and it was only financial constraints that prevented him from pursuing his
dream. Happily, circumstances changed and he joined the 9th Lancers in
1905. Mounted warfare became his passion and he filled endless notebooks
with tactics and observations gleaned from studying at home and abroad, and
observing French and German manoeuvres.

Although a civilian, Rivy shot out to Wiltshire at the mention of war.
Officially a member of the Buckinghamshire Yeomanry, he was a mounted
territorial and not committed to Foreign Service. He talked his way into the
9th Lancers as a reserve officer at lightning speed; determined to go to war
with his twin who was to command one of the regiment's three squadrons.

Douglas Harvey was required to do less fast talking than Rivy, for although
he was still at Cambridge he was already a reserve officer in the 9th Lancers
and he too would be going to war with his brother. Douglas and Francis;
or 'Lennie' as he was known, were considerably younger than the Grenfells.
Both in their early twenties, the Harveys had grown up in an architecturally
eccentric manor house in deepest Sussex, gone through Mr Byrne's house at
Eton together, and then Trinity College like their father before. Lennie, the
elder of the two, was apparently one of the nicest boys his house master had
ever had, with a gentle voice and a firm countenance.

Lennie had joined the Lancers straight after Cambridge and although it is
unclear what Douglas' aspirations were had the war not come, he was now

donning a uniform and pledging his allegiance to the Ninth once it had been declared. It is fair to say that neither of the Harveys were shrinking violets. Both were Captain of their House at Eton and commanded authority. In debates Lennie could argue the most ridiculous of points quite proudly whilst Douglas would beat the table with his pencil to illustrate what he was driving at, whether his schoolmates wished to hear it or not. Both were members of the 'Pop', both were accomplishedftballers and Lennie was a decent cricketer and runner too. Neither fell short academically either. Douglas especially was quite the intellectual, with a gift for sarcasm and a cracking sense of humour.

Although they came from a thoroughly unmilitary background, the Harveys now found themselves together in 'A' Squadron under the command of yet another Old Etonian, Douglas Lucas-Tooth. 'Lucas' had been in Walter Durnford's house with the Grenfell twins in the late 1890s. His temperament made him incredibly popular and reassuring as an officer. A veteran of the relief of Kimberley, he was Australian born and, receiving a Colonial Cadetship, had served in the New South Wales Mounted Infantry in South Africa before being commissioned into the Ninth at 20. A captain eight years later in 1908, he brought an air of serenity into battle with him. Francis Grenfell thought he resembled Stonewall Jackson. 'He said very little, but in any emergency he was the one man to do a great deal. He … had some magnetic influence which filled others with confidence and admiration.'

There was to be no haphazard road trip like George Fletcher's for these cavalrymen. Two days before they entrained their colonel had them parade dismounted to listen to a speech that would have rivalled a modern-day Hollywood scriptwriter. He impressed on them the importance of their role in the coming war and reminded them of all the regiment had achieved in the past. He told them stories of twelve Victoria Crosses during the Indian Mutiny; of marching into Kabul with the praise of Lord Roberts during the Second Afghan War. This was what they had to live up to. 'You are going forth to war with the greatest traditions to uphold,' he declared, and the regiment was duly inspired.

Whilst Colonel Campbell was reciting his litany of regimental glory, George Fletcher was watching events unfold from the window of his room at the Crown Hotel. Southampton was overrun with soldiers of every kind. As many as 80 trains a day heaved into the sidings laden with troops whilst more sweltered in their carriages outside the town until there was room to bring them in. George missed nothing:

> The docks are well guarded and so nobody knows how many transports are being sent off; but fishermen report that enormous ships are leaving nightly. There is a continuous rattle of great motor lorries, ammunition wagons, field guns, etc.; and infantry regiments … but much more cavalry … an immense lot of cavalry.

The scale of it astonished him. 'This is going to be by no means a small business. There are about eight million Germans and Austrians to walk over before we march under the Brandenburg [Gate] …'

As transports filled with men began backing out of berths at Southampton even the ship's masters were ignorant as to their destinations. Secret orders, only to be opened on leaving the coast, revealed ports further south than the enemy expected: Havre, Boulogne and Rouen. The British Expeditionary Force would then make a move towards Maubeuge on the Franco–Belgian border ready for a clash with the Kaiser's army. George and the rest of the Intelligence Corps Motor-Cycle Section were among the first to board ships. On an ocean liner packed to the seams with over a thousand soldiers, he described a perfect summer's evening as they passed down Southampton water with 'cheer after cheer from our men and every boat moored in the water'. Once in the channel, surprisingly, the Royal Navy was enigmatic; hovering protectively but further afield, ready to dispel any German attempts at interference. As night fell George watched a distant searchlight play out across the water: 'We knew we were in safe hands of the Navy after the lights of England had disappeared.' One of those pairs of hands belonged to his elder brother, Leslie, who had carried through the dream of a career in the Royal Navy born through the destruction of George's childhood sailor suit.

George had a more fortunate experience than the 9th Lancers, who had to factor in over a thousand horses on their journey. It took hours to put the cavalry regiment aboard their ships. Both Lucas' squadron, featuring the Harvey brothers and the one led by Francis Grenfell, boarded HMT *Welshman* slowly, walking and slinging the horses aboard. The whole experience was an uncomfortable strain on the animals. The *Welshman* was 'merely a converted cattle-boat' and the officers spent much of their time below with their mounts attempting to care for them. Glad of the fine weather, they then curled up in the open and attempted to sleep on deck. At Boulogne, disembarking was again a particularly trying time. Horses ran off and men gave chase while others lounged on the quay waiting for orders. Finally they faced a 3-mile march to a rest camp littered with bell tents.

The following day a weird and numerous collection of French interpreters turned up. All of the cavalry regiments were receiving such men, who were in the main well-to-do French reservists who would live with the NCOs. Provided by the French authorities, their allocation varied. The 3rd Hussars got a dozen, whilst the Household Cavalry Composite regiment got two, quickly dubbed 'Tired Tim' and 'Weary Willie'. The Ninths appeared with a large supply of maps 'on which it would have been possible to follow every stage of the expected advance of the BEF across France and the Rhine to Berlin, had the fortunes of war not led it in exactly the opposite direction, of which there were few, if any maps available.'

As soon as the troops arrived in France they were met with cheering crowds. Whilst the Ninth had headed for Boulogne, the majority of the BEF would be disembarking at Havre. As some Royal Fusiliers left their ship the French soldiers on the quay cheered them. They tried to show solidarity by attempting the 'Marseillaise', but when they turned to a rendition of 'Hold your hand out, naughty boy' they did so so seriously that the locals started whipping off their hats in reverence for what they thought must be the national anthem.

George Fletcher was overcome by the adoration. At every corner women were blowing kisses. They were showered with gifts: chocolate, fruit and flowers, and wherever they walked he found small children clustering about him and trying to grasp his hand. He would spend nearly a week waiting in the hills at Harfleur in what was, for the most part, blistering summer weather. He watched a continuous stream of regiments pour into camp and one by one move out again in the direction of the front in buoyant mood.

The wait by the coast was frustrating. Some infantry Etonians at Boulogne had been watching famous singers performing in a gymnasium to pass the time. Francis Grenfell had no time for the operatic folly enjoyed by 'the feet'[2]. He had taken to heart the words of Colonel Campbell and was not about to let his squadron put their feet up in the face of the big show. Allowing time for his beloved polo was one thing, but shoddy standards were unacceptable. He found rusty boots and spurs amongst his men and set to work, lining them up. Had they not heard the colonel's stirring words? Was not the best troop in battle nine times out of ten the one that scrubbed up best? They were the Ninth, a fact they ought to remember if they knew what was good for them. The culprits were made to march 2 miles onft and he gave ample warning for the future. Any man who turned himself out badly would have his horse taken away and be made to tramp. Another OE, Algernon Lamb, was charged with the machine gun section of the Household Cavalry contingent and had similar problems. 'I had to speak to the men … about their general slackness and ill-discipline, which has been creeping in the last few days.'

Opportunities for loafing amongst the cavalry turned out to be limited. Their stay at the coastal camp was brief but their train ride to Amiens for concentration with the rest of the BEF was eventful. All along the route they found aged French reservists in bright red trousers asking them all sorts of questions as they guarded stations. One happy trooper of the Ninth managed to fall out of the train. Food and water could only be obtained by adventurous souls willing to struggle from wagon to wagon on floorboards laid between the two. Algernon Lamb's regiment had horses falling over during the journey. There was no method of communication with the driver so one brave NCO had to crawl bravely along the tops of the wagons to get the train stopped.

As these OEs converged on the border between Belgium and France none of the Allies, in these opening days of war, were actually in tune with what their brothers in arms were driving at. The Belgians wanted, understandably, to save their country from oblivion, whilst the French hierarchy imagined them helping to attack their common frontier with Germany. The British had haplessly headed for their original destination at Maubeuge, no matter how foolhardy it seemed to Kitchener in London who seemed to be the only relevant person who had realised that the Germans might swing down a massive force in their faces. When they arrived, to the disappointment of the French, the great offensive to avenge the Franco–Prussian War and take back Alsace and Lorraine was not at the top of their agenda. All of this confusion reigned before the enemy was even factored into the equation.

But the Germans were not superior when it came to the execution of war at this point. On the far right of their line and destined to meet the BEF was the First Army, commanded by Alexander von Kluck. The very definition of a Prussian officer, if he didn't like the orders he received he just ignored them. He was an abrasive personality and a very difficult man to deal with, but he needed this sort of temperament. His men had a monumental task on their hands: to swing down and obliterate the left flank of the allied forces to open up the war for the rest of the German armies. Unfortunately, though, he and von Bülow, commanding the Second Army on his left, hated each other, which was hardly helpful when cohesion and communication were imperative during an offensive. The German High Command had to intervene frequently to settle the verbal sniping between them.

To the south, at the River Sambre, which flows through southern Belgium and a corner of northern France near Charleroi, General Lanrezac was in dire straits at the head of France's Fifth Army. A sharp, practical leader he was also bad tempered and sarcastic with a penchant for foul language. He alone noticed that the heaviest weight of the German offensive was going to charge right into him. Von Kluck and von Bülow had more than half a million men between them. To his right, the Battle of the Frontiers was already raging, disastrously for the French. The situation to Lanrezac's left was no better. The Belgians were no longer there. Their tiny army was saved from point-less annihilation by King Albert, who saw what was coming and dropped out of the line and fell back, taking his soldiers with him. But at what cost? With nothing there envelopment was a haunting but very real possibility for Lanrezac. The British hadn't yet arrived and King Albert's men were being replaced by poor French Territorials. Still, in the face of this insanity, with German armies bearing down on him, his superiors wanted him to attack. The situation was dramatic but frighteningly clear. If he and the British, when they arrived, did not hold their ground and at least stall the impetus of the German advance, all could be lost. The remaining French forces could be encircled and destroyed; the roads to Paris would lay open. The little BEF would be overrun and Britain itself left helpless to an enormous invasion force. The war could be over in a matter of weeks and Europe at the mercy of the Central Powers.

Cavalry patrols had erroneously told von Kluck what he wanted to hear: that the British were landing to the north at Belgian ports. He had absolutely no idea that he was about to march into massed numbers of them whilst he moved in the opposite direction. Germany's first clash with the British Army was about to be centred upon a grim little Belgian mining town named Mons and it was here too, on a hot and sunny Sunday afternoon, in a haze of factories and amongst ugly slag heaps from the mines, that the first Old Etonian to be killed by the enemy was about to suffer his fate.

On 21 August patrols, including men of the 9th Lancers, became the first British troops to enter Mons. Whispers reached them of the fall of Brussels and massive numbers of German troops heading straight for them. The locals were quick to give them information and as battle approached they would give British troops food, tools to dig trenches and would even help building barricades from wagons, furniture, anything bulky that they could get their hands on. The day that the cavalry entered Mons they sighted the enemy: ambiguous, ghostly figures moving in and out of the dawn mist. Uhlans: a nightmare of a word. One minute they were there on their horses, hover-ing by a bridge and then they were gone. General Allenby, commanding the entire cavalry division, offered a medal to the first officer or NCO to stick an enemy patrol leader with a lance.

The strain of the heat on the men, especially the unfit reservists, who formed a large percentage of the BEF was already beginning to tell. With the Irish Guards, Aubrey Herbert and one of his fellow officers had taken to loading his horse with as many rifles and items of kit as he could to lighten the load of those walking alongside, whilst the tired men with their blistered feet clung to his stirrups. Francis, Rivy, Lennie and Douglas, riding with the Ninth, were exhausted. Since Maubeuge, like the rest of the BEF, they had been making their way in stuttering fashion north towards the first British clash of the war.

The Harvey brothers had managed to fashion a single wash out of a local stream, although it turned out to be more of a mud bath. George Fletcher was feeling quite sorry for himself too, not least because a 'disgusting little man' of the Intelligence Corps had refused to give him a horse and sent him off to war on an unglamourous and unreliable motorcycle. 'I have been exceedingly despondent about this business ever since we crossed the sea,' he wrote. 'I felt that a red herring had been drawn across my path.' Had he waited he would have probably received a commission into the Special Reserve of officers but by running off and joining the Intelligence Corps he remained a Territorial. He was suffering many a sleepless night, in the main not because of conditions but because he could not bear the thought of the army fighting the Germans and he himself not being in the infantry. On 22 August, after he and his smell, which was already rapidly diminishing in his estimation had spent a backbreaking day shuttling messages, he had thrown himself into a makeshift bed at ten o'clock. Less than an hour later he was dragged out of it again to find a wandering battalion that was needed for the now imminent clash. 'I spent four hours looking for it,' he bemoaned. 'Being challenged by sentries every half mile, my headlight lighting up their faces and glittering bayonets pointed straight at my nose.'

It had been a trying week for all. In the seven nights since leaving Tidworth one of the Ninth's officers had slept for four of those on a table, in a pub, outdoors on an iron staircase and on the deck of a ship respectively. Their plight was still not over. Having spent 22 August lounging by the side of the road and in fields, as night fell the bulk of the cavalry had orders to switch their position from the right flank of the BEF to the vulnerable left where it would meet the worryingly weak French territorials before fighting commenced.

Mons was almost the last place in the world that a regiment of cavalry would want to end up. Gone were the 'wide rolling downs of their dreams'. It was likened to the Black Country or London's Docklands. The canal itself, black and stinking with chemical refuse from nearby industrial sites, bisected an urban sprawl that went on for miles. The water wasn't deep, nor was it wide, but movement and visibility in the area were appalling. To the north, the Germans were hiding in dotted woods and spinneys. On the south bank, more buildings and slag heaps, pointing their ugly noses skyward as high as 100ft, blinded the troops and made it near impossible for the artillery to come up. Moving around it was trying for cavalry men too as they had to manhandle their horses around tramways and trolley rails as well as artificial waterways, which all lined the banks of the canal like a grimy spider's web.

Even Francis Grenfell, with all of his notebooks, could not begin to make sense of it all. Having covered miles on difficult paved roads on exhausted animals it was a nightmare. A thin drizzle had turned the coal dust that lay everywhere into a greasy slime. 'Our horses, half asleep like ourselves had staggered on, stumbling over unseen cobbles and cinder heaps in the pitch dark, slipping on the endless network of tram and trolley lines.' The Ninth found their animals lumbering, sliding, even falling down. As they rode westwards Belgian men and women 'emerged unabashed' in their nightwear to watch the cavalry as they trudged on their way. They reached their destination, south-west of Mons, just before dawn; their only reward for their troubles a wet field to lie down in. At headquarters, Lanrezac's desperate and ever so slightly cheeky request for the BEF to carry out a suicidal attack on von Bülow's army to give his own troops some relief fell on unsurprisingly deaf ears. And so it was here, where they had stopped in the most unsuitable of potential battlefields that General John French promised that the BEF would hold the British position for twenty-four hours.

Battle commenced, and by mid afternoon on 23 August. Regardless of the dogged nature of the BEF's defence, the overwhelming German numbers and the falling ranks of the British battalions involved had its effect. They began to retreat. All along the secondary front to which they retired exhausted members of the BEF attempted to snatch a few hours of sleep. The wounded were being evacuated as far away as possible and the dead lay where they had fallen. In the aftermath, bodies were buried side by side with the enemy. Today, at St Symphorien Cemetery, one of the prettiest on the Western Front, lie men believed to be both the first and last Commonwealth soldiers to fall in the Great War, the first recipients of both the Victoria Cross and Germany's Iron Cross during the conflict, and with them the first Old Etonian to fall at the hands of the enemy. Frederick Albert Forster of the 4th Royal Fusiliers was attempting to hold off the German assault on the canal at Mons when he was struck down as his battalion began falling back through the town. The first proper clash between the two nations in the Great War was over. More than four years of bloodshed on the Western Front had begun.

Notes

1. It was here, at this time that Eton College suffered its first casualty of the Great
   War. Arthur Hughes-Onslow, a veteran of the Sudan and the Boer War, was
   51 years old when he was called back into service to command the Remount
   Service for the cavalry. Before a British soldier had fired a shot in anger at the
   enemy, he passed away after a short illness on 17 August 1914 and was laid to
   rest in Havre.
2. Cavalry slang for infantry.

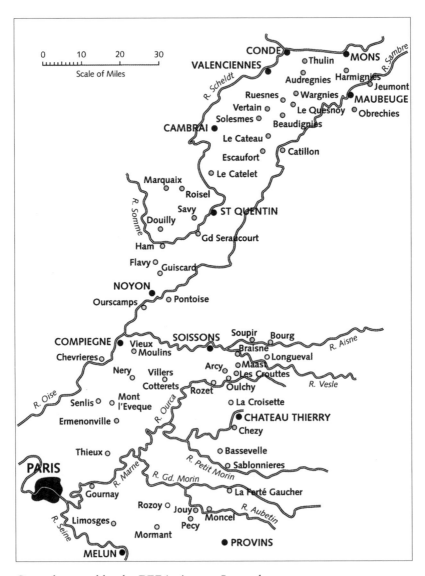

Ground covered by the BEF in August–September 1914.

3

'Shrapnel Monday'

Someone once said of little Charlie Garstin that, with his angelic face, curly fair hair and big blue eyes, had he found himself lost in London in the morning, by nightfall he would have been adopted by a duchess. Had Garstin foreseen the scandalous mess that was to become his childhood then he might have been forgiven for giving this theory a try.

When still 19 Charlie's mother Mary had fallen for a romantically named young army officer, Beau. They spent much of the summer of 1887 on the Kent coast, going for long walks and reading his detailed campaign diaries from Egypt, where he had already been awarded the Distinguished Service Order. He was in his early twenties, serious, about to embark for India and completely unable to consider the idea of marriage. They settled on 'friendship with a capital F' and so it was with a heavy heart that Mary reached Egypt that autumn for an extended stay with friends. There she met Mr Garstin, 'a good looking, fair man with very cold blue eyes and close cut curly hair'. He fell in love with her immediately. She would later claim that the idea of being married (as well as the prospect of more trips to Cairo) enamoured her more than her future husband, but regardless they were married the next year. A daughter, Helen, was born in 1890, followed by Charlie in 1893, but by 1897, citing boredom as one of her excuses, Lady Garstin had begun a very public affair with a married army man.

Charlie's father, Sir William Garstin, was a truly brilliant civil engineer who spent most of his only son's childhood radically transforming the way in which the waters of the River Nile were utilised. Heavily associated with the Aswan Dam, eventually becoming Under Secretary of State for Public Works he was also responsible for buildings and antiquities, and in this capacity oversaw the building of the Museum of Egyptian Antiquities. 'Will's' work weighed heavily on him and took him away from his wife, twenty years his junior. Mary later wrote her dramatic memoirs, casting herself as the 'heroine' and her lover as her 'hero'. So her husband was to play the pantomime villain. He was certainly a very reserved man; she called him the 'pink of propriety' and lamented his inability to let flow any emotional outpouring. Mortified by her indiscretions but even more so by the idea of a divorce Sir William forgave her numerous times and blamed himself frequently before things came to a head at the turn of the century.

Lady Garstin never made any attempt to disguise the fact that she favoured her daughter. Little Helen was diabetic and consequently, before the advent of insulin, almost an invalid. 'With her delicate health and passionate devotion … she so absorbed my love that Charlie had never been quite the same to me.' Being parted from her, as would be the case if she left her husband, was more than she could stand and so she resolved to stay put. Helen sadly passed away in 1900 while her mother was in Cairo attempting to save her marriage. It proved the break she needed. Sir William and his wife mourned their little girl together but in the aftermath her affair was rekindled. Not without floods of tears, Charlie's mother chose her lover over her 7-year-old son. The night before Lady Garstin despatched him in the hands of his beloved nannie to his father for good she watched his 'lovely sleeping face' on her bed. Her very public affair and Sir William's decision to divorce her, not to mention the fact that she would reside with her still-married lover, sealed her fate. Lady Garstin made no attempt to contest the divorce hearing and, as was the norm, was forbidden any contact with her son beyond the concession of a brief note each month to assure her of his continued good health. The matter was taken seriously. On the one occasion that she defied the ruling she was caught out and when Charlie arrived at Eton she received a letter from a solicitor, informing her that if she took advantage of his unguarded presence in the town to make contact with him then he would be removed from the school immediately.

Charlie did not stay at Eton as long as he should have. With a proficiency for modern languages and his father's insistence that war was imminent he spent time in Germany before returning home in 1912 to go to Sandhurst and fulfil his dream of joining the cavalry. Returning to England he had not long begun his training when his mother was coincidentally invited by a friend to stay on the premises. She wouldn't have recognised him. Charlie was a slim young man of 18 now and she was rocked by his resemblance to his father. The ice-blue eyes, the curly hair, the fair complexion. He had inherited some of Sir William's bearing too. Whilst still at Freiburg the local cavalry regiment, much enamoured by their visitor, had thrown him a farewell dinner. He was utterly shocked that the conversation revolved around the deficiencies of the British Army and their impropriety caused him to get up and leave his startled hosts after the soup; an anecdote that was still being passed around Eton with much amusement several years later. But if his father's propriety was high on his list of personality traits, Charlie's mother found that so too was warmth and kindness. He chattered away excitedly with none of the inhibitions that had rendered communications with her husband impossible. He seemed to understand, if not condemn, his father's shortcomings. She learned of his love of languages and how he had recently qualified as a German interpreter.

As Charlie left her, Lady Garstin was full of hope:

> Could it not be arranged that his father and I should, for his sake, [meet again]. Surely, surely it could be arranged? He would write immediately to his father and tell him of our meeting and what it had meant to him. This was only a short parting now, only a very short parting.

Charlie promised her that nothing would keep him from her again. Sir William, however, was furious and threatened to disinherit his boy if he had contact with his mother, and though Charlie walked into the night in his uniform, promising her that they would be together soon, she would never see him again.

Charlie embarked for France with the rest of the 9th Lancers in 1914. The Great Retreat began in earnest the day after Mons. For the OEs, present shrapnel was a hideously recurring theme on Monday 24 August. George Fletcher wrote home, sending his father his tales of 'Blood and Thunder', and lamenting the 'swish of shells' over his head. Blasted from German field guns and exploding above their target, the shrapnel sprayed in all directions, whistling 'like a cat … miaowing over … Bang – interval – whe-e-ew MIAOW! BANG!!' George was not the only one running scared. Aubrey Herbert didn't mind admitting that he was terrified:

> A shell burst over my head. I jumped to the conclusion that I was killed and fell flat. I was ashamed of myself before I reached the ground, but, looking round, found that everybody else had done the same.

The Ninth had not been amongst the troops heavily involved in Britain's opening engagement against the Germans the day before. In fact, whilst chaos descended on the canal to the north, elements of the cavalry restocked their stores. Others enjoyed a relative lie-in and a homely breakfast provided by local nuns. Aside from a quick evening excursion in search of phantom *Uhlans* their cavalry brigade, comprising the Ninth, the 4th Dragoon Guards and the 18th Hussars, had had a quiet day. At dawn on 24 August it was scattered around the vicinity of a small town called Elouges, some 15 miles to the south-west of Mons. Less built up, it was still mining country, with a light, mineral railway dissecting the terrain and more telltale slag heaps dotted around sugar-beet fields. It was more open, but a maze of sunken roads, fences and scattered buildings still made it less than ideal for mounted troops.

Men of the brigade had been standing to all night with their horses saddled and ready to move, listening to the sound of the guns in the distance and watching as the wounded and refugees streamed down the main road. At 4 a.m. Francis Grenfell was ordered to take B Squadron forward to investigate what might be occurring back towards Mons. Cautiously they trotted into Thulin. They came under enemy fire almost immediately, metal raining down on them from where the Germans had taken control of a bridge over the canal to the north. Francis' horse Ginger was killed and an officer was wounded by a flying piece of shrapnel to the chest.

For the first, and as it turned out, the only time, the Grenfell twins came under fire together. In danger of being outflanked by a large body of enemy troops they climbed the high ground out of Thulin and dismounted, unleashing a torrent of rifle fire. The advancing enemy troops halted and B Squadron took advantage of their pause to slip back to the rest of the regiment where collectively they began retiring south-west with the rest of the BEF. For once, the terrain worked in their favour. They were able to move back leisurely, using random cinder heaps and embankments on either side of the roads as cover. Nevertheless the enemy artillery kept coming. More shrapnel exploded overhead, taking chunks out of man and horse alike, wounding one officer and killing another's charger. From their position to the south they remained under heavy fire while they awaited further developments. Aeroplanes buzzed overhead, betraying their position to the German gunners and A Squadron took useless potshots at them with their rifles.

Riding from regiment to regiment, overseeing the whole affair was Brigadier General Henry de Beauvoir de Lisle or, more simply, Lady Garstin's 'Beau'. They had not been in contact since her downfall and he had come a long way since those heady days walking by the sea in Kent. The decision to abstain from marrying her had proved an astute one on his part, for since he had left her in 1887 he had spent a stint at the Staff College, assumed command of a cavalry regiment and served on the General Staff at Aldershot before 1911, when he assumed command of the very brigade that her son Charlie was to join less than two years later.

Halfway through the morning de Lisle sent his orderly officer, an Irish OE of the 10th Hussars named Pat Armstrong, off to a nearby infantry general with a message. When he came galloping back an hour later it was with an urgent appeal for assistance. The last contingent of the BEF trying to retire from Mons was in trouble. A gap had opened in the line and they were in danger of being overrun. Beau's brigade was closest and he burst into action immediately, pushing his three cavalry regiments north again. The Ninth, along with the 4th Dragoons, found themselves deployed to a small village named Audregnies, on the left of two of the troubled infantry battalions.

Lucas, Charlie and the Harvey brothers arrived on the north side of the village, had their men quickly dismount and commenced a sustained, long-range barrage of rifle and machine-gun fire on the advancing German troops. Back with the Dragoons, another young OE named Roger Chance had also arrived. Both regiments had been in the village little less than an hour when de Lisle himself came thundering down the road and drew up abruptly along-side Colonel Campbell. 'I'm going to charge the enemy,' he blurted out. 'The 4th Dragoon Guards will attack on your left.' His instructions were clear. As soon as Campbell saw Roger Chance and his fellow officers emerge from the village and deploy northwards he was to send at least two squadrons of the Ninth with them.

The idea of an all out, Napoleonic-style cavalry charge at this juncture was patently ludicrous. There were no significant bodies of enemy troops close enough to make it justifiable for a start as that left them without a target. Therefore, the logic behind two cavalry regiments riding into the artillery duel between the Germans and vastly outnumbered British artillery was questionable. The ground they would be galloping over was not unproblematic. It undulated, albeit gently; the corn in the surrounding fields had already been cut so only stubble remained, but the crops themselves lay about in piles, or 'stooks'. Add to that all the sunken lanes, railway cuttings, wire fences and quickset hedges, behind or amongst all of which enemy troops could be lurking, then the scenario became increasingly perilous. Nonetheless Colonel Campbell was forced to order his men ready immediately. Under fire, the scene was already chaotic and behind some houses the Ninth mounted up. Meanwhile the 4th Dragoon Guards were jumping into their saddles and tearing off down a cramped, narrow lane towards the edge of the village.

No sooner had Charlie, Lennie and Douglas got ready than the Dragoon Guards were seen emerging from the other side of Audregnies and they were off. They moved off at a trot and rode knee to knee. Campbell wheeled his arm in an underarm circle, the signal for canter, and as their speed increased, they lowered their lances. One of the officers, 'Riffkins', had got caught up in a wire enclosure away from the body of the squadron with an interpreter and almost missed the show. '*I* wasn't behind the house!' he moaned. Suddenly he was under a terrific volley of infantry fire and the French interpreter grovelled beside him. He was being left behind. 'Moving off at a gallop – have a good start of me – What the hell are they doing?'

Beau de Lisle had pushed a dismounted contingent of the 18th Hussars to the north of Audregnies with a battery of the Royal Horse Artillery to take up a defensive position. 'Suddenly there was a tremendous increase in the hostile gun and machine-gun fire to our left,' they noted. The Ninth burst from Audregnies, Francis and Lucas leading their squadrons. The Hussars watched as the rest of the brigade came over the skyline, picking up speed, galloping out across the front of their line. They swept over a gently sunken road, the Ninth leading, the Dragoons slightly behind and to the left. Seeing the cavalry advance with the evident intention of shock action the Germans took cover behind corn stooks and slag heaps, and opened fire with their rifles. 'On we go through a hail of bullets and shrapnel – must be charging,' Riffkins surmised. 'Find my sword and draw it – Cannot see any Germans.'

As they thundered on it rained metal, a dozen shells flashing and bursting at a time. If there had been a coherent target they would not have seen it. The dust kicked up by hundreds of horses blinded them. The crack of bullets and the thumping of shells added to the thundering of hooves. Shrapnel was exploding in amongst them and it was 'a very inferno of shell and small-arms fire'. Next to Chance, a sergeant crouching in his saddle was 'blasted to glory' and Roger felt what was left of him 'go patter to earth' around him. One of the 4th's interpreters, the elegant Vicomte de Varvineur was 'blown to tatters' by a direct hit from a high explosive shell. Horses began to get away from their riders. Roger Chance was clinging on with one hand for dear life. Through 'sleeting bullets' he passed isolated little bodies of German troops in the cornfields but that was it. One man somersaulted down to the ground, another officer's horse was hit and he tumbled to the floor with it. His squadron rode over him, then a machine-gun section and finally a passing horse smashed him in the face before he passed out. The column formations of both regiments were long gone in the melee. One of the the infantrymen on the ridge that they had been sent to assist was up on a bank to their right and he watched riderless horses go stampeding past him down an empty country road in what he called a 'useless waste of life. All to no purpose'.

Rivy Grenfell was not with B Squadron that afternoon. He had been commandeered by de Lisle as a galloper after the morning reconnaissance with Francis. 'A rather weary task on a heavy horse.' He had spent most of the day alone, riding about the Belgian countryside, under fire, looking for staff officers and passing along orders for the brigade. Searching for de Lisle, he rode into Audregnies and found it almost empty. He was told that his regiment had just charged. Then he was engulfed by a herd of wounded horses … 'galloping everywhere … bullets and shells were falling like hailstones.'

With no target in sight, the charge began petering out and self-preservation began to take hold. As one trooper went cascading to the ground, his horse going from under him, he heard Campbell give the order for the mess of cavalrymen to right wheel away from the German guns. As he lay cowering on the floor, they began to change direction 'like a flock of sheep'.

On the main road, a 1½mile north of Audregnies, a red-brick sugar factory with a tall chimney and a large yard dominated the vicinity. It appeared to be their best chance of cover, but as the cavalrymen approached their horses reared. The brick yard itself was bordered by a high fence and all about the property were more wire barriers. Bundled into a corner the horses crowded in and chaos ensued. The factory itself was now being used for target practice by the German artillery. 'We simply galloped about like rabbits,' Francis recalled. 'Men and horses falling in all directions.' In the intolerable heat of mid afternoon the squadron commanders of the Ninth began frantically to try to bring about some order. Any sort of formation had disintegrated completely and there was no telling Lancers from Dragoons. Behind a house where he had taken cover, Francis frantically tried to find a trumpeter to give some kind of signal, but there was nobody in sight. He began blowing on his officer's whistle whilst he 'cursed with vehemence anybody he found out of place'.

Not everybody had made for the sugar factory. Some men, whether by providence or by choice, were dismounted and now they were attempting to keep the enemy at bay with rifles and the assistance of the artillery that continued to pound relentlessly, throwing shells high over their heads. Others had seized a cottage nearby and from there Dragoons were running out into the open to collect the wounded. Riffkins had hidden behind one of the isolated mounds of slag with Colonel Campbell, who instructed their crowd to hold the factory before riding off to find de Lisle. He could make no sense of it at all. 'A few silly fire orders – nothing to shoot at – then the Colonel disappears – for three days.'

Lucas, now the senior officer on the scene, had also found 'scanty cover' behind yet another pile of cinders and like Francis was attempting to organise the mixture of troops that had joined him. He took his ramshackle outfit and attempted to get them out of harm's way to a nearby quarry through yet another tornado of shrapnel. Francis was in a similar predicament. The house he had been using as shelter had been blown to pieces and now, cowering under an embankment, he began attempting to sort out his following. Recalling that on one occasion the regiment had been ordered to trot in South Africa under heavy fire he attempted to use the same method to keep the men together.

In the middle of the afternoon it looked to Campbell and Mullens as if their regiments had evaporated. Coming out of the cover of his embankment with the resilient band that included Lennie and Douglas, Francis Grenfell ran headlong into the 119th Battery of the Royal Field Artillery. They were in a terrible state. Outnumbered three to one, they had been engaged in a duel with German gunners and the results were telling. All about the guns lay the pulverised remains of more than a quarter of the men. Now, ordered to disengage, their Commanding Officer Major Alexander did not have enough men to get his guns out of harm's way. While they were discoursing on this predicament Francis fell victim to yet more shrapnel.

'It felt as if a whip had hit me,' he wrote afterwards. Pain shot through his hand and his leg. One of A Squadron's officers, a young OE named 'Bunny' Taylor-Whitehead, was on hand and got to work with a handkerchief to try to stem the blood spurting from the wound. Out came a copy of the Field Service Regulations. They leafed through the pages trying to find out how to apply a tourniquet. 'Of course we found out how to stop blood in every other part of one's body except one's hand.' Eventually they got it together but by then things had begun to spin a little for Francis. He suddenly remembered that in the wallets of the horse he had inherited he had seen a flask of brandy, so he promptly emptied it. 'I now felt like Jack Johnson instead of an old cripple.'

As well as being mauled by three batteries of German artillery, the 119th and their cavalry helpers were also under a sustained and intense tirade from machine guns and rifles, and Francis' first task, having volunteered to help, was to find a suitable place for them to extricate their guns to. Leaving everybody else under the embankment he mounted his borrowed horse and got on his way, riding out through the silent British guns alone, as the German's continued to shell with enthusiasm. He made it to safety, found a safe place to aim for and then had to ride back. It might have been the brandy talking but he was determined to retain his dignity in front of the troops. 'It was necessary to go back through the inferno as slowly as possible, so as to pretend to the men that there was no danger and that the shells were more noisy than effective.'

Having informed Major Alexander that he had found a way out, Francis was told that the draught horses were gone. The only way to save the guns was to drag them out of the way by hand. Minus a decent amount of blood, ever so slightly influenced by alcohol and having just survived a game of chicken with the German artillery, Francis was full of confidence. Ordering his crowd to dismount in front of their horses he gave a rehashed version of the colonel's speech at Tidworth and asked for volunteers to help manoeuvre the guns to safety. Hands shot up, including Bunny, Lennie and Douglas. In all eleven officers and a host of men offered their hands. Francis glowed with pride. 'Every single man and officer declared they were ready to go to what looked like certain destruction.'

Then they got to work. One by one they ran out into the storm of metal and started attempting to drag tons of heavy machinery out of enemy range. Slowly the guns had to be turned in the right direction and then the hauling began. In direct enemy range, one gun had to be dragged over the body of its fallen gunners. In all, Francis thought that they had managed to accomplish the task with the loss of only three or four men, although they had to return more than once and the enemy reached within 500 yards before the last gun was dragged to safety. He reflected on the actions of his men proudly. 'It is on occasions like this that good discipline tells. The men were so wonderful and steady that words fail me.'

Francis held on, light headed until Lucas arrived and assumed command, and then he began to collapse. His friend was kind yet firm in talking him into the idea of getting into an ambulance. Francis' fingers were badly cut up and a piece of shrapnel had torn a lump out of his thigh. He had a bullet hole in his boot from the morning, another through his sleeve, he had been knocked over by a shell and his horse had been shot; 'so no-one can say I had an idle day', he said drily. A French staff officer took pity on him and drove him to Bavay, where, as luck would have it, his good friend the Duke of Westminster was there to mollycoddle him. Rivy, having been ordered to rally what troops he could on the way south, soon arrived too. Dejectedly wondering what he could do to find news of his twin, he found that he was already in the town. Francis thought much more of his brother's exploits on that first day of the retreat than he did of his own. He told their friend John Buchan, author of *The 39 Steps*, that his twin's 'solitary act of reconnaissance, all alone, was braver than anything he did; a raw civilian riding for hours under heavy fire on a tired horse on missions of vital importance'.

The nation disagreed. In August 1914, specialist publications about the war sprang up. One in particular took its coverage of the supposed exploits carried out by mounted troops to obsessive proportions. The charge led by the 9th Lancers, with all its romanticism and connotations of the charge of the Light Brigade at Balaclava, was irresistible. With truth not getting in the way of a good story, artist's impressions of Francis, leading his men with resolve on his face, in point-blank range of a gun emblazoned the pictorial press. The Germans cower in the foreground, a trooper who had lost his horse charges the enemy on foot, sword in hand. As far as the British public were told, the enemy had captured the British guns and were hell bent on turning them on their owner's troops. Francis and his men stormed to the rescue. Starved of information about the chaotic retreat, John Buchan remembered (and not without irony) how in the confusion of those first weeks of war 'the exploits of the Ninth emerged as a clear achievement on which the mind of the nation could seize and so comfort itself'.

For Francis, convalescing at his uncle's house in the knowledge that not only had none of those guns fallen into German hands but that he himself had not been within a few hundred yards of any concentration of enemy troops, it was embarrassing. Despite his arguable display of bravery, his only concern was his squadron and how they were faring in France. 'I have never felt such a fool in my life,' he declared, by now aware that he had been nominated for a Victoria Cross, which baffled him. 'After all, I only did what every other man and officer did who was with me.' Thanks to a 'lot of rot' penned by 'infernal correspondents' he was receiving fan mail and all kinds of exalted visitors. The king himself had stopped by, as had Mrs Asquith, who was thoughtful enough to ask after Rivy. There were fellow OEs: Prince Arthur of Connaught who sat with him for an hour and the legendary Field Marshal Lord Roberts, who had begun his own cavalry career lifetimes ago, a full decade before the Indian Mutiny. He badgered him for every last detail: who did they charge, how and with what aim? In his weakened state, all Francis could do was watch the clock, entertain well-wishers and take every 'wild story' as it came. In France though, just as he feared, the war continued without him and the Ninth would suffer many more hardships before he managed to find his way back.

On 24 August, as darkness descended and rain began to fall, Lucas took charge of the tattered remains of the regiment. He fell back, taking a third of the Ninth's strength, including the Harvey brothers and Bunny Taylor-Whitehead, over the border into France and on to the town of Ruesnes. Other straggling collections of men were arriving in other little towns along the frontier, like Wargnies-le-Petit, where Colonel Campbell had found 100 more cavalrymen. The BEF had evaded von Kluck again, but to the survivors of the charge it seemed like a catastrophe. That evening, with the men scattered, it seemed as if two regiments had simply disintegrated. The 4th Dragoon Guards could only find seven of its officers and only eighty men had answered one roll call. Not until the end of the week, when the various contingents began collecting at St-Quentin, did it transpire that things were not at all as bad as they had seemed.

As it turned out, one single officer of the 9th Lancers had been killed that day, and it was Charlie Garstin. One late summer morning his mother was cutting out garments for soldiers at her dining-room table, surrounded by pins, patterns and fabric. The door opened and her friend George, 'with *The Times* in his hand and his face working awkwardly', called her out of the room. 'Mary,' he stammered, 'Mary darling.' But he could not say it. He could only point to the obituary column with a trembling hand. Sir William made no contact with her and she died believing he had failed to tell her of Charlie's fate out of spite. In actual fact there had been some confusion as to what had happened to Charlie and the answers lay with a prisoner, which disrupted the flow of information.

Another officer of the 4th Dragoon Guards had crawled into a cowshed with a broken leg and found several other wounded men. Shortly afterwards a German officer appeared 'with a tiny popgun of a pistol' which he kept trained on them as he inspected his new prisoners. More men were marched in whilst, as darkness set in, the Germans set fire to two haystacks and began throwing rifles and saddles into the blaze. 'The merry popping of small-arm ammunition commenced', bullets whizzing in their direction. Their captors brought wine for them and danced about the burning haystacks like demented shadows to the sound of two accordions, 'a weird sight in the fitful light'.

The wounded British men were ushered and carried to a convent in Audregnies. One officer was lying there several days later with some 200 other men when the local priest arrived at the window with an exhumed body. The villagers had buried a British officer in some haste and the father had decided that he ought to be properly identified. It was Charlie. The identification process was repeated for two Cheshire officers and then all three of them were conveyed to Audregnies churchyard.[1]

Charlie Garstin was 20 years old when he charged at Audregnies. Rivy Grenfell had run into Colonel Campbell as he searched vainly that afternoon for Beau de Lisle. On the same fruitless mission they sat together. 'He had been ordered to charge towards Quievrain,' Rivy recalled. 'Why, he did not know, as there was an open space for about a mile and he had lost nearly all his regiment.' 'Balaclava like,' the newspapers called it. If a futile action, with a ludicrous and unrealistic objective that the man who ordered it would try and wash his hands of responsibility for was what was meant by that, then it can be said to be true. That night the commanders of the Ninth and the 4th Dragoon Guards were seething with rage at the man who had issued the order that had seemingly cost them so many soldiers. When someone sought to cheer up Campbell by telling him that he had been nominated for a Victoria Cross he snapped. 'I want my squadrons back,' he retorted, 'not VCs or medals.' In his official write up, Beau de Lisle held firm to the view that he had merely told his regimental commanders that it 'might be necessary' to charge. All of the evidence to the contrary, though, placed the responsibility for this botched footnote in the Great War in his hands; and with it too the death of Charles William North Garstin, his former sweetheart's only son.

Notes

1. The body of Charles William North Garstin was relocated to Cement House Cemetery in the 1950s.

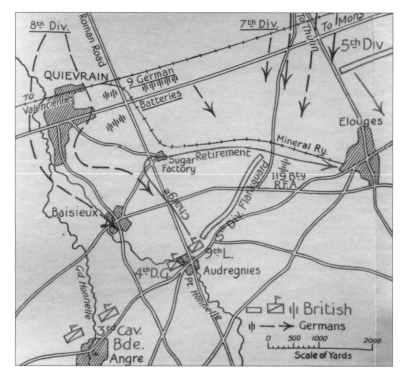

Diagram showing the charge of the 9th Lancers at Audregnies

4

'Our Little Band
of Brothers'

As autumn began, large numers of OEs were engaged in a type of conflict that is unfamiliar to many envisioning the Great War. The timeless image of the war is that of the trenches: stagnant warfare, andarmies scrapping over slithers of mud in Flanders and on the Somme. But this was not the war that governments, generals or the troops involved had anticipated. Combatants across Europe were trained to fight on the move and were conducting the opening throes of the conflict as such: seizing positions, defending them briefly and then moving on. It was a fluid, mobile type of warfare similar to the experience of their ancestors on the battlefields of Europe in the nineteenth century.

Nearly one third of the Old Etonians who fell during the Great War have no known grave. Prior to the BEF's descent into Picardy and the environs of the River Aisne in September 1914 only three of the school's casualties were missing and presumed dead, as opposed to actually having a marked burial site. For Eton the retreat changed this, followed by the re-crossing of the river in pursuit of the enemy two weeks later and the Battle of the Aisne. At the time the reaction of the families of these missing men was not one of muted acceptance. The world had not yet seen the opening day of the Somme, or the vile mud of Passchendaele. The idea of young officers having vanished into oblivion in the opening months of the war was shocking, unacceptable even, and the families of some went to extraordinary lengths to obtain answers that they were convinced had to be waiting for them on the battlefields and from the mouths of those that had survived.

As yet, the Guards Regiments had barely fired a shot in anger. When the 4th (Guards) Brigade arrived in France it comprised the 2nd Battalion of the Grenadier Guards, the 1st Irish Guards and both the 2nd and 3rd Coldstream Guards. For many Etonians these regiments were a family tradition. The Coldstream had been formed by General Monck in 1650 and on embarking for the Great War an OE with the same name boarded the transport; whilst another Etonian travelling to France claimed to be a sixth-generation Grenadier. Between them the four Battalions took 125 officers to war and nearly 60 per cent of them had been educated at Eton College. The presence of such high numbers of Etonians in certain units meant that when they were decimated in combat, large numbers of OEs would likely fall together. On 14 September this trend began, twenty of Eton's old boys fell in one day and of them eleven belonged to one of the four Guards regiments.

Amongst their number was a 22-year-old Old Etonian who had barely been with the Grenadiers for a year when war was declared. Mild-mannered, perhaps a little too laid-back and cheerful by nature, John Manners had it all: intellect, looks and athletic ability in just about every sport he tried. His Eton fame had been secured by the Lord's match in 1910. Partly a brainchild of Lord Byron, it had become tradition that the boys of Eton would take on the boys of Harrow School every summer at the Marylebone Cricket Club's famous ground in St John's Wood. At the time it was a social event to rival Ascot or the Grand National and attracted crowds in the tens of thousands.

The match in 1910 ended in a breathtaking manner. Eton was languishing after the first innings, being all out for a pathetic 67. John himself was ninth in the batting order and had been caught out for 4, the future Field Marshal Alexander of Tunis bowling the offending ball. Harrow had been unbeaten all year but the star of the day was Robert Fowler, the Eton captain. Apart from his 64, the second innings was nothing to shout about either. John made 40 not out, the second highest total, and in desperation Boswell KS, the wicket keeper, had racked up 32 as the last man before Harrow went in to bat needing a mere 55 runs to win.

What followed was nothing short of incredible. The Eton captain led a charge that brought the Harrovian batting line up to its knees. Within half an hour Fowler had taken 8 wickets, 5 clean bowled and Harrow were all but obliterated at 32 for 9. Such was their confidence that Harrow's tenth man, Alexander, was stuffing his face with a cream bun when someone burst into a tent at the nursery end and informed him 'that the Harrow wickets were falling like ninepins and that he might be needed at any moment'. He was still trying to swallow his cake in the pavilion and barely had time to get his pads on and to the crease. Alexander managed just 8 runs before the innings was over and Harrow were all out for 45. Eton had won by 9 Fowler became a national celebrity in an instant. Such was the acclaim that one fan letter, simply addressed to 'Fowler's mother, London' actually found the lady at her hotel.

John Manners had a mischievous sense of humour. He once received a scathing reprimand from Shepherd's Bush Stadium for messing about where he shouldn't have been and went as far as to register his telegraphic address as 'Brainfeg, Oxford'. His father was a sportsman too, but was wary of his temperament and had instilled in John the belief that sporting greatness was not enough in itself. He had won the Grand National on his own horse but he hoped that John 'unlike himself would be remembered for something more' than his achievements on a playing field or a tennis court.

On the outbreak of war John was most amused when arriving in France that he was not supposed to tell his mother anything at all. 'We are not even allowed to say what country we're in which makes letter writing rather difficult!' he joked. 'But I don't think you would be greatly surprised if you knew.' Disembarking at the end of their voyage had been difficult but he was just thankful that the journey was over. He continued to mock the seriousness of his new adventure. 'All the glamour of war was knocked out of me by that beastly departure from London. Bands oughtn't be allowed to play 'Auld Lang Syne'!'

The 2nd Grenadiers first retired across the River Aisne on 31 August just after dawn in sweltering heat. They had marched on for nearly 15 miles, struggling to keep men in the ranks, until reaching the town of Soucy. Major George Darell, or 'Ma' Jeffreys, had left Eton in 1895. There were 'three pillars' to Ma's loyalty: Eton, the Guards and the Conservative Party. The battalion's second in command, having walked over a hundred miles in a little under a week with his Guardsmen, Ma had had just about enough of wandering through the French countryside with an undetermined number of Germans in pursuit. Sleep that night was curtailed after two hours when shortly after midnight came orders to fall back and take up a position at the edge of the forest of Retz, just to the south. At dawn the guards stopped in the shadow of its dense, towering beech trees, which were draped with a thick mist. In a thin, miserable shower of rain the Grenadier and the Irish Guards drank hot chocolate that tasted faintly of paraffin whilst they looked out on dripping lucerne and damp cornfields. Piles of corn lay about, providing potential cover for the Germans. Here they were to stay until mid afternoon, next to Villers-Cotterêts, waiting for the enemy to arrive and hoping that they could keep from being overrun.

This plan fell apart almost immediately. Rumours arrived of German cavalry approaching, and then little pockets of grey-clad men appeared, running between the piles of wet corn and filtering into the forest on either side of them. The Grenadiers opened fire immediately and the Guards prepared to retire into the forest, falling back on the main road and a junction at a clearing in the trees. Into the undergrowth they slipped, amidst a shower of shells from a German artillery battery. The scene was surreal, looking 'for all the world like … the New Forest on a Spring Day'. In one direction, the enemy fire continued and in the other, deer eyed the khaki intruders. Ma Jeffreys' morning was about to get even more surreal. To his astonishment he was ordered to stand his ground for a few hours in order to give the rest of the nearby troops assembling in and about Villers-Cotterêts time to sit down and eat.

With the Irish Guards, Aubrey Herbert was just as bewildered. 'It was evident if [they] took long … we should be wiped out.' Everyone was on edge. There was an eerie lull and Aubrey, ever the optimist, sat down to write two goodbye letters, including a eulogy to his horse Moonshine. Having done so he wandered off to find the Adjutant, 25-year-old Lord Desmond FitzGerald, another Etonian, to have them posted. 'I have the picture in my mind of Desmond constantly sitting in very tidy breeches, writing and calling for sergeants,' Aubrey recalled. 'He never seemed to sleep at all. He was woken all the time and was always cheerful.' On this occasion though Desmond was indignant. 'You seem to think that Adjutants can work miracles,' he snapped at the MP several years his senior. 'You want to post them on the battlefield. It is quite useless to write letters now.' Then he promptly borrowed some of Aubrey's paper and wrote a letter himself, whilst Aubrey passed the time irritating those within earshot with Shakespearean quotes pertaining to cemeteries.

Mid morning arrived. The rising heat combined with the damp to make the atmosphere in the forest stifling and unbearable. At about 11 a.m. there was suddenly an explosion of noise. Ma Jeffreys heard it but couldn't see through the foliage to where the 3rd Coldstream and the Irish Guards had been set upon. The two battalions were over extended, large gaps had opened up between the companies and the Irish Guards were attempting to withdraw slowly down the main road towards Villers-Cotterêts. They could see the Germans coming. As rifle and machine-gun fire fell upon them it was impossible to keep any sense of direction. 'We were together but the wood was so thick that I fear many shot one's own men,' one OE claimed. The terrain was rough. In the half-light there were ferns and brambles waist high, and wide ditches. Aubrey was acting as a galloper, hurtling up and down forest paths carrying information. 'It was like diving on horseback … under ordinary conditions one would have thought it mad to ride at the ridiculous pace we did … but the bullets made everything else irrelevant.' The shower of metal continued to rip through the trees, showering men with leaves and branches. 'The noise was perfectly awful.'

It was impossible to maintain control of the situation. The men of different regiments had become hopelessly confused. Officers took charge of whichever Guardsmen they found. Some orders made it through, others were lost when the men carrying them were cut down. The 3rd Coldstream began to fall back. Hubert Crichton, second in command of the Irish Guards and a veteran of Khartoum and the Boer War, had been at Eton at the same time as Ma Jeffreys in the early 1890s. He had received orders to stay put, but the retirement of their neighbours left him isolated. In the end he fell back too, with German troops just yards from being on top of them.

The brigadier took action. Seizing a company of Grenadier Guards he threw platoons forward, one of them commanded by John Manners. He and his fellow officers charged down a forest path and, taking up the best positions they could, tried to enfilade the Germans. They fought ferociously. Lost amongst the trees they did not receive the order to retire with the rest of the Brigade. Aubrey Herbert watched a man fall to the ground holding a bayonet. Immediately concerned he reined in his horse to see if he could help him but the colonel stopped him. The middle of a chaotic retreat was not the time, he told him. It seemed to the Guards that there was an entire army rolling over them. The Germans were ghostly, flitting out from behind the trees and then back in amongst the greenery.

Shortly after 1 p.m. one of the men coming back to join Aubrey and the colonel claimed that he had seen Hubert Crichton's body lying in the road. Could they be sure? Aubrey was sent forward with directions to investigate. He galloped back through the forest. As he approached the body he realised that it was the man with the bayonet whom he had seen tumble to the ground earlier. A momentary lull had occurred in the firing but the wood was still full of lurking enemy troops. Aubrey jumped from his horse and knelt down. Hubert looked peaceful. Aubrey put his hand on his shoulder and spoke to him for a moment. He leant over his body, mindful of Hubert's wife and two little girls, to check for any letters. Then, hearing German whispers coming from the trees, he fled.

When the Irish Guards finally held a roll call at the end of the regiment's first day of fully fledged battle, the battalion was missing not only its commanding officer, Colonel Morris, and his second in command,

Hubert Crichton, but five more officers were unaccounted for, including
Aubrey Herbert who was in German hands with a bullet in his side. Ma
Jeffreys had assumed command of the Grenadiers and the situation was just as
chaotic in both battalions of the Coldstream. The retreat continued, and the
following morning the Guards moved on, forced to leave the forest of Retz
littered with the bodies of their dead and wounded.

A few days after the clash at Villers-Cotterêts, General Joffre made the landmark decision that would earn him his epitaph as the saviour of France when
he decided to make a stand against the German advance. The Battle of the
Marne followed. Four complete French armies with the BEF, over a million
men, pushed the armies of von Kluck and von Bülow north-east and away
from Paris. By 9 September the Allied forces had succeeded in turning the
tide of the war. Retreat was inevitable and by 10 September it had become
a reality; not a panicked fleeing on the Germans' part; but a sustained retirement nonetheless. The Schlieffen Plan, and with it hopes for a swift, decisive
western victory, had failed.

The war moved back north towards the Aisne. Among the fallen Etonians
left behind on the Marne was Bertrand Stewart who had indeed fulfilled his
threat of coming back to haunt his German captors. Imprisoned under rigor-
ous conditions in the fortress of Glatz he was released as an act of clemency
when George V visited Germany in 1913. By the outbreak of war he had
been promoted to the rank of captain in the West Kent Yeomanry and joined
the cavalry as an intelligence officer, embarking immediately for France. On
12 September, as cavalry patrols pushed on towards the River Vesle, a patrol
entering the village of Braisne was suddenly ambushed. The troops behind
them retired quickly and Bertrand grabbed a rifle and at once assumed command, rallying the patrol and leading it down the slope towards the river to
help the men that had been cut off.

That afternoon a driver attached to the BEF walked the same road, over
pools of fresh blood and dead horses. The view opened out in front of him,
one long line of shell clouds puffing away. The rain came down in sheets: 'the
fight for Braisne was within earshot'. Lying up against a bank by the side of
the road was 41-year-old Bertrand Stewart, his body not yet cold[1].

Aubrey Herbert had been a guest of the German Army for almost two
weeks when the advance came back towards Villers-Cotterêts, liberated him
and saw him evacuated home. Further to the rear George Fletcher walked
alongside his frequently broken motorcycle. 'War is in fact one colossal stink
of dead horse … decay and corruption of every kind – broken harnesses
… helmets cast away and utter desolation,' he told his father. 'We proceeded

with the [stench] of this destruction in our nostrils for a few days till the rains began and then all turned to mud.'

For two weeks the BEF had fled towards the Marne, fighting small rear-guard actions, and it was reasonable to think that, with the German forces now retreating the other way, that it would continue in reverse. By 12 September the BEF had pursued the enemy back to the Aisne itself where miserable downpours had begun swelling the river and the Germans had dug in. Slopes on both sides of the river were covered in wooded areas and foliage that masked movements and troop dispositions. As British and French troops arrived it was unclear whether or not the enemy had left men back to delay them or had thrown everything available into halting their retreat.

Steep hills faced the British troops on the opposite side of the river and more German troops were on their way. Although the armies of von Kluck and von Bülow were not entirely at home in these hurried positions, strung out with gaps in their lines, they possessed heavy artillery with a clear field of fire down to the river where they had already destroyed bridges and crossings. Far from fighting another quick action on the way north, the Kaiser's men had resolved to stay put. What the British Expeditionary Force was seeing were the beginnings of trench warfare and it was to exact a heavy toll on the ranks of Old Etonians beginning to line the banks of the River Aisne.

On 12 September the 9th Lancers were shattered by the cruel loss of Douglas Lucas Tooth. Campbell freely referred to him as his 'most trusted leader'. In private, the sentiment was that the Ninth had 'lost a leader, in whom they had the greatest confidence and belief'. He was experienced, highly competent and universally respected from the ranks of trooper to brigade commander, but his regiment would have to continue without him.

At 2 a.m. the following day the Ninth was roused to begin the action which Sir John French hoped would conclude with the successful capture of the Chemin des Dames, a road running east to west accross the river along a high ridge that was famous as being a prominent route travelled by two daughters of Louis XV. Rivy Grenfell, still without his twin, was amongst elements of the regiment that set out, to cross the Aisne, along with the Harvey brothers. Through the town of Vendresse they climbed on to Troyon, a scattering of cottages and farms overlooked by a dominating plateau. A road wound out of the little hamlet and passed the only landmark in the vicinity, a sugar factory. With high, solid walls and an imposing chimney ideal for observation, the enemy had made it central to their defences in the area. Trenches now branched out from the factory, and artillery batteries had been wheeled into place on either side of the site. Machine guns and troops were ready to drive back any unwanted visitors. It was abundantly clear to the British that any advance to the Chemin des Dames would eventually require the capture of this stronghold.

But another hammer blow was about to fall on the Ninth less than twenty-four hours after Lennie and Douglas Harvey had lost their Squadron Leader. The objective that they had been given was in fact a mile or so behind enemy lines. Without Lucas, the squadron managed to veer off down a stray path and away from the main road. Rivy Grenfell, following with more men, was left exposed and rode right into the path of the enemy. Dismounting, he took a section and bravely went forward, securing a position behind a haystack. He was in good humour, cracking jokes with his men when he was suddenly exposed to enemy fire. The last words his men remembered were 'steady your firing boys we have got them beaten,' before a bullet cut his revolver in two and ricocheted into his head, killing him instantly.

Four miles to the west the 2nd Grenadier Guards, led by Ma Jeffreys, were edging their way down an eerie canal towpath shrouded by fog in a relentless downpour. Tentatively they began to cross a makeshift bridge over the Aisne at 8.30 a.m. Nothing happened. The British were expecting some sort of opposition, but none came. 'Had some German officer blundered or did the enemy not intend to defend the passage of the Aisne?' The fog was in fact providing a protective curtain for the BEF, masking their movements from the German gunners. Edging forward into the town of Soupir, Ma had been given instructions to pass through the town, climb the hill on the other side and secure the high ground above a place called La Coeur de Soupir where there was a substantial farmhouse. Beyond that he knew nothing about where he was or whom he might run in to. 'I was given no information,' he complained, '… either about our own forces or the enemy.'

Thus far they had not set eyes on a German in their wet progress but Ma was cautious. No. 1 Company had been selected as the vanguard and now the decision was made to select bright, young Jack Pickersgill-Cunliffe and his platoon to press on up the road and into the shrouded woods ahead. Jack collected his men and set off. The woods were eerily quiet, with nothing but the sound of the rain coming through the trees. As well as dense foliage, the mist still hid any concentrations of enemy troops from view. Slowly, blindly they made the steep climb up the narrow road, a wall of greenery on either side of them. Robbed of peripheral vision they disappeared from Ma Jeffrey's view. Jack reached the farm. All remained strangely quiet. Around the perimeter of the compound there was no sign of the enemy. They probed cautiously towards a crossroads beyond their final destination.

Jack's platoon was 100 yards past the farm when it came under fire. The enemy came from the north in a surprise attack. The small group of Grenadiers fell in with outposts of Connaught Rangers lurking nearby and together they found themselves on the back foot, being driven back towards the farm where they were overwhelmed and taken prisoner. Further down the road, Ma Jeffreys heard shooting and began sending up reinforcements. His troops were in danger of being outflanked. By mid morning he had almost no men left in reserve and not a clue what was going on in front of him.

Back at the farm, Jack Cunliffe was lying with a badly wounded leg on the floor. Nearly half the battalion had now arrived and the Connaught Rangers had emerged from the farm buildings, which unknown to the Guards they had occupied the night before. The tables had turned. Jack and his men had been saved and their captors were outnumbered and about to become prisoners themselves. The Germans had two choices: fall into British hands or turn and flee. They cut their losses and went with the latter, but not before a despicable act was committed that would send shockwaves through the ranks of Old Etonians at the front and at home. The Germans had an officer among their number. As he was preparing to make his getaway he pulled out a revolver, marched over to where Jack lay hurt on the floor and executed him with a single gunshot wound to the head in front of his men. He was 19 years old.

There were conflicting stories about the fate of the man that murdered him. Some of the men swore blind that they had recognised the officer being led away from the farm at the end of the day with other prisoners. Another story which held weight at the time was that an OE in the 3rd Coldstream had arrived with his company just in time to witness the incident and that his men had taken it upon themselves to bayonet the German on the spot. The Coldstream were, however, still further down the hill towards Soupir and did not arrive until later. Another story, which is even less likely, was repeated by a friend of Jack's, Neville Woodroffe, who was serving in the Irish Guards and not present at the farm when Jack was killed. He claimed that the German officer had been caught 'and having been thoroughly explained why ... he was shot'.

Meanwhile, back near Troyon and the 9th Lancers, Gerard Frederick Freeman-Thomas of the 1st Coldstream Guards had awoken under the cover of some trees to the sound of gunfire raging at the sugar factory. The eldest son of Lord Willingdon, the recently appointed Governor of Bombay, like John Manners 'Gerry' was a talented cricketer and had played at Lord's. His turn came in 1912, two years after John Manners, when the superiority of the Eton XI over Harrow was 'at all times evident'.

Charged with pushing the advance on Troyon forwards after the Ninth had failed, the 1st Coldstream began making their way up, greeted with the encouraging sight of prisoners being led back down the hill towards the river. But they were soon to find themselves in just as much hot water as their Guards counterparts at Soupir.

The beginning of Gerry's advance was similar: a steep uphill climb through wooded heights in driving rain and fog. The going was tough and narrow, and they followed each other up in single file. Once at the top, the true gravity of their task became apparent as they spread out ready to advance into the fray across a flat, open plateau towards the sugar factory. Gerry formed up on the left with the rest of No.1 Company in a line that also included elements of the Scots Guards, the Cameron Highlanders and the Black Watch. An Etonian, John Ponsonby, led Gerry's battalion and had been told to advance straight for the Chemin des Dames.

When, in rotten weather and at the mercy of the German gunners, the British troops went forward into the open it was carnage. Troops that had been involved in the initial onslaught on the factory were crossing their path and in trying to avoid the relentless shellfire being thrown in their direction, battalions ran amongst each other and became immediately muddled. 'Dense mist covered the ground like a pall' and the smoke lingering from the high-explosive shells rendered the men blind and the British artillery redundant. To Ponsonby, the air seemed to be on fire. Out of the mist and rain a shower of bullets and shells swept across the open battlefield, indiscriminately shattering troops.

Ponsonby himself was knocked down twice when shells exploded nearby, but cover was limited to haystacks ripped apart by bullets and holes in the ground. One Guardsman fell wounded and found himself amongst a pile of bodies, another rolled into a ditch to find himself lying in the pouring rain amongst dead and dying men still struggling to shield themselves from bullets flying overhead. All across the plateau men were attempting to patch each other up and get out of harm's way. Gerry Freeman-Thomas was leaning up against a haystack, unable to move and Allen Campbell, another Coldstream Etonian, was attempting to ignore his own injuries as he picked up another officer he had seen fall and carried him a mile to safety. Those that were able to carry on made it to the Chemin des Dames and into German trenches but the strength of the enemy was too great and the men found themselves forced back down the hill to where they had begun.

By 11 a.m. it was clear that as far as the 1st Coldstream Guards was concerned, the attack on the Chemin des Dames was a failure. The battalion lost more than a third of its strength including seventy-seven confirmed dead.

With no reserves and dwindling ammunition they turned and retraced their steps back down the slope towards the river. The attempt to seize the high ground across the Aisne had failed but subsequent German counter-attacks failed to repel allied forces from the river. The initial war of movement was over and a stalemate ensued, one that would last more than four years. At the Battle of the Aisne the Western Front had been born.

In the autumn of 1914, before the vicious fighting over Ypres or the carnage on the Somme, the effect of such casualties and the confusion over the fates of these young officers and their men was traumatising. Half of the OEs who fell in mid September were never recovered, the biggest percentage for a single engagement during the war. Likewise, it was the first instance in which large numbers of Old Etonians were killed owing to their concentration in particular regiments. More than half of the OEs who fell in advancing back across the Aisne came from Guards' regiments. Neville Woodroffe, a young OE in the 1st Irish Guards, was devastated. 'It's awful what the Brigade … has lost and being like one big regiment one knows everyone and feels it all the more … we always just seem to hit the unlucky day to be where the thick of it is.'

Soupir Communal Cemetery was among the early sites begun specifically to hold the remains of British soldiers on the Western Front. Before that, they had largely been buried in plots in French civilian churchyards and burial grounds. Soupir contains the highest proportion of Great War Etonian graves in a cemetery anywhere in the world: 50 per cent of the dead were educated at Eton College.

In such cases as La Coeur de Soupir the fighting had taken place in a relatively concentrated area about the farm and the British had continued to hold the ground. At nightfall on 14 September the Brigade was able to stand still and take stock, treating the wounded and dying on site and evacuating them in organised fashion over the course of a number of days and carrying out burials itself. Jack Cunliffe was laid to rest alongside his fellow Etonians.

At Villers-Cotterêts and by the Chemin des Dames the chaos was on a far grander scale and complicated by the fact that British forces had fallen back, having to leave wounded and dying men on the battlefield. Whether or not the Etonians who fell would rest in carefully tended plots or in complete anonymity mostly came down to sheer luck. In some cases though, those that received news of a confirmed burial in a marked grave, whether it be Old Etonians, their fellow officers or the men that served with them, owed this resolution to the stubborn determination of families who displayed a complete refusal to believe that their son, brother or grandson could simply vanish on a battlefield.

Hubert Crichton's death was a certainty and his body had ended up at the communal cemetery at Puiseux.[2] Lord and Lady Cecil's missing teenage son, George, was not an OE, but he was a grandson of Lord Salisbury, the former Prime Minister, and when they took up the task of finding out what had happened to their boy at Villers-Cotterêts they were also keen to find out whatever they could about his fellow Grenadier, John Manners. The hardest fact to ascertain at first was whether they had actually fallen or were in a German prisoner-of-war camp.

As in the case of Jack Cunliffe's murder, rumours ran throughout the Brigade and beyond until they reached home shores. Lady Cecil referred to a 'particularly cruel' story about John doing the rounds in London. Unsubstantiated, where it began is unclear but she seemed to be referring to a whisper that also appeared in a letter home from Neville Woodroffe. He had heard that having failed to retreat owing to a lost order John found himself surrounded by Germans with just five men and had allegedly shot himself in the head rather than surrender.

On 9 September Lady Manners received a letter from one of John's fellow officers to say that he was missing. He had watched John go up with his platoon and hadn't seen him since. 'My supposition is that he was most likely taken prisoner,' he reassured her; the same fate as officers Buddy Needham and George Cecil. So hope still existed. A few days later though, young Lord Congleton, an OE who had just arrived at the front penned a hurried letter to a friend of his and John's. 'I don't know what news has reached home,' he began, but after the devil of a fight it was apparently clear to all in the battalion that John was dead. Of the three platoons sent to assist the Irish Guards, John's, Buddy Needham's and George Cecil's, only seven men had come back in. 'They report that there are about thirty more wounded prisoners in German hands.' Of the nineteen original sub-alterns Congleton reported the 2nd Grenadier Guards had three left on his arrival.

It would transpire that John had sadly been struck down whilst directing his platoon's fire in the woods, as had George Cecil. Now Lady Manners and Lady Cecil were consumed with trying to find out where their boys had been laid to rest. Lady Cecil arrived in Villers-Cotterêts before September had passed and found herself less than 15 miles from the front, facing a conflict-ing fog of misinformation and confusion. Enlisting the help of the American ambassador in Paris, who gave her a car and a military attaché, she battled her way to the necessary passes to get up to the front where the mayor of Villers-Cotterêts, a Dr Moufflers, had been instructed to provide her with assistance.

She found the town and those nearby littered with caps and men's pocket books. Moufflers directed her to gravesites dug by the French locals and the British prisoners where she was told that any papers identifying the men had been sent to Paris. In the forest itself were two large mass graves dug by the Germans and or prisoners depending on who was giving testimony. One was full of German soldiers and another that seemed, by the amount of khaki caps scattered on the ground, to be full of British troops. Somebody had stuck up a notice indicating that there were twenty men there but nobody knew who.

With his parents in India, Lord and Lady Brassey were pulling every string they could in looking for their grandson, Gerry Freeman-Thomas. It was to be a particularly painful and drawn-out search. Lord Brassey had sent a man to the Aisne and, like Lady Cecil, had approached the American ambassador with no result. By December 1914, however, he and Lady Brassey had managed to accumulate a fair amount of detail about Gerry's part in the advance on the Chemin des Dames by interviewing survivors. A corporal named William Roderick, the son of a Welsh rugby international, had seen Gerry fall whilst advancing across the plateau towards the sugar factory and ran over to him. He found him with a severe wound to his thigh, bleeding heavily. Gerry was adamant that he move on without him and so he continued his advance. His captain, another OE named Gordon Hargreaves Brown, had bound up the wound as best he could to try to stem the flow of blood and he had propped the 21 year old against a haystack where he hoped Gerry would be safe. At some point another injured Coldstream man was placed with him. They were close to enemy lines, as German troops spotted the wounded men and brought them hot coffee and food, although the family also recalled an account that had the enemy setting light to the haystack at some stage. At dusk the other man made his getaway, but Gerry's leg was too painful and he could not follow. The following morning a search party was sent out to bring him back but the young Etonian had simply vanished.

During the course of their investigations the family had for a time believed that Gerry was being treated at a hospital in Cassel, only to have this hope taken away. At the turn of the year, four months after the battle for the sugar factory, the family was 'anxious but by no means hopeless'. By the summer of 1915 though, no more information had come to light regarding his fate. The matter of settling his affairs had begun. It was carried out on the assumption that Gerry had died on or since 14 September, although a reserve was put on his property should he reappear. Lady Brassey, however, had given up all hope of finding her grandson, and 21-year-old Gerry Freeman-Thomas was never seen or heard from again.

At Villers-Cotterêts, desperate families had found the answers they were looking for, but only after resorting to extreme measures. Lady Manners had been given the names of three Grenadiers in captivity in Doberitz and their service numbers so that she could attempt to contact them at their camp. She sent them care parcels and corresponded with them. Two, a Lance Corporal Massey and a Private Bird, claimed to have buried John in a mass grave and described the tree that had been marked up with the details next to the burial site. Another knew nothing of the burial but believed what the others said. Anyone not present appeared to be quoting Massey, who claimed to have been part of the burial team.

Following Lady Cecil's visit, the mass grave in the forest had become the focus of attention in the search for her George, John Manners and their fellow offi-cers. Another member of the Cecil family returned to the area. Accompanying was Lord Killanin, the brother of Colonel Morris, commanding officer of the Irish Guards, who had vanished leaving a widow and a four-week-old son. They appeared on Dr Moufflers' doorstep in mid November 1914 looking for permits to go into the woods. The makeshift grave was located amongst the trees by the side of the forest road leading away from the town. The large plot was marked by a rudimentary cross and some wreaths left by the locals. With heavy hearts and a team of six men they began the grim task of exhuming the bodies, the sound of the guns at the front booming in the distance.

It became apparent that there were far more than twenty men buried in the plot. It was also clear that the burial party had taken little care. The fallen soldiers were tangled together 'as thrown in anyhow, one after the other'. The team began extending the grave, removing identity discs and laying out the men in proper fashion for burial. 'The faces were quite unrecognisable … often smashed. 'These men,' wrote Lord Killanin, 'had been dead for two-and-a-half months. In no case was it possible to identify a body by features, hair, teeth, owing to the amount of time … and the way in which these bodies had been treated.' He was unable to recognise his brother until they found his engraved wristwatch on his remains. George Cecil was identified by his monogrammed vest and his Grenadier buttons, some of which were removed for his mother. Another body was carefully lifted out of the pit and placed on the ground. It was evident that the clothing was that of an officer. Removing the disc from around his neck they were able to identify 26-year-old Geoffrey Lambton, an OE who was known to have been killed early on in the day on 1 September.

No trace was found of John Manners. In desperation his mother began writing to senior officers of the regiment and one was convinced that he was in the same cemetery as George Cecil in the forest. 'I went very carefully into the question in about the middle of September,' he told her. 'I am as certain as I can be that your boy was buried with George Cecil and other British soldiers in the same grave ... The evidence I got was from Grenadiers who knew your boy well and I have not a doubt that they are correct.'

Their testimony was dubious though. The officer admitted that by December, when he wrote to Lady Manners, all of the men who had provided the information were dead or gone from the regiment having been wounded; he couldn't remember which. One who did survive and continued to speak about having been coerced into burying his fallen colleagues was a young drummer boy. He paid a visit to John's grandmother and his sister Betty went to interview him. He was a pleasant boy and he told a beautiful story about finding John's body; his revolver grasped in one hand and his sword heroically in the other with a clean bullet wound to the head. He retold how along with a number of other casualties, including George Cecil, John was taken to the mass burial site and that their German captors removed all personal items and rifled the men's pockets. 'I love to think of him dying as he lived, clasping his sword so proud and triumphant,' wrote Betty.

His story was a comfort, but Lady Cecil was not convinced. '[His] stories were so ... fantastic, as you know ... it really was not evidence until corroborated.' Indeed a full two years later, as the Battle of the Somme raged, another senior officer was adamant that John had not necessarily been buried in the forest. 'I can give you no definitive information,' he commiserated. Certainly no identity disc of John was found when Lord Killanin's team went through the morbid process of identifying the remains and separating the bodies of the likes of George Cecil and Geoffrey Lambton. 'Your son's body was not found in this grave. We have no record at all of where he is buried. I wish most sincerely that I could tell you more, but I fear it is hopeless.' Lord and Lady Manners were still trying to seek clarification as to whether or not John had been buried with his fallen friends when the war was all but over. The waiting was indescribable but the alternative was not much better. 'Grief does not really bring it quite home,' Lady Cecil wrote after she had found all of her answers in the forest at Villers-Cotterêts. 'I still feel as if I were waiting – tho' there is nothing now to wait for.'

John Manners' name joined that of Gerry Freeman-Thomas on the memorial 40 miles east of Paris on the south bank of the Marne at La Ferté-sous-Jouarre. Here 3,739 men who disappeared during the retreat and subsequent advance back to the Aisne in 1914 were commemorated.

John's former house master was shattered by his death. Hubert Brinton would lose twenty-nine of his boys before the war was over. He and his wife were devastated by the loss of John. They hoped and prayed that the rumours of him being a prisoner were true and that he was safe. When confirmation arrived that John had been killed Brinton was beside himself. He couldn't speak his name without tears. 'Three months of war,' he wrote soon after, 'and life changed forever, for so many.' John's parents went to see him at Eton and he thought that he had made an absolute fool of himself because he had sat in front of them in silence. He sought to explain himself in a letter to Lady Manners. 'I *couldn't* talk about him while you and his father were sitting there in the study. It must have seemed strange to you.'

Billy Grenfell had been at Eton and Oxford with John, but their friendship transcended that. Their families were close and they were like brothers. Billy wrote to John's mother in agony. 'I think so often that I owe to him and you the happiest days,' he wrote. Their set, 'our little band of brothers', was falling apart 'and it is such pain for me to think of losing him, to all of you it must be as if the sun has gone out of the heavens'.

In all, the men at Villers-Cotterêts had removed ninety-eight bodies from the German-dug grave including four known officers. All but one man belonged to the 4th Guards Brigade. Pocket books were removed with identity discs and the names of as many as possible recorded. As a result of their determination, almost one hundred men; seventy-eight of them identified, received a fitting burial and commemoration at Guards Grave. Kipling referred to the cemetery as one of the most picturesque in France. The men were cared for diligently by Dr Moufflers until the advent of the Imperial War Graves Commission. 'Irreparable as is the loss suffered by the loss of those officers and soldiers,' remarked Lord Killanin, 'and awful as the work of exhumation was, it is to me an abiding consolation … to know that their remains were rescued from an utterly unknown grave … and have been laid to rest … [with] respect and reverence and affection and honour.'

Of the twenty unidentified men amongst the trees at Villers-Cotterêts it has never been confirmed if one of them was John Manners. At home in Hampshire, an effigy was fashioned of him laid out in his uniform. It forms the centrepiece of a memorial in a private chapel as if it were a tomb. 'It is where he would have liked to lie,' wrote one of his best friends, 'on that lonely windswept hill, looking over the wide expanse of the New Forest that he loved.'

Notes
1. Bertrand Stewart was laid to rest in Braine Communal Cemetery.
2. Hubert Crichton's body was relocated to Montreuil-aux-Lions British Cemetery in the 1930s.

5

'God Won't Let Those Devils Win'

Along with the rest of the BEF, George Fletcher had travelled some 200 miles in three weeks during the retreat, wrestling with his smell and hoping to exchange the 'infernal instrument' for transport of the four-legged variety. He had considered simply abandoning it on more than one occasion, but a last-minute pang of conscience about what the king would think of him if he simply abandoned His Majesty's motorcycle to the Germans inspired him to continue tinkering with it until it jumped back into life. Having been so desperate to get to war, George admitted freely in his letters that he was living a 'pig-like life', destitute as his baggage had been unceremoniously tossed from the lorries to lighten the load. 'A column of sleepless and foodless men staggering along mile after mile is a mighty different thing from a route march at home: and as far as the sight of a horse camp after being surprised by artillery fire, or the road to the firing line in the rear after a big fight, it is a thing not sung of by Homer … or anyone else' he told his father.

'You may imagine me,' George wrote, 'sleeping in a wet trench with bombs bursting all around and the next man grovelling with a bullet through his spleen.' In reality, he admitted, he was curled up in an armchair in front of a fire with a cat purring away on the hearth. The Aisne was a quiet affair for George. The misty mornings reminded him of Eton, 'of early days in the autumn half … and sweaty wall games'. From little igloos made out of brushwood, filled with straw and blankets, George listened to the booming of the guns whilst they sat in reserve. 'During this time our Brigade goes off on manoeuvres in the field like the ECOTC till lunch, after which it reads the papers till tea-time, when it does a little close-order drill and goes to bed. *C'est magnifique, mais ce n'est pas guerre.'*

His period of inaction on the Aisne gave George plenty of time to contemplate how much he missed Eton. His father had moved into his old flat on the High Street and was one of a number of academics volunteering to fill in for younger masters departing for Kitchener's army. George was desperate to hear how he was getting on. 'It is so funny to think of him teaching small boys Latin grammar and I want especially to hear all about my dear stupid pupils.' He could imagine 'thirty ridiculous puppies' gawping in front of his father. 'How they will make you grind your teeth at times, and how you will like them at others.'

One member of the Fletcher family who was languishing even further away from the action was George's younger brother Regie. Five years his junior, Regie too had been a King's Scholar at Eton before going on to Oxford. The fact that he was twenty-two did not stop their father from proudly referring to him as his 'baby'. The brothers didn't look at all alike. George was stocky, whilst Regie was tall and graceful in his movements with reddish gold hair. Where George leaned towards languages and cherished the idea of a pet kitten in his dugout, Regie loved poetry, literature and above all his dog Muncles. Like his elder brother though, Regie was an accomplished oar. Having developed late, he did not feature much at Eton but at Oxford, where he followed George in 1910, he rowed stroke in the Balliol boat for four years, in the Leander Four at Henley and in the University Boat Race in 1914.

Regie's other great pastime was the Oxford University OTC. Much more elaborate than its cohort at Eton, it featured an artillery section and during his four years as part of it Regie rose to second in command. He loved his guns and had already decided on a military career when the Great War came. One of the first of the University men to be called up, Regie was on holiday in Ireland and ended up on a train with 'about 25 carriages carrying a howling drunken mob' to report as reservists to a base. Within a few days a 'rabble' of forty men had turned up and been shoved in his direction. 'I am trying to provide for them; but I should think they will starve fairly soon, as I haven't the faintest idea what to do,' he joked.

Regie had a unique charm. He had a temper; and absolutely no issue with letting anyone, be he a gunner or a general, know exactly what he thought of them. Thanks to his years on the river, which required a certain amount of unique motivational speaking, he had learned to do so in the most innovative and colourful manner. Before he had even landed at Havre in the last week of August, he had established a mutual vendetta with a captain of a Scottish regiment. Once in France it was two native soldiers who made his life difficult that felt the wrath of his sharp tongue by way of 'an assortment of French oaths interspersed with a few sound English damns, to great amusement of admiring crowd of Tommies'. He varied his repertoire when necessary and could do subtlety. Havre was abandoned during the retreat and the base relocated to St Nazaire. Put on a ship and stuffed into a cabin where three other officers, a collection of what he termed 'bores and mangy dug-out Captains', chose to ignore his obvious preparations for bed and continued 'drinking whiskey and talking rubbish' he simply stripped off the shirt he hadn't removed for nearly a month. '*Exeunt omnes.*'[1]

Whatever his capacity for 'abuse' when the situation vexed him, Regie was also noted for his affectionate nature. The first thing he did on landing in France was to go and buy a stock of footballs so that his men might have something to do. Once they arrived at their new base in St Nazaire he was thoroughly disgusted to find that no provision had been made to give the men shelter from the rain. Their constant discomfort angered him to the point that Regie led a raid on the Remount Depot to liberate some tents that they had in stores. 'Owing to stupidity of sentry' he very nearly got away with it. They made off with twelve tents and two poles but were caught. As the only officer present Regie stood and took the earbashing on behalf of all and even put up a fight before he had to yield to a higher-ranked officer and give them back. 'My reputation is quite gone,' he remarked, but the men were grateful for the effort. His worst stream of vitriol though, even more so than those aimed at the Germans, was Regie's reaction to the curators of a park at home. They had been setting out traps and threatening Muncles the dog, whose picture would go everywhere with his master at the front to keep the bullets away. He gave his aunt explicit instructions. 'If my dog gets killed in a trap ... I will come back when this war is over with an 18-pounder gun, line them all up in the middle ... of the cricket field and then bring my gun into action ... "Target, curators of the park, range 100 yards, fuse zero. One round gunfire."' Please give them this message with my compliments.'

For someone as eager as Regie, sitting at a camp in complete ignorance of how the war was progressing and playing no active part in it was not only 'damnable', 'intolerable', but frightening. The camps were rife with unsettling rumours during the retreat. Almost as soon as Regie arrived it began. 'Amiens evacuated? What is going to happen? Suspense awful.' It didn't matter how outlandish the stories were. On this occasion the Germans were supposed to be bearing down on Havre in motor cars laden with Maxim guns. By 11 p.m. this was apparently fact. Packed up and ready to run, Regie and his unarmed men were told in no uncertain terms that if they heard rifles, they

were to flee to the docks. 'Where are we going to? They say not England ...
Is George alive? What has happened to the fleet?' Tales of the annihilation of
20,000 men arrived, along with bloody rifles that were piled in the stores. Ten
days later Regie spotted a piece of artillery; 'sight broken, shield splintered ...
also the limber wheels are broken. There are bloody pieces of meat stuck to
the gun.' He was in no doubt that if the Germans broke through to the coast
they would be done for. 'There will be some sort of massacre ... I have a baby
pistol and a toothpick. Probably shall chuck latter away and use fist.'

The rumours turned out to be false. 'I am sitting here in a rage like a poisoned
rat in a hole,' Regie fumed. 'If only I had joined some damned line regiment, at
least I should be fighting now instead of running away without firing a shot.'
For Regie and those sharing his plight, they alternated between bouts of semi-
optimism ('The war will probably last long enough to kill me and Kitchener's
army as well') and all out despondency ('Every bit of news makes us more miserable and restless'). To make it worse, new arrivals were being sent up to the front
immediately. 'Miserable little squirts ... vile ... little unweaned rats ... boys who
six months ago were fags at their public schools.' It was beyond all things con-
ceivable. 'Our language would make mother's hair turn white.'

In the event, the subalterns at the camp resorted to squabbling with each
other. It was every man for himself and one senior officer had marked Regie
as an Oxford Blue and deemed it sufficient qualification for a speedy posting
to the front. When he informed his brother subalterns that he was off, the
reaction was typical. One officer flew into paroxysms of rage, hurling blasphe-
mies and every swear word under the sun at Regie until he had completely
exhausted his vocabulary. He used more abusive language to Regie's face than
the latter had used in the entire duration of his rowing career. Another officer
didn't have it in him to swear, but said he'd be damned if Regie would go if
he could help it. 'Polite and cheery, aren't they?'

Regie honestly didn't care. On 21 September he and fifty men were sent
off to entrain for the Aisne to join an artillery outfit that had suffered heavy
casualties. Regie was delighted and sat in the door of the train with his legs
dangling out of the window. 'I really am now going to the firing line to take
an active part in the Great War,' he gloated. On his way he learned from fellow
officers that had seen it for themselves that it was deadlocked, an artillery
duel; the Germans heavy guns on one side, British artillery on the other. His
brother George, bored at the front, was in agreement. 'The ... kind of fighting our infantry has done, besides waiting in a trench, has been lying down
waiting for our guns to silence the enemy's guns ... I'm sure Regie has the
real job of the War ... for at present the artillery is the great thing.'

The Royal Field Artillery Brigade that Regie was to join at Paissy consisted of eighteen guns, split into three numbered batteries with six guns each – 116, 117 and 118 – and contained approximately 800 men at full strength. Together they had lost eight of eighteen officers on the Aisne. For much of it, they hadn't been able to get near the guns to fire them, such was the accuracy of their German counterparts. The Scottish rugby international that Regie was to replace was accounted for with a direct hit. Regie detrained and was taken through the woods to a turnip field just by Moulins where Douglas Lucas-Tooth had been buried. There he found the guns surrounded by enormous mounds of earth and concealed by brushwood and large branches. That afternoon they had been discovered by the Germans and shells had been dropping within 10 yards of their precious eighteen pounders, smashing holes in the ground.

Life in the ECOTC had taught Regie the basics in military terms and its counterpart at Oxford had taught him how a gun was fired, but once he got to the Aisne he found that he had much to learn in terms of war. There was the sight of the dead and wounded littered on the ridge, birds circling overhead, and the hardships of life at the front. Some were harder to accept, such as attacks of dysentery and dwindling supplies of tobacco. 'In a couple of days I shall be worse than starving … when my pouch is empty, God help anyone who annoys me.' For the most part Regie bore the rest in good humour. He had had all of his hair shorn off and joked that he would be ugly when he was old and bald. Boredom was abated by frequent rides on one of the two horses he had with him; especially 'The Playboy,' which he had named after a literary character. He rejoiced in getting a rare proper wash. He would sit on a heap of straw with his boots and socks off and wiggle his toes about 'like a baby, in sheer delight at the sight of them.'

Nothing, though, prepared him to being lulled to sleep by the sound of howitzer shells. 'I'm afraid,' he wrote. 'The noise makes one think one is a dead man already.' He panicked at the perpetual banging of the guns and couldn't tell if he was actually under fire. 'It must wear men down to a shadow.' Quickly, Regie learned the absolute necessity of digging. He took up a shovel and fashioned himself a square pit with additional cubby holes at two corners for extra protection. 'The noise is appalling; with your own guns blazing away, a battery … just behind you and the bursting of shrapnel all round.' Within a few days though he had adjusted sufficiently to be pacified by smoking his pipe under fire and was even writing letters whilst the shells rained down.

Their favoured objective was a German battery some 100 yards behind the enemy trenches on the opposite side of the river. All day long they fired at each other while the infantry sat still. Sometimes they were required to jump out of bed and fire at night too and during busy periods they would sleep by the guns. The German gunners were indiscriminate. 'I had not a stitch on my body when she first came … I don't mind when I am fully clothed, but when splinters come whistling round one's bare legs it ceases to be a joke,' Regie commented wryly.

He learned that, to a gunner, aeroplanes were evil; circling about till they spotted a line of guns and then directing German fire on to them. When one buzzed into sight a shout went up and the officers and men scattered into hiding or did their best impressions of a tree. But the most frightening introduction was to the enemy's high explosive shells, 'Black Maria'. She whistled as she came through the air, singing. George had seen it in action. 'One, two, three tornadoes of earth coming nearer and nearer … the crash was awful.' As she exploded she sent splinters: 'great jagged, hot bits of iron' in all directions. Regie was subjected to it constantly and found that some dealt with the threat of it better than others:

> The senior subaltern is married. Somehow he seems to pay little attention to Maria. Perhaps if I was married I should be given the necessary inspiration of bravery; but being just a blasphemous bachelor, whenever the old bitch comes singing through the air I duck my head and drop into my pit.

As well as dodging shrapnel, Regie was also learning that life or death at the front was a lottery. One morning he had climbed into his married friend's shelter for tea when the Germans opened a bombardment and it began to rain shrapnel, shaking the leaves above their heads. He wished to God he could be in his larger, more efficient shelter. At a lull in the fighting he made a dash for his pit. 'What do I find lying in the bottom of it but a great, hot, jagged splinter … about eighteen inches long.' He was resolved to live life for the here and now. In the next hour he might receive a bullet in the head or a thousand cigarettes might arrive in the post, you just couldn't tell.

Finally, Regie had learned that, as sharp as he thought he was, he still had a thing or two to learn from senior officers. He had sent a man to the guard room for answering back and he remained locked up until the major returned the next morning. 'I always thought I was fairly adequate in abuse. But when this creature put up as his defence: "I didn't think a Second Lieutenant could order me to the Guard Room," I just stood and gasped for ten minutes while this old retired Major talked to him. I never heard such [abuse] in my life, and the old man never once repeated himself.'

Regie's induction to life under fire on the Aisne was short; not because of flying shrapnel but because the French were about to relieve the BEF in the area. Sir John French had coveted a move north for some time. In the interests of supply lines and reinforcements it was desirable to be as close to the Channel as possible. Additionally, the German High Command had resolved to push for the Channel to gain a stronger footing in Belgium and threaten Britain itself. A mass logistical effort ferried the BEF north, in large part by rail, and when further troops arrived they would form a line from Armentières in the south all the way up to the area surrounding a little town in Belgium that was about to become engrained on British consciousness: Ypres.

Approaching Belgian shores in the first week of October was a mounted contingent that, like the 9th Lancers, contained large numbers of Old Etonians. The Household Cavalry, comprising the Royal Horse Guards (The Blues) and the 1st and 2nd Life Guards (The Royals) landed at Ostend and Zeebrugge and concentrated in Bruges in pouring rain on 9 October.

Arriving in the SS *Basil* was Charles Sackville Pelham, Lord Worsley. Affectionately known as 'Otto' to his colleagues owing to his resemblance to a famous jockey, he had been an extremely shy child with an intense love of horses when he arrived at Eton in 1899. Whilst not a brilliant academic, he approached everything he did in a painstaking and conscientious manner. He could not abide liars or fools, but had a wickedly good sense of humour. 'He sees a joke at once,' said his tutor. 'Always an asset to a young man with many friends.' Worsley's path to Sandhurst had long since been decided on. With additional tutoring in Frankfurt and Touraine in languages he joined the Blues, his grandfather's regiment, in 1907 and took command of the regimental machine-gun section. In 1911 he became a married man and brother-in-law to Douglas Haig.

From Bruges the Household Cavalry turned south and commenced a tortuous march. It hardly felt like war. 'It all seems so strange,' Worsley noted as he led a machine-gun company south. 'One would think one was on manoeuvres.' In no time at all though, events would take a most serious turn and the Blues and Royals would be in the very centre of the action. As they advanced towards the fray they were cold, wet and tired, but they were all in good spirits. 'Two of my drivers are just like music-hall turns and keep us all in shrieks of laughter all the time we are halted in the road; they are priceless.' They reached Ypres on 13 October and were sitting in the town square under the shadow of the medieval cloth hall. Less than a week later the German artillery would open fire on the thirteenth-century building and begin its systematic destruction.

On 19 October 1914, the battle for Ypres began. As part of an intended Allied offensive to push the Germans back towards their homeland the French had occupied Roulers and the Household Cavalry was ordered to protect them. They set out on a reconnaissance amidst rumours of German troops concentrating in the area. Don't worry, the French told them; there is nothing ahead of you. Within 250 yards they were under fire. Another OE, the Blues' adjutant, watched the brigade retreat west from a burning Roulers in the distance; covered by Worsley and his machine guns. By the end of the day the Germans had advanced up to 9 miles. The population of Roulers was streaming away toward Passchendaele. Worsley and his guns were unscathed, but he was witnessing the worst of the war. In the evenings the regiment billeted in empty houses where they found meals on the table, indicating the speed with which their inhabitants had fled. 'One's heart bleeds for them … leaving every mortal thing.'

Regie Fletcher was not having a merry time either. His artillery brigade had arrived at Hazebrouck where troops were stacking up and tempers were becoming frayed. A body of men, including his own, had been billeted in a farm where the owner was none too pleased about having British troops sleeping in her outbuildings. The men knew exactly which officer to call upon. A bombardier hunted Regie down and complained that the old lady had locked up the water pump and wouldn't let them take anything with which to cook their potatoes. Regie politely asked that she might give him some water personally. No. He tried again, in the sweetest manner possible and still she refused. His temper rapidly diminishing Regie continued to reason with the 'old shrew out of Shakespeare' until he finally snapped. 'I told her in good English that she was the most sour-faced cross-grained old [hag] I had ever met (and one or two other things as well).' The old scold went off obediently and unlocked the pump.

Now the old lady had realised that Regie was in a position of authority she sought him out for all her complaints about the soldiers living on her land. On one occasion she came after him to say that the sergeants had lit a fire in their makeshift mess that would burn her house down. He went to look and ascertained that in fact this was hardly likely to be the case. 'I tell her not to worry herself or me.' She promptly burst into tears, to which Regie was immune. 'Weep on madame; when the Germans come you will have something to weep for.' 'I would rather have the Germans than the English' she spat. He replied, '*Ah taisez-vous Madame; allez-vous en tout suit à coucher.*' ('Be quiet *Madame*; go to bed now.')

The day after the Household Cavalry was pushed away from Roulers, Regie and his guns crossed into Belgium. It was dull and dreary with a miserable drizzle throughout the day. The journey was arduous and Regie amused himself on their halts by making friends with tabby kittens and French soldiers; and putting giggling little Belgian children up on The Playboy and leading him around. Finally, 116th Battery rolled to a stop at Pilckem, some 5 miles to the north-east of Ypres. The country they found there was distinctly unsuited to the workings of an artillery battery. The whole of the area to the east of Ypres was flat. With no high ground to review the terrain, the Germans had taken to destroying any windmills, church spires or vantage points. The artillerymen would have to rely on conducting much of their ranging and observations by walking forward into the lines with a map and a compass in hand. The area around Pilckem already showed signs of heavy fighting on 21 October. Regie's commanding officer had been out to have a look around and had seen French territorials who had been blown to pieces by shells, about twenty of them, mangled and in a disgusting state.

The following day a change occurred. 118th Battery had been sent further east towards Langemarck in pursuit of the Germans. On the way through the town one of its subalterns was struck in the elbow by shrapnel and a reshuffle of the dwindling junior officers was required. Regie had just finished shaving when the major arrived and told him he was required to replace him. 'Great bore this' was all he had to say. He had come to like 116th. 'I say goodbye and reluctantly pack up.' The personnel in his new battery were nice enough though. His new major was apt to be rather too serious for Regie's liking; every time he saw Regie in his non-regulation Leander scarf his face would contort accordingly. Regie was thrilled though to find that the other subaltern was a Cambridge oar. 'He was a Jesus … man and a member of Leander … I doubt if there is another Battery in the army that would hold on to Fawley in a pair!'[2]

His men were raw. Every single one was a replacement for gunners that had been lost in the retreat. 'New sergeants, new men, new guns, new horses.' The first thing he did was sit down and give them some instruction. Half of them didn't know the guns and even fewer knew how to operate the dial sight. This rudimentary lesson had to suffice. At lunchtime they came into action and began blazing away. The Germans came within 1,000 yards of the guns and shells began dropping all around; rifle bullets were pinging off the guns and their carriages. 'The brutes began sniping us … Suddenly one beautiful shot came and burst above my head and the [shrapnel] went crashing into the trees behind.' The order came to retire and 118th Battery limbered up under heavy rifle fire. Regie's men were having a cruel introduction to the realities of war and he was forced to do much of the preparatory work himself. 'My new section did not like it at all … I had to do the final adjustments myself.'

They retreated carrying wounded men they found nearby on their carriages and Regie sympathised with his frightened, inexperienced men. Rifle bullets chased them in the driving rain. Dusk fell early. Men fell asleep in their dinner plates and Regie, who had subsisted on nothing but lumps of chocolate lovingly sent by his mother since 5.30 that morning, couldn't find

the energy to eat a thing. Frantically they attempted to dig in and camouflage their guns. Finding themselves in a cornfield Regie prayed to God that
German pilots knew nothing about harvesting and in late October began
disguising them as giant corn stooks. 'My only hope is that the entire field
does not catch fire when we blaze off.' That day he watched lines of German
prisoners being led past the field. 'I have never seen such poor wretches. Some
boys of only sixteen, some crumplety old men … all the most miserable looking scallywags.' He found it oddly cheering. Surely if that was all the Kaiser
had to offer by way of men then victory had to be just around the corner.

The frenzied firing was not to last. The following day 118th Battery fired
nothing before lunchtime, although they could hear 'a devil of a battle' going on
towards Ypres in the south. Regie even had time to sit down and give his section a lecture on 'The Art of War as Practiced by 2nd Lieutenant R. W. Fletcher,
RFA'. The battle hadn't stopped, and neither had the German gunners, but the
fact was that the British artillery were running out of shells. On 24 October a
limit was placed on expenditure. Regie's battery was equipped with eighteen
pounders and from now on they would be restricted to 120 shells per day
for the four guns in his care. The day before the restriction was imposed he
claimed to have fired 700 in about twelve hours. If he fired this new lower
amount over the same period he would be firing each gun once every twenty
minutes, whereas in the heat of battle on 23 October, he had been timing his
battery's fire at forty-five-second intervals. It was a dramatic reduction.

The shortage was not a surprise. It was apparent on the Aisne that demand
was outstripping supply. The British Army was not guilty of outright negli-
gence. It had two-and-a-half times the amount of shells available in 1899. The
fact was that neither Britain, France, nor Germany, all of whom would begin
to run out of shells, had anticipated just how much modern industrialised
warfare would be dominated by artillery. Along with their dwindling supply
of shells, the theories, tactical doctrine and assumptions of all of the war's
major combatants were being tossed to the wind.

Regie and his brigade left their corn field on 24 October. Rather than listening to the furore of the battle to the south they were being fed into it. The
logistics were absolute chaos. Every time they attempted to limber up the
Germans pummelled them with another barrage. They finally got away in the
early hours of the morning and trudged off into the fog. Men lay sleeping in
ditches, every country road was choked with a cacophony of guns, wounded
men, straggling, exhausted troops, wagons and refugees fleeing for their lives.
Panic reigned. One general was in such a hurry that he charged an entire
brigade of infantry through the middle of 118th Battery, cutting off Regie,

supplies, horses and a gun. Tempers frayed. Precious guns were not supposed to travel in the rear without an escort and Regie told him so, but the high-ranking officer would not let him pass. It was the 'greatest honour' of Regie's young life when the great man labelled him an 'impudent young blackguard'.

Their new home, when they finally got there, was to be in the thickest part of the action as the battle intensified. The guns were rolled up under cover of a small wood at Veldhoek, near Ypres. Within two days GHQ had abandoned any attempts to try to regulate the number of shells being fired. Any hardship Regie had yet faced was about to be magnified considerably. The Germans were about to introduce a third of their armies into the cauldron of noise, chaos and shells in an attempt to make a decisive push towards Ypres, and beyond that, the Channel.

Regie was aware of the rumours of an impending attack, but enthusiastic. The sight of the prisoners had given him hope and convinced him that the Germans were 'obviously' putting their last reserves into the field. He even felt sorry for them. 'These poor German lambs led to the slaughter to gratify the ambitions of a few swollen headed vampires.' He felt even sorrier for his compatriots in the British infantry. He had been dragged out of bed after a full day's work and sent into the line with some Coldstream Guards to spot potential targets for his guns. Regie was 'tremendously impressed' at how they managed to function in the face of the combined threats of snipers, machine guns, shrapnel and Black Maria. A mere month ago he had expressed his distaste for 'foot-sloggers'. Now he thought that the infantry were 'really marvellous'.

British troops were not occupying trenches of the elaborate nature that would follow later in the war. These were ditches, scraped out of the mud with whatever tool they could find. Sometimes they were only 3ft in depth and so narrow that men had to hunch side by side and crouch for hours on end. They were often in exposed positions. Neither did they form a continuous line but rather erratic sections, often divided by hundreds of yards. Once the troops were in them, there wasn't a chance of receiving food or ammunition supplies, or so much as lifting a head into the open until darkness fell again. One OE was bored of it already. Wilfrid Smith had assumed command of the 2nd Grenadier Guards and found it all very ominous. 'I can't see how these battles are to end – it becomes a question of stalemate … no doubt we will kill heaps of Germans but there are always heaps more.' Just as darkness was their friend in terms of being able to move backwards and forwards from the line, so it was their enemy. The Germans could theoretically get into the holes in the line and overrun one set of troops without their neighbours knowing a thing about it.

Regie's new friends in the 1st Coldstream were a far cry from the battalion that had attacked the Chemin des Dames in September. Much depleted, their brigade was now under the command of another OE, 49-year-old Brigadier-General Charles Fitzclarence VC. He had been trying to get to the front since the war began but was originally forbidden to leave the brigade of Kitchener's new army that he had been allocated. A vastly experienced, brave officer, he had been awarded the Victoria Cross in South Africa. Now finally in Belgium, he had posted the Coldstream on the north side of the Menin Road which ran south-east and in a straight line away from Ypres. Strung out over 900 yards it was an awful position; stuck at a crossroads on a salient with a 200-yard gap covered in thick woodland before the line met the Scots Guards on their left. With less than half its normal strength, the Coldstream formed a ragged set of outposts rather than a solid line of defence.

At 5.30 a.m. on 29 October the Germans approached the Coldstream's lines like wraiths and burst from the fog. The British were expecting an attack, but further south. Masked by the mist, enemy troops got within 50 yards of the British trenches before they were spotted and the Guards opened fire. In their weakened state and in their weakened position it was over almost immediately. Two machine guns jammed and the Germans washed over them like a wave, flooding through gaps in the line. Of eleven officers present in the trenches, four vanished into German hands and seven, all of them Old Etonians, were killed in one strike. Amongst them were Gordon Hargreaves Brown, who had tried to patch up Gerry Freeman-Thomas on the Aisne, their machine-gun officer and Charles Williams-Wynn, 18 years old, who had been at the front for less than forty-eight hours. The battalion was so depleted that eventually Fitzclarence would withdraw it from the line so that it would not be wiped out entirely.

Any help that Regie and his battery might have provided was nullified early that morning by seemingly ridiculous orders. The artillery had been instructed to fire on enemy batteries and told that the German infantry should 'be allowed to come on'. On the south side of the crossroads the 1st Grenadier Guards, not long arrived from England, were oblivious as to what had been inflicted upon the Coldstream. That was until, in the gradually clearing fog, at about 7.30 a.m., rifle fire began pouring into their lines from behind. Straight away they realised that the enemy had come through the gap between the two battalions. After a brief attempt to hold their front-line trenches most of the Grenadiers fell back to their support lines. Major Stucley, an OE and second in command of the battalion, dashed off immediately to fetch the King's Company, the only troops that they had in reserve. Having collected them he bravely led them across 200 yards of open ground back to the support lines, where he realised just how dire the situation was.

The King's Company had already taken heavy casualties in its advance. The two companies in the support trenches, one of them led by Captain Lord Richard Wellesley, the Duke of Wellington's great-grandson, were under sustained machine-gun fire and the last remaining company, led by another OE, Captain Guy Rennie, were still stuck up in the original firing line. The rush of enemy troops was 'like a crowd coming on the ground after a football match'. The problem was not hitting the advancing Germans. There were so many of them that 'there was not the slightest difficulty', but that there were so many that 'the futility of killing a few out of such a crowd' made the men panic. Stucley fell, dashing forward in a hail of bullets. Lord Wellesley followed, similarly trying to save the situation. Guy Rennie was so overrun that he and his men had no choice but to try and abandon their front-line trench. He was never heard of again.

Since being driven back from Roulers, the Household Cavalry had been busy digging makeshift trenches with their bayonets. Large numbers of their horses had been killed by one lucky shell burst and valuable machine guns were systematically being put out of action. Whilst Regie was arguing with the general, the Blues and Royals were also being moved southwards, towards the village of Zandvoorde, south-east of Ypres. In such flat country, any piece of high ground was coveted greedily and Zandvoorde sat upon a mediocre ridge that nonetheless became the focus of German attention as they sought to gain an advantage.

Even by the primitive standard up at the Menin Road, the trenches that the Household Cavalry occupied were 'from first to last … a death trap', dug in on forward slopes and leaving them in a particularly vulnerable position. Again, the lines were interrupted, with no lines of communication to reach the troops in reserve. It was a struggle to get enough food up to the lines and Worsley divided his supply of chocolate up and shared it between his men so that they might all have something to eat.

As the Blues and Royals rotated in and out of the front line, he consistently remained. Some 50 per cent of the brigade's machine guns were lost or damaged beyond use and he was simply indispensable. He had the propensity to try to make the best out of any situation, but on 26 October he admitted in a letter to his wife that he was struggling. The adjutant was sure that there was 'nothing to prevent the Germans breaking through at any time'. The cavalry was holding a line far too long for its numbers and with nothing to respond to the enemy's guns.

On 29 October, as darkness set in, the Blues were relieved. Worsley had barely jumped out of the trenches when the brigade major, another OE named Cyril Potter, broke the news that he was required to stay behind yet again, this time to assist the 1st Life Guards. He had now been crouched in the front line for seven days and nights without respite, managing to take three hours' 'rest', not sleep, each night. When he heard the news he characteristically grinned and remarked that it was 'all in a days work', but Potter was not convinced. 'It must have been a bitter disappointment.' As elements of the Blues turned out of the trenches, leaving him behind, the Royals arrived to join him, led by Lord Hugh Grosvenor; son of the Duke of Westminster and yet another Etonian. They settled down to a night in the open as the heavens opened and soaked them to the skin. In artillery terms it was ominous, silent.

At 7.A.m. on 30 October the Germans opened a terrific cascade of high explosive and shrapnel shells on the Household Cavalry's pitifully exposed trenches. The infantry attack was just as swift and just as brutal as the one that the Guards had faced further north. By 9.A.m. they had been bombarded out of their trenches and as they were forced back into an older set behind, to the right of Worsley the line simply collapsed. Messages were sent out to Grosvenor to get him to retire but if they ever reached him he was unable to act upon them. Two whole squadrons simply vanished whilst the tiny number of troopers or NCOs that were not killed outright were hauled off to prisoner-of-war camps.

In just four hours the Germans had secured Zandvoorde and the entire ridge, leaving the Blues and Royals to retire slowly down the hill towards Klein Zillebeke. They sat waiting, hoping that stragglers would file in after them, but not a single man did. Lord Grosvenor and seventy of his men never returned. Alec Vandeleur of the 2nd Life Guards, another OE and a great friend of Worsley's, also disappeared with sixty more and another six Etonian officers who added to the school's rapidly growing list of casualties.

In the aftermath of the attack, Oberleutnant Frieherr von Prankh was wandering through the British lines. Lying in a shell hole on his route were a number of fallen soldiers. Inspecting the bodies he rifled through the pockets of the officer he found among them. The effects that he found identified Lord Worsley. He and his entire machine-gun section had been wiped out in the attack. Von Prankh thought that an English lord should have a grave, so he had his men dig one by the side of the road south of Zandvoorde. The German himself was killed within a matter of weeks.

These desperate attacks, with their astonishing casualty rates, were to prove to be just a prelude. The BEF and its French counterparts would reach the height of desperation on 31 October 1914 and events would reach crisis point

at the village of Gheluvelt, just west of the crossroads where the Guards had
been hit so hard on the Menin Road. The only thing standing between the
British Empire and ruin were 'haggard and unshaven men, unwashed, plastered with mud, many in little more than rags'.

The British artillery began firing early. Rather than taking potshots at
enemy batteries, Regie was ranged on a wood, inside which enemy troops
were massing for an attack. At 8.a.m. a massive German bombardment began
to pave the way for an fierce attack on both sides of the Menin Road. An
hour later they rolled more batteries into action. The Menin Road was
packed with British troops attempting to retire. Artillerymen squirmed their
way westwards having abandoned their guns – others were attempting to drag
theirs through the crowds. The noise of the bombardment was phenomenal.
Wounded men, wagons, confused troops and the guns jockeyed for space to
retreat. The British were swamped but shot back so fiercely that the advancing
Germans were convinced that they faced large numbers of machine guns. By
midday though, they had seized Gheluvelt, which was ablaze, also infiltrating
the grounds of the nearby chateau. To make matters worse, shortly afterwards
a chance shell hit a building where several staff officers had congregated,
throwing command into disarray. The British line had been breached and the
road to Ypres, and beyond it the English Channel, lay open.

As devastating as the situation at Gheluvelt was, the Germans would throw
the heaviest weight of their attack that day on the British line on the Messines
Ridge to the south. The line there was held by cavalry, including the 9th
Lancers. The point had arrived when the cavalry had ceased to be mounted
troops who occasionally got off their horses to fire their rifles to become
dismounted men 'occasionally using their horses to move from one part of
the battle to another'. A passionate cavalryman, Francis Grenfell did not like it
at all. 'We have become mounted infantry ... with very little of the mounted
about it.' The burden of doing two jobs at once was a heavy one. 'If you see a
man carry a lance, sword, rifle, spade and pick he looks just like a hedgehog.'

The Ninth had only arrived back in Messines on the evening of 30 October.
Large numbers had gone off to a remount depot and they were depleted. Out of
a full strength squadron of 130, Francis had forty men. He was back in command,
having returned to the front in mid October and was clearly not himself. He
was yet to accept his twin Rivy's death on the Aisne. He savoured the moments
when the men still confused them and called him by his brother's name. The
Harvey brothers, aside from a case of toothache that had earned Lennie a few
days in Paris, had come through unscathed thus far. That night the regiment
remained awake, listening to the the Germans shuffling about in front of them.

The attack came at 4.30 a.m. on 31 October. German bugles began to sound and lanterns began flashing. 'With the first dull streaks of light' they came on. Nine hundred cavalrymen, strung out on a ridiculously long front with newly arrived Indian troops, faced some 6,000 Germans. Driven out of the trenches east of the village, the British fell back into Messines itself. Enemy troops followed, dragging a battery with them. Francis and his men retired, crawling from house to house, surrounded. The Ninth convened on the road by the local cemetery. German shells had set the village around them on fire. 'Smoke clouds rose from every quarter of the town. A dozen houses were ablaze, the flames leaping high in the light breeze.' The air was a 'mass of rending flashes. Shock succeeded shock, and deadly missiles fell like hail.'

Francis found Lennie Harvey and his troops and gave him orders to hold the position to his left. At the edge of the town, Francis himself turned with some of his squadron and began heading back down the approach trench. One trooper was baffled. 'I didn't know where the Captain was going, but he said, "come on". It looked to me as if he was starting off to take the bally trenches back with a bloomin' pistol.' Francis had heard that men had been left behind and he was determined to go to their aid.

The first territorials had already arrived at the front, including the Queen's Own Oxfordshire Hussars. Amongst their number was Valentine Fleming, MP for Henley. He had been hanging about Dunkirk and St Omer for a number of weeks before, on 30 October, in pouring rain the regiment was told to saddle up and move. After riding all night they dug reserve trenches all morning behind Messines. This he described as disagreeable whilst shells whizzed overhead and exploded 'with a disgusting regularity'. Exposed, the shrapnel shells fortunately exploded behind them whilst Black Maria fell short in front, so although 'horribly frightened' they were lucky not to be far more severely hit. As they held fast on the left of the 9th Lancers, the Germans closed to within 500 yards. 'They kept pooping away at our squadrons on the left of the barricade' Fleming complained. 'We began to wonder how to use the bloody bayonets with which we had been issued two days previously!' As Gheluvelt fell, the British at Messines battled on.

Back at Gheluvelt, Sir John French, commanding the BEF, was talking about going up to the front and being slaughtered with everyone else. Douglas Haig's Chief of Staff, another Etonian and Victoria Cross recipient named 'Johnnie' Gough was holding it together slightly better, declaring something along the lines of 'it [don't] matter a damn what happens, God won't let those devils win'. Fitzclarence too, commanding the 1st Guards Brigade, was of a mind to halt the impending doom rather than morbidly embracing it.

Shortly after Gheluvelt was overrun, Regie Fletcher had been sent up to the lines to try and range 118th Battery's guns. On the way he met an officer of another unit with two NCOs who were off to do similar work and they walked together for about a mile to a dugout behind some trenches being manned by the Cameron Highlanders. When they got to the front they realised that the telephone wire was broken and so they set to work trying to repair it.

Behind them, the remnants of the 2nd Worcesters, some 350 surviving men and seven officers, had been sent to Fitzclarence to reinforce his rapidly diminishing brigade. Shortly before 2.p.m., determined to try to rectify the situation, he led them out, south-east and back towards the Menin Road. Leaving him at the edge of some woods, the ragged battalion advanced bravely towards the chateau and Gheluvelt itself. As soon as they reached the open country men began to fall. Decimated, they advanced past bodies, equipment, shell holes and other battlefield debris. Shaken, the Germans began to fall back. The gap in the line had been plugged at a cost of almost 200 men. The Worcesters were heroes. Fitzclarence would be credited as the man who turned the tide. The German line would eventually reform further back, but disaster had been averted, for now.

In the meantime, nearby, an excitable Regie Fletcher and his colleagues had just about finished ranging their guns when news came through to say that their batteries were to retire. They were to return at once. Jumping out of their dugout they made a dash for the woods. Seventy yards into their sprint there was a rush overhead, followed by the telltale miaow as a shell burst and sent a cascade of shrapnel flying overhead.

The situation at Messines remained grave. The regiment on Valentine Fleming's left was all but wiped out, the 9th Lancers on his right badly battered. He and his Oxfordshire horsemen were finally relieved at 4.30 a.m. on 1 November and staggered 2 miles back to find breakfast. Their food was just about ready when Beau de Lisle arrived to inform them that the line had been broken and that they must participate in a counter-attack. 'This bloody prospect made us sick,' recalled Fleming. He was categorically not impressed. The trenches they stepped into were bloodied and full of corpses. 'You can have my share of glory in exchange for one Turkish bath, one game of squash,' he commented drily. His opinion of war did not get any better. He told a friend that, while it may be 'bloody' in England it is positively 'f★★king in France'.

The line around Messines finally stabilised. Nobody had seen a thing of Lennie Harvey since Francis had met him by the cemetery and Francis himself had been wounded again. Having been pushed out of the town Douglas Harvey and the remainder of the 9th Lancers helped to dig in to the west of the town. His family had been shrouded in tragedy. A sister had died in 1897, followed by his mother whilst he and Lennie were at Eton in 1908. Just a few months later their younger brother Ian had caught pneumonia and died in the sanitorium at school aged 13. His father had now to contend with the loss of his eldest son, for Lennie was never heard of again and nobody was able to shed any light upon the 23 year old's fate. If he had an inkling that his brother was dead, Douglas would never know for sure. On 3 November, just three days after his brother vanished, a high-explosive shell whistled across from the direction of Messines and scored a direct hit on him and several of his men. Douglas, 22 years old, was carried out of the battered trench and laid to rest in Dranouter churchyard three days after his brother was killed.

The first battle for Ypres cost the British dearly. In just over six weeks nearly 60,000 men were wounded or taken prisoner and 8,000 killed. The BEF had been wiped out. Only nine of eighty-four battalions had more than 300 men and eighteen were at cadre strength; less than a hundred. Amongst the fallen were well over a hundred Old Etonians, almost the same figure as for the whole of the Boer War. They came from forty-five different units. Sixteen had died on 29 October alone; the vast majority of them at the crossroads on the Menin Road. Not surprisingly, the Grenadiers and the Coldstream suffered the heaviest losses of OE; the four Guards regiments accounted for forty-eight casualties alone. Owing to the heavy toll exacted on the Blues and Royals more than half of Eton's deaths from mounted regiments came from the Household Cavalry.

There were the more experienced casualties, such as Fitzclarence, nearly thirty years in the army, who became the first Etonian general to fall during the Great War. His grave was lost in the subsequent fighting and he became the highest-ranked soldier of the 54,406 men commemorated on the Menin Gate at Ypres. There were veterans of the Boer War such as Lord Wellesley, whose wife was six months pregnant with their second daughter when he fell and there were volunteers, such as Gerald Anderson, the Olympic hurdler and reservist who was killed assaulting a German trench. Then there were the youngest casualties: nineteen-year-old Jack Lee Steere, who had fallen just weeks after learning of the death of his best friend Jack Cunliffe on the Aisne; 24-year-old Lord Congleton who had sought to solve the riddle of John Manners' fate, mischievous and adventurous; he became the first member of the House of Lords to fall in the war. Neville Woodroffe, 21, who had survived Villers-Cotterêts and the Aisne was killed advancing side by side with the Household Cavalry on 6 November; another of Hubert Brinton's boys. Carleton 'Laddie' Tufnell, 22, had been the biggest blood at Eton in 1911, a sporting great and captain of the XI. He was shot through the throat whilst trying to hold back the advancing enemy on the same day. The list being read out in the chapel at Eton went on, and on, and on.

In all, fifty-two Old Etonians would fall serving with the artillery during the war, three quarters of them with the Royal Field Artillery. Reginald William Fletcher was the first. The efforts to save him after he was struck by shrapnel running back to his battery failed. He died within two hours, at about 5 o'clock on 31 October 1914. That evening, one of his best friends, serving with another artillery unit, dug him a grave and laid him to rest under a tree in the gardens of the chateau near Veldhoek. Like Fitzclarence, four years of dogged fighting in the area destroyed any marker and he was ultimately commemorated on the Menin Gate.

Whilst still on the Aisne, Regie had sat down to contemplate death in his diary. At the front he thought it was 'a cheap and common thing' and that it was no use trying to avoid it. 'If you avoid today a road … being shelled,' he reasoned, 'you may be caught tomorrow by a splinter of Black Maria while you are washing … Something always manages to come along when I have got nothing on but one sock and an identity disc.' He recalled chatter at Balliol after a heavy night of drinking champagne when the subject had come up. '[Death] seemed an awful thing; complete extinction and the end of everything one enjoyed on earth – a thing to prepare oneself for all one's life with much thought and meditation.'

War had changed Regie's outlook:

Now, when the prospect … of a very speedy end is ever present, one does not spend time thinking about it … One realises that it is not really an awful thing … but one event of small significance that may happen at any odd time. It is not so much extinction as the consummation of life, and can make little difference to one's real existence.

He was almost resigned to it:

I am convinced that if I am killed tomorrow, I shall still be able to realise some satisfaction from the sight of my Sam Browne belt suspended from my oar-handle in the den … and shall still be able to talk to Muncles. Its queer how circumstances will change one's ideas completely.'

Regie died convinced that victory was imminent. The author of a nationally accepted history textbook, the poignancy of that moment in time was not lost on his father:

Regie was hit at the very hour on the very day on which the future of the first battle of Ypres turned with the successful charge of the Worcesters on Gheluvelt. In that turn of fortune hung the whole future history of the world.

Notes

1. Exit all.
2. A bend on the course at the Henley Regatta.
3. Valentine Fleming would fall on 20 May 1917 whilst defending an advanced post at Guillemont with his men outnumbered nearly three to one. He left behind a widow and four sons, including the future creator of James Bond, 8-year-old Ian.

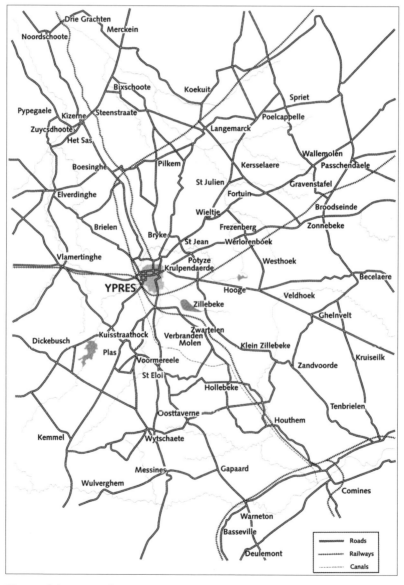

Ypres and the surrounding area.

6

'To Die Would Be an Awfully Big Adventure'

More Etonians with literary connections played their part in the Great War too: Charles Dickens' grandson went straight to France in 1914 and Alfred, Lord Tennyson's would serve with the Rifle Brigade, whilst Arthur Conan Doyle's son Kingsley would also serve; but it was a less conventional connection that dragged one of the writing celebrities of the day into the conflict.

James Matthew Barrie was born in Scotland in 1860. Relocating to London in the early 1890s he eventually moved to Gloucester Road with his wife and their dog Porthos, just a short walk away from Kensington Gardens. A large, sprawling escape for Londoners, it was full of nannies wheeling perambulators whilst their elder charges scampered alongside. One day in 1897, by which time he was becoming an established writer, Barrie was walking his dog when he made the acquaintance of two little boys wearing distinctive, red tam-o'-shanters. The eldest, George, was a beautiful, dark-haired little boy; cocky, obnoxious, honest and inquisitive without a hint of self-consciousness; all the qualities that Barrie thought wondrous in small children.

As his star rose, the author had all the time in the world for his friends' children, filling the void where his own might have been. One of his first cohorts had been Bevil Quiller-Couch, who in 1914 was the young officer who had dug his friend Regie Fletcher's grave in the gardens of Veldhoek Chateau; but the Llewelyn Davies brothers would become increasingly influential in Barrie's eyes. He became acquainted with their parents; their father Arthur, a handsome barrister who had been a master at Eton for a single year and their mother, the beautiful Sylvia Du Maurier, sister to Gerald and aunt of Daphne.

Engaged within weeks of meeting, the couple's family grew quickly after they married. George was born in 1893, Jack, the only brother who would not go to Eton, followed. Peter joined them in 1897, Michael in 1900 and the family was complete when 'Nico' was born in 1903.

Barrie had long been incorporating friends and acquaintances into his work. With George he would concoct stories, the little boy pressing his hands to his temples to 'remember' what it was like to be a baby. In 1902 Barrie published *The Little White Bird*, based on their friendship. On a family holiday in Surrey in 1901 the three eldest boys were given the roles of 'the boy castaways' and he took innumerable research photographs of how they might behave on their own little island. He played the evil pirate, George hunted with a bow and Peter walked the plank. Once again, in 1903, based in part on their castaway games, Barrie sat down to write; this time a play. Rehearsals began in October 1904 under a blanket of secrecy. Actors hardly knew the title of the work as they underwent 'flying' lessons on wires above the stage.

The curtain rose on *Peter Pan, or the Boy Who Wouldn't Grow Up* at 8.30 p.m. on 27 December 1904 at the Duke of York's theatre. Each of the Davies boys, who had attended rehearsals and practiced flying for themselves, had lent their name to a character; George Darling, Peter Pan, Michael Nicholas Darling and John Darling. The eldest three in particular had been Barrie's inspiration. The 'spark' had come from them and the play had been forged by 'rubbing the fire of [them] violently together, as savages with two sticks produced a flame'. Barrie himself was completely unsure as to how this labour of love would be received, and yet *Peter Pan* was a success before the curtain fell. When the actress playing Peter asked the mainly adult audience to clap if they believed in fairies the response was so overwhelming that she burst into tears.

For George and his brothers, the frivolity of fairies and pirates, and their childhood, receded into the background when their father was diagnosed with cancer in his jaw in 1906. Barrie dropped everything and put himself entirely at the family's disposal; assuming all the financial burden for the excruciating treatment that Arthur Llewelyn Davies would undergo. Despite a brutal operation that removed a large portion of his jaw and the roof of his mouth, the cancer spread. George was by now 14 and remained at home, but his father's 'last selfless gesture' was to send the little ones away so that they would not see him die. He passed away in 1907 at the age of 44; a few months before George was despatched to the house of his old friend Hugh MacNaghten at Eton.

In 1909 further tragedy engulfed the Llewelyn Davies boys. Their mother Sylvia collapsed and was diagnosed with inoperable cancer. A number of relatives were to act on behalf of her boys, but she did not want them separated and therefore it ultimately made logistical sense for the wealthy Barrie to adopt them and for their faithful nurse to remain in a prominent position. Sylvia died in 1910, aged 43, and that autumn Peter arrived at Eton, not as an Oppidan like his brother but as a Colleger.

George was an unmitigated success at school and found a happy home with MacNaghten, far happier that Peter who lived in the teasing shadow of the character to whom he had given his name, wishing that somebody else had had the honour. George was a fine cricketer and, like Gerry Freeman-Thomas, had been a member of the XI that took on Harrow at Lord's in 1912. The prospect of him appearing at Lord's had excited his late mother. J.M. Barrie told George that she talked about it 'with shining eyes'; and two years after her sad death her eldest son did not disappoint her. When Gerry was caught out for 64 on the first day it left his team at 116 for 4. Then Eton took a risk. For the Winchester match, the traditional precursor to Lords, George, primarily a bowler had sat at ten in the Etonian batting order. He had had a successful match. As well as taking four wickets for just eighteen runs, when George went in to bat in his only innings he had hit a curiously impressive 42. As a result, he had been bumped up to six in the order, a decision which was considered dubious by some.

George had already made a fantastic left-handed catch that found its way into the national press along with his photograph, but it was for his batting that George was to be commended that day. He began a little shakily, nerves perhaps, and in the face of one of Harrow's better bowlers he was failing to inspire the sweltering July crowd with any confidence. He should have been stumped for a single run, but luck was with him. Given a little time, George began to hit freely; beautifully even. Harrow had no fielders in the deep and in that situation he could begin swinging away with little risk of being out. He began hitting over the boundary and put together a string of fours, two of them in one over in 'a most dashing innings'.

Peter described George as having 'absolutely no vanity at all'. He quite clearly idolised his dashing older brother. In a lot of ways George resembled their father, and was quite reserved. He was never very vocal, in fact he was rather shy, but he was charming. His sense of humour was 'exquisite' and when Peter arrived at Eton he was left open mouthed and in complete wonderment at his brother's colourful language.

George went up to King's College, Cambridge in 1912 and Peter was about to follow when war was declared. He was at the OTC camp at Mytchett Farm and when it was turned out he hurried to Scotland where George and the rest of his brothers had joined Barrie for a fishing holiday. In his hand he was brandishing a circular from the adjutant of the Cambridge University OTC, 'pointing out that it was the obvious duty of all undergraduates to offer their services'. Dutifully, that night the two brothers boarded a train going south.

To say that every young man in Britain was dying to join the army would be an exaggeration. George and Peter would be partly buoyed by their fellow passengers. They sat in a carriage full of reservists overflowing with a 'pack up your troubles' mentality, but it had begun to ebb by the time they were redirected to the rifle depot at Winchester. George had served in the ECOTC too but never took it seriously, which was a common sentiment before the war. He joked about his awful shooting and was more vocal about the 'topping rag' on the way back to school in the train than serious military matters, although he thought it was all rather fun 'seeing an enemy skulking along about 500 yards off, and potting at him'.

Peter had 'odd sensations' in the pit of his stomach as they climbed the hill from the station. George had a funny turn outside, 'something between a fainting fit and a sick headache' and had to sit down and pull himself back together outside the barracks. Peter was all for running away back to London 'humiliated but free', but George took a deep breath, steadied himself and marched them both through the door.

When George and Peter entered the rifle depot they found themselves face to face with a lieutenant colonel who appeared to be busy and showed little interest in their presence. Where were they at school? Eton. Were they in the corps? Yes. Did they play games? As soon as he established that George was *the* Davies who had made that 59 at Lord's in 1912 in front of his very eyes, for his old school, this fellow OE who himself had been in the XI changed his tune and immediately became more congenial. Peter met his approval by way of being related to George and with that, they were in the army.

When George and Peter reported to Sheerness to join the King's Royal Rifle Corps in September it was in a depressed mood. They watched baby-faced officers being sent off to replace those who had fallen in the early days of the war and as they undressed in their tent to go to bed that first night, George said: 'Well, young Peter, for the first time in our lives we're up against something really serious. F★★★ me if we aren't.'

Life in the Intelligence Corps had not been entirely plain sailing for George Fletcher, even if he was far removed from the action he craved. He had been grazed by shrapnel during the retreat but it could have been far more serious. 'A man a few yards off was biffed … I stole his Greatcoat which kept me alive.' He had even been arrested. One night he was rattling along on his smell when he ran into a party of Germans. Thinking quickly, he started chattering away in German and they failed to notice that he was not one of them. Unfortunately for George he was overheard by a British contingent lurking nearby and dragged off for incarceration as a spy. There he sat until a fellow OE chanced by and asked him what the devil he was doing locked up.

In fact, George had become so tired of motorcycles and of intelligence work that he had been 'touting' to every staff officer he could get within earshot to try to secure a transfer to an infantry battalion. George was attached to the 2nd Royal Welsh Fusiliers. 'Henceforth I march on my feet like a man instead of scorching on my tail like a monkey.' He had arrived in time for the beginning of the battle for Ypres in October but they occupied a section of the line to the south, away from where Regie was involved in the thick of the action. George was still unaware of his brother's death when he and his men were pulled from the lines in November. He set to work shaving off the scratchy beard that had grown in the fortnight spent in a cramped, makeshift ditch.

As the snow began to fall the men of the BEF who had survived the slaughter got ready for a winter of inactivity as far as large-scale battles were concerned. George sat 'begloved and bemittened', wearing every item of clothing he possessed at once, draped in all of the blankets that he could find. He was convinced that he and his men would remain where they sat until the following March. 'We shall stay facing one another in trenches the whole weary winter,' he suggested to his parents, 'and in the Spring, we shall go for them.' If this was the case, then the lines hurriedly scraped into the earth as the battle had raged around them simply wouldn't do as accomodation.

One of the first priorities was to make a solid bottom to the trenches, by whatever means possible in the worsening conditions; be it brushwood, bricks, sacks of straw, timbers or ammunition crates. The digging of communicating trenches was also important so that the men could move to and from the firing line in safety. George was in a trench only 100 yards or so away from the Germans, so barbed wire entanglements were especially vital to keep the enemy out of their lines. George was trying to construct a dugout. He had an old door as a roof, which leaked; three more forming walls with the last side made out of ammunition crates. The entrance was hung with a waterproof sheet and he had found a long box to act as a bed and stuffed it full of straw and blankets. As yet, trench was an elaborate description for their home. They lacked a parapet to shield them and the addition of one of these was absolutely vital, as any attempt to dig down brought more water into the trench. Any attempts they were making to pave the floor with bricks were useless as they just sank into the thick, glutinous mud.

On his 27th birthday George was supervising the construction of a communication trench that filled up with water as soon as they dug it. It had rained continually for over a week and when he tried to walk to and fro the water nearly went over the top of his gumboots. He had been tying them on with webbing straps so that they did not get left behind when he lifted his feet but it was a losing battle. By the end of January pumps had arrived to bale out the trenches. The worst of it was that the water had nowhere to go, wherever it landed on the clay-like soil, it stayed. They had taken to pumping it out of one trench and into an old communication trench which had been barricaded with sandbags, but no matter what the men of the Royal Welsh Fusiliers tried, the water found a way to trickle back in.

The amount of mud shocked new arrivals. Ian Henderson left Eton in the summer that war was declared and subsequently joined the Argyll & Sutherland Highlanders who were in the same brigade as George Fletcher's battalion. Still a teenager, he was cloaked with a sometimes painful naivety. The crossing was wonderful, the men were wonderful, the weather fine and all was dandy until 'beastly shells' turned up and put him in 'the most awful funk'. In one of his letters home he admitted to an 'awful discovery' he hoped that they wouldn't be shocked, but he had found *two* lice in his vest, and he was not the only one. 'I haven't had my shirt off for eight days now or my boots. And terrible to think of, I haven't had a bath for very nearly a month.'

On 11 November George reported that his feet had been wet for three days despite his new habit of rubbing vaseline all over them to try and keep the water out of his skin. His men had stood in a trench for three days. With almost nowhere to lie down and rest they spent day and night trying to bale out the trench with buckets only to see the water find its way back in. The men with the buckets were exposed all day long to German rifles, 'but they, poor things were just as badly off'. It had created a sort of uneasy truce. They did not snipe at the Germans whilst they battled the water and vice versa.

One young woman who knew George Llewelyn Davies well said of her own Etonian brother, who would be killed in May 1915 with the 19th Hussars, that he thought the war was going to be 'one long cavalry charge, everyone waving their swords – Smash the Kaiser! Terrific!'[1] George Davies was never, she knew, under any such illusions. 'He knew what he was in for from the word go.' In early December the brothers had been separated. Peter, still seventeen, was left at Sheerness whilst George was sent to the 4th Rifle Brigade. The battalion had arrived home from India in preparation for being sent to war and he was to go with them. Leaning out of the train as it pulled from the station, George waved goodbye to his younger brother, calling out 'Till our next merry meeting!'

George was subsisting with holes in his pants almost as soon as he arrived at the front but that was the least of his concerns. He had had a harrowing walk up to the trenches one night through thick mud in complete darkness. He was bringing up the rear and accidentally found his way into a silent, abandoned communication trench. He waded into mud up to his knees. There, unsteady and perhaps with a hint of panic setting in, he toppled over backwards. 'Behold me sitting with exceedingly cold water trickling into me everywhere, unable to move and shouting for help.' Another OE had told a similar, horrific story of a 'missing' man who had vanished whilst relieving troops one night. They assumed that he had stopped a stray bullet in the dark. Two days later when the same men came out of the trenches they heard groans coming from a waterlogged communication trench. They found the missing man up to his shoulders in mud. He had got lost and sank. It took them more than four hours to extract him and get him help but he died of shock and exposure almost immediately.

The spectre of death was always lurking in the trenches. The men of George Fletcher's battalion used to sit discussing the spirits of dead men. They used to say that when the war was over, the ghosts of dead troops would be marching over their fields every night 'cursing and grousing' as they were moving along and that no farmer would be able to use the land again. They talked about whether or not the soldiers already claimed by the war could wander through space and look down upon them. One of their number was dry in his response when he replied that he 'wouldn't mind betting' that at that very moment they were looking down and 'dancing a two step and clicking their heels together in holy glee to think that they had scrounged out of this blasted misery'.

Dead, rotting men were turned up all over the Ypres Salient area when troops tried to drain or extend their lines. Many were in an advanced state of decomposition and the smell was harrowing. George Fletcher was sat right across from a turnip field that was full of dead Germans and he told one of the other Eton masters that it required 'heartiness' to see every day the remains of human beings laying face down on the ground 'in lumps and rows' right opposite where they slept and ate. The smell reminded them that they were there even if they could not see them.

Life was cheap. Just because there was no fighting going on, it did not entirely remove the threat of death. George talked about four consecutive sergeants getting 'biffed in the head' by sniper fire in a short space of time and shell fire still accounted for the lives of many. Every now and again something brought home to the OEs in the front lines that it was a human life like their own that they were referring to. George Davies went to great lengths to shield 'Uncle Jim' from the horrors that he was enduring, but he wrote home on one occasion of having seen 'violent death' just a few feet from him. He had been underneath a parapet when a man had exposed his head to a German rifle and George watched the top of his head taken off. 'I oughtn't write about these things ... but it made an impression.' Just four days later Barrie replied and informed him that his uncle, Guy Du Maurier, had been killed a few miles up the line. He urged, begged George to stay safe. 'I don't have any little desire for you to get military glory ... You would not mean a featherweight more to me [if] you come back a General. I just want yourself.' He ended on a desperate note. 'I have lost all sense of war being glorious, it is just unspeakably monstrous to me now.' At home on leave, Peter watched Barrie walking up and down in his room, 'smoking pipe after pipe, thinking his dire thoughts'.

George Fletcher found it especially hard to have to utilise his German proficiency to read through the letters of dead enemy soldiers to try to glean information. Military relevance aside, he found it awful to have to read what their mothers had sent them. Finally though, he was confronted with his personal loss. Ten days after his brother's death he was lamenting his broken wristwatch and that there was no Regie close enough to fix it for him. He supposed that he was still to the north, where he heard the artillery was busy. Nearly a week later, he was complaining that he had had no news. 'I don't know what he has done since going to his new battery ... I expect Regie has had a fearfully exciting time ... *Please send me all his letters.*'

He finally received the news that his brother had died on 16 November and it was brutal, shocking. All he could do, isolated in his trench with plenty of time to contemplate his loss was find solace in the fragments of poetry that he had stored inside his head. 'This does not make me in the last more revengeful against the Germans except that I feel more willing to push the war right home to a decision'. Any murderous feelings he had went towards the pacifist MPs criticising the war and to the crowds who went to football and, in his opinion, cared 'not two straws' how many lives were being claimed, the best of men dying 'while defending their worthless lives'.

Boredom was rife on the British front. George had been 'snaffling' in Armentières and managed to find a skipping rope and an eclectic collection of English books in the classroom of a school including *Brer Rabbit* and *Robinson Crusoe*. He was, he said, flabby and fat. By spring his men would be 'as fat as Wiltshire hogs', or worse still, as fat as Germans. His captain apparently had already begun morphing into a frog, 'so podgy has he become'. He just wanted to hibernate until spring when he might be of some use. His father was sending him more reading material from his flat in Eton but it did little to alleviate the monotony. It was a blessing to have a vivid imagination. George Davies was dreaming of a family reunion at the Ritz when he got home, and Ian Henderson was imagining a posh dinner with his parents, a crisp white tablecloth, polished silver and lovely food. George Fletcher's imaginings had transcended to a whole other level. He had been having a vivid dream about a talking goat wearing medals and causing a stink in his room. It disappeared eventually with a clap of thunder and he woke up to find that the thunder was in fact the artillery shelling German trenches in front of him.

The men of the Royal Welsh Fusiliers sang to keep themselves occupied. One of the corporals had a penny whistle and the rest would sing along. George thought that the Germans were better at it. It was 'eerie and wonderful' listening to their harmonies as they drifted across no-man's-land. He sent home snippets of sights and sounds that coloured his image of life at the front. The rattle of maxims 'like a very loud motorcycle'. Rifles made a double report when they were fired. There was a 'pleasant hiss' as British shells went overhead on their way to the German trenches. Aeroplanes buzzed above him, men chatted around him; their frequent blasphemy had a strangely contented ring about it. Then came the crack of a sniper's bullet, the singing of the cat-like shrapnel.

His daily routine was not inspiring. George would get up just before dawn and stand to, barging his way down the trench, dragging out 'snoring lumps of humanity'. He went stamping up and down with a pipe in one hand and the other shoved deep into his pocket, a light-hearted impression of his father. The day was spent supervising the men; making sure that they cleaned their rifles, arranging digging parties, wood-fetching parties, sawing parties, guard duty. Then he would have to censor the men's letters. Before dark there was more organising, dictating who was going to fetch water, who was going to fetch rations, who would be put in one of the outposts. Any gaps in his day he attempted to fill with eating, drinking lukewarm tea or jumping up and down to keep warm. At night they waited for 'water-cart' – not only literally water but the nickname for the gossip that came with the drinking rations. (Most of the time it was fanciful. On one occasion it was rumoured, via a friend of Regie's, that Kitchener's army was to be equipped with knuckledusters with long spikes and with daggers; the officers were to get miniature axes.) Finally, George had checks to do at 9 p.m., midnight and 3 a.m. before he could attempt to sleep, before beginning all over again, until they reached the end of their five-day stint and were relieved for a similar period.

This stuffy atmosphere of course made for bickering and antagonisms. Most of George's rage was aimed at the Scottish battalion that rotated in and out of the lines with his men. This was on the grounds that their only occupation was to undo any of the work that his men had done and he even took to drawing flaming red dragons on parts of the trench to make it clear whose territory it was.

It was symptomatic of his gift for endearing himself to his men. One hardened reservist in his battalion claimed that they were wary of young subalterns who were shunted into their path. They were judged by whether or not they showed guts in the trenches. On this score, George impressed immediately. The same man claimed that his men thought him 'the bravest man in France', with 'more brains than all the battalion officers put together'. George had heard them talking about him in the close confines of the trenches: 'T'aint 'arf a lark bein' in that there Fletcher's section … 'E speaks to the bastards in their own bloody language!' In return George was already quite fond of them. He was massively amused by a conversation he overheard one morning between two of the soldier servants:

> 'You go and wake Mr Fletcher.'
> Mess servant: 'You go and wake adjective Fletcher your adjective self; I've got this 'ere adjective bacon to serve up.'

They might have moaned a lot, but he thought they were remarkable. 'They can carry any weight through any mud and dig any amount of wet clay all through the night.' They required prodding, but as long as he was standing there cursing over their shoulders they were very efficient and thorough. One day he was marching them through Armentières when he decided to cheer them up by pulling out his penny whistle and playing the 'Marseillaise' in the highest possible key with electrical effect. After that they cheerfully swung through the 'echoing and desolate town' just like the mythical soldiers in the *Daily Mail*.

George had a somewhat unique perspective as far as the enemy was concerned. Having lived and worked in Germany, he couldn't bring himself to hate an entire nation based on the indiscretions of a few. In the wake of Regie's death, their eldest brother Leslie was raging. He wanted to hurt the Germans but George's response was measured. He seemed to think that his brother's position on a ship, isolated and not face to face with the enemy, had fostered this attitude. He was sure that Leslie would change his mind when he was required to rescue them from struggling in the sea, especially if he had suffered the same fate. It was different for him, 'biting the same ground', suffering the same hardships as the Germans. News had arrived at Oxford that Regie had fallen in British territory; that Bevil Quiller-Couch had buried him with his own hands. It caused some relief to their parents and to Leslie that he had not been touched by the enemy, but George's mood was not much altered. It made little difference to him.

His command of the German language and his sense of humour meant that he became well known to the troops across no-man's-land. The lines were only 100 yards or so apart and George held daily chats with the enemy; in this case Saxons. In mid December the battalion heard that three German ships had been sunk. The commanding officer decided that their opponents ought to know and so George chalked it up on a board in German and they waved it above the trench. The men began hollering to attract attention. There was a momentary pause, clearly whilst the Germans digested the information; and then bullets began to fly at their sign. The men tied a red flag to a long pole and waved it to signify hits or misses: 'Yah! Put it down as a bloody miss!'

Christmas approached and presents began to flow in. His parents couldn't send him the kitten he wanted to make his billet homely, but they had found him a penknife with cats engraved on the handle and he stuck it in the ground opposite his brazier so that they could warm their theoretical paws. George had ordered chocolates for his men and his parents were sending them pipes and tobacco. He was jumping at every package like it was his Christmas stocking in the 1890s.

George had been dreaming of integrating with the Germans for a Christmas party since the beginning of December and had no intention of leaving it to chance. He had been trying to persuade the men across no-man's-land to partake in a 'beer and sausage evening' on Christmas Day. 'You will provide the sausage and beer,' he informed them, 'and we will produce the plum pudding.' All he got initially was loud guffaws in response. By Christmas Eve his plans had been downgraded to the erection of Christmas trees on the parapet and a meeting in no-man's-land at midday, so he was still slightly hopeful. That was until his company commander forbade anything of the sort.

Despite the captain's best efforts though, and perhaps as a result of George's efforts, at about midday on Christmas Day two Germans appeared, rolling two enormous barrels of beer towards the Royal Welsh Fusiliers. Two men jumped out and went to fetch them. Before George knew it, white hankies were waving on both sides and men were streaming out into the space between the lines. They shook hands, cheered, laughed and exchanged cigarettes and food. George even saw one of his men emerging from the German lines smoking a fat cigar with a brazier under each arm. Some of the Germans had climbed out to start burying their dead and the Fusiliers helped. The lines were extremely close together and the company commander was wary of the Germans being able to see inside their defences. Too much 'prowling about' might have dire consequences at a later date and so he sent George out to put an end to the fraternisation. The men retreated into their lines and resumed waving their hankies in good spirits.

Miffed at the lack of festivities, George wandered off down the lines to the 2nd Argyll & Sutherland Highlanders to find a friend of his. There the trenches were much further apart and almost everybody was out. George joined them and found himself surrounded by kilted Scottish soldiers scampering about wearing German foraging caps. He and his friend went armed with cigarettes and newspapers to make friends with the German 133rd Regiment. They barely talked of war. Six of the men they met had won the Iron Cross and one of them let George examine his. They discoursed on football and exchanged calling cards for after the war. George thought their men rather 'pipsqueaky' but the NCOs were tall, intimidating fellows. They talked for nearly an hour before a bark came from the German lines and their men scurried home. At dawn the following morning a captain in George's battalion pulled down the white flag and three shots were fired. The Germans put up a board saying thank you and fired three shots of their own. Heads went down. War had begun again.

Anything that could remind the men a little of home was a welcome diversion in the New Year. George Llewelyn Davies had long since had a ruse running at Eton whereby he would feign starvation and Barrie would promptly despatch hampers of treats from Fortnum & Mason. War was no different. He showered George's mess with boxes and boxes, whether solicited or not. 'I ask for the devil of a lot,' George admitted, but Barrie did not care. 'It is always a blessed thing for me when you want something, if you don't want, go on inventing.' The truth was, that whether it be food, cigarettes, mittens for men, pipes, writing letters to the wives of their men or even visiting them in hospitals at home when they were wounded, parents, grandparents and extended families just longed to feel useful.

Shades of Eton followed her old boys about the front as they cherished familiarity in their depressing setting. George Fletcher was able to walk down to the Rifle Brigade battalion and talk 'tug-shop' with another old Colleger. Billy Congreve's position as an aide gave him a mobility that meant he could drop in on even more friends up and down the front. He found one old school friend 'exactly the same as when we were at Eton together'. OEs swapped news of each other. Reggie Hargreaves was, so he heard, 'disgustingly brave, so I suppose he is bound to get hit sooner or later'. George Fletcher, of course, was still fully connected with the school and had been fairly grovelling for

news. His school colleagues had obliged. 'It is very good of them to let me
have a whiff of Eton in the middle of … blasphemous war,' he told his father.
Charles Fletcher had returned to Eton in January and was proudly showing
George's letters off. For the boys and masters who remained he became their
window to the war. His tales of being arrested, of doing his daily rounds of the
trenches with a cat on his shoulder, and the sights and sounds of the trenches
became common knowledge amongst the various boarding houses.

Eton was, after all, his home for much of the year and George missed it
sorely. He would have loved to have seen it just for one ordinary evening.
'[A] College kickabout … or the hum of boys going into 5 o'clock school',
his father leading the way to the classroom with an enormous key in his
hand. Masters made sure he had the *Eton College Chronicle*; bits of news that
had reached home rebounded back out to him. One of his old College and
Balliol friends, he heard, was on his way to the Dardanelles, 'lucky devil'. The
boys were sending papers and socks for his men along with sheaves of letters
for him. 'Curious little letters, full of the infinitely remote details of Eton life.'
George adored reading them. He took one batch on a march up to the lines
and read them as he moved along. 'The two worlds clashed strangely together',
house colours and football with the noise of rifles and artillery shells.

Now all George wanted was a real tabby kitten to sit in front of his brazier.
He intended to feed it on tinned sardines and stash it in a gumboot when they
advanced, but he feared that the censor wouldn't pass it. But George's prayers
were answered. In January he got out of the trench one day to stretch his legs
to the rear and was wandering past Stinking Horse Farm when he heard a
little mew behind him. George invited the cat up on to his shoulder and took
it for a walk. It ran up and down his arm, wandered off numerous times but
came padding back again to climb on to his shoulder and rub his face against
his stubbly beard. It ran off knowingly as he re-approached the trenches. 'I will
not forget you, o' cat – visitor of comfortless mortals,' he sighed.

One bit of work that George seized upon to break the spell of inactivity was night patrols. They at least made life more interesting. George was
renowned for his 'brave and brainy deeds' and went out frequently. Usually
with one other man to keep it simple, he went to 'see what the Germans were
up to'. He would pull on a Burberry, remove his underwear from under hia
trousers (the less clothing that was soiled the better), put a pistol in an acces-
sible pocket, wire cutters in another and finish off his outfit with a knitted cap
and gumboots.

Gathering information was the intention. On one occasion some men up
the line were convinced that they had heard noises coming from underground.

Fulfilling the colonel's request for information, George set off with ten men. He didn't like taking out large groups and it disappointed him immensely when the men he took out didn't share his enthusiasm. The ones that had a tendency to 'lie doggo' and wait for him to baby step them through the adventure ruined his fun, although if they lay petrified he knew they were 'in a worse funk' than he was, which was marginally satisfying.

When a patrol went out, word went up and down the lines and no shots were fired until they returned; unless it was a flare telling them to return. Off George would go, 'bellying and elbowing along like a worm', scraping through his own barbed-wire defences. It was a filthy, slow job and the first thing he would do was look for cover. One night he found a good ditch 'not exactly a commodious lying place', for it was full of water: 'however we stopped and lay for a few minutes every ten yards. Elbows soaked, knees and legs immersed.'

Avoiding searchlights was a priority that George considered 'great fun'. The most powerful searchlight one of his men saw in the entire war was in front of them. Every time it was switched on as they were carrying up to the trench they stopped dead in their tracks, 'sinking our heads on our chests so that we would resemble stumps of trees, or posts'. Once it shone within inches of George, who rolled under some cabbages and hoped to God they wouldn't move the beam over him.

If all went well he would get close enough to hear the Germans snore and the guards whispering. On these instances the noise of wire cutting was too risky so they lay listening to their conversations. The Germans, of course, were playing the same game. They would send out twenty–thirty men, spread out like a fan, and it was easy to get caught in the middle of a patrol coming the other way. Communications sometimes went awry and George could be in danger from his own men. One night he found a lovely looking bucket which he claimed eagerly to take home only to find that it was a British trap that rattled. When he lifted it men of his own battalion began shooting at him.

Of all the surprises that one might come across on a patrol, bloated, decaying corpses were the worst; a stark reminder of what could happen if you didn't make it home safely. One night, George had made it about a 100 yards along a particular ditch when he came upon a German who had evidently tried the same things days before. George retrieved his helmet for the den at home. Bobbing about in the North Sea, his brother was desperate to have one. 'Leslie will be disappointed, but the den is the real depot for all the common gear of "the boys". He shall have the next.'

On another occasion George encountered a far more grizzly sight. He was crawling along when he saw against the skyline an ominous bayonet and the tip of a German *pickelhaube* helmet. 'My revolver came out and I silently worked up to the helmet till I touched it with the barrel.' The man wasn't asleep, he was dead. Crawling along the rim of the trench, which ran back to the enemy lines George was greeted with a horrific sight. Much of the ditch had been roofed over but it had now collapsed. 'Everywhere there were [bodies], German rifles, equipment, spades and other tools.'

The trench continued for some 30 yards, sometimes disappearing underground. It was impossible to count the dead. George found some sitting, some leaning, some lying down. He couldn't imagine what had happened to them or why nobody had come to claim them. It was far too grim to think of pinching a helmet for Leslie and instead he focused his attentions on climbing along without disturbing the remains. It reminded him of climbing, like the holiday on Skye he had taken with Regie the previous summer: 'working from point to point and saying so far, so safe, and now for the next part.'

Gareth Hamilton-Fletcher, who had had such bold ideas about Britain's pre-war relations with Germany and another member of the Eton XI at Lord's in 1912, arrived at the front in January 1915 with the Grenadier Guards. Sometimes, rather than keeping their distance, patrols turned into raids and unlike George Fletcher's outings the onus was very much on making contact with the men opposite. Attached to the Scots Guards because they were completely devoid of officers in the aftermath of Ypres, Gareth went into trenches near La Bassee. Every single officer in his company was borrowed from another regiment. Gareth had been there precisely a day before they were the subject of a fierce, small-scale German assault. Situated in front of a number of brickstacks that had been reinforced to create a keep of sorts, at 6.30 a.m. on the morning of 25 January a German deserter came in and declared that in half an hour the enemy would begin bombarding them and blowing up mines planted under the British trenches prior to an attack. The deserter proved as good as his word. Sure enough mines went up and shells followed. Then came waves of hundreds of German troops. As the enemy came on the Scots Guards began retreating towards the keep to form some kind of makeshift defence. Gareth had been holding the right flank and they were knocked out almost immediately. Two Etonian officers fell in his company. One was Geoffrey Monckton, aged 19. His brother Francis, 24, had already been lost at Ypres some ten weeks before. Neither brother's body was ever recovered. Gareth fought 'like a hero' and was wounded, carrying on until he too was cut down. Seven officers and well over a hundred men were lost. In just six months of war a second of the Lord's heroes of 1912 was dead at the age of 20.

In mid January George Fletcher and his men were moved to Bois Grenier and found that the same care and attention that the Royal Welsh Fusiliers had lavished on their lines had not been spent on what was to be their new home. They found themselves in shoddy lines again and slowly began building. The weather that month was appallingly wet and by the end of it the River Lys had risen 6ft in a mere twenty-four hours. Two months later, just as they had finished a monumental effort aimed at making their lines suitable for living and working, to their utter dismay they were moved from them. To George's disgust they found themselves shunted further along exchanging spots with a Scottish regiment who now moved in to reap the benefits of their hard work: comfortable dugouts, a firm parapet and even his cat.

'What are your old trenches like?' the departing Scot enquired. George laid it out for him. 'Bulletproof parapet … thick wire entanglement, good dugouts for men, a nice mess for the officers, stores, tables, chairs and importantly, a proper construction of latrines and fully connected trenches to be able to move about in daylight.' George then watched as the officer looked increasingly uncomfortable; knowing that in return the Welshmen would find next to none of the above in their new home. 'May the devil stick a fork through their noses,' George wrote. Despondent and exasperated at the thought of the work, his men began to dig, again.

For George, the only consolation was the prospect of new ground to skulk about in in the darkness. At the end of a diagonal ditch that ran in front of the Fusilier's new line across to the Germans was a French flag fluttering on a pole where it was fixed to a tree. 'The Sausagers had evidently pinched it from the Frogs,' and as far as George was concerned it was taunting him. The Scottish captain passing the sorry-looking trenches over to him had offered five shillings to the man of his company who could shoot down the pole with his rifle. Five shillings did not make this feat in the slightest bit realistic. There had to be a better way. At midnight one night, a message went along the companies telling them to be careful of their fire. 'Mr Fletcher and one man gone out on patrol.'

George had grabbed a willing apprentice and hoofed it out over the top of the crumbling parapet into no-man's-land. He found a convenient furrow in the ploughed field and they dropped into it. It was a dark, dark night but he foresaw frequent flares being sent up and appreciated the additional cover. Keeping low, George and his man crawled across to the clump of trees and worked their way along them. At last they came upon the tree with the flag tied to it. They were on the wrong side of the ditch. They lay flat and still 'for perhaps half an hour … listening to the spittings, coughings and grunts of the German sentries'. It was impossible to think of grabbing it whilst they were being periodically lit up by coloured flares. George lay there, scoping out his prize and noticed that as well as being tied, it was also nailed in place and tied by several bits of string to a tough-looking branch. If he wanted to grab it he was going to have to climb the tree under the noses of the mocking enemy and untie it with both hands. Having come so far, George was adamant. He'd be 'jiggered' if he was going home without his flag now.

Waiting for a bright flare to die down, he leapt up and swung into the tree with a 'swish'. Another ball of light went up and he threw himself back into the mud. Waiting for darkness to resume again he shot up 'like Israel Hands' with his penknife between his teeth. Cursing under his breath, heart pounding, balancing on a tree trunk on one leg George slashed away at the strings one at a time. Finally the pole came loose in his hands. He threw it to the ground and swiftly followed it down as more flares were shot into the sky. The next morning he penned a note home. 'The flag is now being waved over B Company's parapet by a delighted Tommy, and is being shot at by infuriated sausage-eaters.' His men were thrilled and his legend cemented.

The British Army was adjusting fully to the idea of complex trench construction and as George and his men began working at Bois Grenier there were sandbags, barbed wire and duckboards in abundance. Equipment to aid the day-to-day practice of surviving the enemy had begun to emerge too. Periscopes began to arrive; little mirrors were stuck up on the back of trenches and by day, sentries could sit on the fire step and observe no-man's-land without putting their heads into the line of fire.

One Etonian who was going to find himself at the forefront of new technology as far as weaponry designed with trenches in mind was concerned was 'Jack' Haldane. Born in November 1892, John Burdon Sanderson Haldane came from a family of highly individual academics. His father John, a brother of the War Minister who instigated Britain's pre-war army reform with a European conflict in mind, was a scientist and intensely interested in the nature of gases.

Precocious was an understatement as far as Jack was concerned. At 3, the same year that his father began using him as a guinea pig for his experiments, he cut his head open and asked if the blood dribbling down his forehead was oxyhaemoglobin or carboxyhaemoglobin. At 4, he was with his father in London as the latter hung out of windows on the Underground. Jack remembered the grime and the smoke breathed in as his father tested the atmosphere by collecting it in glass bottles. By the age of 8, Jack was fully engaged in helping his father analyse gas during his experiments and soon moved on to making simple mixtures for Haldane Sr to use.

It was always going to be a struggle for Eton to further the education of this prodigious talent. Arriving in 1905 he was that good a mathematician that it was rumoured that he taught the masters as opposed to the other way around. The headmaster was frequently frustrated with him; threatening him with the notion of becoming 'a mere smatterer' instead of being exceptionally good in one field if he continued to jump about between different specialities. Some of the masters just couldn't comprehend him. 'He is a baffling boy,' one wrote in a school report, 'and I shall be glad to be rid of him.'

When he went up to Oxford, Jack continued to help his father, who strove to expand his son's scientific knowledge in a continuously unique way. Down a mine in Staffordshire he taught Jack the effects of breathing methane. He had him stand and recite Mark Anthony's speech from Julius Caesar. 'Friends, Romans, Countrymen …' He soon became short of breath and 'somewhere about "the noble Brutus"' Jack's legs went from under him and he collapsed onto the floor, where of course the air was clear. 'In this way,' he explained pragmatically, 'I learnt that [methane] is lighter than air …'

After fiddling with his degree and characteristically changing from maths and biology (he claimed that nobody could study mathematics for five hours a day and remain sane) to arts he came out of New College with a First to absolutely no raptures at all because the date was 4 August 1914. Like its Eton counterpart, the OUOTC was in camp. Jack had joined the Signallers with the express intention of grasping wireless telegraphy and was busily engaged with it when 'the angel of death on a motorbike' arrived with news of war. Jack volunteered immediately and asked for a commission in the Black Watch. The War Office duly obliged. After four months of training he crossed to France and joined the 1st Battalion as their bombing officer in February 1915.

Jack Haldane was fully aware that he might be killed at the front, and that 'a huge waste of human values was going on there' but it did not anger him. He rather enjoyed the whole thing, which he knew singled him out from most of his contemporaries. Neither did he appear to be afraid. In fact, he lacked any sense of fear to the point of recklessness. This endeared him to the men at least, who gave him nicknames like 'Bombo' and 'Rajah of the Bomb'. He would crawl out alone into no-man's-land at night to watch and listen to the enemy scuttling about their trenches. One night he had been gone for some time when a loud bang went off at the German lines, 'succeeded by a tangle of very lights' and the sound of rifles and machine guns. Silence fell and they waited 'with some apprehension' to see what would happen. In time a torchlight appeared and a filthy Jack climbed over the parapet. 'The Boche was saying unpleasant things about us,' he drawled. 'So I just tossed a bomb over to them.' On another occasion, to prove a point, Jack seized a bicycle and cruised across an exposed gap in full view of the Germans; stating that they would be too shocked at his brashness to take a shot at him. He was right.

His eccentricity, sometimes bordering on insanity, made him immensely popular, but his duties with a new weapon had the reverse effect. Other officers loathed the sight of Jack after he was appointed Trench Mortar Officer for the 1st (Guards) Brigade. Men would be sitting quietly in a portion of trench and along he would come with his team and their mortar. Unceremoniously they would plonk it down and begin firing its shells at a high trajectory with the intention of having them drop into the German lines just in front, attracting unwanted attention from the enemy. George Fletcher described them: a large bang, then 'a slight swish in the air, and then an almighty roar'. Whenever they were 'biffing' in his sector the Germans threw a powerful searchlight on them looking for the offender or showered them with machine-gun fire. By the time this retaliation had started, Jack and his men would have packed up and moved along the line, leaving a distinctly nasty taste in the mouth of those who remained. Retribution occasionally found him. One day Jack was pulled up for not wearing his Glengarry and had to admit that it had been ruined when a neighbouring battalion had taken offence to his visit and pushed him into a ditch.

Haldane's bomb squad, so to speak, was a funny little outfit. He had an NCO from the brigade's Coldstream Battalion and a small team of hand-picked men that constituted his own little army. They were largely left to their own devices and spent their days playing with explosives. They were exempt from certain duties and didn't turn out for guard duty, being focused on thirteen muzzle-loading mortars. Jack was in his element when Douglas Haig came across him and labelled him 'the bravest and dirtiest officer in my army'.

As well as trench mortars, hand-held bombs were becoming a mainstay on the Western Front. Jack thought that they were fantastic. 'The best people at it seem to be the reckless kind. The average man does not seem to like it.' Ian Henderson had been on a training course on how to use them and seemed to fall into the latter of Haldane's two categories as he returned to start imparting this new knowledge to the men. 'They are beastly things,' he complained. 'Likely to go off at any moment. I live in deadly fear of them.'

Of all the weapons unleashed on the Western Front in the spring of 1915, the one that instilled the most fear and caused the most horrific damage was yet to come. In April and May the Germans used poisonous gas for the first time on French and then British troops. Peculiar yellowish-green clouds formed and began to drift towards the Allied lines. Chemical warfare had been outlawed at the Hague but every major combatant in the Great War at this juncture had been guilty of experimenting with it. In the opening days of May gas attacks were relentless. A battalion of the Lancashire Fusiliers ceased to exist as a military entity with not fifty men available because of it. Thousands of British casualties were accumulating in medical posts where the baffled staff stared at them in dismay.

The British hierarchy immediately assumed that they were dealing with chlorine. The effects of this gas were horrific, to say the least, stripping the bronchial tubes. As the victims subsequently began gasping it proceeded to fully infiltrate the lungs. Tissue turned to mucus and the lungs filled with fluid. Throwing themselves to the ground did nothing for those that had been exposed as the gas sank. Men grasped at their throats and died with their fists clenched in agony. Casualty clearing stations were flooded with men who were quite literally blue, the result of their blood being starved of oxygen. The worst off died coughing, spitting and gagging as they drowned on dry land. British troops were promptly instructed to soak field dressings in bicarbonate of soda and use it as a respirator. Soaking it in some kind of alkaline solution was also thought to be effective; the most readily available source was latrine buckets full of urine.

As soon as he heard what had had happened Kitchener consulted Jack Haldane's uncle who telegraphed his brother in Oxford. Within twenty-four hours Haldane Sr, with all of his specialist knowledge of gases, was on his way to France.

In the first week of May, Jack Haldane was promptly ripped from his unit and ordered to join his father at a large school in St Omer with a selection of other volunteers. In one classroom a miniature greenhouse had been constructed and they took to sitting in it and pumping it full of chlorine gas. Jack assisted as they compared the effects on themselves in various quantities; with respirators, without them; 'it stung the eyes and produced a tendency to gasp and cough when breathed'. Having inflicted this horror on themselves, Jack and his colleagues sat in the greenhouse trying to crank a hand turned wheel as their respiratory system began to break down, they then burst outside and began doing 50-yard sprints in the grounds with respirators on to see what the effects of the gas were. When they had had enough they traded out and the next man rolled up for punishment.

'None of us [were] … in any real danger,' Jack claimed as they ultimately came up with a stop-gap form of protection for soldiers in the trenches. But a few men had to 'go to bed for a few days'. Jack found himself short of breath and incapable of running for a full month or so after their experiments. Unfortunately for the young scientist, however, in a matter of days he was advancing across no-man's-land in pursuit of the enemy.

On 8 May Jack Haldane was despatched back to Black Watch for 'special duties' in connection with the gas menace; there was even a suggestion that he might be named as some sort of advisor on the subject to Douglas Haig, but the point became moot. When he arrived back at his regiment, he found that his men were about to go into action and he was absolutely determined to go with them, at the head of his own platoon if at all possible. This push, known as Aubers Ridge, was a disaster. In the spring of 1915 the British had resolved to push towards Lille and this offensive followed a failure at Neuve Chapelle. Still suffering from the effects of the gas, Jack set off 'with all the urgency of an old gentleman with chronic bronchitis'.

Years later he still had a distorted version in his mind of what happened. He mustered the reserves of Black Watch and was advancing through an orchard under heavy fire when he was hit by debris and fell to the ground. Dragging himself up, Jack resumed command of his depleted platoon and raced for the parapet. In no-man's-land he went down again under the shock of another shell blast. He remembered, or so he thought, staggering back through reserve trenches towards a dressing station, caked in mud and blood, with his right arm and his left side bleeding.

Wandering through the ranks of wounded and dying men another Black Watch officer caught hold of him and flagged down a car to ask the driver to take Jack on to another dressing station. 'Oh it's you,' the driver remarked casually when he saw Jack. They had met in 1913 at Oxford and, bleary eyed, Jack recognised that his chauffeur was the Prince of Wales. He was so far gone that in the days after the battle he 'remembered' reading about his own death in *The Times*. In 1961 he told Robert Graves that he thought it quite plausible that he had died that day in pursuit of Aubers Ridge and that the succeeding forty-six years had been a vivid dream.

In the early evening of 14 March 1915 a terrific bombardment opened. The German target was a small, loosely defended village on a crossroads named St Eloi, sitting midway up a gentle hill some 2 miles east of Ypres. The Germans had begun their attack by setting off a mine in the vicinity and news shot up the line that the enemy had managed to blow up several sections of the British front and rush men into their trenches. Approaching midnight a significant part of the British defences had fallen and the village too.

At St Eloi itself, George Davies' battalion of the Rifle Brigade and the Princess Patricia's Canadian Light Infantry were ordered to support a counter-attack that was being planned. The counter-attack failed and at 3 a.m. on 15 March George and his fellow officers received orders to make the main attack in an attempt to retrieve the situation. Billy Congreve's insanely brave schoolfriend, Reggie Hargreaves, was their sniping and bombing officer. By the end of their failed attempt to drive the Germans back out of the village and the British lines Reggie would be lying in the ruins of St Eloi, shot in the chest and the leg, with a broken arm and his left foot and right hand mangled by shrapnel. During the retreat he was left behind but four of his snipers ignored orders the following night and went looking for him. Reggie was barely breathing when they began dragging him on to a stretcher in full view of the enemy.

It was the middle of the night when George Davies' youngest brother, 10-year-old Nico, was woken by the sound of the doorbell frantically ringing in the aftermath of St Eloi. He sat up in bed and listened to muffled voices drifting up the stairs. 'Then I heard uncle Jim's voice, an eerie banshee wail and an outburst: "They'll all go Mary," he cried to the boys' nurse. "Jack, Peter, Michael, even little Nico – this dreadful war will get them all in the end.' A little while later the door opened to Nico's bedroom and Barrie silently entered and sat on the end of his bed. 'I don't think he spoke,' Nico recalled, 'but I knew George was dead.'

As George Llewelyn Davies' battalion was advancing to drive the Germans out of St Eloi, he was not with them. He had marched up towards the fray with another OE, none other than Alfred Aubrey Tennyson, explaining a morbid premonition that he had had about being killed. On the way their colonel had sat them down in the early hours of the morning to explain the advance. Resting on a bank, George had not realised that he was sitting in an exposed position. A sniper's bullet was the result. His colleagues took him back along the main road to Voormezeele, a sad, battered little village and buried him, covering his grave in purple flowers; his favourite colour.

A few days later, in amongst a bundle of black-edged condolences, a little envelope arrived on James Barrie's doorstep. George had written one last letter just hours before he was killed. To the end he tried to console his guardian. He was not afraid, he claimed, nor taking any unnecessary risks. 'And if I am going to stop a bullet, why should it be with a vital place? … Keep your heart up Uncle Jim and remember how good an experience like this is for a chap who's been very idle before.'

It was five days later when another sniper struck a further blow at Eton. George Fletcher popped up to take a quick look over the inadequate parapet at Bois Grenier and was hit in the head. He died almost instantly. One of his men, Frank Richards, claimed that in the whole of the war, which he himself survived in its entirety, he never saw the battalion so cut up about an officer's death. When another OE took over later in the year he found he was still living in George's shadow. Charles Fletcher, who had lost two of his three sons in under five months, indirectly blamed the French flag for the attention it had drawn to the Fusiliers' section of the line. At home, the den became a shrine to his two lost boys but George's flag, the offending object, hangs today in the ante chapel at Eton.

But aside from this memento, George's death was still to have a far more poignant legacy. Devastated, Charles Fletcher sent word of his middle son's death on to Shrewsbury School. Evelyn Southwell, an OE himself, was mortified. To George's former colleagues he was still part of their household, their extended family. Evelyn could not walk into their shared house without thinking of him. When he broke the news to his form, the boys responded with a loud burst of applause for George. 'What else would you have?' It was the cruellest blow that the war had yet sent him. 'His personality lies stamped on all the little institutions of our life, and his name is mentioned almost every time we sit down together. He was, and is our d'Artagnan.'

With no interest in military matters and no practical experience, the next letter Evelyn wrote was to his own father: 'You will have heard the news of Fletcher's death. I think you will agree with me that the matter is now closed. I must go and take his place.' To George's father he closed with a final sentiment for the road. 'I hope I may catch some of his spirit and show one hundredth part of his courage.'

Notes
1. Lieutenant Gilbert Mitchell-Innes died aged 20 and lies in Vlamertinghe Military Cemetery in Belgium.
2. 'Tug' was another term normally used by Oppidans to describe a King's Scholar.
3. Geoffrey Valentine Francis Monckton is commemorated on the Le Touret Memorial. His brother, Francis Algernon Monckton, is remembered on the Menin Gate. The third Etonian to fall in Gareth Hamilton-Fletcher's company was Harold Sterndale Entwistle Bury, 26. He too is commemorated on the Le Touret Memorial.

7

'The New Argonauts'

Patrick Houston Shaw-Stewart passed through Eton and Balliol College, Oxford, at the turn of the twentieth century as part of an exceptional group of young men. The losses amongst them during the war would spur many a conversation about the waste of the Great War. Patrick himself was never at a boarding school until he went to Eton in 1901. The son of a general, he found, to his disappointment, that he was far from the only genuinely gifted King's scholar. He would spend years tussling for prominence with another Colleger named Foss Prior, who had returned as a master by the outbreak of war, eventually suffering defeat in the competitive environment amongst the scholarship boys. Never gifted at games, Patrick however found sporting employment as a cox of the house four, but described it as 'a thankless office from every point of view' for it associated him with 'a ridiculous set of scugs and scamps'.

Patrick longed for status and fretted frequently over it, at one point so much so that his hair began falling out. A hammer blow was when the mechanics of school life ensured that Foss and not he would one day be Captain of the School. This to Patrick had seemed his 'only chance of cutting a figure'. He did get his recognition though in 1904 when he beat both his rival and the famed Ronald Knox[1] to the Newcastle Prize, the premier academic contest at Eton. 'This was … fame indeed,' he concluded. 'I was greatly petted and applauded, and tremendously happy.'

George Fletcher was on the fringes of this bright set all through Eton and Oxford but his background was very different. Patrick was at the very centre. Alongside him was Julian Grenfell, eldest son of Lord Desborough 'with his intellectual contempt of intellect' and wild high spirits that would be followed by bouts of depression. There was Edward Horner too, 'most generous of hosts and most enthusiastic of companions … despite all protests from his friends an unabashed Whig'. His sisters, one of whom had married Raymond Asquith whilst Edward was still at Balliol, nicknamed him 'the popinjay' because he was so preoccupied with his state of dress. Born five weeks after Julian Grenfell he grew up in Somerset before being sent to Summer Fields Preparatory School in Oxford, where he became friends with both Ronald Knox and Julian. Edward was not ecstatically happy at Mr Impey's house at Eton and struggled. His mother wrote to him in a disappointed vein which almost caused him to break down completely and he referred to one half as 'long, stormy, troublesome and unsatisfactory'. He wrote once to his sister that 'I never seem to have succeeded at a single thing since I came to this beastly place … and I've disappointed Mother and Daddy ever since I came here.'

And then there was the Hon. Charles Alfred Lister. The eldest surviving son of Lord Ribbesdale, his brother Thomas had been killed during the Somaliland Expedition in 1904. Charles was equipped with 'generous enthusiasm … reckless fun … nervous breeziness of manner and [an] embarrassing conviction that every second person he met was a "good chap".' He was relentlessly cheerful even when the authorities at Oxford sent him down for a term. He went off and worked at a mission in East London. 'Self-critical, self-conscious but brilliant', his wit was sharp and getting into an intellectual dogfight with him was not advisable.

Not even his parents could quite fix why, but Charles had found his way into the Labour Party. He was leaning towards socialism at Eton, coinciding with civil unrest in Russia and his sympathy with her people in 1905. He even took up a collection for the Russo–Jewish fund and managed to extract £60 from his schoolfellows. His views were never militant, nor did he force them on others or take them out on the landed gentry that were his own, but he favoured options such as nationalisation of industry. His mother was somewhat troubled by Charles' political affiliations, although former prime minister Arthur Balfour sought to comfort her with the reasoning that 'Charles would get all sorts of experience and some sort of special knowledge which might be of more use to him than if he … ran an actress'. By the outbreak of war, however, he had left the party. Disappointed by 'recent methods', he still believed in the cause but had 'lost faith in most of the remedies' that he used to believe in.

Whilst at school this set, Charles, Patrick, Julian, Edward, Ronnie Knox and two other contemporaries, set up their own newspaper at Eton titled

The Outsider. It ran for six issues, to both positive and negative reviews before they all began departing for Balliol in the summer of 1906.

On leaving Balliol Charles embarked upon a career with the Foreign Office, firstly at the embassy in Rome and then in Constantinople where he still resided when Britain declared war on Germany. Charles began making a dash for home but his conscience got the better of him and he returned to his post. His determination to get into the firing line did not subside though and he began applying for leave from his job to join the army.

'The Turks are very cross with us now,' he reported in August 1914, 'and we may all have to come home if the Germans manage to rush them into war with Russia. That is now the game ... You can't imagine what a state of suspension we are in here.' By mid September things still hung in the air and Charles was completely unaware of what was happening as far as his own family was concerned. Unbeknown to him his sister, married to another OE (a grandson of the Duke of Westminster named Percy Wyndham) was already a widow. Wyndham was already in his grave when Charles wrote, 'Percy must have already done a lot; I hope he will get a VC or something.' He wouldn't find out the fate of his brother-in-law or of his younger acquaintance John Manners until he reached England at the end of the month. He was urged to stay on in a diplomatic role but Charles was firm about leaving Turkey. 'The date of my birth determines that I should [take] active service,' he declared as he left for home.

After Oxford, Patrick Shaw-Stewart embarked on a career in finance and characteristically excelled. Still in his mid 20s in 1914 he was already a director of Baring Brothers. The powers that be in the organisation thought that given his age it might be prudent to broaden his life experience. At the beginning of the year he was sent travelling in North America, which was a culture shock for him. 'Someone wrote to me as "Dear Patrick",' he exclaimed. 'I have only seen her *once!*' Wide eyed and dismayed by over familiarity and uncouth language he went from Washington to Arizona and then, via the Grand Canyon, to Los Angeles, San Francisco, Oregon, Seattle, Vancouver and Calgary before travelling back east through the Rockies, via Iowa, Illinois and Kansas; by which time he had somewhat fallen for 'this bustling, simple-minded, gaseous, rather incompetent, hospitable nation.'

Patrick returned to England in the summer and when war broke out he was back at Bishopsgate. That August his 'warlike soul' prompted him to enquire about joining the Inns of Court OTC and the following month he obtained leave to join the war effort. With a familiar, fierce determination he aimed at getting to the front as soon as possible. 'Baring Brothers have been perfect angels,' he wrote. He spent a week cramming languages and after twenty-three days freezing in various passages in the War Office trying to attract someone's attention he was finally employed. Now an official interpreter he would find himself thrown in at the front in a matter of days, sent with the new Royal Naval Division to try to save Antwerp.

At the outbreak of war Winston Churchill, as First Lord of the Admiralty, found that with the Fleet Reserve, the Royal Naval Reserve and the Royal Naval Volunteer Reserve, he had far more sailors than he needed. A number of battalions of land forces were formed from this excess of manpower, named after prominent figures in naval history and combined with the regular battalions of Royal Marines to form this new division. With extremely limited infantry experience they did not expect to be sent away for some months but as desperation rose over the situation in Belgium they were despatched before the war was more than a few weeks old. Royal Marines aside, ramshackle did not even begin to describe them. 'Most' of the men had a rifle before they left although at least one OE was practically a novice at firing his and the press was erroneously reporting that their bayonets were tied on with string.

Patrick remained at Dunkirk throughout September and October, no closer to the front than when he first stepped off the transport. The cheering crowds and adulation from the native population, who were convinced that they were a precedent for a huge British Army 'which was to drive the hated Germans from the country', wasn't enough to cheer him up. 'My sword, revolver and wire cutters are honourably rusting ... I use my silk pyjamas,' he quipped. Returning to England the haphazardly formed Royal Naval Division went to Crystal Palace for proper training where Patrick was told that he marched like a Chelsea pensioner and where he was shunted into the Hood Battalion with 'Oc' Asquith, the prime minister's son and the poet Rupert Brooke.

The men themselves came from marine depots, the various reserves, the Merchant Navy and numerous shipping hotspots such as Glasgow, Newcastle, the north of Scotland, London or Bristol. 'I have got the queerest command ... a platoon of old stokers!' Patrick reported. This rugged band came equipped with 'extremely fruity language' and 'cunning almost inexhaustible'. They had character though. He thought he could get used to them even though he suspected that they had 'a sort of standing grievance in the back of their evil old minds that they wanted to be in their steel walled pen yelping delight and rolling in the waist, instead of forming fours under the orders of an insolent young landlubber.'

By February 1915 the men of the Hood had been served pith helmets and rumours flew as to where they might be going. 'Egypt, East Africa, South

West Africa, Cameroons, Persian Gulf all freely mentioned' and Patrick was quietly impressed as he was of the opinion that if he was going to see any of the world at his country's expense he would much rather it was somewhere like Egypt than the squalor of Flanders. Rumours heightened again when their commanding officer had them solemnly practice forming squares. 'It may be only to puzzle the poor stokers,' thought Patrick, 'but it seemed to him to smack of 'fuzzy wuzzies and other crude foes.'

In the third week of February the Hood had confirmation. 'It is the Dardanelles,' Patrick reported excitedly. 'All the glory of a European campaign ... without the wet, mud, misery and certain death of Flanders.' He was resolved to take his copy of Herodotus' *Histories* with him as a guidebook. The connotations, with his classical education, were not lost on him at all. 'Think of fighting in the Chersonese, like Miltiades' or, alternatively, 'if it is the Asiatic side they want us on, on the plains of Troy itself!'

Turkey had procrastinated over entry into the war but nailed its colours to the wall at the end of October 1914, a month after Charles Lister left for home. Winston Churchill had already had the Royal Navy strike at the Turkish forts at the entrance to the Dardanelles, the straits forming a barrier between Europe and the East. They came under bombardment at the beginning of November but the dire state of events around Ypres on the other side of the continent ensured that nothing else transpired as the focus was on the Western Front.

On New Year's Day 1915 Russia requested that Britain make some sort of aggressive move against the Turks. Given the strain on all aspects of the British war effort at the time it was a big ask, but nonetheless the idea of an effort that did not involve large bodies of troops was suggested by Kitchener and wholeheartedly pushed by Churchill. The latter's plan was to force the straits open using naval forces exclusively. This was a failure though and following this lack of success, despite the strain on British resources, in March 1915 land operations to try to conquer the Dardanelles were approved. General Sir Ian Hamilton was put in charge of what was to be dubbed the Mediterranean Expeditionary Force.

The Turks had established their defences at key areas on the Gallipoli Peninsula and if the Allies had a mind to land on the Asiatic side of the straits, further men were stationed at Kum Kale near the site of Troy. In the northwest, near the neck of the peninsula, more troops were stationed near the Gulf of Saros. The peninsula itself was hardly hospitable to an occupying army either. It was dry, sparsely populated, and mountainous in places with barely any shelter. Given the position of the Turks and the previous attempts to force a way through there was also no element of surprise either. The enemy was fully aware of Allied intentions.

The British contingent decided against trying to land on the Asiatic side. The ground was a lot more open which would leave them extremely vulnerable if the Turks decided to come at them in large numbers. Gaba Tepe or 'Z Beach', midway up the western side was picked as one landing point; an easier alternative for an invasion and not as securely defended as other potential sites. It was also decided that there would be a number of landings all around Cape Helles, the southern tip of the peninsula, on the premise that any Turkish troops lurking on the beach would be hammered by naval guns prior to the assault on three sides.

So, rather than picking one good plan, it appeared that the Allies would try everything at once and hope for the best. The Australians and New Zealanders would be landing at Z Beach, whilst the Cape Helles landings would be attempted by British troops on V, W, S, X and Y beaches. Whilst they were at it, the French were to create a diversion by landing at Kum Kale on the Asiatic side and the Royal Naval Division, including the Hood, was to feign another landing in the Gulf of Saros to confuse the enemy. The aim of this over-complicated lunacy by the British was to take Krithia, a village at the ft of a large, flat hill named Achi Baba on day one. On day two the British would link up with the Anzac troops to the north and storm the higher ground and on day three the Royal Navy would weigh in, steam up the narrows and barge their way through the straits. Ambitious was an understatement.

Whilst Patrick was bored in Dunkirk, on his return to England Charles Lister had joined the 1st City of London (Middlesex) Yeomanry under the command of his brother-in-law to act as an interpreter, as it seemed entirely likely that they would be embarking for France imminently. Charles' dreams of active service, however, were well and truly scuppered. The regiment was sent to take up a coastal defence role in distant Norfolk. There they dug sorry-looking trenches into the sand cliffs and practiced with a machine gun. 'A certain amount of spy-hunting gave spice to the early days ... but later, when this flagged, the tedium grew intolerable.' The only highlights occurred when the men spied supposed lights being flashed out at sea by potential spies.

Charles was fully aware of the concentration of Eton friends and other acquaintances; the likes of Shaw-Stewart and Rupert Brooke massing in the Royal Naval Division, 'The New Argonauts' heading for the Dardanelles. In February Charles shot to London to talk his way onto their staff and sailed aboard the Cunard Line's *Franconia* when they departed for the east. 'I shan't regret this stunt, whatever happens,' he wrote gleefully. 'It is the most exhilarating feeling to be again on the sea of the ancient civilisations … I feel like a pinchbell Odysseus – longing for the same things, but with the limits and valour of some little city clerk.'

When Charles reached Malta on 10 March he found that the SS *Grantilly Castle*, carrying the Hood Battalion, was already there and he met his friends for dinners, the opera and 'generally razzled'. Charles had seen enough of the ship, with its happy mess, full of familiar faces and complete with piano, to know that he quite fancied being a part of it himself. It would beat hands down the role he had been given with the staff, where he was 'neither fish, flesh nor fowl, being viewed with suspicion as a Headquarters man and yet not sharing in the glories of the red hat and lapel tabs.'

The Royal Naval Division was sent to Egypt to prepare for the campaign. When they docked at Port Said they found Aubrey Herbert. Passed fit following his gunshot wound at Villers-Cotterêts it became apparent that the same basic ruse of sneaking into a regiment was not going to work again as far as active service was concerned. Owing to his linguistic skills and his experience of the east he took up a post at the Arab Bureau with T.E. Lawrence, but was not enamoured of either the work or their superior officer. Whilst Patrick was full of enthusiasm it was a completely different story for the intelligence officers in Cairo. Amongst themselves they talked about it freely. 'There was, as far as I saw,' Aubrey recalled, 'unanimity between military, naval and political officers … who deplored (not to use a stronger word) the idea of attempting to land on the Dardanelles; which the Turks had been happily fortifying and they preferred, on the whole, the idea of Alexandretta far, far to the South.'

In the spring Aubrey sought a permanent change from his unpleasant environment and joined the New Zealand contingent of the Australian and New Zealand Division. Acting as an interpreter/intelligence officer he began preparing for departure to the Gallipoli peninsula to fight the Turks he knew so well. When the Hood arrived Aubrey was happy to find old friends amongst the officers. The razzling continued and they gathered for dinners, lunches and a tour of the pyramids by moonlight. Charles and Patrick had combined to learn precisely one phrase in Turkish: 'Do not kill me, I am a friend of Herbert Effendi.'

By 2 April Charles Lister had managed, 'employing the most subterranean methods' to get himself into the battalion with his friends. Shaw-Stewart claimed that his friend had pulled as many strings to get off the staff as other people pulled to get on it, but his deviousness worked. Within three days Charles had command of a platoon and found himself in the same company as Patrick and Rupert Brooke, both of whom were presently laid up 'weak as kittens' with dysentery. Sadly for Patrick, it meant that he missed the wonderful spectacle of his friend elegantly attempting to command his men through drill in his special parade voice. Now experiencing camp life for the first time, Charles felt rather 'a sort of baby' amongst his band of hardened naval reservists, many of whom were advancing towards forty. The orders he attempted to bellow out he only understood 'through a glass darkly'. He had a mind to try to impress those around him and attempted to learn signalling; 'a useless accomplishment, I fancy, but I must above all give the impression of zeal, as I always feel my position is risky and my accomplishments far behind those of my brother officers.' Their best officer was an ex-cavalryman and a veteran of Queen Victoria's wars in Africa. Charles, by his own admission, had seen service on a hillside in Norfolk.

On 10 April, Patrick hauled himself back aboard the *Grantilly Castle* to find his Eton friend firmly ensconced in the Hood with no intention of leaving. Their dinner table in the mess included Oc Asquith, Brooke, Charles, Patrick and another slightly older OE named 'Cleg' Kelly; an Australian-born talented musician who kept them entertained en route.

Everyone referred to them as 'The Latin Club' and they remained up after everybody else had gone to bed every night, drinking wine and chatting away. Their conversation flowed from Byzantine emperors to music, to Turkish prisoners. Every destination, every island glimpsed along the way brought to the fore ancient connotations for Patrick and Charles. Lemnos, where Philoctetes was left behind during the Trojan War, Samothrace where Poseidon sat to watch the fighting. Unlike Aubrey, they were firm in their conviction that the campaign would be over swiftly and successfully, the Royal Naval Division at the fore. The dangers of modern war seemed alien. 'I don't think this is going to be at all a dangerous campaign,' Patrick scoffed. 'We shall only have to sit on the Turkish forts after the fleet has shelled the unfortunate occupants out of them.'

In the third week of April the Hood landed at Skyros, the island of Achilles; where his mother was said to have dressed him as a girl so that he would not be whisked off to Troy. Training continued, but life was merry. They swam, sunbathed; the sub-lieutenants even threw a fancy dress ball for the men. Most of them scraped together odds and ends to dress as old dames or painted themselves black, but one 'vain spark' in Charles' platoon cast himself as Queen Elizabeth. 'His skirt,' Charles wrote, 'is my burberry, his stomacher my cabin curtains; his wimple (non-historic but one must wear something on one's head) is a boot bag and his veil a blue antiseptic bandage.' When not ragging with the men, Charles and Patrick managed to get off the ship one day and on to the island to chat with the locals and ramble about taking in the scenery. They returned to find Brooke, who had taken their watches so that they could stay out as long as possible, hanging over the side and bombarding them with sarcasm.

The following day, though, their friend fell ill. Patrick was frightened by the sight of him 'so motionless and fevered' as he was lowered over the side and taken to a French hospital on the island. Blood poisoning claimed the poet, before he caught sight of Gallipoli. 'I shouldn't have thought,' wrote Patrick, who had only met Brooke since joining the battalion, 'that anyone in three months could come to fill so large a space in my life.' Three petty officers performed the challenging feat of carrying Rupert's coffin for a mile across rugged terrain, along a stony path where they buried him in an olive grove. Charles, who had known the poet for much longer, helped to dig the grave and stayed behind after the service to cover it with pieces of white marble in the shadow of a bent olive tree leaning over it 'like a weeping angel'.

When they returned from the burial Cleg Kelly composed an elegy, trying to introduce the feel of Greek temples and the movement of the olive trees as opposed to religious undertones that wouldn't have suited their friend at all. Perhaps, Charles reflected sadly 'the Island of Achilles is in some respects a suitable resting place for those bound for the plains of Troy'.

Despite his complete lack of enthusiasm for this new endeavour, Aubrey Herbert had no complaints about his trip save for the fact that the 'puritanical' New Zealand Government had ordained that their ship was to be dry of all alcohol. After a three-day voyage they docked at Lemnos where the mood from ship to ship was buoyant. By now he was aware that the New Zealanders would be attacking the central part of the peninsula and Aubrey had been despatched onto the island to buy as many donkeys as he could get his hands on. Some things never changed. His adoration of animals led him to rescue a miniature one that would have been useless for military purposes to keep as a mascot for the division.

On 23 April he watched a magnificent procession of boats depart for the new front. In the afternoon the New Zealanders left in a stiff breeze and the island sparkled behind them in the sunlight. 'With the band playing and flags flying, we steamed past the rest of the fleet. Cheers went from one end of the harbour to the other.' The sea was calm all the way across to the Dardanelles. Some of the officers intended to get up early and watch the Australians attack from the deck. Aubrey didn't want to. 'I thought that we should see plenty of the attack before we had done with it and preferred to sleep.'

He eventually emerged two hours after the off at 6.30 a.m on 25 April. to the continuous roar of artillery from Cape Helles in the south. Behind the sands at Z Beach the ground rose steeply into cliffs and hills towards the imposing peak of Chunuk Bair and from the shore he could hear the crackle of rifles. At 8.30 a.m. he received his orders and was loaded on to a small craft to be towed ashore. Aubrey eyed it suspiciously as they were herded in. There was no shelter of any kind and as they drifted along bullets splashed into the water alongside them. They watched the outline of bodies on the beach loom larger as they approached land. Aubrey 'floundered ashore' and scrambled on to 'that unholy land' amidst a shower of bullets. 'The word was then, I thought rather unnecessarily, passed that we were under fire.'

At Z Beach, which would become known as Anzac Cove, there was initial success but it came at a price. They had been landed in the wrong place, right in front of Chunuk Bair instead of further south where the ground was easier. At about midday the Turks turned their guns on them. The Australians got right up on to the high ground before the enemy counter-attacked under Mustafa Kemal and pushed them back. Aubrey Herbert was running backwards and forwards past hordes of wounded men looking for (fictional) Turkish prisoners that he was supposed to be interviewing. He was appalled at the conditions that he saw and wrote in his diary of 600 wounded men loaded on to one ship and despatched to Egypt in the care of one veterinary surgeon. The commander of the Anzac forces, General Birdwood, wanted to evacuate, citing in particular the plight of the New Zealanders, who had been heavily hit. General Hamilton didn't want to hear it. He told him that the only option was to 'dig yourselves right in and stick it out'.

At Cape Helles in the far south the attacks had been a collective disaster. Meanwhile, Charles Lister, Patrick Shaw-Stewart and the rest of the Hood Battalion were carrying out their false landing in the Gulf of Saros. Shortly after dawn on 25 April, transports carrying the naval men began playing about with a collection of rowboats and pretended to set up for an attack. Patrick then listened for two days to 'the most prodigious bombardment that ever was' going on to the south whilst they bobbed about on their ship. He couldn't believe that any Turks would survive such a storm of shells 'but they have the devils', he wrote miserably. Rumours had reached the Hood that all was not playing out well on the peninsula and he was glad that they hadn't formed part of the original landing force. 'Though our men will probably be very steady,' he remarked, 'I doubt they are quite the raging fiends the Australians seem to be when they are raised.'

By the end of April the Hood had been moved down to V Beach to land at what had been a scene of unprecedented slaughter just a few days earlier. Bodies lined the sand and the *River Clyde*, the modern day Trojan horse that had run aground to land troops by way of holes cut in the side and gangways attached to the hull, dominated the scene. There were ships everywhere and in the dark they reminded Charles of the illuminated Brighton Pier. Occasionally he saw tiny little figures ashore; they looked like ants creeping and crawling about the cliff faces and hillsides. Achi Baba loomed hundreds of feet above them as they waited to come ashore. The noise of the guns was deafening and the Turkish artillery retaliated. Charles, Patrick and their men camped near the shoreline for the night and shivered whilst they watched the red haze of fires on the skyline. The Gallipoli campaign was now well under way.

What followed for the next month and a half was a systematic attempt to carry out the original plan to seize the straits. It began with a massed renewed attack on 28 April which failed; a huge blow to the British idea of a swift victory in this new theatre of war. Having suffered Turkish counter-attacks, on 6 May the assault was thrust again towards the village of Krithia and above it the already familiar Achi Baba.

At midnight on 5 May the Hood were awoken by a crescendo of noise. Charles, buzzing at the idea of actual fighting, was convinced that the enemy was right on top of them. They marched across a soggy ravine, 'overgrown with lovely water weeds and olives, grey in the moonlight' to a line of trenches that awaited them. They tucked in behind the firing line. Dawn revealed the Allies in front of them advancing over hoards of Turkish dead.

Charles' platoon moved off in support. The men in front had gone 2,000 yards when the Turks opened fire with shrapnel. The lines were still primitive and there was no time to improve their positions. The Hood was isolated on the flank and orders came up to retire, but not before the enemy had singled them out for a heavy barrage. The Hood had managed to effect some sort of advance but gains were minimal and the casualties to the Royal Naval Division were shocking. Charles' company was amongst the last to retreat. As they moved back, a shell exploded sending a shower of shrapnel at him, lodging in his water bottle, his coat and, most ignominious of all, in his backside. There he was, 'bleeding like a pig' and limping along when he wanted to be rallying his men. 'I never saw a Turk within shooting distance,' he remarked drily. Patrick agreed with his statement.

Charles managed to disguise his injury well until his trousers became soaked in blood. He was deposited on a stretcher, carried down to the beach and sent off to Malta. His company remained in the firing line without him. He likened his battle experience to foreplay. 'I should like to get back quick, because I have seen just enough to tantalise.' It hadn't been glorious, but as far as he was concerned they were not to blame. If the commanding officer had not instructed them to retire then Charles thought that they could have been cut off and annihilated. 'That day they showed great steadiness for raw troops, but their situation was impossible.'

The New Zealand Brigade had been moved round to Cape Helles to take part in the assault too. The dead lay everywhere. The wounded cried for water in between the trenches. Aubrey Herbert had seen enough. He located medical officers and had them approach General Birdwood about some sort of ceasefire to attend to the situation. The general did not think that the Germans would allow the Turks to carry through such an idea. Aubrey was disgusted. He had been out with a megaphone, which Birdwood quite rightly thought was a futile exercise, trying to convince the Turks to surrender. He was shot at, laughed at and otherwise ignored. He had the same effect as a trench mortar. Every time he stopped to speak he elicited a volley of rifle fire. Unperturbed, Aubrey continued with his ploy to effect a temporary ceasefire to take care of the dead and wounded.

Patrick was one of the few sub-lieutenants who came through unscathed but his love affair with the war was already over. Men around him had been struck and a bullet had lodged in his Asprey steel mirror, which he thought almost as good an advert for the manufacturer as Oc Asquith's wound had been for the government. The war was a thing that he didn't think a man ought to miss, but now he had seen it and participated in battle he began to wonder if this was any place for a civilised man.

On 8 May the New Zealanders made their own attempt on Krithia and gained about 400 yards before they were pinned down. Despite this, the battle's commander, Aylmer Hunter-Weston, ordered them to attack again that evening in pursuit of Achi Baba. The effort failed amidst catastrophic casualty figures for Ian Hamilton's force.

The smell of bodies had now become unbearable in the stifling heat. Aubrey tried again but was refused permission to try to negotiate a truce. Aubrey was relentless, demanding to board Hamilton's ship to speak to the MEF's commander himself. He had no love for Hamilton at the best of times but this was to enhance his distaste. Aubrey labelled him a vain fool and the dislike was mutual. The general, though, did approve a pause in hostilities for burials, providing that it did not appear that the British had asked for it. Aubrey managed to make both sides believe that it was the other who had wanted a ceasefire. A colleague and an Oxford friend remarked that 'Liman von Sanders says we did, Sir Ian Hamilton says they did. My own opinion is that Aubrey Herbert was responsible for it.'

On 24 May Aubrey's stomach was in knots, paranoid that something was going to go wrong. He climbed upwards to 400 Plateau above the beach at

Anzac Cove through a field of poppies. He had just reached another plateau full of tall corn when the 'fearful smell of death' hit him. Corpses were scattered all over the place. He climbed through gullies of thyme and it was 'indescribable'. A Turkish Red Crescent man gave him a dressing doused in antiseptic to cloak his mouth and nose from the smell. As the soldiers went about their burial work, they were visibly distressed. Aubrey came across two wounded men 'in all that multitude of silence, crying in the gullies'. He approached one, who lay in the middle of a pile of bodies, pulled out a water bottle and helped him to drink from it. A Turkish captain with him was feeling reflective. 'At this spectacle,' he said, 'even the most gentle must feel savage and the most savage must weep.'

Amongst the bodies the damage done by machine guns was evident by the injuries that the men had sustained: 'their heads doubled under them with the impetus of the rush and both hands clasping their bayonets'. Aubrey was required to alleviate a fair amount of bickering throughout the day. The Turks argued that the Australians were making off with rifles and the Australians levelled their own charges at the enemy while Aubrey tried to pacify both sides. Craftiness did occur. One chaplain managed to get a trench that had been the source of much bother used as a grave so that it was taken out of use and both sides spied when they could.

Aubrey, being Aubrey, managed to make friends with some of the Turkish troops. The sultan's men were gleaned from all over the Ottoman Empire. He had a Greek try to surrender to him, an Anatolian gave him a fierce stare to send chills up a man's spine and the Albanians took to him immediately. They knew Aubrey by name, for after all he had nearly become their king and men began clapping him on the back and cheering. Unfortunately this was in the midst of funeral services occurring across the battlefield and Aubrey quietened them all down quickly. The truce was due to end in the late afternoon and Aubrey joked with the enemy troops that they would shoot at him the next day. The Albanians found the idea ridiculous. That night Aubrey was dousing his throat with whiskey to get rid of the taste of death and coating his legs with iodine where barbed wire had slashed at his skin.

The following day HMS *Triumph* was sunk in full view of the beach. 'There was fury, impotence and rage on the beach and on the hill.' Aubrey heard a captain ranting, 'you should kill all enemies, not give them cigarettes!!!!' Men were crying and cursing. 'Very different from last night when they were all wishing each other luck.'

On 4 June the British and French launched another massed attack on Achi Baba. The 3rd Battle of Krithia was the final attempt to carry out the original plan of attack on the peninsula. At 8 a.m. a bombardment began, concentrating on strongpoints before it became a general barrage on all the Turkish lines three hours later. The French to the right of the Hood were also pummelling the Turkish lines but unfortunately for the allies, the wind blew the smoke from their shells right back into their faces and obscured their view at midday when the Hood burst forward.

As soon as they emerged men began to fall back dead into the trench in a hail of Turkish fire. Those that survived poured into three enemy trenches taking an obscene amount of casualties. They were in dire need of support. To their right, the French were completely mown down by machine guns and the Royal Naval Division was therefore exposed to enfilading fire. Setting off behind the Hood, the Collingwood Battalion fell in their droves before they could even get to the front line. Butchered and in a state of confusion, at lunchtime they were ordered to retreat. As if this was not crushing enough, the following day the Turks launched a forceful counter-attack. The whole offensive ground to a halt and all hopes of an advance evaporated.

Patrick went into battle having just received word that Julian Grenfell and Edward Horner had fallen foul of the Germans and ended up in the same hospital in Boulogne. He had been abruptly pulled out of the line at the very last moment to replace a fallen French interpreter dealing with the troops next door. There was simply no time to think of his friends when the Hood was being slaughtered all around him. The battalion suffered severely on 4 June. Of fifteen officers, six were killed and five wounded, including Cleg Kelly. Patrick was one of only four to come out physically unscathed. He was 'filled with disgust and rage' at the folly of it. Trenches were captured but they got nowhere near the summit of the hill. The Hood had lost twenty-six of thirty officers since 6 May and finally attempts to carry out the initial intentions on the peninsula were abandoned. It all appeared to have been for nothing.

Charles Lister was fit to re-join the Royal Naval Division a few days later. His return was mortifying. He sailed in at dawn and the fleet was nowhere to be seen. Just a couple of hospital ships bobbed about with a destroyer or two. The green keel of the sunken *Majestic* stuck out above the waterline lit by a single lamp, reminding Charles of the oil lamps put on the graves at San Lorenzo cemetery in Rome on All Soul's night. He found the Hood much changed. The survivors were working on the beach, grossly under-officered and digging saps, sniping, lugging supplies and even carrying out guard duty for high-ranking officers. As on the Western Front, stagnant warfare now kicked in on the Gallipoli Peninsula.

Aubrey's mood was desolate. He found the inactivity and the calm awful. The likes of his own general, Godley, were not unpopular, but Hamilton was another story. Aubrey despised him. He reported that he had been to the area precisely twice in the early stages of their occupation. 'I think for a quarter of an hour each time and has never been around the positions at all. GHQ are loathed.' Aubrey grew more and more bitter towards him. In June he wrote to his wife that Hamilton had 'the obstinacy of weak men'. He continued his appraisal: 'I have had one or two instances when I have seen how he and his staff believe what they want to believe in the face of all sense and evidence.'

Neither did Aubrey reserve his venom for General Hamilton. Although an MP himself, he did not refrain from criticising the politicians at home for the ineptitude that he believed was responsible for the army's plight. Thanks to his wife he had intimate knowledge of what was being said inside 10 Downing Street and was distinctly unimpressed at how miserable Churchill was at his failure. Apparently he had said that if he was Prime Minister for twenty years then it would not make up for the failure of the Dardanelles. 'I would like him to die in some of the torments I have seen so many die in here,' Aubrey spat. 'But his only "agony" you say is missing PM.'

Despite the failure of the expedition thus far, Kitchener, in the face of a disastrous scenario in Flanders, was not about to let the campaign fold. During the summer the beaches on the peninsula were swarming with activity. Sitting in a rest camp with the rest of the Hood, Charles Lister claimed to be quite enjoying himself. 'I look forward to the rum nights with all the zeal of an old sea dog,' he reported. He had a light-hearted approach to war but it did not sit well with everybody. Certain occupants took life on the beaches very seriously but he couldn't. He likened one of them to Blackpool but then noted that 'its inhabitants take the shells rather seriously and would resent this flippancy'.

There were opportunities for swimming, which Charles loved, although one had to become adept at dodging the bloated corpses of dead horses. Animals of the living variety differed greatly from the tabby cats of the Western Front. Patrick Shaw-Stewart was repulsed by 'centipedes and other monsters'. Flies were by far the worst irritation. It was impossible to sleep during the day without some sort of protection and Patrick had frantically employed his whole family on thinking up ideas to defeat them. 'Fly papers, fly whisks, some sulphuric apparatus for smoking them out' anything that they could think of. 'Flies by day and flies by night, flies in the water, flies in the food,' bemoaned one Etonian.

OEs relied on care packages from home as, unlike the Western Front, it was impossible to pop into the nearest town for supplies. The alien climate also disturbed the men's health. One OE in the Royal Engineers was lucky to have a stash of chlorodyne with him which he began getting his mother to supplement. With it he had managed to cure most of the diarrhoea/dysentery that struck down his sappers. He was also maintaining a stash of arrowroot for similar purposes. 'I have to harden my heart and be really brutal,' he wrote, 'as I think every man in the section has been upset by the heat and unsuitable food at one time or another and any who have a little gut just lie down and collapse.'

Patrick was tired of the squalid existence that he claimed reminded him of the Selli tribe in the *Iliad* who crouched on the ground and never washed their feet. He had let his red beard grow through and according to Charles he looked like a holy man who had dyed it with henna. The situation was not, of course, helped by the many dead bodies lying about decomposing. Patrick had a pile of them in front of his trench. 'At dawn a lark got up from there and started singing. A queer contrast. Rupert Brooke could have written a poem on that, rather his subject.'

By mid July the Hood was in the trenches; old Turkish lines. 'It is fairly whiffy,' Charles Lister wrote; on account of the bodies that were close by. 'With the tell-tale stocking or end of boot' sticking ominously out of the trench walls. They were at risk of snipers during the day and at night when the men were led up and down the communication trenches they tripped over the bodies of unlucky colleagues who had exposed themselves. 'It is an awful job getting our men past them,' Charles explained. 'They have a sort of supernatural fear of trampling on their own dead.'

The lines themselves were cramped and Charles complained that he had had his toes trodden on 'by every officer and man of a Scotch territorial division' who came past in driblets, lost and wandering. Patrick managed, even when the trench was 'a seething mass of humanity', to remain lucid, but Charles lost his temper and ultimately began jumping up and down on the parapet 'kicking dust on their heads and … using the most violent language'.

On 1 August he wrote home once again from a sickbed to say that, having been told that they would be taken off the peninsula at the end of the month, suddenly not a man was allowed to leave. 'So I suppose there will be something doing.' And indeed there was. The British government had approved the sending of tens of thousands of reinforcements to Gallipoli; New Army and Territorial men; basically whatever they had to hand. This massive influx opened up all kinds of possibilities for Ian Hamilton.

Cape Helles, already the scene of so much devastation, was a write-off. Anzac Cove still looked like the better option but it was now that Suvla Bay to the north, previously ignored, came into play. It had been deemed too far away from the original objectives in April, but now fresh (but inexperienced) troops were ordered to assault it on 6 August under dubiously defined and overcomplicated orders. Men, unready for battle, were thrown into an overly optimistic attack which failed to recognise just how much trouble the Turkish resistance had caused. Not surprisingly they failed.

Aubrey missed the onset of the new offensive as he was off on nearby islands in his capacity as an intelligence officer. He arrived back on 7 August and spent the day interrogating prisoners. The following day he watched the attack. 'It looked so cruel I could hardly bear to see it.' It seemed like a horrible dream sequence to him. '[I]n the beautiful light, with clouds crimson over them, sometimes a tiny gallant figure in front then a puff of smoke would come and they would be lying still.'

Again the sight of the wounded distressed him greatly. Outside a hospital of sorts he came across an acquaintance who had been wounded during the battle and spent an excruciating day lying out in the sun. 'He recognised me and asked me to help him, but he was delirious. There were fifty-six others with him.' It was unbearable having to walk past them all. The smell was appalling as none of the wounded men had been cleaned and he heard some of them call out, 'we are being murdered.'

One of the objectives in the August offensives was the peak of Chunuk Bair in the Sari Bair range. Aubrey Herbert's New Zealanders, in his absence, had forged a path towards the summit before they were relieved by the British and trudged back over tall cliffs, deep ravines, and dry river beds and through wooded country in the dark. Early on 10 August Mustafa Kemal launched a counter-attack and thousands of Turks came pouring over Chunuk Bair and tore the British infantry to shreds. The fighting was hand to hand, 'so desperate a battle cannot be described'. The enemy came at them in waves, washing the British aside.

Down on the beach the wounded on the sand and the men attempting to treat them were under sustained rifle fire from the Turks above. It seemed that nowhere was safe. In his capacity as an interpreter Aubrey didn't have a specific job to do at that precise time, so once again his concern for the broken men being brought down from the battle came to the fore. They lay in rows, 'their faces caked with sand and blood'. He grabbed another officer and together they commandeered 200 exhausted New Zealanders of the Canterbury Battalion who had not slept in three days and began carrying them to safety. They passed around all of the water they could. Nobody was of a mind to move the wounded Turks, but Aubrey could not bear their crying. An order had come that they were not to be evacuated until all of their own men had gone. 'This is natural but was of course an order of lingering death.' Aubrey went back with water and tried to drag the wounded Turkish soldiers into some shade. He wanted to go up to the battlefield where more men could be heard, of both sides, crying for water but the general refused him permission. What right did he have? Aubrey fumed. 'Tempers have got very short.'

He found General Birdwood and learned that the prognosis was not good. The Turks had pushed the invaders off Chunuk Bair and the battle appeared lost. The enemy, he said, had been magnificent and Aubrey feared that the New Zealand Infantry Brigade had ceased to exist. 'The lines of wounded are creeping up to the cemetery like a tide,' claimed Aubrey, '... and the cemetery is coming to meet the wounded.' On 13 August Aubrey himself contracted a fever. He was full of resolve to carry on, but eleven days later he was put on a hospital ship. Struck down with dysentery he was still claiming to be fit enough to stay when he fainted during an interview with a doctor. Having had three week's sick leave in Egypt he did return in September but lasted approximately a fortnight before his health completely broke down. As he left Gallipoli, this sideshow of a front, Aubrey wrote 'I never want to see again a mule, or a backdoor, or a sideshow, or Winston, or flies or bully beef.' 'Sooner or later,' his granddaughter wrote, 'he saw them all again.'

Meanwhile Charles Lister had returned to the Hood, again sitting in reserve. He had already proved his worth to the men's morale when he had come back to them after 4 June. Cleg Kelly recalled just how miserable and depressed the battalion's survivors were until Lister arrived with his irrepressible spirits to charm them back into acceptance about their situation.[2] Charles was flagging though. 'I feel that we shall never fight or move, and I shall not know what has happened if I wake up one morning and don't see Achi Baba on the skyline.' His thoughts had already wandered to what he had lost; whether it be on the peninsula or on the Western Front. 'It will be sad coming back.' So many friends had died and their old haunts would be 'full of ghosts'. Things would never be the same again.

On 19 August Charles and his men were preparing to go back into the firing line where he hoped that they would sit tight and forego any more fruitless attacks. This played out when he reported from the trenches a few days later that he was catching up on his reading, but soon afterwards the Turks began tossing shells at them. He shuffled his men along to safety and then went back down the trench thinking the show was over, only to be hit by a piece of flying shrapnel which struck him on the pelvis, damaging his bladder and causing slight wounds to his legs. Charles was operated on immediately but remained unsure as to what exactly had been done as he bobbed up and down on a hospital ship. His doctor, however, was quite pleased with his progress.

After the failure of the August attacks inertia had set in. General Hamilton became a victim of his own failure and ineptitude and was relieved of his command. Patrick was no longer with the battalion, having replaced a liaison officer with the French who had been badly wounded. He was ensconced in 'inglorious safety on the gilded staff … speaking French for dear life'. A few days later news reached him that Charles had worsened and he died on 28 August. He was devastated. At the time 'Lord Lister', as his men called him, had been fending off, despite Patrick's encouragement, approaches from intelligence people contriving to give him work away from the trenches. He was laid to rest on Mudros.

By October, Patrick was convinced that he too would die on the peninsula, quite possibly of old age as his residence there seemed to be 'smacking of eternity'. He was soon put out of his misery though. A new front had opened up in the Balkans and it was decided that enough was enough. Patrick Shaw-Stewart was one of the last men to exit this doomed theatre of war as a line was drawn under a disastrous campaign and the Allies prepared to depart. 'It is pretty sad when you think of what it has cost us,' he wrote in January 1916, although he was convinced that it was the right decision to go. Of the French contingent only he, the guns and his commanding officer remained, lighting fires and burning anything the Turks might use. 'I have burnt some queer things, including a bowler hat.'

As Patrick prepared to board the *River Clyde* the Turks continued to shell them from the direction of Troy. On the beach it was 'as quiet as the grave'. Not a man was lost during the evacuation of the Gallipoli peninsula, which is more than can be said of the nine months before. There are twenty-nine Old Etonians buried or commemorated on the peninsula as testament to a shambles of a campaign. Herodotus was useless as a guidebook to Patrick now. Each island, each beach, each objective was marred by death and stained with the sacrifice of his friends. As he turned his back on the Dardanelles he wondered what was next. He left behind the ghosts of Charles Lister and Rupert Brooke. In 1915, at Gallipoli and on the Western Front, almost his entire circle of friends would be slaughtered.

Notes
1. Ronald Arbuthnott Knox, the famous theologian.
2. Lt Commander F.S. Kelly was killed on 13 November 1916 on the Western Front. He is buried at Martinsart British Cemetery.

8

'I Feel an Outcast to Be Alive'

Field Marshal Lord Horatio Herbert Kitchener was a national hero. The victor of Omdurman and a commander of British forces during the Second Boer War; he accepted the role of Secretary of State for War on 5 August 1914 with the sentiment, 'May God preserve me from the politicians.' Convinced from the beginning that war would last at least three years and isolated in this opinion, he understood better than most that Britain would need men and a coherent structure to bring them to arms. Almost immediately he made the bold decision not to raise troops for the war effort through the existing county scheme for territorials, but by way of separate recruitment, forging a 'new army'. Scenes at recruiting offices in London were mayhem and enlistment fever rapidly spread. By 25 August 1914 Kitchener could count his first 100,000 volunteers, soon to be dubbed K1, and appeals went out for another 100,000 men. K2 was raised in less than a week, and the queues of men intending to enlist had not yet diminished.

Richard Selby Durnford, or 'Dick', came from a thoroughly Etonian family. The great grandson of the fabled headmaster, Dr Keates, his uncle, Walter, was also a master for nearly thirty years. Dick himself had arrived at school in 1899. Captain of the Oppidans, captain of his House and an editor of the *Eton College Chronicle*, he was good-natured, 'highly principled' and enthusiastic. He went from Eton to King's College, Cambridge, where he was a feature of the dramatic society and began a career as a schoolmaster at Lancing College. It was perhaps always inevitable that he would end up back at Eton and that he did in 1909. Dick, 29, loved every minute of his life at the school, from

teaching lessons and pupil-room to his participation in games and the OTC.
Nevertheless, as soon as war broke out, he felt compelled to go.

As a territorial Dick should have waited for a summons to his regiment but
instead he raced off and managed to offer himself for service in a New Army
battalion of the King's Royal Rifle Corps. The logistics of training so many
men were proving horrifying. There were massive shortages of accommodation, uniforms, weapons, bedding and food. Nearly half-a-million men had
enlisted in the army and Dick sat waiting for his uniform to turn up. Most
of the men were in khaki, but there were missing caps throughout and only
one-third had a rifle. The King's Royal Rifle Corps and the Rifle Brigade
had each stumped up three new battalions of volunteers immediately the war
commenced; the 7th, 8th and 9th of their respective regiments. They were
some of the earliest formed of Kitchener's first 100,000, so if they were lacking any equipment or comfort, Dick didn't feel that they were particularly
hard done by when he considered K2 and K3 further down. 'Picture what is
happening lower down.'

Aldershot, where the two regiments were based, was fast filling up with
Eton masters who were abandoning their posts at school. In all sixteen of
them had now left and numbers amongst the younger men willing to carry on
teaching whilst their friends went into uniform were continuing to dwindle.
Foss Prior was one of George Fletcher's closest friends at Eton. He was a brilliant scholar as Patrick Shaw-Stewart, his academic rival, found to his chagrin.
His grandfather was bishop of Westcott and very fond of Foss and his siblings.
Whilst taking tea when he was a little boy, the bishop would draw railway
engines for them. 'I remember his lifting up his hands in amazement,' another
relative recalled, 'as he reviewed all the animals of the Noah's ark arranged in
procession round the dining-room table, and how he delighted the children
by pretending that the camel was an elephant ... so as to leave behind an
agreeable impression that he was a well meaning but sadly ill-informed old
man.' He would even descend to the floor to assist in building operations. In
1900, Foss and several siblings and cousins accompanied their grandfather to
a picnic at Bolton Castle where the old man found little Foss peering into
a dungeon. The bishop stooped down to look too and remarked, 'Do you
think that is where we are to have tea?' When Foss laughed and replied that it
wouldn't be in that dark hole, the bishop professed to be much relieved.

Foss could come across as quite rigid and shy when first met, but he was
a treasured companion amongst his closest friends; always of a gentle temperament. Whilst at University College, Oxford, he was offered a clerical
Fellowship and he had been considering holy orders with some seriousness.

He spent several months at the theological college at Wells but in 1912 he decided 'after grave searching of the heart' to postpone the idea of ordination. This coincided with a job offer at Eton and he put his religious ambitions on hold and returned to his old school gladly.

Although he was willing to go to war within a few months, everybody knew that Foss was not born to be a soldier. This was not based on ability but on his temperament. He wrestled greatly with his conscience at the outbreak of hostilities but ultimately could not bear inaction. He was massively enthusiastic about all aspects of his life as a master at Eton with the exception of his involvement in the corps; which as an officer he found boring and loathed that it required him to give up parts of holidays. Nonetheless his sense of duty banished his reservations and as soon as war began he went to spend his summer helping the Cambridge OTC at Royston. He returned to school at the end of September for little over a month before he packed his things and joined the new 8th Battalion of the Rifle Brigade. He was joined by another Eton colleague, Arthur Sheepshanks. He may only have stood 5ft 3in but 'Sheep' was to prove that stature was not dictated by a tape measure on a battlefield.

Dick Durnford was ensconced at Blenheim Barracks where his battalion, the 9th King's Royal Rifle Corps, was sharing barracks made for one unit with the 9th Rifle Brigade. They were muddling along without too much discomfort. The most pressing concern, so far as he could see, was a disturbing lack of junior officers and NCOs to command these new battalions.

Kitchener was by no means ignorant of this issue. At the outbreak of war he had available to him a shade under 30,000 officers, but with the number of men he had raised he would need to double this figure. However that did not take into account replacing those who were by now beginning to fall at the front in high numbers. There were a few hundred officers at home on leave from India in August 1914 and he seized them before trying to smooth things over with the Indian Government. Dick's battalion was initially lucky as they had inherited some Gurkha officers who reported for duty but they were liable to be called off at any moment, leaving them extremely short handed.

On 10 August an appeal was published for 2,000 junior officers to join the army until the conclusion of the war. This appeal was liable to appeal to many an Old Etonian as it sought to find men between the age of seventeen and thirty who were cadets or ex-cadets in university OTCs, and other highly educated young men. Kitchener got more than he asked for but these volunteers could not instantly be turned into competent officers. It became a constant trade-off between keeping them at home to train them as much as

possible and using this precious stock to replace the fallen at the front. Foss
Prior was one master who would actively try and direct boys he had taught at
Eton to join his own battalion as officers when they had determined to go to
war but it was a frustrating situation. The enthusiasm of some men who were
potential officer stock to get to war meant that they had enlisted in the ranks.
One Scottish regiment had whole swathes of men from Glasgow University
in the ranks. Worst of all was the huge shortage of experienced men to command brigades and divisions, numbering thousands of men, in the field.

Dick was hoping that the shortage of sound company commanders would
earn him his own company as the prospect of life as a second lieutenant did
not excite him. His experience in the Eton OTC meant that he was used to
ordering people around and the thought of going backwards was concerning,
as was the idea that the War Office would summon him back and send him
off to where he ought to be in the first place, as the lowest of subalterns. 'Then
I shall have to make a fuss.'

Part of Patrick Shaw-Stewart's set, the Hon. Julian Henry Francis Grenfell,
as born in March 1888. His father, Lord Desborough, was an Old Harrovian,
but he would send all of his sons to Eton. Going up in 1901 Julian was, along
with his friends, an editor of *The Outsider*. 'No one was fuller of the rather
misdirected but not wholly deplorable spirit of levity and mischief which
animated that paper than Julian.'

When his younger brother was born, Julian had demanded that they name
him Billy, and although their parents declined and christened him Gerald
William, 'Billy' he remained for life. Julian was just as forceful about his own
nickname. When endeavours were made to affectionately call him 'Max', he
retorted, 'Call me Julian Grenfell, Taplow Court, Buckinghamshire.'

The Grenfells were closely associated with the Manners family, who termed
the brothers 'the curly heads'. Billy went up to Eton in 1903 and was one of
the rare Oppidans to win the Newcastle in 1909 as well as being editor of the
Eton College Chronicle for two years. He was a big, solid young man standing
6ft 4in, a boxer when he went up to Oxford; but his build contradicted his shy,
gentle nature.

Julian, a shade shorter than his brother, was a regular in the cavalry, although
his regiment of Dragoons was in South Africa when the war commenced so
he was not among the first to depart for the front. Billy waved John Manners
off to war on 7 August 1914 and promptly delivered himself to the War Office.
Six days after finding out about John's heart-breaking disappearance at Villers-
Cotterêts he received a commission of his own and became one of the OEs
joining Foss Prior and Sheepshanks in the 8th Rifle Brigade.

Despite the urgency and enthusiasm with which the lines of he and Dick Durnford delivered themselves into Kitchener's hands, there was then a long period of training and inaction. In fact, to begin with it was not certain that they would be needed at the front at all. Billy was busy trying to turn 'unlicked ruffians' into soldiers with furious sham fights by both day and night. Dick was still waiting patiently to be given his own company. His biggest trial was adjusting to a military diet ('You may imagine my pampered stomach's disgust'). He also enlisted his mother to produce 250 pairs of khaki-coloured mittens for his men. The 9th King's Royal Rifles had been moved to Petworth where he was as heartily sick of Sussex as the Sussex locals appeared to be of them. The battalion was to be inspected by Kitchener who was bringing politicians to see some of his New Army. It had become necessary, Billy thought, as the politicians were said to believe that it was mythical.

The misinformation and rumour circulating as to when these volunteer soldiers might see action at the front was overwhelming. Dick's advice to his mother was not to believe a word of anything, from anyone. Put quite simply, an army such as theirs was 'comparatively valueless minus rifles' and so, as they lacked them, whatever she had heard they were not ready to go anywhere yet. Billy Grenfell was far more laid-back about when they might be leaving for France. 'Some say March; some say next Thursday.' He thought perhaps April but he was not at all disappointed to be kicking his heels in England at first. 'We shall have plenty of time to exhaust the pleasures of war,' his remarked. 'The men are a trifle impatient, which is a good sign: but they are not really slim enough to face the German machinations at present.'

Lord Shuttleworth's son, the Hon. Edward James Kay-Shuttleworth, was referred to as 'Ted' by his friends. He had followed his elder brother Lawrence through Mr Bowlby's house at Eton and then gone up to Oxford full of the joys of life but with a serious, religious edge to his outlook. He too had found his way into a New Army battalion of one of the rifle regiments. Whilst the 7th Rifle Brigade prepared to go to war he married his sweetheart Sibell. His new wife stood with a friend at Aldershot in May 1915 and watched a cloud of dust coming towards them; their men on the way to war. Ted brought up the rear as they filed past, giving her a big smile and waving goodbye. Surely now, she thought, with the Kitchener's men taking to the field the war would come to an end soon.

Dick Durnford and his men crossed with a ship full of Sikhs and Gurkhas, landing at Havre in the dark and stumbling into camp having not eaten properly since England, laden with heavy packs. They could hear the artillery far away at the front and whilst the men practised getting their new respirators on and off lest they be gassed, he planned to climb to the top of the nearest steeple and watch the flashes of the guns to the east.

Billy Grenfell too was getting ready to depart with the 8th Rifle Brigade and Lord and Lady Desborough planned to leave for France at the same time. His sister Monica was working at a hospital in Wimereux on the coast and they had gained permission to look it over and see what she was up to. Just before their planned departure though, a cable was received from their daughter to say that she was in Boulogne with their eldest son Julian, who had picked up a minor head wound and was awaiting a berth on a hospital ship back to England. A blood-stained letter arrived from him, cheerfully boasting that he had (partially) stopped a German shell with his head. 'We are practically wiped out,' he said of his regiment 'but we charged and took the Hun trenches.'

Despite his good spirits, Julian's condition deteriorated swiftly and it was suggested that his parents might want to advance their plans for their French crossing. They left Taplow Court seven minutes after receiving permission and found scruffy but gratefully appreciated passage on an ammunition boat. It transpired that a shrapnel splinter had penetrated Julian's brain by an 1½in. An operation was carried out and he awoke with every hope of making a full recovery. They spent much of their time comforting the Marquess of Lincolnshire and his wife who had journeyed out in a similar manner to be with their son, another OE, Viscount Wendover, 'Bob'. He had gone into the Royal Horse Guards in August 1914, an only son after five daughters, always smiling. His hip had been smashed up along with his arm and he passed away at the age of 20 at Boulogne[1].

Meanwhile Billy was making his way to France with his battalion. When the ship docked and the men sat down to rest he rushed off to the hospital. He was 'terribly overwhelmed' by his brother's decline but his appearance cheered Julian. 'I am glad there was no gap,' he said. He meant that as he fell out of the line, his brother was to walk into it.

Coincidentally, Edward Horner was languishing in the same hospital, horribly wounded. After some indecision he had joined the North Somerset Yeomanry but had coveted a move to a regular cavalry regiment. He had the watchful eye of Sir John French on him at the front, who apparently couldn't sleep for worry when Edward was in the trenches. This did not save him from a severe abdominal wound caused by shrapnel. It was not considered fatal but it had damaged a kidney. Like the Desboroughs, his parents managed to get permission to go to France and took a surgeon with them. They found him 'drunk to serenity on morphia'. When he saw them he raised his head pathetically and said, 'O' darlings, the fun of it.'

Edward's condition was to improve and he was soon bound for London and a lengthy convalescence but Julian was not so lucky. He held his mother's hand to his face and passed away a few days after Billy arrived in France at the age of 27. He was buried in what would become a vast military cemetery full of British graves in Boulonge, with a letter from their youngest sister Imogen and flowers that she had sent him from her little garden at home. John Manners' sister too was nursing and she wrote a brief letter to Julian and Billy's mother that tried to make sense of their mutual loss. 'I try to feel that we have been lucky and blessed in having these glorious beings, and being loved by them ... but my heart is aching for you, because I just do know what it is; nothing can be the same.' In Gallipoli Patrick Shaw-Stewart was grief stricken ny his friend's loss. They had been so different. Julian was 'all for letting things happen to him' whilst Patrick planned everything to the last detail. They quarrelled frequently, but when Patrick threw himself into the Royal Naval Division it was Julian who had come to him in London to show him how to put on a Sam Browne belt. Charles Lister was similarly distraught over Julian when he received the news on his sick bed in Malta. 'It is the bitterest blow I have had since the war and am likely to have,' he wrote to Lady Desborough. 'I can't write what I feel about poor Julian; the void is so terrible for me and the thought of it quite unmans me ... He stood for something so precious to me, for an England of my dreams made of honest, brave and tender men.'

Before she departed for England, his mother went for a walk and sat down to try and write Billy a letter. She glanced up to find him standing in front of her. He had received their telegrams and borrowed a car to get back to Boulogne. He stayed with her for three hours and when the time came for him to leave and return to his battalion she almost couldn't let him go. Having buried one son, Lady Desborough might have done well to cling on, because she would never see Billy again.

Dick Durnford had found his church steeple and had been watching star shells and gun flashes at the front, acclimatising himself to the constant noise. With his feet back on the ground he sadly pondered the growing casualty lists in *The Times*. He was now one of the wide-eyed newcomers that his friend George Fletcher had spoken of, gaping with surprise at the state of the men he saw coming back from the lines. They were 'fearfully untidy' in their battered uniforms with their straggly beards.

As Dick's bewilderment highlighted, some sort of training in trench warfare was required for this army of volunteers before they went into action. Accordingly, at the end of May, the 9th King's Royal Rifles were informed that they would be introduced into the lines in stages; the first of which was a lot of digging. Within a fortnight they had progressed from daytime excursions into the reserve lines to forty-eight-hour stints. These rotations were supposed to be in what were considered 'healthy sections of the line', but nonetheless Dick's battalion did not emerge unscathed. The officer who was second in command had lasted precisely ten minutes before a bullet grazed his head and he had to be taken away again.

Dick's first impression of trench warfare was that it was noisy, with 'monstrous' shooting going on day and night. He was, he felt, handicapped by a 'constitutional ineptitude of all mechanical devices'. He loathed the 'unsportsmanlike' nature of bombs, howitzers and mines. There was no peace from these menaces though, even in the reserve lines, for all the shells that overshot the front line or fell short of the artillery batteries landed on them. At night they served the front trenches and carried them 'anything from barbed wire to a biscuit, stumbling about in shell holes … and being shot at'. Once they had delivered the goods and were thoroughly worn out, inevitably some threat became apparent that required them to stand to rather then sleep, or the battalion in front would complain about something that was missing and off they would have to go again. He reported at the end of June that such menial work had cost them 140 men in three weeks. 'This shows you the wastage,' he wrote home, 'and it is rather sad.'

Billy too was becoming used to 'every form of frightfulness'. The smell of manure behind the lines was a godsend after living 'in a cage' with a host of German corpses in different stages of decomposition. In July a trench mortar scored a direct hit on the 8th Rifle Brigade and a young Etonian officer named Arthur Ronald Backus was buried alive with two sergeants by the blast. Born in Peru and a member of the VIII in 1913, he had gone up to Cambridge before departing to join the army. Some fifteen Germans clad in greatcoats had come sidling towards them with bombs in hand and while Billy and his men caught them with rifle fire as they turned and ran, 'Ronnie' Backus dug himself out of his grave with his hands.

Billy was growing used to the dirty tunnellers, walking about the trenches ahirtless with their picks. He was not impressed by the visiting generals though. He had a good way to get rid of them: 'Excuse me, sir, two men were shot dead by snipers just there; for God's sake, sir, keep your head down and move along at the double'. Off the senior officer would go 'lathering with fear, never to reappear'. One such officer had offered Lord Desborough's son a supernumerary role as an aide to remove him from danger, but Billy was disgusted. These roles were, to his mind, reserved for 'all the tufts and toadies' and the scorn that he saw heaped on these 'extra' aide-de-camp's was not unjust. His battalion was already five officers down; he was not about to leave the rest and his 'glorious' men to kick his heels in a job of no real use.

As part of a carrying party Dick got his first glimpse of Ypres. At the beginning of July he saw first-hand the destruction that had befallen the medieval cloth hall and the cathedral. The ghostly ruins were shrouded in gas that hurt the men's eyes. Billy, quietly going about his business amongst this terrifying spectacle and bearing the 'grievous shock' of Julian's death bravely, painted a picture with words of his own: a town of rubble and broken bottles. 'Darling Julian is so constantly beside me,' he wrote, 'and laughs so debonairly of my qualms and hesitations. I pray for one tenth of his courage.'

Despite the fact that no major offensive was immediately pending as far as British plans went, intensity was rising around Ypres as the summer approached. Another OE who found himself moved into the area was Francis Grenfell. He had returned to the 9th Lancers following his wounds at Messines on 21 April to find the regiment at a reduced strength. He was moved up towards Ypres immediately. In the middle of May, the dismounted Lancers were subjected to the fiercest fighting they had yet seen and his squadron was moved into the lines at Hooge.

Empire Day, 24 May, was to dawn clear and sunny, with not a cloud in the sky. The Ninth were hustled into a stretch of trenches straddling the Menin Road, bolstered by the remnants of some infantry battalions placed under their officers' command. With his men Francis occupied the road itself. A light breeze was blowing when at 3.a.m. the cavalry saw four red flares shoot up and then a 30ft-high thick, yellow haze rising in front of them. It rolled down the ridge towards the British lines. With no experience of gas and having been issued with new masks only two weeks before, the cavalrymen flailed as the pungent smell overcame them. The masks became saturated and were rendered useless as men began dropping to the ground, gasping for air, stumbling blind through the trenches and clutching at their throats.

Then the German guns opened fire and troops poured towards them. The line broke on either side of the Ninth but they tried desperately to hold on although pounded by shells and trench mortars. Under the intensity of the German attack they fell back, abandoning the trenches. Casualties were continuous and heavy, the Germans poured past them, overrunning the British lines and pushing the survivors back towards Ypres.

In the early hours of 25 May, following their 'greatest day of glory and sorrow of the whole war', forty-odd men came stumbling down the Menin Road from Hooge with a yellow tint to their faces, wearing ragged uniforms, caked in mud. They carried Francis Grenfell's body with them. They were all that was left. The 9th Lancers as he and his twin Rivy had known it, as Lennie and Douglas Harvey had known it, had ceased to exist.

Nearby Hooge, by the side of the Menin Road south-east of Ypres, was dominated by the ruins of a chateau that had been blown up by shellfire during the fierce fighting on 31 October 1914. This poisonous area was to become fiercely contended as the summer progressed. British tunnellers had managed to dig underneath a farm and carve out a gallery below what they hoped was a significant tangle of German trenches; stuffing it full of ammonal. On 18 July an OE nearby was awaiting what ought to be a decent-sized explosion that would rupture the German lines and enable elements of the Middlesex Regiment to flood in and take the void that was left, strengthening the British position.

The following day the mine went up with some force. But by the time the Rifle battalions arrived a few days after the explosion, it had still proved impossible to build a trench into the crater as planned. It now formed an unsightly gap in the British line, garrisoned at each side by men laden with bombs ready to lob their ammunition at anyone who might try to overrun the area. Wet weather was turning Hooge into a liquid mass of mud and slime and preventing any further extensions to trenches and other fortifications being dug properly.

Dick Durnford began hearing rumours of a German offensive; indeed they were not exactly concealing their efforts in front of him. He had been subjected to a full week of perpetual shelling and was extremely frustrated by the notion of having to sit still whilst the Germans took potshots at him. To make things worse, the trench on their right was not fully joined up so that they lived under constant threat of the enemy exploiting the gap. Dick had even neglected to eat, which he admitted was a very significant thing for him. As he was relieved from the line, exhausted, on 26 July there was little going on, 'but you never know your luck,' he said cautiously. The situation at Hooge was indeed about to take a dramatic turn for the worse.

The 7th Rifle Brigade had, until this point, been occupying a length of trench near the ruins of Hooge Chateau and the crater which they had taken over from some Highlanders. On the evening of 29 July they prepared to switch places with the 8th Battalion, who set out to relieve them at 9.p.m. Foss Prior and Arthur Sheepshanks had been among the senior officers in the 8th Rifle Brigade who had been scouting the area for some days, acquainting themselves with what they were about to let themselves in for. They were not impressed; lack of wire, overly deep, narrow trenches and the proximity of the German trench mortars were to hamper them. Additionally they would have to contend with bad communication lines and support trenches so mangled that weren't fit for habitation, not to mention the giant crater dividing their lines.

As their battalion took up residence, twenty-four officers and a shade under 750 men, the 7th Rifle Brigade marched back down the Menin Road in the opposite direction. Waiting for them at the other end was Ted Kay-Shuttleworth, who had been at a nearby hospital with a minor ailment throughout their last stint in the trenches. He had heard news of severe losses amongst his men, through artillery bombardments and the lines being peppered by trench mortars. They had lost one hundred men in a week, including two officers. Like Dick, he had heard of an impending German attack. He sat up discussing the rumours with some fellow officers before going to bed.

At about 2 a.m. he almost woke up, half aware that his 7th Rifle Brigade had begun arriving and tramping into billets for a well-earned rest. The weary footsteps continued for an hour, but just as the last of them petered out he became aware of a particularly violent bombardment going on nearby. He pondered whether or not it was at Hooge. Now fully awake, Ted listened as it grew more and more intense. Then a message arrived from Brigade headquarters. The 7th Rifle Brigade were to get back out of bed and be ready to move off immediately.

The noise had indeed been coming from Hooge. At 3.A.m. the 8th Rifle Brigade were settling in to their new home and going through the pre-dawn ritual of standing to. Suddenly a hail of shells pounded them for a few minutes. But this was nothing against the new force the Germans were about to bring into play. Sheets of fire began erupting from the enemy lines. Foss Prior was in command of C Company and it bore the brunt of the attack near the crater. The Germans were unleashing a torrent of liquid flame 'like water coming from a large hose'. At the same time a massive bombardment of everything that the enemy could fire, trench mortars, shells and bullets, opened up on the communication trenches, no-man's-land and the support lines in the woods where Sheep and Billy Grenfell were settling in. The Belgian countryside had been transformed into a vision of hell on earth. Flames blanketed the front lines and they were enveloped in fire and thick, acrid black smoke, rising from which was the smell of flesh, burning.

Foss and his men were overrun with Germans wielding bombs. They came at the British soldiers from all directions, rushing the crater to break the British front line then fanning out behind the men occupying it. The scene was chaos, with charred bodies littering the scene and men turning and fleeing. The Germans had established machine guns in the ruins of Hooge and as the British turned and made for their support lines and the woods behind they sent a torrent of bullets crashing through the retreating soldiers.

One of the front companies tried to counter-attack, but they were pinned down by the machine guns and had to fight hand-to-hand to get out of the area. Whole platoons were overwhelmed and almost wiped out. The Germans tried to bomb their way down the communication lines, nicknamed Old Bond Street and The Strand; but the way was blocked and they were held. Back in the wood, Sheep and Billy had avoided the flames but were struggling under the weight of the German bombardment as what was left of the trees came crashing violently down around them.

Meanwhile, back towards Ypres, as soon as the order to get ready arrived, Ted Kay-Shuttleworth leapt from his bed and got dressed. Ted went outside and listened to the bombardment as the battalion prepared to move. The noise seemed to be gradually subsiding. He began to think it was all over and took off his equipment to lie down again. He had barely reached his bed when he heard the words: 'Prepare to move at once'.

The 7th Rifle Brigade got underway at 6.30 a.m., shoving chunks of bread and chocolate into their pockets. As they walked the 3 miles towards Hooge, ammunition wagons galloped past on their way to the battle. They heard false whispers that almost as soon as they had been relieved the Germans had exploded a mine under the chateau stables; that they had taken six lines of trenches.

Back at Hooge at noon orders were received to mount a counter-attack at 2:45 p.m. after a hastily arranged forty-five-minute bombardment. The 8th Rifle Brigade was to lead the attack, bombing their way past The Strand and parallel to Old Bond Street towards the Menin Road. A Company and C Company had suffered so heavily from the flames that they were in pieces; the latter, Foss's, had all but ceased to exist. B Company had also been heavily hit when it tried to counter-attack. And so it fell to the last company, D, commanded by Arthur Sheepshanks and containing Billy Grenfell as one of its subalterns, to make the main assault.

Sheep was summoned and told to send half of his men up the trenches to dispel the assaulting Germans that had been penned up in them since the morning. These front platoons were then to move into position ready to attack. Dick Durnford's battalion was to attack too; the 9th King's Royal Rifles had been ordered to charge along the Menin Road towards the Chateau ruins and the stables.

Sheep was given instructions not to attempt to make contact with the 7th Rifle Brigade as the gap was too great. Ted Kay-Shuttleworth and his men

were next to him, but they were having a difficult time getting to their communication trench. They had orders to lie down and play dead in the event
that any enemy aircraft passed overhead, thus three or four times they were
compelled to stop and throw themselves down on the Menin Road, which
held them up. Ted walked up with another OE, 'Bones' Drummond[2], commanding one of the 7th's companies and they grew more and more anxious
about their timing. Finally, they reached Zouave Wood, to the rear, at 1.55 p.m.,
just five minutes before the artillery bombardment was about to start.

At 2.p.m. the British artillery opened up as planned. The Germans retaliated
in kind. Zouave Wood was in chaos, and had now become a mass of shell holes,
splintered trees, battered foliage and mashed up trench lines. Faced with a walk
through it all to be ready to advance at 2.45 p.m., Ted and his men had to begin
climbing over the carnage, attempting to stay in some kind of military formation. They staggered over the debris, exhausted men awake for thirty-six hours
breaking down and crying with the roar of shells intensifying overhead.

Organisation was in complete disarray. Ted continued climbing over fallen
trees, tangled foliage and splintered branches in the direction of the communication trenches. The atmosphere was so thick with dust and smoke that
they could hardly see where they were going. The men became scattered and
the earth shook beneath their feet. At 2.10. p.m. a bullet pinged off of Ted's
wristwatch and his ability to time their counter-attack was gone. Together
with a fellow officer he crawled to the edge of the wood and they decided on
a plan. They would lie there until they saw everyone else move and then take
their men and run after them.

Sheep and Billy were also having trouble co-ordinating their attack. Billy
had crawled right to the point from which they were to begin. His company
commander was attempting to do the same when a bullet went through his
thigh. He attempted to crawl down to tell Billy that he had been put out of
action, but was in too much pain. He was vaguely aware that Billy was wearing a watch, but insured himself by sending a rifleman along to find him. He
never arrived.

At exactly 2.45 p.m., despite the fact that the enemy did not appear to have
been in the slightest bit silenced by the bombardment, the 8th Rifle Brigade
commenced their counter-attack. Billy Grenfell's platoon was to bomb their
way up The Strand, ejecting the German squatters before lining up in front
of their own barbed wire to advance towards the crater where the British
lines had stood before the flame attack. The bombing went off successfully
and Billy charged up the trench, but as soon as they advanced into the open,
the ground in front of them was swept by bullets. Billy made it a little over

70 yards up the hill before he was hit and his large frame pitched forward and hit the ground with a thud. Sheep, who ascertained that 25-year-old Billy must have been dead before he hit the ground, was hit twice in the face by flying debris but carried on regardless; an act of valour that was not to be an isolated occurrence in his war.

Ted Kay-Shuttleworth was lying in wait along the edge of the wood waiting for something to happen. At last he saw another subaltern of the 7th Rifle Brigade making a run for it to his left and so up he got and rushed out from the battered trees towards the Menin Road, followed by his men. It was baffling. Somehow in the confusion they found their own men in front of them, and then they ran right up against their own barbed wire in full view of the German machine guns. A shell knocked them down and wounded Ted's colleague in the thigh.

There were so few of them left that Ted decided they ought to wait for reinforcements. He could see nothing happening to either his left or his right so he began scraping at the ground, trying to make some cover. The man next to him had his head split by a bullet; Ted grabbed the dead man's entrenching tool and continued digging. He and his wounded friend had a discussion. Should they attack? There were ten of them left. It seemed madness and almost all of them were carrying some kind of wound. They were in full view of the enemy and so there was nothing for it. They crawled back and fell into a soaking wet, abandoned trench behind. Ted was one of only three men unhurt and he began attending to the wounded, binding up bleeding arms and legs. More and more broken soldiers were dropping into the trench.

Ted moved off to explore his surroundings, helping to drag more men in and ordering them to stay put, trying to form a line of defence. A machine gun was playing along the top of the trench incessantly and it had become lined with corpses and moaning, broken men. It transpired that they had taken up residence in an old communication trench, far too narrow to be used effectively under fire. Ted had to get the men he passed to kneel down in 1ft of water so that he could climb over their backs without exposing his head.

Right at the end of the line, holding on with what was left of his company, Ted found Sheep. Dick Durnford's contingent had been luckier. At 2.45 p.m. a subaltern led out a party of bombers and was followed by two companies. Taking heavy losses they managed to take some trenches but could go no further so they began consolidating their position.

As evening approached, Ted decided to find his colonel. On his way down the trench he found Ronnie MacLachlan, an OE and commanding officer of the 8th Rifle Brigade instead; he was frantic, in a state of total shock. Ted tried to fill him in as to what had happened and by the time he returned to his own men he found that their second-rate trench was overflowing with wounded men being brought in from the darkened battlefield. Stretcher bearers were trying to move them along, but the numbers were overwhelming and they lay unattended everywhere. Survivors struggled across the battlefield dragging their wounded friends whilst others, including Bones Drummond, were never heard from again. The 7th Rifle Brigade had walked something like 20 miles and had one meal in twenty-four hours, notwithstanding the actual fighting, and finally they were relieved. Overcome by sadness and their loss they began the long walk back down the Menin Road.

If the carnage at Hooge was hard to comprehend for the likes of Ted Kay-Shuttleworth and Ronnie MacLachlan, then it was impossible for those at home. Dick Durnford's company had been in support as the 9th King's Royal Rifles retook the trenches to the left of Hooge. They were busy consolidating their position when Dick came up to offer to help. He was greeted by a friend who then turned away to give directions to a bombing party. He was just walking back down the trench when he saw Dick fall, hit by a chance bullet. Dick's poor mother could neither comprehend the manner of his death nor the subsequent loss of the grave his men had dug for him. In her grief she became fixated on the whereabouts of one item, his revolver, and why it could not be found and returned to her. It fell to one of Dick's fellow officers to try to convey the horror of Hooge to her without causing her more pain some months later. In the mayhem, John Christie, another Etonian master, had passed Dick's revolver to another OE in the Rifle Brigade as he didn't have his own.[3] Christie had not seen the grave himself. He had been the last man of the 9th King's Royal Rifles to leave those trenches. By then anyone who might have known the whereabouts of the grave had fallen too. 'Conditions were very bad,' he told her. For example, in his bit of trench he had had to live with the body of a young subaltern for days as it was too dangerous to try to bury him. He could not so much as find a shovel and they had not so much as a field dressing to try and treat the men bleeding next to them.

Ronnie MacLachlan's 8th Rifle Brigade was relieved and when he arrived in billets all he wanted to do was sit and sob. He began the agonising task of writing to the families of his officers. Nineteen out of twenty-four of them were dead or unaccounted for and hundreds of men were gone. Billy Grenfell, to his father's desolation, had to be left where he fell owing to how far forward he had managed to get. The idea of his boy lying abandoned on the battlefield would haunt Lord Desborough.

A fortnight after the German attack at Hooge the situation had improved somewhat and Ronnie MacLachlan began badgering the authorities about the prospect of recovering Billy's body. He was told that it was not safe for him to send up a search party but that the troops in the vicinity would do as much as they could. Sheep, however, had absolutely no intention of leaving his young subaltern on the field of battle. Attempts to find him and lay him to rest at Vlamertinghe with his relative, Francis Grenfell, had failed. On 15 August the 3rd Rifle Brigade moved into the area. A sergeant had seen a body in no-man's-land but snipers meant that he could not approach it to find out who it was. A corporal tried and managed to retrieve the identity disc. It was Billy. After dark they went out, collected him and managed to bury him just to the north of a trench dubbed Fleet Street, 250 yards due south of Hooge[4].

Barely two months after losing their eldest son, Lord and Lady Desborough had lost their second. He had been at the front for a little over two months and his and Julian's deaths rocked the upper echelons of society. Lord Kitchener had no family of his own; he was uncomfortable socially and he thought of Taplow Court as a home of sorts. When the news of Billy's death arrived it was the only time that the Secretary of State for War was known to break down. He left his desk, on which sat a photograph of Julian in a silver frame, and went for a walk to pull himself together.

Foss Prior was lucky to be alive. Shot in the back the bullet had narrowly missed his spine and come out the other side. It was finally deemed safe enough to ship him home in the middle of August aboard the SS *St George*. Ted Kay-Shuttleworth had found himself the only officer left across two companies. Only seventy men remained in his own and of his officer's mess, his jolly mess, he was literally the only one left. He sent a list of the fallen home to his wife, including his best man and overflowing with the names of OEs who had been claimed by this one solitary German attack. He had lost as many friends in a day as a man might expect to lose in years.

Walking towards Ypres, Ted came across a quartermaster that he knew. When the man told him how glad he was to see that he survived, Ted burst into tears. He ate breakfast and tried to get to sleep but it was impossible. He rolled over and over, absorbing the day's events. Their proud battalion was in tatters, almost half of them dead or missing. Disconsolately, he wrote to his wife: 'I feel an outcast to be alive.'

Notes

1. In a rare occurrence they took his body back to England and buried him at home in Buckinghamshire in Moulsoe churchyard.
2. Captain Spencer Heneage Drummond.
3. By the time Christie wrote his letter, this OE too had died. Gerald Boswell KS was severely wounded and died on the Somme in 1916. Aged 24, he was laid to rest at Abbeville Communal Cemetery.
4. With both of their graves lost in subsequent fighting, Billy Grenfell and Dick Durnford are commemorated on the Menin Gate at Ypres.
5. Edward Kay-Shuttleworth survived his friends by a little over two years. In the summer of 1917 he was killed in a motorcycle accident in Essex. His brother, the Hon. L.U. Kay-Shuttleworth had been killed on 30 March 1917 with the Canadian infantry and laid to rest at Villers Station Cemeterey.

9

'Till Berlin'

The instant that war was declared the world of European finance was plunged into turmoil. Embroiled in the mayhem was J. Henry Schröder & Co. The company had been established in London in 1818 so, despite its German roots, it was no stranger to the City. Baron Bruno von Schröder had lived and worked in London for years at its head. His children had been born in England and his two sons educated at Eton, but his nationality meant that on the outbreak of the Great War the company could be seized by the government.

His business partner went to work immediately to try to rectify the situation. The fate of von Schröder's company was of great importance. In August 1914 London's financial hub was in a state of meltdown; should it be sequestered von Schröder had £11m in outstanding acceptances that it would not be able to honour. As such the governors of the Bank of England were onside and took the matter up with the Home Secretary. It would be, they said, 'a disaster if the doors of Baron von Schröder did not open on the following morning.' Separate appeals were made by friends to the Prime Minister and Baron von Schröder was given immediate naturalisation. As early as 7 August 1914 he had received both a certificate confirming his status as a British citizen and a licence to trade and reside in the country from George V himself.

That von Schröder and his colleagues had curtailed the possibility of being sequestered did not alleviate all of their commercial issues. In many circles there was outrage at his rapid conversion to British citizenship. In October the aldermen of the City of London passed a resolution of protest and the Home Secretary was forced to continuously bat away the issue in Parliament throughout November. At the forefront of the howls of protest that were latched on to by the press was the fact that Bruno von Schröder's 19-year-old son and heir, a territorial, was mobilising for war and heading for the Western Front – with the German Army.

Born in Kensington in 1895, Rudolph 'Bruno' von Schröder arrived at Mr Hill's house at Eton in 1908 and made his way through the school relatively quietly, not surprisingly making off with school prizes in German. In 1913 he went straight into the family business and headed straight to his father's native Hamburg to learn his trade. Once there Bruno immediately joined a cavalry outfit, Dragoner-Regiment 18 or the 'Parchim Dragoons' as an *Einjährig Freiwilliger* or one-year volunteer.

It was a regiment with a proud heritage. The Parchim Dragoons had close ties with the city of Bremen and had helped to besiege Paris in the Franco–Prussian War. Hamburg citizens were not obliged to join the PRussian Army, but Bruno's father had served with the regiment in his youth so there were familial connections with this Mecklenburgian regiment. Gefreiter (Fahnenjunker) Bruno Freiherr von Schröder, his rank that of an NCO acting as the lowest rank of officer was already on the Western Front attempting to wrestle Liege from Belgian hands when his OE counterparts in the British Army had yet to cross the Channel.

With the arrival of the BEF in France and Belgium in the middle of the month began the only recorded instances of Old Etonians fighting against each other in the Great War. In fact Bruno and his men were pursuing cavalry regiments packed full of his fellow OEs, including at least one boy who had been in the same house with him, through the French countryside.

Bruno von Schröder was not the only Old Etonian joining an illustrious mounted regiment in a foreign army. Russia had at her disposal what seemed like infinite reserves of manpower. The Tsar could put literally millions of men to war against the Central Powers inside a month at the outbreak of war. His army was mobilised on 31 July 1914 and Germany declared war the following day. In the east the immense might of three powers; the Kaiser's, the Tsar's and that of Austria–Hungary, were lining up on an immense Eastern Front to do battle.

George Schack-Sommer was the son of an established merchant. Suffering from delicate health as a child, he radiated charm and had impeccable manners. He arrived at Eton in 1903 and was a keen member of the OTC, leaving school four years later bent on being a mining engineer. He started off right at the bottom in Cornwall, working as a miner himself to get a feel for it. Experience gained, he went off to the Royal School of Mines and three years later, at 20, he finished his studies and went out into the world. He had worked in Norway and India, where again he had volunteered for territorial service with the Kolar Goldfields Mounted Rifles, but ultimately had become an assayer and a cyanide operator at the Tanalyk Mine in the Urals. He was an animal lover and had much experience with Siberian ponies. In spring 1910 he had interviews with Robert Falcon Scott for his South Pole expedition but ultimately Scott felt that George was too young for the rigours of the expedition. Ultimately he took Lawrence Oates to maintain the ponies, an older OE who had the added advantage of offering substantial financial support.

In November 1914 George left his job in Siberia and embarked on an epic journey to offer his services to the Russian Army, as he rightly thought it would be faster than travelling home to apply for a commission. He began his 1,700-mile odyssey with a thirty-six-hour troika ride to get to the nearest railway station. Eventually he rolled up at the Grand Hotel d'Europe in newly renamed Petrograd having travelled via Chelyabinsk, Ekaterinburg where the Tsar would be executed in 1917, and Vologda. It would be no more dangerous than going down into the mine, he attempted to convince his mother 'Think of the Russian people I live with going off ... surely it would look terrible for an Englishman to sit tight and leave it to others.'

As a foreigner George had to petition the Tsar to be allowed in to the Russian Army as an ordinary soldier and doggedly stuck at it until they let him into the ranks. Numerous regiments turned this thoroughly determined Englishman down, but he was on familiar terms with a minister who introduced him to his brother; a colonel of a cavalry regiment, who agreed to take George down to Kiev to join the 12th Artirsky Hussars. 'If anyone asks why I went to scrap from this side,' he told his family, 'tell them it was because I thought it would be the quickest way to get to the front.' He was bullish in backing up his decision against those who may scorn him. 'Jump on anyone who thinks I have in any way sunk my nationality. I have your Union Jack in my breast pocket,' George assured them, 'and it is going to fly somewhere, before I've done with it.'

George entrained for Galicia to join his regiment. Here four Russian armies were lined up against Austro–Hungarian forces fighting a war of movement. Whilst the war on the Western Front was grinding to an industrialised halt, this was a throwback to a bygone age. Cavalry performed in traditional role, skirmishing and scouting.

The journey had been incredibly arduous. He had covered nearly 2,500 miles since leaving the mine. George arrived in Lviv[1], recently liberated from the

Austro–Hungarians, just as the fighting around Ypres was subsiding at the end of 1914. It appeared to him, thus far, to have been a walkover for the Russians. He thought the residents of Lviv 'poor devils', mostly Polish Jews seemingly fairly pleased with the outcome, 'chiefly because they were so neglected by the Austrian government'.

By 3 December[2] he had finally reached his regiment at Samborzec. He found the Hussars billeted in the village, covered in snow. They didn't anticipate any fighting soon. There might, perhaps, be skirmishes, but nothing serious until they had gone through one of the Carpathian passes which was a ludicrous idea in such weather.

He was being made to feel welcome. Several of his officers spoke English; in fact one even spent much time living in London when he was not at war. George was not the only 'gentleman ranker' either, so socially things were not as trying as he might have feared. His fellow troopers found this cheerful little foreigner immensely interesting, rather like an exotic pet. 'After talking to a group of them for about half an hour, one man said "your language is nearly the same as ours".' George thought it was hilarious. 'The dear lad thought my Russian was English!'

Ludicrous as the idea was, the Austrians set out to traverse the forbidding Carpathians in the depths of winter. George found himself south-east of Krakow in the far corner of Russian Poland at Lesko. The Russians had arrived as a precursor to advancing into Hungary and up into Silesia but the balance of power was changing. Germany had rushed reinforcements down to bolster the crumbling Austro–Hungarian armies who were racking up hundreds of thousands of casualties on this front and against Serbia who were pinning them back in the Balkans.

It was a bitter winter. The men of the Artirsky Hussars found themselves facing Austrians on raised banks either side of a stream in some woodland over the festive period. Whilst his namesake George Fletcher was swapping cigarettes on the Western Front, George Schack-Sommer spent Christmas 1914 gnawing on a chicken leg in the snow and eyeing the Austro–Hungarians in the trenches opposite. His cavalry regiment was a prestigious one and had as an honorary commander the Tsar's sister, Grand Duchess Olga. Gifts flooded in from well to do friends and families, in fact so many boxes had arrived that some were passed on to regiments who had not been so fortunate.

The snow and the terrain made it impossible to work like cavalry, except as occasional scouting parties. There were repeated skirmishes as small groups harassed the enemy with rifle fire and there was a consistent exchange of artillery fire from mountain batteries but little else. Russian suspicions were soon raised though when the retorting Austrian guns grew feebler and feebler and one afternoon stopped altogether. Perhaps they had retired completely? The officers of the Artirsky Hussars got together and considered a move forward to see what had become of the enemy. Under the confusing circumstances it was considered rather reckless. Instead it was decided that they would send out some scouting patrols under cover of darkness to see if they had properly retired or were bluffing. George volunteered to go immediately and with eight companions set off that night.

They crawled through the trees until they arrived at the bottom of the slope on the banks of the stream. 'From there another chap and I crept forward, trying to look like stumps,' he later retold. 'There was no moon and it was snowing but the snow on the ground made it light enough to faintly see and be seen.' They got to within 20 yards of the Austro–Hungarian lines and heard muffled voices. They lay low for almost half an hour, counting several enemy soldiers. Suddenly two of them looked up and spotted George. 'I beat a hasty retreat. They fired twice but either very wide or low as I didn't hear the bullets.' For this excursion George received a promotion and a recommendation for the Cross of St George. Reserved for non-officers who had acted with conspicuous bravery, there were four classes, two silver and then two gold. A colonel arrived to distribute his and several other medals and went down the line, asking each man what he had got it for and handing them out. Then, to George's bemusement, he gave each man a kiss: 'most embarrassing when you haven't had such a mark of affection for so very long'.

After a few weeks working as a sapper of sorts George re-joined his squadron to take up normal duties. He soon went out on a scouting party with a dozen or so men. They went with the intention of taking any stragglers prisoner as the village they intended to infiltrate was still occupied by Austro–Hungarian troops. They trotted through the town and then galloped full pelt in a mad charge towards the enemy troops that they found dotted about amongst the buildings. 'They started to run but we soon caught them up.' Their little flurry of activity soon became violent. Two horses were wounded. Of their prey, five were struck by lances and as George so eloquently put it, 'It was necessary to chop one about a bit to make him drop his rifle.'

'I'm glad to let you know I was well up with the hounds,' he wrote to another Etonian. The enemy soldiers had apparently taken them for the leading men of a larger cavalry force. Thrown into a total panic by the frenzied Hussars galloping towards them 'spurs in and hell for leather' they fell apart. In all, fifty-three of them surrendered but George had not finished yet. 'I spotted some on the other road and with two fellows galloped over and bagged fifteen.' They put up no resistance at all. He then trotted back into the town and rounded up twenty more of the enemy they found scurrying about. So eight Russian cavalrymen had taken eighty-eight enemy prisoners. A second St George's Cross was struck in George's name. 'It was a fine rush,' he claimed proudly, but recognised that it had played out largely owing to the confusion and panic amongst the surprised enemy troops, 'as the idiots instead of running along the road could have run into deep snow.' But they didn't. As George surmised, 'nine galloping horses, not to speak of cold steel is a formidable spectacle and so we bagged our game.'

George was soon involved in more daring enterprises. On another occasion he and three other troopers were sent with cases of ammunition to supply other Russian troops at a critical moment in battle. His three companions 'funked at running the gauntlet' and declined to carry out their orders. George, perturbed though he might have been, was not about to follow suit and resolved to go on his own instead. 'All very well, but the next time I have to run to music I hope it won't be through snow, with a long coat, sword and five cases of ammunition.' Luck remained with him. 'Don't be anxious,' he gloated to his mother, 'these Austrians can't shoot for nuts.'

The 12th Artirsky Hussars eventually came to a bedraggled stop just to the north of Kolomea. Shivering and with empty stomachs they rounded off non-stop fighting with nearly forty-eight hours in trenches during a blinding snowstorm. Visibility was so bad that George described it as dangerous to go more than a few yards from the trench for risk of being completely lost. During this lull in the fighting he found time to sit down and pen a letter to a fellow OE serving on the Western Front. Charles Le Blanc-Smith, imaginatively nicknamed 'Blanco', had been in Mr Radcliffe's house with George before moving on to Trinity College, Cambridge where he was president of the University Boat Club. He was about to embark for France with the 8th Rifle Brigade and would survive the horror of Hooge in July. George wrote to him excitedly. 'I shall look forward to saluting you in Berlin,' he began. Excitedly he told him about the circumstances surrounding the award of his two medals as he gave absolutely no hint of regret at having joined the Russian Army instead of making the journey home to offer his services against Germany and her allies. He was quite at home and found that he was not the only British subject now serving the Tsar. He had found two in the Motor Division and a former Dragoon Guard in the British Army was also serving with a friendly but mad Caucasian cavalry regiment nearby, although George thought it rather tactless to ask why.

The Gallipoli campaign was about to commence and they had some inkling of what was going on on the Eastern Front. 'We await with the greatest excitement the fall of Constantinople,' George told Blanco excitedly, 'which we all here think will make a great difference and hasten the end ... No one expects the war will hang on longer than July, so you will probably shoot grouse as well as Germans this summer. Well my old dear pal. Till Berlin.'[1]

By the end of March 1915 the regiment had moved again; south-east to a spot on the River Dniester where it wound backwards and forwards on itself. Employed to spy on the enemy across the river, one particular scouting trip was a rather trying ordeal of four days and nights. Whilst the regiment proper was engaged in a fierce battle at Zalishchyky several miles back upriver, a dozen men and a single officer had been told to protect 6 miles of the Dniester down towards Moldova. Opposite were three villages all occupied by the enemy and five boats tied up for their use. It was clearly impossible to man this entire stretch with such a small unit, so four men were allocated to watch each village.

'For three days and three nights I didn't once close my eyes,' George explained. 'By day we occupied points of vantage where we could see but not be seen and at night lay on the bank of the river approximately opposite the boats, all eyes and ears strained to be ready to prevent a crossing. In the middle of the river it was light enough to see and aim at a mark, but all the banks were quite dark and we feared they would move the boats to another place and cross.' Whenever they heard a noise at the boats they blazed away with their rifles in their direction and then got out of the way. 'They certainly misjudged our forces,' George said, 'because they always cleared off and only once seriously tried to get over.' In time an entire infantry regiment arrived to relieve them of their posts, which gave some indication of just how big their task had been.

'Tell Winston to hurry up and take Constantinople,' George instructed his family. On 22 March over 100,000 Austro–Hungarians who had been besieged at Przemyśl finally surrendered. This triggered an offensive by the Tsar's armies in Galicia aimed at putting the beleaguered and tortured Austrian armies, who had already suffered more than two million casualties, out of the war. On George's front he was awaiting orders to push east through Russia proper and attempt to come round and outflank the Germans before turning north to Czernowitz. Then, if things progressed rightly, they would clean up Bukovyna which was proving troublesome with its Austro–Hungarian inhabitants.

First though Zalishchyky must be secured. On Easter Sunday George experienced his most brutal action yet. In front of the Artirsky Hussars were solid Austrian trenches protected by barbed wire, eight pieces of artillery and a dozen machine guns. The regiment was ordered to dismount and at 4 a.m. 130 of them contributed to some 1,600 men making an attack on the position. As dawn broke they surged forward and overran the defenders, taking some 1,200 prisoners who were mostly Serbian but obliged to serve in the Austro–Hungarian army. However, ninety-four Hussars were killed or wounded, some three quarters of those that had gone forward. The enemy though had proved reluctant, perhaps unsurprisingly given their ethnicity. Many turned and ran when they saw the extent of the Russian attack and the conquerors also took a gun and several machine guns before seizing the palace on the riverbank where they found some forty horses and stores of ammunition, provisions and barbed wire.

Unfortunately for the Russians, their victims had already phoned through to Czernowitz 30 miles away and by mid afternoon reinforcements had arrived in the shape of heavy guns which began pounding the Tsar's troops. Infantry followed in the early evening, fiercely and overwhelmingly outnumbering the Russians. At 6.30 p.m. they were forced to retreat. Few were killed but they lost nearly a thousand men to captivity. 'It was heart breaking after our brilliant success in the morning,' lamented George.

The collapse of the Austro–Hungarian forces appeared imminent and Germany had no choice but to begin pulling men from the Western Front in an attempt to bail them out. By 10 April the Russian offensive in Galicia had come to an end. Shortly afterwards George was plastered all over the British press as the young Etonian gentleman who fought for the Tsar. He wasn't over keen on the fame but his antics, which now included another Cross of St George for carrying the ammunition crates alone under heavy rifle fire, could not fail to get him noticed.

The fighting petered out for now. Spring had arrived and George was tortured by the sight of the Dniester sparkling in front of their trench so invitingly. 'I am all for challenging the enemy to a game of water-polo – stakes five prisoners, or a machine gun, or something.' They were now guarding the Dniester from Zalishchky east to the corner of Galicia. Officers returning from leave were full of optimism. 'We should take the Dardanelles in a month and Austria should breathe her last by June,' George claimed emphatically. There was talk now of getting him a commission, almost unheard of for a foreigner. Nobody in the regiment objected at all having seen his conduct and in fact he was essentially living as an officer already, dining and sleeping with them, and walking in and out of their quarters at will.

At the beginning of May, after many attempts to distract and deceive the Russians, the Central Powers launched an assault. They rolled over the Tsar's force, sending them cascading back towards their own borders. Entire Russian corps to the north were evaporating and the Austrians were sweeping through the Carpathians. Insufficient defensive preparations had been made and raga-muffin remnants of regiments and nearby men scraped together were all that existed to stem the tide.

To the south, George's sector had not yet reached such a parlous state. By mid May they had in fact claimed much of Bukovyna as the Central Powers attempted to push them over the Dniester and failed. Indeed by the end of the month the Artirsky Hussars had got as far as the Prut, 30 miles south of Czernowitz by way of a strong advance steering well clear of Kolomea, which was still occupied. Czernowitz itself had been cleared, but as it lay in a valley it would have been dangerous to occupy it when the enemy could have begun shelling them. By night they watched the river and by day they slept out in the open. George was in his element despite a shortage of food. 'I'm brown as a chestnut and very fit and cheerful.'

Sadly for George and the Artirsky Hussars, their gains were largely irrel-evant in the grand scheme of things. The enemy advance further along the front was relentless and Russia was in trouble. On 4 June the Germans took back Przemyśl. The Tsar's forces had no reserves, no shells; their only option was a large-scale retirement. George and the entire 8th Army began heading east. They had reached the environs of a small hamlet named Halych when at lunchtime on 7 June, as they were fighting their way back, he was hit in the stomach by a rifle bullet.

As darkness fell on the battlefield a hospital train screeched to a halt at Halych. As they unloaded the wounded a sister was called to where George lay on a stretcher. Too much time had passed and his wound appeared to show signs of infection. There was no hope of saving him and moving him would have caused him immense pain. A Sister Rymaschevsky sat down beside him so that he would not be alone. George groaned with pain. He wanted to know if he was going to die. 'I knew it was absolutely impossible to save him,' she wrote to his mother, 'but ceaselessly made efforts to calm him, saying that naturally he would pull through.' As his condition worsened she called for a doctor who gave him an injection of morphia.

The retreat was still in full swing and that night it became necessary to load George and the entire clearing station on to a new train bound for Ternopil. A sister was designated to travel with him and as the train rumbled along he passed away quietly before they reached their destination. George Schack-Sommer was buried in his Russian uniform in a common grave at Ternopil three days later with six comrades. He had passed his 25th birthday just one month before. The sister sent his medals to his mother and the contents of his pockets to a young OE friend of his acting as an attaché in Petrograd. 'Your son died far from you,' she was determined to tell his mother, 'but ... during the last moments of his life he was never alone. Around him were people, who were deeply concerned for him and wanted to help him with every power they possessed. Everything possible was done to save his life. Our sisters remember him very well ... he died in *our* ranks as he would have died in his own.' Any notion that George Schack-Sommer had had that people might disapprove of his choice to serve in a foreign army bore no witness at Eton. 'We are all so proud of him,' wrote Hugh MacNaghten as he lead the tributes.

The same would not be said of Bruno von Schröder, for there are no contemproary references at Eton to his war service. Whilst the southern end of the Eastern Front was largely propped up by struggling Austro-Hungarian forces, the northern sector was a fully German affair. The Parchim Dragoons had arrived some 60 miles north of Warsaw in mid November. At the onset of the war the Russian armies had planned to advance either side of the Masurian Lakes in Russian Poland, some 100 miles south-east of Kaliningrad and the Baltic Coast. It was done haphazardly by two armies whose commanders cared for each other not in the slightest, but they managed to bulldoze their way well into East Prussia. This was a terrifying prospect for the Germans as, beyond the western borders of East Prussia, lay Berlin. However the disorganisation of the forces helped them to bludgeon the Russians at Tannenburg before August 1914 had drawn to a close and the Kaiser's men managed to force them back over the Polish border and out of Germany. The Russians resolved to try to push into German Silesia but their consistently shoddy intelligence served up their plans for the Germans on a plate and the Kaiser's men were able to strike first, pinning the Russians at Lodz. Bruno spent the weeks surrounding Christmas scrapping around Warsaw whilst the Germans dug in west of the Vistula.

By spring the 18th Dragoner-Regiment had relocated north-east. In the middle of April Germany resolved to try and get Russian reserves away from Galicia where they planned to strike. They did this by launching attacks in the Baltic region, pushing further north-east towards Riga. There had been no serious fighting in the area thus far. The two combatants sat 10 miles apart in a string of posts as opposed to proper lines. The Germans could not afford to send men there and the Russians were relying on the fortress of Kowno to watch over the area, so the region remained underdeveloped as far as the Eastern Front was concerned.

The situation was ideal for cavalry to perform in a traditional role and Bruno had been skirmishing right on the coast 100 miles north-east of Kaliningrad. At the beginning of his offensive, Ludendorff launched a strong cavalry force forward including the Parchim Dragoons. The Russians were barely interested in this mostly mounted advance but it would prove to be their undoing in the area. Suddenly it looked like Riga might be under threat and there were even horror stories about the Germans landing on the Baltic Coast and making for Petrograd.

Conforming to the general advance, Bruno and the Parchim Dragoons had been moving north-east, skirmishing all the way. In June they reached the wooded area around the fortress at Kowno just as Russian reinforcements finally arrived. Three large-scale attacks were being planned for the following month up and down the Eastern Front, including one in the Baltic. In August Kowno itself came under siege and when it fell just over a fortnight later it took the Russian commander Grand Duke Nicholas with it and resulted in the Tsar assuming ultimate command of his own army.

In early September the Germans set out again, this time for Vilnius. It fell on 18 September but it was to be their last major achievement during the offensive. Bruno and his regiment crossed into Belarus, but a German attempt to take Maladzyechna 50 miles north-west of Minsk failed. The Parchim Dragoons had pushed out beyond this target to the area around Daŭhinava another 50 miles north-east where they reached the limits of their advance.

Late on 24 September the regiment arrived at a small collection of villages and hamlets bordered by a stream named the Wilija to the east. The Dragoons immediately began setting out posts in the area to secure their position and at dawn they sent out patrols. Each village in the area had been secured by cavalry and a single machine gun, but the road running east across the stream from Pahost, where Bruno was situated, ran right into woodland that was occupied by unknown numbers of Russian troops.

Everything remained ominously quiet throughout the morning of 25 September but at lunchtime the inhabitants began packing up and running away. At 2 p.m. Russian artillery began pounding the entire area and patrols emerged from the trees. Bruno's squadron, No.2, was one of two allocated to hold the road running back to Pahost but quickly they found themselves pushed back towards the Wilija. Pushed back again, Bruno took up the defence of the southern half of Pahost itself. In front of them another squadron held the bridge over the Wilija.

At dusk a prolonged scrap began over the crossing. The German defenders fell back as the Russians sent in more and more reinforcements. It was not until midnight that the cracking of rifle fire halted and an ominous silence descended on the isolated German cavalry.

It was only to last a few hours. At dawn the Russian guns boomed back into life. The Parchim Dragoons began spreading out and the horses were led away to the rear. As the Russians emerged towards the Wilija with their artillery support, Bruno's regiment steadied itself to put up a fierce defence. Suddenly they realised that the enemy was already across the stream to the south. The German cavalry was rapidly becoming surrounded. Pahost and it's surroundings were catching alight. The fighting became more and more violent and the burning buildings blocked the path west. With great difficulty men were attempting to get the horses away, chased down by Russian cavalry that emerged from behind their advancing troops.

In front of Bruno the Russians had been held on the eastern side of the Wilija, where, in the face of heavy casualties, they began digging in. The entire village was now ablaze and runners could not get back to headquarters at Daŭhinava. In Pahost itself, in command, with no instructions, and seeing the situation deteriorate around him, Rittmeister von Massow gathered the dwindling squadrons and headed for the high ground behind the village. One squadron had suffered heavy casualties in the northern part of the village and had just got to their horses to try to effect this controlled retirement when Russian horsemen came barrelling towards them from the south. They caught the squadron completely by surprise, broke their ranks and completely overwhelmed them. Massow could not see a thing through the rising smoke from the village and he continued to wait for his men to arrive.

The Russians were now advancing on Pahost from both sides, so high ground or not his position was futile. He gathered up all the men that had managed to join him and began heading west to Daŭhinava with anyone else who had managed to survive. The numbers were low. It was apparent that the Parchim Dragoons had been badly hit. Leutnant von Bulow, commanding Bruno's squadron, had been taken prisoner along with scores of men.

Rudolph Bruno von Schröder never made it to Daŭhinava. No account of him being a prisoner of war came to light and his body was never recovered. The 20-year-old was never seen or heard from again[3]. Up and down their part of the front, the German cavalry was being repeatedly checked. In fact, the entire Eastern Front front was stabilising. The following day Ludendorff ordered the construction of permanent trenches. As it had on the Western Front, static warfare had kicked in in the east. It had come less than twenty-four hours too late to save the only Old Etonian to fall whilst serving with the German Army in the Great War.

Notes
1. For ease of understanding, place names on the Eastern Front, with the exception of Petrograd, have been given their modern names.
2. In 1914 Russia still operated on the Julian calendar, so 3 December was actually only 20 November as far as George was concerned. All dates in this chapter are given in the Gregorian calendar used in Western Europe so that the reader can connect events with those on the Western Front more easily.
3. Bruno von Schröder is commemorated on the regimental memorial for Dragoner-Regiment 18 in Parchim.
4. Charles Le Blanc-Smith was killed in November 1915. He was buried at Essex Farm Cemetery.

Progress (left to right) on the Eastern Front, 1915.

10

'Pitifully Humorous in its Imbecility'

By the autumn of 1915 the pool of combatants that had been educated at Eton had widened once again. As well as regulars, territorials and men who had volunteered at the onset, it now included boys who had been too young to run off to war in 1914. Teenagers who had left the school early in 1915, desperate to play their part, now began arriving at the front.

John 'Robin' Blacker and his elder brother, Carlos or 'Pip', were the sons of an American mother and a part Spanish–Peruvian father who moved in literary circles. Pip had been born in 1895 and Robin in 1897. The elder of the two made his way to Eton but it was originally intended that Robin, the shorter, stockier of the brothers, should enter the navy and therefore he was to go to Osborne and then on to Dartmouth. After being 'acutely miserable' at the former he settled down and did well; but as he reached his mid teens it transpired that he was developing problems with his eyesight that were not debilitating in an every day sense but which would make life as a naval officer impossible. By this time Robin had passed the usual threshold for admittance to Eton and lacked the grounding he would need for a classical education, but Hugh de Havilland, his brother's housemaster, took pity on him. Having been put through a Latin bootcamp of sorts at Vane Tower, the beautiful family home overlooking Torquay harbour, Robin passed the necessary entrance exams and 'stretching things to the utmost' joined Pip at Eton in 1914. It was a rare occurrence for boys to share rooms, but an exception was made for the brothers in order to squeeze him in at de Havilland's, in a room at the top of the house. They bickered and fought until another boy suggested Pip fight it out with his sibling. One punch in the face later, Robin looked a little the worse for wear but their differences were behind them and they became the best of friends.

The Blackers had spent many happy childhood days in Germany where their aunt had settled and where their cousin was an officer in the German Army. This caused an unusual rift in the family on the outbreak of war, their father being unable to bring himself to join their mother in her conventionally anti-German views. Both brothers were at Mytchett Farm when war began. 'For someone who had been to a public school,' Pip said, 'the moral pressure was well nigh irresistible.' Robin was immediately desperate to get to the front but Pip hardly felt the same. Although he went straight to try to join the Devonshire Regiment, he spent much time inwardly debating whether it was braver to go to war or to say to hell with it and refuse to play a part.

The Devonshire Regiment would not take Pip; he had far worse eyesight than Robin and they rejected him three times based on the medical examination. In the end it was an Eton housemaster, Mr Churchill, who suggested a courier position shuttling between London and Belgium for one of the British voluntary hospital units. Robin, 17 and two months, reluctantly returned to school.

Yvo Alan Charteris was the third son of the Earl of Wemyss. Tall, fair haired, with broad shoulders, a slender waist and a tendency to look rather solemn he had arrived in College in 1910. He was a gifted public speaker, with a distinctive deep voice and possessed diverse passions, from modern English poetry to medieval alchemy.

Slightly older than Robin but still not 18, Yvo Charteris did the same. He was fed up before he even got back to Eton. He had waved his eldest brother, Hugo, Lord Elcho, off to war in August and half of the staff at Stanway, his family home, had gone by the end of the month. Even the women in his life were fully involved. Two of his own sisters were nursing, as were John Manners' and Monica Grenfell, both of whom he was well acquainted with. When one of his sisters admitted to going down with 'khaki-fever' – crushes on soldiers – his flippancy could not mask his foul mood. 'As everyone is in khaki it seems hopelessly indiscriminate and rather banal.'

Yvo sat shivering through early school on a dreary morning before breakfast, rueing the fact that all of the best people, including Peter Llewelyn Davies, had left for the war. Yvo felt 'crushed with ennui'. Not even the OTC could satisfy his military appetite because it no longer offered the opportunity for buffoonery that it used to. It was all horribly efficient. Eton seemed pointless, people left almost daily to take up commissions, so that reading classics and playing games just felt horribly irrelevant in the grand scheme of things.

He returned home for leave at the beginning of November but no amount of grovelling could make his parents back down. They had agreed to let him leave at Easter, but no sooner. Yvo returned to school after Christmas and was miserable half a day later. His desire to join the army, and he was not alone, was becoming an obsession. 'I have been extremely happy here and it is a pity to leave with a nasty taste in one's mouth.' Anyone with any 'gumption' as he put it had already gone and he was beside himself. He had already decided on joining Peter Llewelyn Davies in the King's Royal Rifles and ordered a uniform. In February his parents relented and he left in the middle of the half. As the cab pulled away from the school Eton receded into the fog and Yvo felt that he was leaving perhaps the happiest years of his life behind, but he was content. He had done the right thing.

Across the road at de Havilland's house Robin Blacker was similarly being driven mad by the routine of school life whilst it seemed that all those around him left for the war. The thought of joining the army was all consuming, as was the desperation to accomplish this feat as swiftly as possible. During his last year at Eton Robin had specialised in history and become close to Foss Prior. Acting as an unofficial recruiting agent of sorts for the 8th Rifle Brigade, Foss arranged for Robin to join him, and shortly after Yvo he too departed Eton College for good. He was not yet 18 years old.

Thus far 1915 had yielded nothing but misery for the allies. Neuve-Chapelle in March had been the first solo effort of British troops against the German lines. That and Aubers Ridge in May, again aiming to make a decisive break-through in front of Lille, had failed and resulted in long lists of casualties being telegraphed through to the War Office. The Russians had been trounced on the Eastern Front and Gallipoli had been a catastrophic waste of time and resources.

The BEF had continued to expand rapidly with the arrival of Kitchener's recruits and by autumn it held a line from the Ypres area down over the French border to Lens. A large-scale battle had been in planning since the beginning of the summer but where the British would play their part was a contentious issue. The French intended to make a large push in Artois and Champagne. They therefore wanted their allies to push just on the north of their lines. Unfortunately this area, around Lens itself, was appalling as a potential battlefield. It was flat, dreary mining territory littered with houses, giant slag heaps and pit heads. The British still wanted to pursue the Lille objective but ultimately the government line had to be toed, and that was, in the end, an order to co-operate fully with the French.

Knowing that they were attacking in a spot that was far from ideal did not put the breakers on Haig's enthusiasm. The BEF was by now split into two armies and it was his that would undertake this main offensive. They were to push over the area around the town of Loos and advance 5 miles, taking what had been dubbed Hill 70, to the east of the town. Bursting through the German lines they would create a gap to pour into, flood behind the German lines and send them running for their lives.

The planning was awful. There were no stages to the advance. It was a free-for-all that lacked artillery, men and experienced officers. The attack was due to begin at dawn on 25 September with a forty-minute release of gas followed by the boldest British advance of the war so far, despite the fact that the big French offensive it was originally supposed to be a subsidiary of had now drifted off miles to the south. Unit commanders had been given objectives but generally vague orders, so remained unsure of how they were supposed to achieve them. Just to crown the ludicrous situation that senior officers and battalion commanders now found themselves in, the Germans were dug in in strong lines of defence with many machine guns lined up ready to rip through the attackers.

Yvo Charteris left Stanway on 16 March 1915, had his portrait taken and delivered himself to Sheerness. It was his first time out in the real world proper and he promptly bought a large motorcycle over which he had no control whatsoever. His mother referred to it as 'that infernal machine' with due cause. He had never so much as sat on one before and now he was excitedly running amok on the Isle of Sheppey, his golden hair blowing in the wind, and running an unfortunate rifleman off the road. 'However, saluting from the dust he apologised profusely, thus showing the glorious spirit of discipline that pervades the British Army and will eventually bring the Kaiser to the doom he deserves,' Yvo reported cheerfully.

Lord Wemyss soon decided that he would much rather his young son served in the Grenadier Guards. Yvo was not entirely happy in the King's Royal Rifles anyway. His mother thought it was more to do with being so far away from all of his friends and family for the first time. There was a chance he might be viewed as fickle by colleagues but he wasn't too bothered. In actual fact he thought he would much prefer the Grenadiers, who were based in London. He left it to his father to work out. 'I should like papa to take the responsibility as no one could mind his asking.' Yvo did have a 'most awful fit of indecision' as it all went through. As casualty lists poured back from the front necessitating officers being sent out to the King's Royal Rifle battalions he asked his mother for advice; but the countess felt 'so lacking in conviction, or the knowledge or the power to judge' that she abstained from getting involved.

Robin Blacker had made the journey away from his rifle regiment too. When the 8th Rifle Brigade left for France in May 1915 he was still 17 and they had enough officers to be able to leave him behind. The simple logistical fact was that the regiment had so many battalions that he could find himself waiting for some time to be sent out to replace a casualty. He received a letter from an Eton friend, Willie Edmonstone, who pointed out that the Guards regiments had far less battalions. Thus it stood to reason that if he transferred to join him in the Coldstream Guards he had a far better chance of getting to the front. That was all the convincing that Robin needed and he was off back to Windsor with new insignia on his uniform. Not only did Robin Blacker take Willie Edmonstone's advice and transfer the to the Coldstream Guards at Windsor, but he had convinced Pip to try to do the same. The elder of the two brothers had been considering forsaking the idea of the Devonshire Regiment in favour of one that was a little less choosy but in the end it was one of the old Eton masters who facilitated his way to a commission in the army. Mr Conybeare pointed him towards a 'broad-minded' doctor who Pip was sure had purposely set up his waiting room in front of the eye chart so that, with his glasses on, he might memorise the letters before his eyes were 'tested'.

One morning at the beginning of August, Pip returned to the room that they were sharing at the White Hart Hotel opposite Windsor Castle to find Robin in a complete state. The news of the 8th Rifle Brigade's plight at Hooge had reached him. 'Torn by grief and frustration,' Robin learned of the deaths of his former friends and men. And he had transferred, so he would not be able to replace them. What if Foss, Sheep and the others thought that he had moved to 'shirk' the fighting? He wanted to go back to the Rifle Brigade. The authorities forbade a second transfer but Robin, aged 18 years and 2 months, managed to get his move to the front expedited. Their father begrudgingly signed a letter of permission and on 26 August, having been marked for the 1st Coldstream Guards, he waved goodbye to Pip. His elder brother returned to the White Hart and got out his diary. 'I put the chances four in ten that I never see him again.'

The day after Hooge, Yvo Charteris bid farewell to Stanway and went for a walk there with his mother. His hands were deep in his pockets. They walked largely in silence, 'charged with deep emotion and thoughts beyond all words'. Soon afterwards, she watched him sleeping in front of her on the train as he returned to London for the last time, laid out across the seats opposite. She was overcome with fear at a vision of his cold, dead body laid out in a similar manner.

All of the Guards regiments had been pulled back to St Omer to form their own specific division. Lord Cavan had been at home with his sick wife when word reached him that it was to be his. Yvo was all calmness and serenity as he boarded the train to join them. As he did so he took a small embellishment from his uniform out of his pocket and pressed it into his mother's hand. As the train moved slowly away from the platform at Charing Cross his travelling companions crowded the window and the last glimpse that the Countess of Wemyss got of her boy was him leaping above them to see her.

By the third week of August Yvo had found his way to his battalion, the 1st Grenadier Guards, where he was beginning to feel at home. The new Guards Division was marking time, playing drunken games of 'hunt the slipper' and throwing Perrier water at one another. Yvo came away from one gathering with the remnants of a pigeon egg on his forehead. The guns rumbled low in the far distance 'like distant breakers' reminding them of what lay in store.

At 6.30 a.m. on 25 September, after spraying gas and wafting a smoke screen not wholly effectively towards the German lines, the first waves of British troops went over the top at Loos and streamed eastwards. Fighting was fierce all morning and success varied. Generally things went better in the southern part of the attack but the difference in how individual commanders had planned, interpreted and carried out their orders was telling. To the north, back towards La Bassee, some troops got absolutely nowhere whilst others got bogged down heavily after initial gains.

By mid morning, Haig's army had had the best of the success that it was going to encounter that day. The decisive break had not been made and what was needed now was quick exploitation of the gains to be able to push on. But the errors and failings of attacks earlier in the year came back to haunt them. Communications had fallen apart and therefore the artillery support was failing because it lacked information while the organisation of the troops in reserve that were supposed to be brought up was dire. They had broken in, but breaking out the other side and having the Germans turn and run for the border was going to be an entirely different story.

William Winterton was another Etonian who had done his very best to try to get to the front as swiftly as possible. Born in January 1896 he was 19 years old, his recently widowed mother's eldest son. He had arrived at Heygate's house in 1909 and appeared to have it all. He was a talented athlete, oarsman, footballer and a cadet officer in the OTC. Whilst not a genius academically his scholarly qualities were sound. He worked hard, but he was most memorable to the younger boys he had left behind for a selfless attitude and his 'indefatigable efforts' to support them as they made their way through the school.

William had been nominally attached to the Royal Berkshire Regiment in 1914 but when he left Eton at the same time as Robin Blacker and Yvo Charteris, he had opted to take a commission in the 11th Royal Scots. In May 1915 the SS *Invicta* carried the battalion to war and by the time the Battle of Loos commenced on 25 September they were in the thick of it. They had been working day and night under the watchful gaze of the Germans, digging additional trenches, improving communications and lugging stores to various dumps. The digging they hated, but it beat hands down carrying heavy stores through muddy, slippery trenches. Worst of all though was transporting the gas cylinders to the front lines by hand. The weight was not the concern, it was 'the nerve wracking fear' that a chance shell might explode nearby and set one off, resulting in horrifying death for the whole party.

William's battalion were in support on the first morning of the attack. The Highlanders in front of them had carried the advance forward towards the village of Haisnes through the pit head known as Fosse 8 and the forbidding Hohenzollern Redoubt. They had then begun pouring eastwards towards the next objective: Pekin Trench.

All the while the 11th Royal Scots had been moving up towards the forward trenches. At dawn on that miserable soggy day, twenty minutes before the gas was due to go off, they began their struggle to reach the front lines. The instant the battle commenced the communication trenches leading to the scene of the fight were crammed with howling, bleeding men and parties carrying supplies up. William and his men had been scheduled to occupy these lines as soon as the Highlanders in front left them but in the reality of the battle the plan evaporated.

It was illustrative of problems occurring all over the battlefield. It was a nightmare. Not only was William's battalion exhausted by the halts they were compelled to make every few minutes, but constant shell fire decimated their ranks. By 8.a.m. they still hadn't made it up the communication trench and their commanding officer began to panic that the 12th Royal Scots to their left would have gone out over the top on their own without support. The attack on William's flank had collapsed so that in their way were all of the surviving men who had been part of that failed advance. Their approach was completely disrupted and eventually they were forced to turn off into another trench at about 9.30 where they finally managed to make some headway, but only after a battalion of the Argyll and Sutherland Highlanders stopped to let them pass.

Already thoroughly spent, as soon as they set foot into no-man's-land William and his company came under a deluge of bullets from the high ground to the left that their compatriots had failed to secure. The Germans on the rise were free to rake the ranks of the Royal Scots with bullets so that 'every few yards of progress were purchased by a mounting list of dead and wounded'.

At about 11.a.m. the two battalions of Royal Scots formed a single line with what was left of their ranks and finally reached Pekin Trench where they ran into the back of the Highlanders who had made the initial advance. The men had marched for five hours just to begin advancing and now they were faced with lines of Germans who had gathered themselves after the first push and were sending up reserves for a counter-attack. William's battalion tried to creep forward in small groups, each of them providing covering fire for the other. With no artillery support; for they had no information as to what was occurring in front of them, the superior German numbers held them at bay as the rain began cascading down. The slightest movement brought on more enemy fire and in the end, cold, wet and famished, realising that no support was forthcoming, they withdrew to Pekin Trench with their rifles so clogged with mud that they would no longer fire.

The 11th Royal Scots were in such disarray that they could not even fathom what had become of their commanding officer. William Winterton was amongst those that simply vanished into the mud. A major evacuated to a London hospital confirmed that he was wounded, but that was as much as was known. It was not until 1916 that two men who had ended up injured in the Boulogne area were able to shed just a little light on what had happened to the teenager. One recalled that he had been one of those who picked up an early wound when they first attempted to go over the top and that William had turned to the corporal next to him and said, 'Am I not going to have a shot at these beggars?' The corporal said that he had been the first officer to fall when they went charging towards the German lines, which suggested that William had been able to get on his feet and at least attempt to advance. The two could not agree though, on whether he had been struck down by machine-gun fire or a shell.

William had penned a letter home in August as soon as he found out that he was leaving for the front. 'Dear People,' he began, 'I am not going to make a will as I am not of age.' If he was to 'kick the bucket' then he left them to ensure that anyone who wanted one should have a little memento of him. At 19 he had little to give save for all of the photographs of his 'chums', which he wanted his sister to have. His younger brother Frank was to have the rest. His body lost, all that remained of William Winterton were his sports' trophies, his school photographs and his watch chain.

As darkness fell on 25 September the British were exhausted, freezing and soaking wet. The night brought counter-attacks from the no-longer ruffled

Germans, who had brought up their reserves and trained their machine guns on the British troops before they could take advantage of any advance. The initial bombardment had failed, leaving strong defences unscathed. Men were ill informed and unaware as to what they were supposed to be doing and how they should do it and things were not about to get any better.

Problems with communications, the impotence of the artillery and the shocking planning of the day before all repeated themselves at horrific cost. At nightfall on 26 September it had become clear that Haig's ambitious plans were in ruins. They had not even taken the German second-line positions and in certain areas the hold that they had achieved was getting weaker by the second. All the Germans had to do was remain organised and sit and watch the farcical tragedy being played out in front of them.

The Guards contingent, including Yvo Charteris and Robin Blacker, had been marching towards the battlefield for days. On 23 September they marched off through a moonlit night, tired-looking locals lining the road outside their cottages, silently watching them pass. The following day Robin was summoned, as his battalion's bombing officer to a conference where they were given an outline of the offensive that was to come. In the background the preliminary bombardment, 'a continuous roar', rumbled on.

On Friday 25 September, as the first assault began, the Guards wound up a rain-soaked march and collapsed to try to rest. By lunchtime though, they had been given an hour's notice and warned that there might be no food for thirty-six hours. If the attack was successful, and there was every indication that so far it was, then they would be going through the gap punched in the German lines. At 2 p.m. they moved off again and marched for seven and a half hours in the pouring rain. On their way they passed wounded men being ferried back from the front in motor-ambulances. Their spirits were buoyed though as they stopped to let several cavalry contingents overtake them; surely that pointed to a real advance?

There were continual checks on the road, and Yvo was exhausted by the time that they reached a village named Houchain. It was 'seething' with troops, and after much bad language and hollering he managed to find some sheds full of straw for his men to use as shelter from the downpour. Someone had procured a cottage for the officers and Yvo went to sleep on the brick floor on an air cushion, with his wet overcoat as a blanket, to the tune of a terrific bombardment going on up at the front.

There was little hope of any significant rest. At 6 a.m. on 26 September they began marching again. That morning the entire Guards Division was put under Haig's control when his secondary attacks failed. Orders were issued for them to march to Vermelles. Then they were halted and told to sit in a swampy field in the rain, not knowing if they should just seize the initiative and press on owing to the great congestion of troops ahead. Yvo and Robin were issued with circulars to read to their men: 'On the eve of the biggest battle in the world's history the General officer commanding the Guards Division wishes his troops God speed'.

By now the severity of the situation had become apparent and the plan was changed. At 2.30 p.m. they were shifted on again. Robin was bound for the old German trench lines whilst Yvo and his battalion would be part of the brigade left in support. Yvo was beside himself. 'Oh! What a march!' They walked for nine more hours, or rather walked then stopped, walked then stopped in the rain, held up by long lines of cavalry. On they went, on and on all the time thinking that there couldn't be much further to go. Then it became apparent that nobody knew where they were going. 'It was terrible to see a gaunt railway bridge looming in the distance that we had left hours ago,' Yvo complained. 'Altogether a brilliant piece of Staff work.'

His battalion was winding ever closer to the lines. The roads grew more and more congested as they moved towards Vermelles and great lorries lumbered continuously by. All the 'sweat of war', the wounded men, the prisoners, the supplies, greeted them on their way. As darkness fell the guns grew louder and louder and the flashes brighter. Yvo grew more and more excited. Every building that they passed seemed to be 'battered to bits'. Streets were laid out with the wounded. They sat with their bayonets fixed; exchanging battle stories and always there was 'the jolting of limbers on the road as the transport lorries bumped by'.

Robin and his men quit marching, exhausted, at 9.p.m. and he shed his pack, wrapped himself up in his trench coat, drank some tepid tea then sprawled out on his waterproof sheet and tried to sleep. At last, Yvo and his battalion turned into Vermelles, a 'wreck of a town'. Yvo promptly got separated from the rest of his brigade. He had been heading the rear party, walking at the back and trying to rally stragglers who had fallen out, 'an awful task'. He ended up wandering about the town with a different Guards brigade until he found his fellow officers and spent the night lying in the bottom of a soaking wet ditch drinking a mixture of rum and brandy to keep warm. All night long, the artillery hidden in amongst the ruins pounded away. Robin was despondent. 'All this served to prove that there had been no very great advance, and things were more or less as they had been.'

His enthusiasm to get to war no longer came hand in hand with the 'smash the Kaiser' philosophy. 'On the contrary, he talked of it as if it would be never-ending.' He had assumed a fatalistic attitude towards the war before he had even left England. In mid July the Blacker brothers were at the RAC Club when Pip picked up a newspaper and saw that his best friend from Eton had been killed three days before. He took the paper over to Robin and silently put it in front of him. His younger brother just handed it back. 'Don't worry about this. We are *all* going to get killed. You and I and everybody else.'

By the time he had arrived in France, Robin's nonchalance had devolved into all out bitterness; ostensibly since the decimation of his brother officers in the 8th Rifle Brigade at Hooge. He was in France, so he declared, 'to partake in that universal lapse into barbarism and inhumanity (not to say imbecility and madness)' that was the Great War.

'There is one subject on which I try not to let my mind dwell as it irritates and disturbs me,' he fumed. 'That I, a human being 18 years old, the product of untold ages of evolution in humanity, should be in this place with the sole intent of putting to death other human beings ... and with what object?' Clearly, to Robin at least, removing 'militarism and tyranny' from the face of the earth was never going to be achieved in this manner. 'Never!' He had decided that the whole sorry mess was 'pitifully humorous in its imbecility, in its hopelessness'. If he ever lived to see another war, well, he stated his intentions forcefully: 'I will have sufficient moral courage to proclaim my sentiments and to wash my hands of a pack of idiots of which I regret to say I am at present one – unhappily.'

After the disaster of 26 September plans for a mass push had faded, but the idea of simply abandoning the battlefield and leaving the French to it on the right was not an option and so planning for smaller advances continued. From Hill 70 on the southern end of the battlefield the enemy commanded Loos and in its environs. Opposite them there was a chalk pit and a nearby mineshaft which gave the enemy a superior view of the area. The importance of these positions was apparent and at dawn on 27 September the plan for the Guards, the only reinforcements available to Haig, was that they would take both along with Hill 70 itself. One OE was serving with the 4th Grenadier Guards and remarked that neither he, nor indeed any of the other subalterns, received the slightest bit of detailed information as to what they were supposed to be doing. Their orders were still being amended even after they had set out to attack the Germans.

Robin's battalion was to support an attack being made towards the chalk pit, the narrow strip of woodland next to it that had been thoughtfully dubbed 'Chalk Pit Wood' and a distinctive chimney by the mineshaft. Robin was ordered out of bed at 2.30 a.m. and pushed on in the dark over barbed wire

and empty British trenches on the way to occupy the old German line abandoned in the preceeding days. Before the fighting had begun, there had been
a large gap between the trenches. In the initial attack British troops had had to
advance across this open stretch of ground under heavy fire and Robin found
himself tripping over dead bodies. 'The scene is not pleasant,' he remarked. 'The
battlefield has not been touched … and there are many, many dead.' He found
himself sitting in a scruffy German dugout surrounded by German correspondence and it sent shivers up his spine. He couldn't wait to leave Loos behind. It
was 'a blighted and poisonous land' and it made him sick to look at it.

The 2nd Irish Guards took Chalk Pit Wood as planned with the aid of a
smoke screen thrown up by more Guards to the left; but when they emerged
out of the other side of this shield they were easy targets for the German
machine guns across the road in a little bit of woodland known as Bois Hugo.
They were eventually forced back with heavy casualties. Robin's battalion
had been sitting in wait and were now sent up to help and together with the
Irish Guards they took back the wood[1]. At 6.30 p.m. the Coldstream were
ordered to advance on the Chalk Pit itself and so two companies, including
Robin's, set forth and did so without too much difficulty. Darkness found
them digging in and consolidating their position.

On the evening of 27 September, Lord Cavan did his rounds, assessing
the situation and decided against a further move on Hill 70. What he did
want, though, was a fierce effort to consolidate their positions. The Guards
were ordered by Haig to repeat the attack on the chalk pit, however, and
at 3.45 p.m. on 28 September they set off from the southern edge of Chalk
Pit Wood to try to take the mineshaft. At the time Brigadier-General John
Ponsonby, the Etonian commanding Robin's brigade, was still trying to get
the attack postponed, at the very least till it was dark, but zero hour came and
he still had no word in reply, so he was forced to commence the advance.

The attack had been entrusted to the 1st Coldstream Guards and again it
was Robin's company that was in the thick of it. They were to push south
and all available machine guns were to be utilised to cover their advance,
concentrating their fire on Bois Hugo across the road which was packed with
German firepower. As soon as they set out they were showered with shells and
bullets from the machine guns in Bois Hugo. Just ten men, two of them officers, managed to reach the objective. The rest were swept away. A withdrawal
was ordered. When a roll call was taken at the end of the day, the Coldstream
Battalion found thirteen of its twenty-three officers and over 200 men either
dead, wounded or missing on the battlefield. The whole of that night was
spent digging in and scouring the nearby ground for wounded men.

On 3 October a casualty list arrived at Windsor with Robin Blacker's name on it as 'missing'. The same day his brother was put on notice to leave for the front. At Vane Tower the desperate wait for news had begun. Pip later heard that their father had swung from extreme pessimism to bouts of optimism, slowly convincing himself that his youngest son was certainly alive and taken prisoner. Pip himself was wandering about Windsor and Eton in a daze. It was agony. Was it better or worse that they had heard nothing? If nobody had found him then he must have surely been alive; or no, he could have been blown to pieces by a shell. Perhaps there was just a delay whilst Robin encountered all the bureaucracy of becoming a prisoner of war or was it because he was one of the cold, dead bodies littering no-man's-land?

Two days after the list arrived Pip crossed to France in a draft of 100 Coldstream reinforcements. It was radically different to the embarkation of just a year ago. Most of these men were returning to a front they had already experienced. There was no cheer. As soon as he arrived he began interviewing any survivors of the attack on the Chalk Pit that he could find. Robin had last been seen carrying a rifle and bayonet well ahead of his platoon. Fifty men had gone in and so far fifteen had come out, but where was he?

Robin Blacker was found by a party of South Wales Borderers on 14 October. It was a misty morning and they took advantage of the cover to go out looking for bodies. He was lying by the side of the road just to the south of Chalk Pit Wood, his body torn apart by machine gun fire; at 18 years and three months he was among the very youngest Etonians to fall during the war. They returned for him in darkness, carrying him back to their lines and digging a grave behind their trenches. They had made a duplicate cross by accident for one of their own men who had been killed and so the Welshmen scrubbed out the name, wrote Robin's on it instead, and marked his final resting place.

Confirmation of his death reached Vane Tower on 19 October. George Bernard Shaw, a family friend, was in Torquay and hurried to Robin's parents to find that Robbie Ross[2] had coincidentally arrived the night before: 'Just the right man at the right time'. Leaving Ross with Robin's mother, Carlos Blacker was whisked off for a walk by his friend. Shaw listened while Blacker damned Vane Tower and said that he would shut it up with all of the memories it held of his teenage son and let it all rot. Shaw exploded and argued that anything associated with Robin should be 'blazing with life and triumph'. When he calmed down Carlos said instead that he would kill himself if not for the pain it would cause his wife. Shaw listened, he joked, they laughed, philosophised and talked through his grief. 'I played all my stage tricks to keep him going.' Only when he was satisfied that the Blackers would make it through that first, awful night did he leave them; Robin's mother with her eyes full of tears and his father agonising over a still-sealed letter from the front lest it contain some horrible description of his boy crawling, wounded through no-man's-land and dying a long, painful death. Robbie Ross took it away.

Four days later Pip had spent a frustrating day trying to get baths for his men organised at a colliery with a broken water supply. He was just sitting down to dinner when the post arrived. He stopped reading his mother's letter halfway through and staggered unnoticed outside to stand in the rain. He decided to go to bed and, lying down but unable to sleep, he realised that he was an only child. Robin was no prisoner, there was no guaranteed safe return when the war ended. Pip had no choice now but to survive for his parents. That was his only thought. 'Now their anxieties were wholly focused on me.'[13]

With the offensive petering out life gradually settled down to a tedious routine, just as it had in the Ypres area the year before. Having been spared the attack on Hill 70 Yvo was becoming used to life in the trenches. The weather was dire and Vermelles had become a 'sea of mud', hideously ugly and squalid. Loos was disgusting, nothing but a heap of ruins and piles of corpses. 'We have a delightful sight in our graveyard here,' he wrote home. 'From one of the graves the tombstone has been laid open by a shell – the coffin lid has been torn off showing the skeleton of a man – a toad is playing on his chest and little brown mice are playing on his bones. RIP says the tombstone.'

Yvo had plenty of time to contemplate his surroundings and he still had a childish view of things. The flares and shell flashes reminded him of the annual fireworks display on 4 June at Eton. He was mesmerised by them. He favoured the flares, which were better than his favourite roman candles. They hung and then fell slowly in red, white or green. How were they ever going to repair this land once the fighting was done? He rather thought he'd like to buy up Vermelles and turn it into a theme-park type establishment that would resemble White City. He would make a maze out of the trenches, and rifle ranges with dummy Huns 'peeping from the windows of ruined houses'. Overhead shells would burst and dispense chocolates at various intervals to amuse the guests. The biggest concern Yvo had about being wounded was that if he was sent home everybody would see his shaven head. This idea was mortifying for one blessed with such flowing blonde locks. He would have to make sure that he received a light scalp wound so that he could 'swathe his head in an impressive bandage' until his hair grew back.

Every now and again the reality of the grown-up world he found himself in was visible through the cover of his jokes and light-hearted quips. The chances of him getting his conveniently distinguished wound were increasing as Yvo had been rotating in and out of trenches around the town of Hulluch. Up he went through what seemed like miles of communication trenches 'everyone getting entangled in telephone wires', past old German lines with deep, comfortable-looking dugouts equipped with beds. The first sight of blood at the bottom of a trench made him sick and he felt a little out of his depth. On the first evening he had had a map thrust at him and was told to take a party off to improve a communication trench. Bewildered, he picked up a revolver and his broken compass, which was about 'as useful as Nelson's blind eye' and went off to give it a go with no faith in his own ability.

He spent his nights sitting on an old gun emplacement drinking brandy and supervising (though he claimed he knew nothing about it) the digging of trenches. He spent the beginning of his nineteenth birthday picking at a can of bully beef that he had found on the floor of the trench while he waited to be relieved 'for lack of a better occupation'. As soon as it was open he was engaged in his own personal war with an army of rodents who could smell breakfast. 'The war seems weary of its own melodrama,' he wrote, '... but it does not not know how to give up.'

A final British attack a week later was aimed at taking the Lens–La Bassee road; a humble objective compared to the original aims of the Loos offensive. Yvo went back into the trenches on 14 October to relieve some territorials who he claimed had 'made a mess of things'. It was a particularly unhealthy spot, an old German trench near the Hohenzollern Redoubt within 150 yards of the enemy.

On 17 October the 1st Grenadier Guards were given orders to bomb a trench that connected the British line to a German one. Exquisitely named 'Slag Alley,' they were to force the enemy out of the other end. At 5.a.m. Yvo's company commander sent a party of bombers out. The trench turned out to be shallow after the first few yards and although they made some progress the men walked into the path of two machine guns that were spraying bullets up and down the trench. A little time passed and the captain ordered Yvo up the line to see what was occurring and why the advance had ground to a halt. He succeeded in shifting them along, returned to report his success and then went back up to continue supervising work.

As he was walking up the line the German machine guns opened fire and in one spray of bullets both Yvo and another promising young officer were killed. The company commander went running up to see what could be done but for his trouble had the top of his skull shaved off. A huge portion of the battalion's strength was wiped out in one tiny assault that failed in its entirety;

for as soon as Yvo was killed his men abandoned the fight, having no direction, and turned for home. That evening they went back to collect his body, carried him back to Guards headquarters in the town of Sailly-la-Boursem and buried him next to the churchyard.

Yvo's mother's worst fears had been realised just eleven days after his nineteenth birthday. She had sat with Julian Grenfell's father, Lord Desborough, her heart aching for him after he and his wife had returned from burying their son. 'He looked so crushed, so seared, so patient and so brave.' But now, following the experiences of the Grenfells and the Manners it was her turn. 'I have felt, superstitiously, that things might have gone differently had he not changed his regiment,' she wrote. But he had, and now she could do nothing but try and put such thoughts out of her mind to stop herself from going mad.

At a cost of 3,500 casualties the advance on the Lens–La Bassee road typified everything that had been wrong with the autumn campaign and crowned a truly awful year for the allies. Operations officially ceased at Loos on 4 November, by which time fifty more Old Etonians had had their names read out in the school chapel and many hundreds more were irreparably scarred or lying in hospital. From here on out, the average age of the school's casualties was to get younger, for as 1916 dawned the boys leaving Eton College no longer had a choice about whether or not they went to war.

Notes
1. It was on this day that Rudyard Kipling's only son, John, vanished in the midst of battle with the Irish Guards.
2. The long-time friend and companion of Oscar Wilde.
3. The Blackers visited France in 1919 to find their son's grave but after three years of subsequent fighting and artillery action in the area there was no trace of it. John Robin Blacker is commemorated on the Loos Memorial with 20,602 others lost on the battlefield, including Captain the Hon. Fergus Bowes-Lyon, uncle of Her Majesty The Queen.

11

'We Had Not Been Taught to Surrender'

Just before the outbreak of war the 10th Earl of Wemyss passed away at the grand age of 95 and Yvo Charteris' father succeeded to the title, leaving that of Lord Elcho for his eldest brother. Almost twelve years Yvo's senior, Hugo Francis Charteris, 'Ego' to the family, was born prematurely on 28 December 1884 at his grandparents' house. As a little boy his angelic long, flaxen hair, big blue eyes and long lashes belied shrewdness and a sensible manner that coloured the way he saw the world. He was at a birthday party at the age of 5 when one old lady went overboard in her appreciation of him and his looks which led him to ask his mother, 'I'm *not* such a sweet as that lady says am [I]?'. Soon afterwards she was hat shopping with him in town and he was listening to the staff ('Oh Moddom, you do look well in this' or 'Oh Moddom, this suits you fine'). When they stepped out on to the street all little Ego could say, with intense scorn was 'vile flatterers'.

The age gap between Ego and Yvo meant that the former was away at school by the time his younger brother was born and so they were not close. Ego's confidant was the brother in between them. If Ego was pragmatic and sensible, then Guy, eighteen months younger, was a dreamer. When they were still quite young Ego was heard to remark that on Christmas morning Guy's future children would get no presents because his brother would still be waiting for Father Christmas to show up.

As children they were well acquainted with Julian and Billy Grenfell and they were frequent visitors to Taplow Court. Following a spell at prep school in Cheam, Ego went up to Eton in 1898 where the size of the place was a shock to him and his most exciting observation was that the organ had a funny way of going moooo like a sick cow in the middle of chapel. Ego eventually began to settle in and adjusted to the bustle of life in Mr Impey's house where he would just about be a contemporary of Edward Horner. Guy followed him and managed to crush him somewhat. As only a brother could, he proved to be an awful 'facetious' nuisance. Ego had got issuing pompous commands to his fags down to a fine art. 'You might boil these eggs,' he instructed regally one day. 'Boil your face,' remarked his brother and Ego had to sit whilst everyone in the room laughed at him.

Capable enough but not always enthusiastic at his studies he joined the Eton Volunteers in 1901 in time to participate in the funeral of Queen Victoria. Ego spent the whole solemn occasion stuffing chocolate into his mouth when the officers were not looking. He was a talented cricketer too, just missing out when it came to Lords in 1902.

As he grew into a young man Ego had a strain of self-consciousness that could make him appear 'taciturn and aloof' in his mother's words. Having persuaded himself that he was a social and intellectual failure, he would try and convince everybody else by telling them stories that made him look silly, in which he figured as a 'rabbit' or 'whatever word was then in vogue for general ineptitude'. In comfortable company he was laid-back, sometimes to an almost alarming degree. Violet Asquith once said that it could be difficult to shake him out of it but 'then it was as if a smouldering fire had burst into brilliant flames' and a stream of 'passionate eloquence' would flow.

Just as Yvo entered College in 1910, Ego informed his parents that he wished to marry Lady Violet Catherine Manners, 'Letty', the daughter of the Duke of Rutland. They duly wed at the beginning of 1911 and set off on an extended honeymoon cruising the Mediterranean and travelling back to England overland via Madrid and Paris. Married life suited Ego immensely. 'Happiness shone out of him.' A son was born in January 1912, David, just as Ego began reading for the Bar and another little boy, Martin, arrived in 1913.

Two days after the outbreak of war, Ego bid his family goodbye and, in his capacity as an officer of the local Royal Gloucestershire Hussars Yeomanry outfit, joined his regiment. It all seemed surreal. It wasn't until his mother saw him at church parade three days later in uniform that her heart sank at the prospect of him and his men, with their 'quiet earnest faces' going off to fight. This was not occurring for the foreseeable future though. At the beginning of December 1914 the Gloucesters remained on British soil. 'The Front seems farther than ever from us now.' Ego complained. They had not heard so much as a whisper about a departure date, but rumours were circulating that included the possibility of a departure to Scotland or even Egypt.

Ego had inherited a somewhat unwilling servant. 'Scorgie,' a native of Cheltenham, was 'well over 50' and not exactly enamoured with the idea of becoming a soldier servant as he thought that it would make the other men look down on him. Ego was in a dilemma. If he could not get a man of his own troop to take on the job, he reasoned, he would look like an unpopular officer. Scorgie agreed to give it a go. 'If you do my horse as well as you do your own,' Ego told him, 'I'll be satisfied.'

It was not until the beginning of April 1915 that the Gloucesters finally left for war, their destination Egypt. Ego's departure was an emotional affair. He said goodbye to his sons and Letty hung the cord with his identity tag around his neck, whilst his mother, who had recently capitulated and agreed to let Yvo leave Eton, raced to the regiment at Hunstanton to see him off. The night they were to leave he came and lay beside her and she struggled to contain her emotions. 'Ego had never failed me and I could not fail him then.'

They left a few hours later in darkness. At midnight the Gloucesters filed past the Countess of Wemyss, Letty and the other assembled well-wishers 'singing or crooning a wild, rather lovely song which mingled with the tramping of the horses and the clinking of their bits'. Then the singing faded and the procession passed by silently. As Ego approached he managed to pause slightly for one last goodbye. Then he and his men rode off into the night. The transports rumbled by and then the Gloucesters were gone; 'the place was utterly deserted'. The countess turned sadly for home. In just a few weeks she would be making her way to Charing Cross with Yvo.

By January 1915, 70,000 troops were in Egypt, not including the Egyptian Army which was there to protect the country and defend the Sudan. The troops were there to maintain the security of the Suez Canal following Turkey's entry into the war. Linking the Mediterranean to the east and therefore far-flung Imperial troops to the war, it was the 'jugular vein of the British Empire'. In itself the Suez Canal was a hindrance to any invading army. Up to 148ft wide and 100 miles long, it ran from the Red Sea to the Mediterranean, which unfortunately made it difficult to defend. The plan had always been, in the event of hostilities with Turkey, to abandon the Sinai desert and fall back on its banks. The British had promptly started digging trenches along both banks of the Suez and strung up barbed wire.

Meanwhile the Turks were planning an invasion of Egypt largely in the hope that when they arrived the native population would revolt against the British. They moved off in the middle of January 1915 from Beersheba with a paltry force (given the task and allowing for the fact that the Egyptians might not be spoiling for a fight) of 20,000 men. They tried to cross the canal, failed, tried again and then gave up. By the time that Ego and the Gloucesters had boarded their transports at Avonmouth the canal had re-opened to merchant traffic and everything had returned more or less to normal.

It had become apparent that the whole set up about the Canal was perfect for employing mobile cavalry. Roads were lacking, a very limited railway ran to and from Cairo and there was a vast amount of territory to try and keep tabs on. The arrival of the Gloucesters coincided with a reduced Turkish interest in the area. The burden of Gallipoli, a front in Mesopotamia and one in the Caucasus against the Russians meant that the Turks shelved any plans to conquer Egypt until at least 1916.

All of this meant that when Ego arrived in Egypt with his regiment and a number of other Yeomanry units, nothing much was occurring. Aubrey Herbert was a little shocked by the frivolity of Cairo when he arrived at the end of 1914 to take up his intelligence role. The social life in Egypt was intense. By now his brother Mervyn had arrived too and Aubrey joked that it felt like the whole of the peerage and House of Commons had travelled east. 'This place was as grotesquely unreal with Christmas trees and race meetings as the war was grotesquely real.' In fact, the scene was so relaxed and un-warlike that many of the officers had their wives follow them out to take up residence in Alexandria or Cairo. Letty, along with Ego's sister Mary and Mary Herbert, Aubrey's wife were all involved in nursing work in Egypt in 1915, treating the wounded as they came off hospital ships from the Dardanelles. If their wives were busy the Gloucesters were beside themselves with boredom. 'We seem never likely to hear a shot fired in anger,' Ego reported in June 1915. 'Poor old Yeomanry.' News of what was transpiring on all fronts came in only through his mother.

Whilst he kicked his heels in Egypt the disaster at Gallipoli was being played out, casting its shadow across to northern Africa and the troops stationed in Egypt. The broken men being stretchered off hospital ships brought with them stories of an ailing campaign. 'You don't realise the awful waste,' Ego told his mother. 'The horror and the hopelessness of the Dardanelles stunt.'

In August things took a serious turn for the regiment with a surprise order to get ready to depart for Gallipoli for the assault at Suvla Bay. However, four officers and a hundred men of each Yeomanry regiment were to be left behind with the horses in Egypt. Ego was to be in charge of the contingent left out for the Gloucesters and it was heart breaking for him. 'I was sulky at being left,' he recalled, 'but the Brigadier would not hear of anything else.'

The morning before his regiment left they conducted a practice route march and Ego shed a few tears. His colleagues all boarded the *Ascania* and made for Suvla Bay. Their lot, as one of them put it, was to take part in the 'fag-end' of the expedition, when for all of the bravery and enthusiasm they could have no impact on the campaign.

All of the sketchy accounts Ego received portrayed the peninsula as 'the last word in Hell'. Egypt was clouded in pessimism and willing the whole Dardanelles stunt to be over. 'You never hear anything but bungling and ghastly casualties' and it was rumoured that the only Gloucester man to have actually killed a Turk was the A Squadron cook. Aubrey Herbert arrived in Alexandria much to Ego's joy for his three-week convalescence. He was full of anecdotes about life on the peninsula, making Ego laugh with the story of his respirator. 'He did not know how to work it ... so he handed it on to his Greek, who used it as a poker mask ... on the beach!'

In mid October, news of Yvo's death at Loos reached Egypt. Their sister Mary, especially close to him and in Egypt still, was shattered. All Letty could remember was him kissing her two little boys goodbye before leaving for the Western Front. Ego could articulate nothing at all on the subject. 'When your own mother and brother are concerned it is futile to talk about sympathy.' His father had adored his youngest son and he was 'awfully sorry for Papa'. As for his mother, she had sat beside Lady Desborough just weeks before and comforted her on the loss consecutively of both Julian and Billy. 'A woman with sympathy loses many sons before her own,' he remarked. 'The only sound thing is ... to expect absolutely nothing for oneself ... to write down everyone one loves as dead and then if any of us are left we shall be surprised.'

In a matter of days Ego was drinking champagne and playing bridge with another OE, a colonel in the Australian infantry, as they sailed towards the peninsula. It was his companion's third trip. He had been hit four times and had a suppurating wound in his knee. No medical board in England would pass him fit for overseas service so he had bought a ticket to Egypt, where nobody knew about his injury, and contrived to get back out to the fighting. Champagne, with regular doses of morphia, ensured that he could sleep through the pain.

Ego spent the rest of the voyage separating British soldiers (who were apparently gutless) from Australians (who were accused of being ill-disciplined yobs). It was the closest he came to a real fight, as the Yeomanry were recalled to Egypt. Letty's prayers were answered when the ship reached Mudros and he was told that he was going to be sent back. 'Poor Ego,' he said of himself, 'destined to be a buffoon in life, could [it] have happened to anyone else?'

On 10 January 1916 General Sir Archibald Murray assumed command of the Mediterranean Expeditionary Force and having taken over, the policy in Egypt became markedly more progressive. Most notably he started a railway line and a freshwater pipe from the canal out into the desert towards Palestine and Ottoman territory. The Gloucesters were to find themselves remounted and part of a large cavalry force being pushed into the desert on reconnaissance and raids.

The British hierarchy had come to realise that placing all of their defences on the west bank of the Suez Canal meant that they could not stop the Turks from approaching the waterway and harassing the canal and its traffic, even if they were only approaching in small numbers. The effort was moved to the east bank and three defensive lines were formed. Closest to the canal were fortified bridgeheads on the bank itself; just over 3 miles further east was a defensive position and further on from that the front line was formed.

'We are still by the old pyramids,' Ego reported soon afterwards. 'But alas soon moving out to some lonely spot in the desert.' He found himself second in command of A Squadron behind another OE, Michael Lloyd-Baker, and they foresaw long months of training and toil before the regiment would drill its replacements sufficiently and the Gloucesters would shape up again. Ego was realising more and more the loss of his younger brother. 'I used to like to make him laugh, and often think of him when certain things strike my sense of humour.'

His work was cut short by a particularly virulent bout of flu and Ego found himself first in hospital and then sent to recuperate. Lady Quenington, whose husband 'Mickey'[1] was an OE and a Lieutenant in the Gloucesters, had fallen foul of the same thing and was far worse off. She had been suffering an excruciatingly high fever for several weeks. Poor 'Mickey' came and went, keeping vigil at her bedside but all of the inoculations that she had had in England did her no good at all and pneumonia 'sadly destroyed her in the end'. Ego's fellow Old Etonian was absolutely devastated. Ego himself got off comparatively lightly and even managed to cram in some sightseeing with Letty before he was signed off as fit to return to the desert. Their tour guide through the sites of ancient Egypt was Howard Carter whose work in the Valley of the Kings, funded by Aubrey Herbert's elder brother Lord Carnarvon, was on hiatus because of the war. He spent his time instilling in Ego a brand new passion for Egyptology and hieroglyphs which the latter carried in the shape of new books back to the regiment.

By the end of March the Gloucesters were a few hundred yards to the east of the canal. From their vantage points the high banks made it look like the great ships passing up and down the waterway were cruising through the sand. The only thing they lacked, in fact, was an enemy. 'Not a sign of one yet,' Ego said of the Turks. His squadron was engaged in pretty menial work, escorting camel convoys and patrolling alongside the precious new water pipes.

Two weeks later Ego and Tom Strickland, an Etonian in the regiment who had married Ego's sister Mary whilst they were all in Egypt, managed to finally catch sight of the enemy. They located a couple of camps and took one prisoner in raids, but the others made off as soon as they saw the British Yeomanry coming. The Gloucesters were rather pleased with themselves. The British pushed on to a new base at Romani; a palm grove just inland that had all the prospects of becoming a centre of operations in the area.

Affairs, as Tom put it, then began hotting up. Once the new canal defences were in place, and the grinding monotonous work done, the British struck out south-east from their main camp at Romani towards Qatiya on the old caravan route towards Palestine through Sinai; an oasis 25 miles east of the canal.

There had been rumours that the Turks were planning to use the Qatiya region as a base for further operations so the British seized it first. It sat at the western end of a series of oases that extended 15 miles to a place named Bir el Abd and had drinking water in abundance; making it the nearest point to the canal that could sustain a significant force. For now aeroplane reconnaissance seemed to intimate that there were no significant bodies of enemy troops in the area, but things were about to change.

In mid April 1916 the Turks despatched 3,500 men, six pieces of artillery and four machine guns into the sands and set them on a collision course with the Warwickshire, Worcestershire and Gloucestershire Yeomanry scattered throughout the Romani area. They began creeping across the desert and by 19 April they had reached British outposts. When they attacked it came as a real surprise to the three regiments scattered throughout the desert as aeroplanes had yet to pick up the enemy presence. The Turks brought with them a contingent of mounted Arabs that terrified Tom; Four hundred men of the Hedjaz, so he had been told, known as the Mecca Camel Corps wearing long red cloaks and apparently famed for being fanatically anti-Christian. 'They gave one a cold shiver to look at ... Dark skinned individuals with gleaming teeth, waving curved swords, riding swift camels and thirsting to kill!'

On 21 April the Gloucesters were told that they would be leaving Romani for Qatiya to replace the Worcesters, who were in turn moving out to another new site further east named Oghratina. As far as Ego was aware, they would only be at Qatiya a day or two until a contingent of Australians arrived and by the end of the week they would be back at the canal, which he was anticipating eagerly.

The following day intelligence reports, all of which may have been lies concocted by native camp followers who were spying for the Turks, reported the enemy as only being present in very small numbers. Meanwhile at Romani, preparing to leave for Qatyia, Tom described the scene as getting 'rather unpleasant'. German aeroplanes had been dropping the odd bomb on them. They also now had Arabs shooting into their camp, 'an infernal nuisance … damned impertinent … It's getting rather warlike here'. The natives within the camp were restless. Mainly employed as camel transport drivers they were suddenly acting as though there was somewhere else they would much rather be. Tom was quick to notice. '[It] seemed to show that something unusual was afoot.'

That morning the Gloucesters moved off. A Squadron, with Michael Baker leading, Ego as second in command and Tom Strickland as one of three subalterns, was heavily populated with OEs. On their arrival they found a contingent of the RAMC in charge of a Red Cross marquee and some forty bitter men of the Worcesters who had yet to move, reluctantly, east. The Worcesters resented being sent to Oghratina which was on the fringes of British occupation, with infantry support more than 20 miles away. To make things worse they were taking with them a contingent of Royal Engineers to dig a well, who were not mounted. This stripped them of their ability to jump on their horses and make a run for it should they come into trouble.

Michael Baker immediately doubled the watches at Qatiya. Officers were put in charge of establishing their horse lines. Ego was put in charge of improving the primitive trenches but it proved to be a hopeless task. The irony, in the middle of the desert, was that they had no sandbags to shore up their lines. As fast as they dug, sand poured back again. By nightfall though the camp, set on rising ground, had dugouts that could hold some six men each at the end of the trench. The horses and the medical tent sat in the centre and the limited sandbags at their disposal had been used to construct a shelter for their lonely machine gun. A few hundred yards to the west lay the well, surrounded by a clump of palm trees.

The morning of 23 April, Easter Sunday and St George's Day, dawned misty, 'a dense sea fog' that wrapped itself around the dunes and left them with no visibility at all. The soft sand meant that anyone approaching the little camp would have their movement completely muffled. At Oghratina the Worcesters were taken completely by surprise at dawn. The Turks, so it seemed, stumbled upon them as they passed westward along the old caravan route towards Qatiya. The new camp held out for three hours, but two whole squadrons of Yeomanry and their well-digging counterparts vanished into the desert, including two OEs.[2] The Turkish troops eyed their surroundings clinically, left some men to deal with the prisoners and then headed for Qatiya and the Royal Gloucestershire Yeomanry Hussars.

Tom Strickland had gathered up his men at 3.30 a.m. They saddled up their horses and stood to arms in the thick fog. Ordinarily a mounted patrol would have followed an hour or so later, but blinded by the mist, Michael Baker called it off until the weather improved. A little while later ghostly spectres loomed silently up in front of them, just a few feet in front of the part of the line where Ego was stationed. The men called out, but when no response came Ego ordered them to open fire. A few shots were exchanged and the ghosts faded back into the mist. Just a few moments later, the crackling of rifle fire opened up 5 miles away at Oghratina, just as the Gloucester's main telephone wire back to the larger camp at Romani was cut.

At 6.30 a.m. the fog had cleared slightly but, urged on by the sound of fighting nearby, Michael Baker managed to get a patrol out. They returned having seen nothing. As daylight came on and havoc was being wreaked on the unfortunate Worcesters several miles away, the Gloucesters began cautiously taking their horses down to the palm grove in groups and small parties went to breakfast. Tom went off with Ego and they sat discussing the incidents of the morning so far and talked up their chances of a proper mounted infantry action against the Turks. They ate nervously. One of their men was halfway through his meal when he got word that more figures were emerging from the dissipating mist but after a few shots were fired, again they faded away. The last telephone message came in from Oghratina at 7.30 a.m., news that the Worcesters were surrounded on all sides. Shortly after this silence fell over the desert.

Michael Baker immediately began sending outposts to points a mile from the camp to attempt to detect the enemy, NCOs with three men each. One corporal, Smith, was immediately suspicious of the behaviour of the Bedouins. He sent a message to Baker who ordered him to take no risks: 'Shoot and shoot to kill'. Then he heard a sniper's bullet whistle past his ear. Smith was off of his horse taking vengeful potshots in the direction of his assailant when he saw a dark crowd coming towards the camp. Jumping back on his horse, Corporal Smith and his companion scarpered. The fog was still thick enough that most of the patrols could barely see a few yards. 'Shots were flying all round us and no one to be seen!' One of the patrols ominously failed to return.

Tom Strickland took out five men, tentatively edging towards Oghratina to see whether he could make head or tail of what had happened to the Worcesters. They softly edged across the sand on horseback for a mile, when a scout he had sent out in front came galloping back in a panic. Hundreds of Turks were heading towards the camp at Qatiya. Tom climbed up to the top of a small ridge in front and sure enough, coming out of the mist less than 500 yards away were, it seemed, well over a thousand men advancing towards them. There were lines of cavalry and twice as many infantry in extended order, with a trail of men on camels behind and, worst of all, artillery. Under a smattering of rifle fire, Tom turned and galloped for Qatiya where Lloyd-Baker ordered all the horses out of the way and all the men ready to defend their position. Scrambling back into camp the first officer Corporal Smith found was Ego, who told him to pass his horse over to the men detailed to hold on to them and then start scratching himself some cover in the sand.

Shortly after nine in the morning, having annihilated the camp at Oghratina, the Turks began a full on assault of the Gloucesters at Qatiya with long-range rifle fire. Ego took up a position next to their one and only machine gun, Tom was 30 yards away to his right. Within moments the Turkish barrage opened, the first twenty shells burst high and then the artillery corrected their range with the help of aeroplanes buzzing overhead.

It came as an utter surprise, according to Tom Strickland, as the Gloucesters had been led to believe that the Turks had no artillery at all in Sinai. Shrapnel began pouring into the camp and burst amongst the horse lines. Michael Baker crawled up to Ego and Tom. He had telegraphed brigade HQ to ask if he should retire and fight a rearguard action back to Romani, but he was told to stay where he was and get as close to the guns as possible and he would shortly be relieved. Both Tom and Ego began cursing headquarters as 'showing a complete misunderstanding of the situation'. They expected one 100 men to hold on in the face of over 1,000 troops plus artillery when they still had horses available to mount and ride away in a controlled manner back to Romani.

Just before gunfire erupted at Qatiya another OE, a Colonel Coventry, commanding a second contingent of the Worcesters, had set out in the direction of the Gloucesters. They got halfway there when the shrapnel began to fly. Coventry had been ordered to reinforce 'if necessary' and he immediately decided that it was, but as he and his men came up on the left of Ego, Tom and A Squadron at about 10.30 a.m. the artillery suddenly ceased. Having dismounted and approached cautiously on foot, Coventry took in the scene. Looking at the piles of mangled horses, and bearing in mind that another Turkish force was apparently advancing which could encircle them, he decided that for him retirement was the only course of action.

Meanwhile, having learned that they were expected to return to their posts and stay there, Ego and Tom had done just that. They were thrilled to see Coventry and his men gallop into the palm grove to their rear, dismount and begin to approach the camp. In front of the Gloucesters, the Turks had begun advancing in short, sharp rushes, taking cover in between whilst officers in uniforms that looked suspiciously German galloped about on horseback orchestrating proceedings. Casualties began to mount, worst of all amongst the tied-up horses, whose ranks had been devastated by shrapnel. It seemed, though, that help was at hand as in addition to Charles Coventry's Worcesters, the remaining squadrons of the Gloucesters had come into sight a mile off to the left. More firing was heard in the distance and Tom assumed it was the Warwickshire Yeomanry somewhere nearby. For a few moments the Turkish advance seemed to stall. Then everything fell apart.

Coventry was ecstatic to see the rest of the Gloucesters appear and eagerly awaited some kind of communication. As far as he could make out they were setting up a machine gun. But then, to his astonishment, just as the Turkish guns restarted their deadly barrage using an aeroplane dropping smoke bombs to direct their fire, the relieving party turned and headed in the opposite direction.

As soon as they had come on to the scene, the Turks had turned all their fire on these Gloucesters who found themselves in a futile position and turned for home, lest they be annihilated. Poor Micky Quenington had survived his wife by a matter of weeks. Carrying a message back towards brigade headquarters he was struck in the thigh and died before his colleagues could get him back to Romani. Now, to make things worse, more Turks were arriving from the direction of Oghratina, riding the horses of the slaughtered Worcesters.

Ego's soldier servant Scorgie had been badly hit whilst carrying up batches of ammunition. 'I've got it,' he told Ego. 'Where have you got it?' 'Through the groin,' poor Scorgie replied. Having ascertained that he was able to crawl, Ego dispatched him in the direction of the Red Cross tent. Scorgie had been lying there about an hour when Ego himself came in, minus his coat and with a red, silk handkerchief tied around his bleeding shoulder. Tom had watched his brother-in-law retire and he was out of sight long enough for his men to begin to panic, but shortly afterwards Ego reappeared with his arm properly dressed. Tom crawled over to find out if he was all right and Ego assured him that it was a simple rifle bullet through the fleshy part of his upper arm. It didn't even hurt, apparently, and he was ready to come back into the fray. He went back to giving his men their ranges, cheering them on and encouraging them, scrabbling in the sand from place to place and looking through his field glasses to direct the men's fire.

The Gloucesters were rapidly becoming exhausted. Sand had got into their rifles and the sun became so hot that the men were burning their hands trying to operate them. They felt as if they were being cooked alive. Tom Strickland's men were running out of ammunition and Ego began tossing bandoliers over to him from some boxes surrounding the machine gun, 'delighted when he made a good shot … and equally annoyed if he made a bad shot'. Both of them, when they were not passing out ammunition or directing fire, were grabbing the rifles of their dead men and joining in the shooting.

At lunchtime Ego was wounded for a second time when a shell fragment knocked him off his feet and again he trotted 50 yards back into the RAMC tent. Scorgie was dismayed. 'Oh sir,' he sighed. 'Why do you not retire, you are twice wounded?' Ego was adamant that his continued presence would show courage and boost the dwindling ranks, so having had his thigh bound up he told Scorgie not to bother about him and he went back outside.

Shortly afterwards a shell came flying over, scored a direct hit on the tent and set it on fire. Ego crawled back with a few men to help the doctor rescue the badly wounded, including Scorgie, from the blaze, dragging them to relative safety behind some bales of hay. The situation had become dire and, watching from afar, Colonel Coventry could render no assistance. The Turkish artillery fire had been creeping closer and closer to his Worcesters and, without the assistance of the other two Gloucester Squadrons, approaching the scene meant certain death. There was nothing he could do but sit and hope that further reinforcements would turn up, but this was not to be. The enemy was within 400 yards and Coventry's priority now was to load his own wounded on to camels and horses and evacuate them from the scene. Any hope of assisting Ego and Tom's shrinking squadron had gone.

They watched as the Turkish infantry came closer and closer. They were within 150 yards. Shells rained into the camp, disrupting the attempts of the few survivors to keep firing on the approaching enemy. After six hours fighting in the blazing heat, the Gloucesters were fully aware of what was coming next. Their telephone operator had bravely kept up communications, but now he sent out a call saying that they could not hold out much longer. The Turks had closed to within 50 yards. They fixed their bayonets and charged what little remained of the camp at Qatiya. Tom ordered his men to keep firing until they were swamped, outnumbered three or four to one, in a hand-to-hand fight.

The surviving men had waited for an order to charge, but instead Tom took the initiative and surrendered, ordering a ceasefire. Ego's squadron was baffled. Nobody had taught them what to do in the event of surrender. The

Gloucesters began throwing their hands up and for an awful moment it looked as if they might feel the sharp point of a bayonet anyway, but then Tom was relieved to see German officers arrive and take charge.

Watching from afar, Coventry was sulking at the sight of Tom's white flag because nobody consulted him before throwing it up. The Turks busily packed up ammunition, tents, water, rifles and anything else they could carry and began loading it on to camels. They arranged the wounded in rows, dressing the injuries of the men that they intended to take as prisoners. Once they had moved off, 'Arabs' arrived and they were far less accommodating. They stripped the dead and badly wounded of their clothes and their weapons and even their helmets so that they had no shade. Some were garrotted. One lucky trooper had telegraph wire wrapped around his neck but it snapped so they just left him lying there. Another trooper was beaten with a sword. 'They made me take my coat off,' he complained, 'and then went away with it. I never had any water and one of them came to me and said "English finish, Turk Port Said …" and some of the women were spitting at us.'

The Australians and New Zealanders who had been marked to take over the area arrived a few days later to find the wounded still strewn through the desert. All about the camp men and horses lay still dying whilst others half burrowed into the sand looking for shade. Heaps of spent cartridges lay next to the bodies; some of them garrotted and others bayonetted or tortured by the Bedouin. One trooper had been lying next to a wounded officer,;shot through the neck, he kept trying to speak, despite his injuries. Men were crawling through the sand, delirious and looking for water. The nights were so cold that they lay shivering and unable to sleep.

Scorgie lay in the sand for three days. All he could talk about when the Australian Light Horse found him was whisky and Ego. He kept telling them to look for Lord Elcho, that he might be alive and wounded elsewhere in the sand. 'Search, oh search everywhere. Please go and search until you find him.'

It was decided that Micky Quenington ought to be taken to lay beside his recently deceased wife. Men of the regiment acted as his pall-bearers and he was given a funeral in Cairo. Michael Lloyd-Baker was amongst the fallen; shot through the stomach he was much maligned for not withdrawing his force but, as Tom Strickland bore witness, his fellow OE had been expressly told to stay put and that help was on the way.

Tom had remained unscathed until the last five minutes when he got 'a slight touch' on the elbow and a wound to the shoulder. The Turks were in a hurry to leave with their prisoners, edgy about a counter-attack. They refused to let Tom or his men get their overcoats from their tents, forcing them to line up in fours, including the walking wounded. A German colonel then appeared speaking English and removed their papers. He even commiserated with Tom when he saw a letter amongst his things saying that he was a couple of weeks away from a month's leave to England. Hungry, tired and scared about what would happen to them next they moved off.

The German officer was a 'decent sort of man'. He praised the Gloucesters for their courage and when he found out just how few of them that there had been 'he thumped his fist into his hand and said, 'You *have* put up a good fight!' Tom watched his colleagues hobbling pitifully along towards Beersheba. Unknowing British airmen dropped bombs on them to compound their misery, inflicting further damage on the wounded .They were marched along, day and night for hours at a time. The Mecca Camel Corps passed them, taunting them with fierce songs. Even their German leader admitted that he was afraid of being pushed aside with his Turks and that his bag of prisoners would be murdered.

The Countess of Wemyss, still mourning the very recent loss of Yvo at Loos, was of a spiritual nature. On the night before the Turkish attack, she recalled, she had had an odd nightmare at Stanway: 'I felt the stress and the strain and saw, as if thrown on a magic lantern sheet, a confused mass of black smoke splashed with crimson flame; it was like a child's picture of the battle or explosion and in the middle of it I saw Ego standing.'

A few days later, before the Anzac troops had found the survivors at Qatiya, the family read that there had been a scrap east of the canal where the Gloucesters were known to be. News of Viscount Quenington's death arrived immediately but for the rest, there was a strange silence. Letty telegraphed from Egypt to say that Ego and Tom were both prisoners and that Ego had been slightly wounded, but that was all she knew, which was agonising for his wife who couldn't bear the thought that Ego was most likely being marched further and further away from her.

An officer from one of the other Gloucester squadrons went out to Qatiya to interrogate the Australian troops who had taken over the camp. He returned supremely confident that none of the bodies found could have been Ego. Letty was now ecstatic, for he would at least be safe until the end of the war. Mary too, frantic for news of her new husband Tom and of her brother, sought and was given permission to interview the wounded Gloucesters now lying in Egyptian hospitals. They also had the US Consul in Cairo wire the American embassy in Constantinople before she and Letty packed up and returned to England to be with the family. A few days after the officer returned from interviewing the Anzac men, a note arrived from Tom, merely telling her that he was alive. To Letty's utter despair it said nothing of his brother-in-law; his captors had forbidden it.

On 10 June the telephone rang when the countess was sitting in her husband's sitting room to say that the Red Cross had found Ego; that he was a prisoner of war and had ended up in Damascus. 'We were wild with joy.' Then, silence. No further information was forthcoming 'and hope began to fade again'. Lord Wemyss repeatedly called at the American embassy, desperate for news, but then a telegram arrived from the Red Cross. It nullified their previous statement and confirmed that Ego was killed in the dying moments of the fight at Qatiya. Letty assumed a position of complete denial. Ego's eldest sister, Cynthia, rushed to her and together they survived 'that first dreadful night'. A padre with the Australian Light Horse came to tea and claimed to have found Ego with two volumes of Herodotus beside him and to have buried him himself. The Turks and the Arabs had stripped him of his clothes and he covered him with sand until they could go back and conduct a proper burial. It would be weeks before Tom could get a proper letter off. It was soon corroborated by the testimony of one of the troopers who wrote: 'Lord Elcho wounded twice then shell blew out his chest, *acted magnificently*.' 'He was killed instantaneously,' Tom was finally able to reveal. 'Michael Baker was killed quite early on and Ego took command … The men put up a splendid fight until an hour after he was killed, when … [we] were surrounded and had to surrender.' Tom had watched as, when the Turks had approached to within 150 yards, a shell came careening towards the machine-gun post and burst exactly where he had seen Ego lying. When the smoke cleared, neither Ego nor the man that had been with him was anywhere to be seen. As the Turks had rounded up their prisoners Tom had gone to the spot, but Ego and all traces of his equipment had vanished. The Countess of Wemyss had now lost two sons in the space of six months. Ego's once reluctant servant, the gruff Scorgie, recovered from his wounds and answered her invitation to visit Stanway. When he arrived on her doorstep in Gloucestershire to talk to her about her eldest son's last hours he was in floods of tears.

Ego's grave was lost and he was commemorated on the Jerusalem Memorial along with 3,298 other men, including five more Etonians, all of whom were lost in the campaign in Sinai and Palestine before the end of the war. Patrick Shaw-Stewart never told Letty what he thought of Ego because he found it hard to articulate his feelings. 'She might perhaps not think it flattering.' But he thought that he was much like Charles Lister. 'Fools to the world and philosophers before God', neither had yet achieved great things in the conventional sense of the word. But perhaps they had the last laugh and knew what life was really all about. 'They formed, for me,' he wrote, 'a little sect apart from the hustling, intriguing, lusting, coveting, money-loving herd of us.'

Notes

1. Michael Hugh Hicks-Beach, Viscount Quenington.
2. Captain George Robert Wiggin and Lieutenant Sir John Henry Jaffray. Neither man was recovered and both are commemorated on the Jerusalem Memorial.

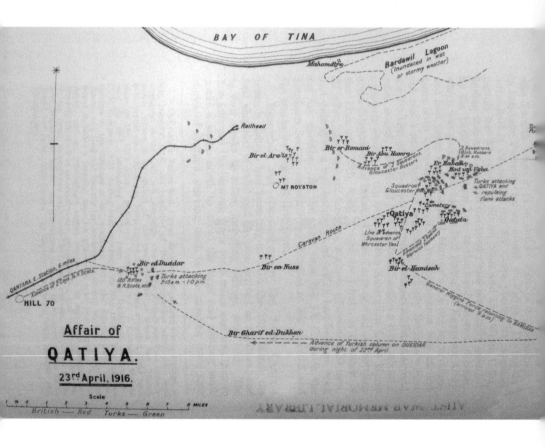

Affair of QATIYA.

23rd April, 1916.

12

'To Hugh or Blighty'

At the onset of 1916 the BEF was some ten times bigger than the initial contingent that had been dispatched in August 1914. Regulars and territorials had been joined by a multitude of personnel, from New Army men to troops from all over the empire. At the end of 1915 a crucial change occurred. The failure at Loos was devastating and did not come without consequences. On 19 December 1915 Sir John French was removed from command and replaced by one of his subordinates, Douglas Haig.

Despite the large numbers of troops now at his disposal, like his predecessor, Haig was still expected to conform with the French command, which was of the opinion that the British should be shouldering more of the burden on the Western Front. Shortly before Haig assumed control a conference was held at which it was established that a joint Anglo–French offensive would commence in summer 1916. Haig himself favoured a push in Flanders, where if it was successful they could eradicate the German presence from the Belgian coast, but General Joffre was insistent on another path. Planning began for an attack in Picardy at a point where the British and French lines met by the River Somme. For all the organisation now underway on the part of the Allies, the German Army was not idle. It had been making its own offensive preparations.

On 21 February 1916 the German Army launched a colossal assault on the fortress at Verdun which dragged France to the brink. Joffre's men suffered hundreds of thousands of casualties. By the time the Germans were finished, there was no way that the French were able to launch a full-on assault alongside the

British on the Somme. In fact, it became more realistic to describe the assault as a British offensive to ease the pressure on the French further south.

The Germans had been digging themselves in on the Somme since 1914 (see map p. 213). The front line incorporated several fortified villages with names that would become synonymous with British hardship during the battle. The front line itself was actually a whole system of trenches and strong-points that had been massively fortified with elaborate dugouts installed to protect their occupants. Behind this was another system and beyond that yet another had been begun so a formidable task lay before the Allied troops. To take up the task, Haig picked two subordinates, both OEs, to plan the offensive: 53-year-old Hubert Gough was the elder brother of 'Johnnie', the Victoria Cross-winning Etonian general who had been so adamant that the Germans would not break through at Ypres in October 1914. Hubert had left Eton in 1888 and embarked on a cavalry career. It was curtailed by his threat of resignation during the Curragh incident of 1914 but he had been steadily climbing the ranks since the outbreak of war. In July 1916, in command of a reserve army, Gough would be waiting with his men to capitalise on the anticipated success. But the man charged with smashing through the German trench systems in the first place was his fellow Etonian, General Henry Seymour Rawlinson.

Rawlinson was born in 1864, the eldest son of a famous Assyriologist whose deciphering of ancient texts was only outdone by the translation of the Rosetta Stone. 'Rawley', as he was known to certain friends, arrived at Eton in 1878, high-spirited and good at games. He had a passion for horses inherited from his father and a corresponding one for art and sketching that came from his mother, whose family was descended from that of Jane Seymour, third wife of Henry VIII.

Rawlinson was placed in command of the Fourth Army, which was in fact a unit aimed at breaking up the administration of the now huge BEF rather than an independent organisation. By the time the summer offensive commenced he would have at his disposal some half-a-million men. Rawlinson was to lead the planning himself. He opted for caution. What he came up with was a series of stages to be executed with pauses to reposition the artillery for maximum effectiveness. All of this was based not only on his own tours of the area but on experience honed throughout the war so far.

Unfortunately Haig threw it out straight away as a soppy effort to kill a few Germans and gain a bit of ground. He wanted much, much more; namely the first and second German trench systems taken in one swoop with a diversion further north chucked in. He wanted to smash the enemy and overrun them.

Haig was relentless, but Rawlinson did not challenge him sufficiently and so Haig got his way. Rawlinson's huge force would be responsible for a main assault whilst men of another army attacked at Gommecourt, further north. Rawlinson's half a million men, along with over a thousand guns, would try to decisively break the Germans north of the River Somme. The preparations were elaborate and the Germans watched huge numbers of troops and masses of equipment arriving on the front in the weeks running up to the opening day of the attack, knowing that all of it was about to be thrown at them.

Hugh, Guy and Harry Cholmeley were the three surviving sons of a solicitor from St John's Wood. Following the loss of two baby boys both named Robert, Hugh was born in 1888, Guy followed in 1889 and Harry, the youngest, was born in 1893. All three boys passed through Mr Somerville's house at Eton. Hugh arrived in 1901 but suffered from rather severe asthma. Forbidden from taking part in games he indulged his passion for music instead. Instead of university, their parents sent him off travelling to try to improve his constitution. He returned to London to be articled to the family firm where he was due to be made a partner when war was declared.

His brother followed a different path. On leaving Eton in 1908 Guy followed the century-old Cholmeley tradition of going up to Magdalen College, Oxford, where their father had been a contemporary of Oscar Wilde. Whilst studying architecture he joined a number of young men at the college who had joined up as territorials in the London Rifle Brigade. His despatch to the front, therefore, was swift and Guy arrived in Flanders in November 1914.

Harry, the youngest, left Eton as late as 1912 and followed Guy to Oxford. He had decided to take Holy Orders when his studies were complete so the idea of seeking a commission might have seemed odd. Nonetheless he had spent time in the OTC and decided not to return to his college in the autumn of 1914; instead joining one of the university and public school battalions of the Royal Fusiliers.

Hugh 'wistfully' watched his brothers join the war effort. He shared their sentiment, but had failed a medical with the Guards. He joined the Inns of Court OTC, however, and eventually, by way of a special medical board, managed to convince the Grenadiers that he was fit for overseas service. He proved as good as his word, for apparently not a trace of his asthma was seen once he got to the front.

By the time Hugh got to the front his two brothers had already seen plenty of action. Guy had witnessed the Christmas truce of 1914 before getting himself a 'Blighty'. He had been wounded and shipped home in 1915 from

Le Gheer where a German sniper had hit the trench periscope he was holding. He returned to France in the summer, but Harry had by then been sent
home in far worse shape.

After joining the Royal Fusiliers with the intention of getting some extra
training under his belt as an officer cadet and undergoing what turned out to
be a rather dubious 'Course of Instruction' at Shoeburyness, Harry had been
commissioned into the Border Regiment on 31 October 1914. He disembarked in France on 11 January 1915 with a draft of poorly equipped men.
He was sent off to join the 2nd Battalion, which was languishing in reserve
with only a handful of its original numbers after having had a torrid time on
the salient in the battle for Ypres the previous autumn. When he reached his
company Harry found that aside from himself there was only one other officer.
The colonel had sent a batch of them back to England, claiming that they were
'diseased' and complained 'very bitterly' about the standard of men coming
out from home. Having been completely unimpressed by the organisational
structure of their despatch, the lack of preparation of the men arriving to fight
and the quality of the course he had completed, Harry was not at all surprised.

At the end of January 1915 he arrived in a sector that was in a truly awful
state. Less than 100 yards away from the Germans, they were sniped at in
miserable weather. The men were far better than their officers, he thought.
'They all do nothing but grumble.' He remained completely unimpressed
at the standard of officers. Even if they were inexperienced in tactics 'they
should know,' he wrote, 'what the men are supposed to do in the trenches and
be really good disciplinarians before they come out here.'

Harry had arrived just in time for the assault on Neuve Chapelle. Sat in the
pouring rain, he continued to articulate his concerns about the inexperience
of the officers, including himself. 'I should like to have been one of those
who had some decent training and valuable experience ... I consider that a
great deal could be taught to people before they come out ... There are new
forms of attack now and new ways of digging oneself in ... Also the power of
shell fire and its danger should be taught.' Leading a platoon on 10 March, the
opening day of the assault, Harry advanced towards Neuve Chapelle itself. He
and his men dropped into a trench that had just been vacated by the enemy
and had now come under heavy enfilading fire. Initially ordered to cross a
portion of open ground with his men to try to extend the British line, they
had no supporting fire and so instead were ordered to lie down.

Baffled by the change, Harry decided to dash back and ascertain what his
orders really were. He was running when he felt one arm go stiff and something hit his chin. He got into a trench and lay there for several hours until

friends stumbled across him and helped him limp, with his jaw shot away, to a dressing station. Within a few weeks Harry was spied at Magdalen 'with his face and head bandaged up and a plate in his mouth' but it was to be a long path to recovery. Not until February 1916 did he arrive back in France, patched up and ready to fight once more.

Just as the third Cholmeley returned to the Front, tragedy befell the family. Hugh had undergone a period of training and become machine-gun officer for his brigade. On 7 April he was standing by a dugout when a shrapnel shell screamed overhead and exploded. One officer was wounded in the shoulder, another fatally in the leg; a guardsman was killed and sixty men wounded. Hugh was killed instantly when a shard of shrapnel penetrated his chest. He was 27 years old. At the threshold of the infamous Battle of the Somme two of the Cholmeley brothers now remained in the firing line.

Henry Rawlinson's 'army' was divided into corps and four of them would attack on 1 July. In the very south, where the British sector met the French, one would be attacking Montauban and the surrounding area. To the north of them, another corps would be attacking La Boiselle and Ovilliers to the right of a third who had been allocated the daunting Thiepval Ridge. On the far left of Rawlinson's army, VIII Corps was to attack the area around a fortified village named Beaumont Hamel. Amongst its number was Harry Cholmeley. The man in charge of this assault, Aylmer Hunter-Weston had had a disastrous campaign in the Dardanelles and this was his return to action.

By now Harry was in the 1st Battalion of the Border Regiment, which had been moved to France after the doomed Gallipoli campaign. Harry would be advancing straight across the valley that contained the village of Beaumont Hamel, then attempting to climb uphill to attack the Germans' second set of defences. To aid them on their way the Royal Engineers had put a mine underneath a particularly strong German position known as the Hawthorn Redoubt in front of the village. Some 40,000 pounds of explosives were ready to go up in front of the battalion as it went over the top.

To the north of Harry his brother Guy found himself part of the attack that fell outside Rawlinson's jurisdiction and was intended as a diversion. The London Rifle Brigade would not be trying to obliterate the Germans and send them running for the hills. Their task would be to court the enemy artillery fire and the attention of troops at Gommecourt which might otherwise concentrate on the northern part of Rawlinson's attack.

The London Rifle Brigade was part of a well-respected division of Territorials from the capital; it was to attack around the southern edge of the village. Gommecourt had been chosen as an objective because it formed a salient and stuck conspicuously westwards from the rest of the German line. A division from the Midlands was going to attempt a similar move to the north of the village. The London Rifle Brigade would first reach Gommecourt Park, which was in fact a wooded area swarming with enemy troops and all manner of weaponry. Also in the way was a strongpoint known as 'The Quadrilateral' which contained 'veritable nests of machine guns'. Behind that lay the village itself and here they were to join up with the Midlands division.

Attacking with the London Rifle Brigade was another battalion of the London Regiment nicknamed the Kensingtons. Amongst their number was another OE, Major Cedric Charles Dickens. 'Ceddy' as he was known had followed his brother to Eton in 1903, yet another of Mr Brinton's boys and a grandson of the famous writer. There he was remembered as a diminutive boy who played the cello in music recitals with exquisite skill and emotiveness. Having gone up to Cambridge he had then become a solicitor in London and, like Guy Cholmeley, was a keen pre-war terrier.

Like Guy's outfit, the Kensingtons had been at the front since November 1914. Cedric had been wounded during the winter and the battalion had gone on to see action at Neuve Chapelle and Aubers Ridge. They were eventually re-routed to the Gommecourt area in May 1916; making themselves at home in previously French lines. Their trenches ran through orchards and gardens on the outskirts of the town and they found that much improvement was needed.

The Kensingtons were fully aware that a large scale offensive was coming. Dumps of ammunition kept springing up in the area and discreetly camouflaged guns could now be picked out in the overgrown fields to the rear. The battalion was employed ceaselessly to prepare for the forthcoming offensive. In addition to improving their positions ready for the big push, the Kensingtons also underwent further training to get ready for the attack. They were marched to the tune of a fife and drum to Halloy for intensive practice in trenches that had been modelled on the German front line in their sector. Nothing was left to chance; everything was rehearsed in detail including the use of smoke clouds to veil their advance.

The Cholmeleys were not the only Etonian family who had been devastated by the war already. Towards the southern end of Rawlinson's army one of the New Army battalions of the West Yorkshire Regiment had as its second in command Major James Knott of a prominent Northumbrian shipping family. At the outbreak of war James had been the managing director of the Prince Line. His brother, Henry, several years younger, was also following in their father's footsteps as a shipowner, colliery owner and merchant. Having left Eton in 1910, Henry had immediately applied for a commission on the outbreak of war and having joined the Northumberland Fusiliers had died of wounds in September 1915 at the age of 24.

James and the 10th West Yorkshires had left the Armentières area at the end of May for a period of training and joined Rawlinson's force in mid June. Their objective on 1 July was to be Fricourt, another fortified village where a supposed weak spot had been identified. They would be making a frontal attack and then forming a defensive flank to protect the troops coming up on their right.

A massive amount of firepower had been collected to participate in the preliminary bombardment. More than 1,500 guns would be firing shrapnel and high explosive shells to cut German wire, put enemy batteries out of action and to smash the German front, thus making an easier path for the assaulting British troops. The bombardment was to last for days until zero hour when the barrage would, broadly speaking, bunny-hop across the battlefield on a timetable, pounding German objectives whilst the infantry followed in its wake. This, of course, depended on the barrage wiping out anything that might hold up the assault and that the advance itself would go exactly according to plan. If not, the timetable would be irrelevant.

On 24 June the bombardment opened and it was earth shattering. There were so many guns packed along the front that the noise could be heard in London and some guns were firing over the heads of other terrified crews in front of them. The Germans, so it appeared, were doomed. In front of the West Yorkshires, the enemy trenches were pounded day after day and then again at night when it was thought that they might be trying to relieve the troops in the front lines. In front of Cedric Dickens and the Kensingtons the barrage 'burst into a roar of sound'. In the days running up to the attack, as the Germans clearly knew they were about to be attacked, smoke was discharged in an attempt to 'cry wolf'.

One OE who was destined to become Governor-General of New Zealand, reported that it was 'very hot-stuff here', but unfortunately for the British, the Germans had remained largely safe in their deep dugouts whilst their surroundings were smashed to pieces. Despite the heaviest artillery barrage the world had ever seen – a million-and-a-half shells fired in seven days – the length of the front had diluted the impact and the result was patchy and short of expectations. This and heavy rain led to a delay in the grand offensive, so as the day, now fixed as 1 July approached, the bombardment began to slacken.

Meanwhile the troops awaited the carnage. In front of Harry Cholmeley controversy raged over the detonation of the Hawthorn Redoubt mine.

Hunter-Weston, for some odd reason, wanted it detonated a full four hours before his men went over the top into battle which, to say the least, detracted from the element of surprise. Haig wasn't having any of it, but eventually a ridiculous compromise was worked out whereby the mine would be sent up at 7.20 a.m. This would give the Germans ten minutes; ostensibly just enough time to regroup, man their machine guns and brace themselves for impact when the attack began. Hunter-Weston had also arranged for the artillery bombardment to be lifted off the enemy as the mine went up. To add to Harry's problems, the random achievements of the week-long artillery bombardment had not been kind to his sector. The momentous nature of the upcoming attack was not lost on Harry Cholmeley. Three days before he went up to the trenches in preparation for the attack he wrote to his brother Guy further up the line: 'Well, here goes – we either go to Hugh or Blighty'.

At 6.30 a.m. a final flurry of shells was thrown towards Beaumont Hamel and now the Germans, who had quietened their artillery to keep its remaining strength under wraps, unleashed a torrid fire back in the other direction. In front of Harry barbed wire had been removed and ladders put up to help the men out into the fray. At 7.20 a.m. the earth heaved and the Hawthorn Redoubt mine was detonated. It obliterated those close by, but for the enemy troops sitting in their deep dugouts it was far from devastating and now they knew full well that the British were coming. The chalky ground was blown sky high and when it came back to earth it looked like it had been snowing. When the attack came the Germans, now on alert, would be far closer to the crater that had been blown and far better positioned to occupy it.

All along Harry's part of the front it was devastating. From the second that they mounted the parapet and went over the top they were sprayed with machine-gun fire, shells and rifle bullets. To compound their misery, large amounts of enemy barbed wire remained uncut and needed to be traversed in the midst of the German onslaught. Dead men lay on it whilst others tried to cut their way through and begin climbing the ridge, exposed to everything that the enemy could throw at them. The timed British artillery barrage left them behind and wandered forward of its own accord. The attack did not even reach the German front lines before it utterly failed.

Sir Edward 'Harry' MacNaghten had arrived at Hugh MacNaghten's house some eighteen months after George Llewelyn Davies in January 1909. On 1 July 1916, just across the River Ancre from Harry Cholmeley, the 20-year-old was waiting to go over the top with his platoon of the 12th Royal Irish Rifles. It was apt that the battalion belonged to the 36th (Ulster) Division, as it comprised volunteers from County Antrim where his family home was situated. He and his men had been given a monumental task for the opening day of the offensive on the Somme: attacking two solid lines of German defences on the high ground at Thiepval, which was daunting in itself without the obscene concentration of machine guns and fortifications in the way. If they could take it, it would be a hugely significant boost as the British would then overlook German positions to the north and south, but the bold plan of attack had them sweeping the German front-line in one hit. To the right of Harry another division was attacking Thiepval itself and if they failed, the knock-on effect could have catastrophic consequences for the Ulstermen who would be exposed if a gap opened between the two forces.

Until 7.30 a.m. the Germans were treated to 'a perfect hurricane of shells'. As soon as the barrage lifted Harry helped lead the attack at the head of his platoon. He was one of the first to jump in to the enemy trench as they rushed the front line, which baffled his old housemaster back at school: 'as you will remember he was very slow at Eton'. The German wire had actually been cut quite effectively but after their initial surprise the enemy found their feet and turned their artillery on supporting troops coming up. Behind the front lines the German position was strongly held and Harry's men were now taking very heavy machine-gun fire. The enemy stood up on the parapet of their second line and threw bombs into the trench while the platoons coming up behind were subjected to more heavy machine gun fire and half of the platoon coming up to support Harry had been lost before they even jumped into the trench. An order to retire was shouted but as Harry clambered out of the trench to relay it to the men he was shot in the legs by a machine gun just a few yards away and fell back into the trench.

In front of Fricourt, James Knott and the 10th West Yorkshires were due to attack in four waves. They waited anxiously in position at 7 a.m., listening to the final bombardment sailing over them and furiously crashing into the German lines. At 7.30 a.m. the guns lifted and the battalion swept over the top. The village itself was to be skirted rather than attacked frontally and the two leading companies got across no-man's-land relatively unscathed. They were, unfortunately, compelled to wait for a battalion of the Yorkshire Regiment so that, together, they could drop into trenches and bomb their way towards Fricourt.

The artillery was to keep up a bombardment to assist in pinning the enemy in their dugouts, but it was insufficient and the Germans flooded towards them. James Knott left with a second wave of West Yorkshires in the company of the battalion's commanding officer. As they proceeded the whole contingent was met with a scathing machine-gun fire. The men were simply cut down.

The attack collapsed. That night, the survivors had to crawl back to where they had started from. They had been left with no support and they were all but surrounded. Split up and confused they were picked off one by one by German rifles. Elements of both the Yorkshire Regiment and the East Yorkshires tried to get to them but German fire held them back.

Just to the north of James Knott was yet another OE and an unlikely soldier. Desmond Darley was a musician, a pianist and hardly seemed to have a temperament suited for war. None the less he was one of a number of Cambridge University men who had joined a New Army battalion of the Suffolk Regiment.

Like Harry Cholmeley, Desmond sat opposite a large mine at dawn on 1 July, this time at La Boiselle. At 5 a.m. his battalion, who had yet to see battle, left the shelter of a wood for their jumping off point. At 7.28 a.m. 80,000 pounds of ammonal blew a permanent hole in the French countryside just to the left of the 11th Suffolks but it soon became evident that the enemy at La Boiselle was entrenched in a particularly strong position. In front of Desmond and his battalion the 10th Lincolns led the brigade out into the face of a monstrous storm of enemy fire. The leading men had hardly climbed out of the trenches when they were cut down. They swung around dead and dropped back into the trench behind them. The casualties mounted before the Suffolks could even get into formation. Isolated survivors began to join together to try to advance hopelessly towards oblivion.

After just half an hour the assault on La Boiselle was a write-off. The odd few men who tried to rush a German strongpoint were ignited by liquid flames as they climbed out of the parapet. 'The sight of their crumpled figures staggering back from the tongues of flame and smoke, tearing helplessly at their burning clothes and then falling one by one was terrible to behold.' Survivors sat isolated in no-man's-land for two days until reinforcements were scraped together. Not until 4 July was their ordeal over.

Although the attack at Gommecourt was a subsidiary one, it did not mean an easy time. On the evening of 30 June Cedric Dickens' men were issued two hot meals before being led up to an assembly area, picking up extra ammunition, shovels and sandbags along the way.

Cedric had command of A Company and rather than a straightforward attack he had a special task. Whilst Guy Cholmeley and the London Rifle Briagde would be attempting to help execute the southern part of the pincer movement around Gommecourt, Cedric would be going out into no-man's-land to dig a trench that would face the main attack on the Somme and act as a defensive flank. The 27 year old had under his command snipers and observ-

1. Aubrey Herbert MP.
(Author's collection)

2. George Fletcher (right)
with his brother 'Leslie',
c.1892. (Private collection)

3. A leaving breakfast at Eton in summer 1913. Major John 'Marcus' de Paravicini (left) and Ronnie Backus (right) are just to the left of the centre pole, their backs to each other. (Private collection)

4. From left to right: Hugh, Guy and Harry Cholmeley. The strapping on Harry's jaw hides wounds received at Neuve Chapelle. (Private collection)

5. 2nd Lt Walter 'George' Fletcher, 2nd Royal Welsh Fusiliers. (Author's collection)

6. Captain Francis Octavius Grenfell VC (left) and his twin Captain Riversdale Nonus Grenfell, 9th Lancers. (Author's collection)

7. 2nd Lt Charles William
North Garstin, 9th Lancers.
(Author's collection)

8. Detail from a fanciful
portrayal of the 9th
Lancers saving the guns
on 24 August 1914 as it
appeared in the pictorial
press. (Author's collection)

9. Lt The Hon. John
Neville Manners in his
cricket whites at Eton, 1910.
(Private collection)

10. 2nd Lt John Reynolds
Pickersgill–Cunliffe, at Eton
c.1908. (Private collection)

11. Men of the 2nd Grenadier Guards are saluted by the king, August 1914. Jack Pickersgill-Cunliffe is marked by a cross. (Private collection)

12. George Llewelyn Davies, 4th Rifle Brigade. (Author's collection)

13. Guards Grave Cemetery as it looked after the war, when Rudyard Kipling described it as 'the prettiest cemetery on the Western Front'. (Private collection)

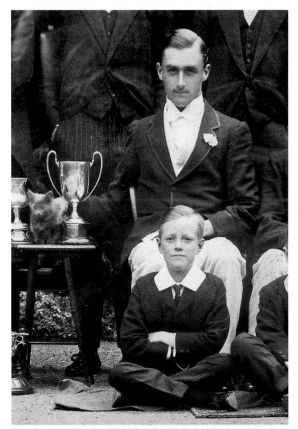

14. 2nd Lt Gerard Frederick Freeman–Thomas, 1st Coldstream Guards (rear) with his brother Inigo at Eton in 1912. (Author's collection)

15. 2nd Lt Reginald William Fletcher, Royal Field Artilley. Taken at Oxford in 1914. (Author's collection)

16. George Fletcher (right) shares his love of climbing with his brother Regie on the Isle of Skye, summer 1914. (Author's collection)

17. Lieutenant Lord Worsley, Royal Horse Guards. (Author's collection)

18. An officer tries to make his way down a waterlogged trench in George Fletcher's sector at Bois Grenier, spring 1915. (Author's collection)

19. Lt Douglas Lennox Harvey, 9th Lancers. (Author's collection)

20. The staff of *The Outsider* pictured at Eton in 1906. L–R: Patrick Shaw-Stewart, The Hon. Julian Grenfell, Ronald Knox, Robin Laffan, Edward Horner, Cecil Gold and The Hon. Charles Alfred Lister. (Eton College/Private collection)

21. 2nd Lt The Hon. Gerald William ('Billy') Grenfell, 8th Rifle Brigade. (Author's collection)

22. Captain The Hon. Edward James 'Ted' Kay-Shuttleworth, 7th Rifle Brigade. (Author's collection)

23. 2nd Lt The Hon. Yvo Alan Charteris, 1st Grenadier Guards. (Author's collection)

24. 2nd Lt John 'Robin' Blacker,
1st Coldstream Guards. Pictured just
before leaving Eton in 1915. (Private
collection)

25. Captain Lord Elcho (Ego Charteris),
Royal Gloucestershire Hussars. (Author's
collection)

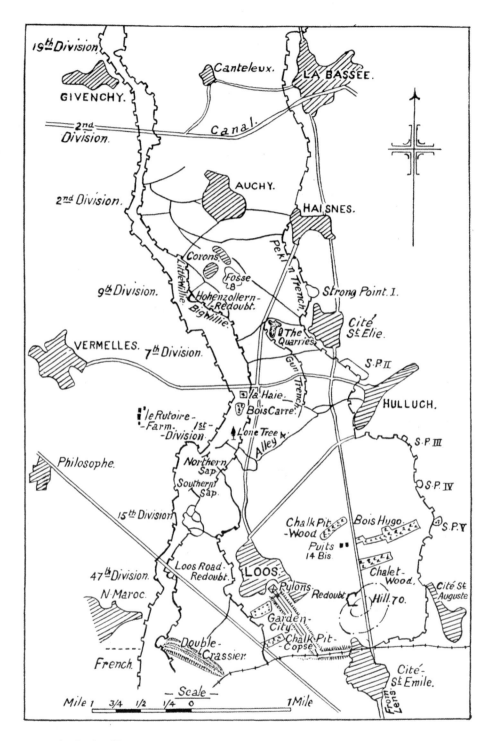

26. The Battle of Loos.

27. Captain Alexander Dobree Young-Herries, 2nd King's Own Scottish Borderers. (Author's collection)

28. Captain Henry Nevill Lancaster Dundas, 1st Scots Guards. (Author's collection)

29. Major William ('Billy') La Touche Congreve VC. (Author's collection)

30. Wounded men struggle
across the barren landscape
around Ginchy, September 1916.
(Author's collection)

31. A group of officers of
the 8th Rifle Brigade 1915,
including 'Ronnie' Backus,
(back right), 'Foss' Prior (front
right), and Arthur Sheepshanks
(front centre). (Private
collection)

32. 2nd Lt Richard William Byrd Levett, 1st King's Royal Rifle Corps, pictured in his Eton OTC uniform c. 1914. (Author's collection)

33 Captain Ian Patrick Robert Napier (left) and Lt John Hay Caldwell, RFC, pictured outside Mr Byrne's house at Eton c.1912. 'Jack' Caldwell's body was found in the Mesopotamian desert in 1918 just a few miles from home after he crashed, fled Turkish capture and tried to find his way to British lines. (Private collection)

34. Ian Napier watches on as a
mechanic works on his aeroplane
on Agars Plough at Eton. (Private
collection)

35. Logie Leggatt as a child in India
c.1897. (Private collection)

36. Logie Leggatt at Eton in 1912. (Private collection)

37. 2nd Lt Logie Colin Leggatt, 2nd Coldstream Guards. (Private collection)

38. Lt Marc Anthony Patrick Noble, Royal Field Artillery. (Author's collection)

39. Cambrai, 1917.

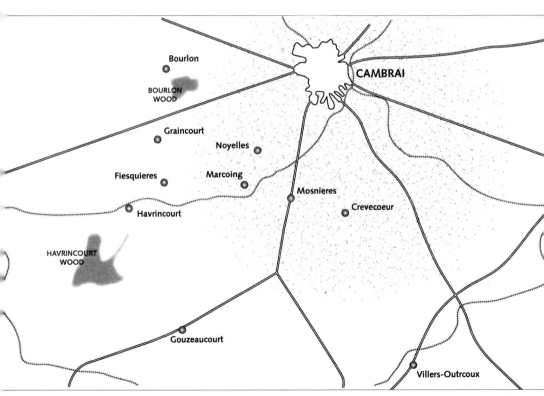

40. Lt Col Eric Beresford Greer, 2nd Irish Guards. (Private collection)

41. Example of one of Eric Greer's sketches that appeared in the national press in tandem with Henry Dundas' poems during the summer of 1917. (Private collection)

42. Eric Greer's bride,
Pamela Fitzgerald, pictured
before her marriage.
(Private collection)

A Quiet Day at Corps' Head Quarters.

Observe a simple rustic scene,
The Corps Head Quarters' Croquet green,
stretching in beauty far below
The windows of the old château:
And here, worn out by ceaseless work-
Which not a man would deign to shirk -
The General and his friends are playing,
The Staff, for once, is holidaying.
Most days, when all the work is done,
It 's much too late for outdoor fun,
And there is nothing else to do
But play at ping-pong, whist or loo,
Or, if the General 's in form,
Some blind man's buff to keep one warm.
To-day however all is glee,
The birthday of a D.A.G.
Has banished toil and all are free
To snatch one afternoon of leisure
And neath the trees to roam at pleasure.
The General and a G.S.O. -
School playmates in the long ago .-
Swollen with lunch and draughts of Tokay,
Engage in mimic strife at croquet.

----

43. Excerpt from one of
Henry Dundas' satirical
poems, typed at brigade
headquarters in 1917.
(Private collection)

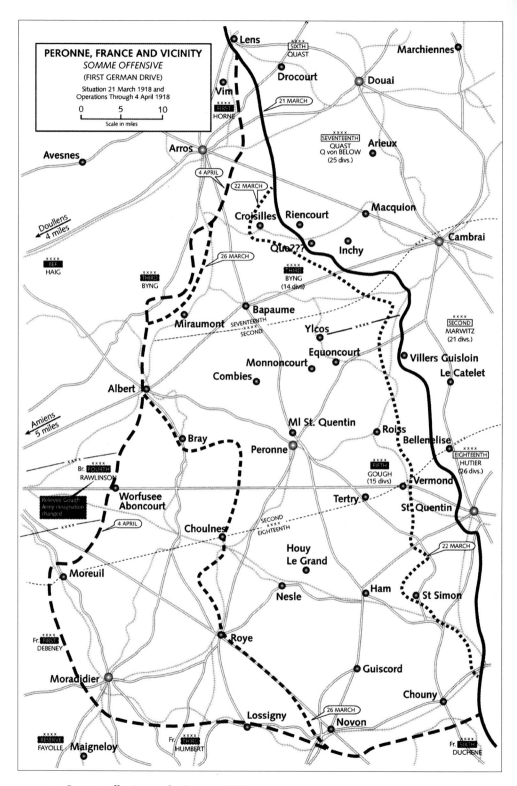

44. German offensive on the Somme. 1918

45. Captain Ralph Dominic Gamble, 1st Coldstream Guards. Pictured just before leaving Eton in spring 1916. (Author's collection)

46. Ralph Gamble a little over a year later. The strain of war is apparent. (Private collection)

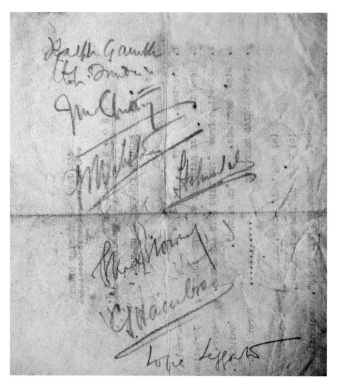

47. Logie Leggatt's menu from the elaborate 4 June dinner at St Omer, 1917, signed by Ralph Gamble, Henry Dundas, Viscount Holmesdale and Charlie Hambro, among others. (Private collection)

48. Henry Dundas (far left) instructing a group of Guardsmen in bombing. (Private collection)

49. Men of the Guards Division cross the Yser Canal, 31 July 1917. (Author's collection)

50. Captain Victor Alexander ('Teenie') Cazalet, Household Cavalry Regiment. Pictured at Eton in 1915. (Private collection)

51. RMS *Lusitania*. The torpedo struck between the first and second funnels on the side shown. (Eric Sauder Collection)

52. Lieutenant-Commander Geoffrey Heneage Drummond VC. (Private collection)

53. HMS *Invincible* on fire at the Battle of Jutland, 31 May 1916. (Author's collection)

54. Henry Dundas with his blackthorn stick. (Private collection)

55. 2nd Lt Reginald 'Rex' Mendel, Royal Field Artillery. (Private collection)

56. Lt David Stuart Barclay, 1st Scots Guards. (Private Collection)

57. 'Audley' Drake. (Private collection)

58. Charles Fletcher pictured with dog,
possibly Regie's Muncles. (Private collection)

59. 2nd Lt Charles Austin Pittar, Coldstream Guards. Pictured after the war at Oxford. (Private collection)

60. Bruno Schroeder, the only Old Etonian known to have fought with the Kaiser's army during the Great War. (Private collection)

61. Etonian Generals pose for a group photograph with the school's hierarchy on a visit to Eton, 20 May 1919. Back Row: Lt Gen Sir T. D'O. Snow, Maj Gen J. Ponsonby ('General John'), Maj Gen R.L. Mullens, Maj Gen The Hon. E.I. Montague-Stuart-Wortley, Maj Gen Sir H.S. Jeudwine, Maj Gen A.E. Sandbach. Middle Row: Dr A.J. Butler, Sir Henry Babington Smith, Maj Gen C.R.R. McGrigor, A.B. Ramsey, Maj Gen C.F. Romer, Lt Gen Sir W.P. Pulteneny (front), Maj Gen Hon. Sir W. Lambton, Lt. Gen Sir W.T. Furse, Maj Gen H.R. Davies, Lt Gen Sir F.J. Davies, Lt Gen Earl of Cavan, Lt. Gen Sir C. Fergusson Bt. Front Row: Gen Sir H.S. Rawlinson, Dr M.R. James, Gen Sir H.C.O. Plumer, Rev C.A. Alington, Gen Hon Sir J.H. Byng, F.H. Rawlins. (Eton College)

62. Hubert Brinton. (Private collection)

63. Henry Dundas' father looks out over Canal du Nord on a trip to the battlefields in the early 1920s. (Private collection)

64. Pam Greer with her daughter Erica just weeks before her own death in 1918. (Private collection)

ers to protect his digging party, covering fire from two more companies of the Kensingtons, and a platoon of another regiment ready to wire the trench when it was done.

At 6.25 a.m. 'the clamour of the guns shattered the quiet of the summer morning'. German shells began dropping into the assembly trenches. 'The roar of the guns and the crash of bursting shells rose to a fury'. At 7.26 a.m. the smoke cloud was discharged.

The leading companies of the London Rifle Brigade, including the one led by Guy Cholmeley, formed up at lines of tape which marked their starting point and waited for the whistles to sound. Into the enveloping smoke they went towards Gommecourt, just as the Germans turned the full weight of their artillery on to them.

Cedric Dickens was nervously waiting. He was to sit tight until a battalion of the London Scottish reached its objectives, then venture out and commence his trench-digging expedition. Unfortunately that battalion was wandering lost in its own smoke, which had turned out to be far thicker than the veil that they had encountered in rehearsals. That and German opposition contrived to leave them in utter confusion. All the while, whilst they waited for word to proceed, Cedric and his men were being shelled. Their assembly trenches had been dug in a hurry and lacked sufficient cover. Casualties began to mount.

After a positive beginning things were taking a turn for the worse for Guy Cholmeley. The London Rifle Brigade had reached the enemy trenches quickly and relatively unscathed despite the horrific shellfire being flung at them. Their formation was somewhat disrupted but they had managed to get into the German trench system as planned.

Just after 8 a.m., John Somers-Smith, another OE in the London Rifle Brigade, set out in Guy's direction to try to make sense of what was occuring. Captain of the VIII in 1906, the same year that George Fletcher was present in the crew, John had gone up to Magdalen College and had the misfortune to be the spare man for the Oxford VIII in the Boat Race twice. A solicitor by trade, he had married a matter of weeks before Britain declared war on Germany, but nonetheless departed for France in 1914 with the rest of his territorial battalion. He was awarded the Military Cross just as his elder brother, Richard, another Old Etonian, was killed with the King's Royal Rifle Corps on the Salient in 1915.[1]

John had crossed no-man's-land with one of the rear waves of troops on 1 July to oversee events in the enemy lines. He sent a message back to say that all companies bar Guy's were in position and that his fellow OE looked to be having a hard time in the park, which was swarming with Germans. A small number of men were sent out to assist him but could not get across. Guy, commanding the left-hand side of the assault, had been wounded in the shoulder as he went over the top, but he carried on regardless. He eventually managed to get his men into the park area before going back to report that the whole wood was in tatters and still populated by Germans.

At battalion headquarters they began to doubt, quite rightly, whether Somers-Smith had enough men to clear the park. They sent a message to find out but, like other runners being wiped out across the battlefield, the man never reached his destination. The scene was chaotic. The maze of trenches had been reduced to a collection of large mangled shell holes and the system was falling in on itself. Rifle fire came from every direction and nobody could figure out if from friend or foe. Bombs sailed randomly into the trenches. One German burst into view waving his hands in the air and they shot him anyway. 'There was no time to figure out whether it was a ruse or not.'

John Somers-Smith had ordered the prisoners rounded up and either herded into dugouts or escorted back across no-man's-land. Their efforts though, to secure the German strongpoint were hampered by the British artillery, which was still firing on the position. At about midday the situation began to get critical. The assault that was mirroring their own to the north of Gommecourt had spectacularly failed and this enabled the Germans to turn their entire barrage on the Londoners approaching from the south.

The troops in the trench system had begun to run out of bombs and using venetian shutters they frantically began signalling back for more. The Germans began a fierce counter-attack and the London Rifle Brigade was forced back, inch by inch, trench by trench. The prisoners they had been holding simply ran away.

Slightly to the south of Guy, Cedric Dickens had carried on waiting. The London Scottish had been well and truly raked by the machine-gun fire from the park and the first that Cedric heard from them was a desperate cry for more bombs. He immediately started sending men of his company up to them with supplies through the shower of German artillery until the intensity of the bombardment made it nigh on impossible. Another company of Kensingtons attempted to help but their commanding officer ended up dead for his trouble.

The fate of the London Scottish and the result of its attack was completely unknown so a patrol was sent out. The officer leading it saw his entire platoon wiped out but eventually made it up to them on his own to find survivors clinging on for dear life. Gaps had opened in the line but the weight of the barrage was such that sending any more men up to fill them was tantamount to suicide.

Cedric, who in this bewildering scenario had not even come close to his allotted task of digging a trench, sent a message back to say that he had just fifty men left. The rest had all been picked off or blown apart by artillery fire. Unaware of whether or not his messages were getting through, he sent another at lunchtime reporting that the trench he was in was practically untenable. What should he do?

Half an hour later it was impossible to move in Cedric's trench owing to German shells. 'Every party that enters is knocked out at once,' he informed battalion headquarters. 'Our front line is in an awful state.' Digging the trench was out of the question. Fifteen minutes later Cedric's despair had increased. 'I have as far as I can find only thirteen men left besides myself. Trenches unrecognisable. I am the only officer left. Please send instructions.'

As evening approached survivors crawled with the wounded on to the road behind. At 5.30 p.m. the German bombardment finally began to slacken and then died away. The battalion finally gave up at about 7.p.m. and made a run back in the direction that it had come from.

The scene as dusk descended on Gommecourt was just as pitiful as far as the London Rifle Brigade was concerned. John Somers-Smith had simply vanished. He was still alive in the middle of the day because he sent a message back ordering another officer to withdraw to the German front line, but after that he was never heard from again. He left his widow with a 1-year-old little boy named Henry.

Guy Cholmeley was the only officer to go over the top at 7.30 a.m. that the commanding officer of the battalion ever laid eyes on again. His war was over. After carrying on with his wounded shoulder Guy was hit in the chest by shrapnel, similar to his brother Hugh. Despite surgery a large splinter remained in his lung and he was never cleared for active service again. He became an instructor at home and eventually joined the family firm in 1921.

At the top of the tree and completely misinformed, Rawlinson thought that casualties amounted to just a third of their actual numbers. 'I feel pretty confident of success myself,' he had written the night before the battle.

His confidence did not bear fruit. At Gommecourt too the attack was a failure. The London territorials had faced unprecedented levels of artillery fire and the enemy troops in the park had wreaked havoc. The Kensingtons had lost sixteen of twenty-three officers and 300 men out of 592. Cedric Dickens had somehow managed to survive and with the remainder of the battalion he spent the night dragging badly wounded men to safety and attempting to bury the dead where they had fallen.[2]

At Beaumont Hamel poor or unsuccessful preparations doomed the likes of Harry Cholmeley to failure before they even set out. Statistically the worst fate of the day had befallen the central part of the offensive. The troops commanded by Hunter-Weston met with total disaster, many of them massacred as they staggered over the bodies of their own men before they reached their own front lines. Harry Cholmeley was yet another OE whose fate was utterly unknown. Fate had sent Harry to Hugh and Guy to Blighty.

La Boiselle was also a dismal waste of men and resources. What made it worse was that given the terrain and the failure of the preliminary bombardment, it was inevitable, and that inevitable failure cost Desmond Darley his life. The raw 11th Suffolks suffered the highest casualties in their division: 691 men and eighteen officers in its first action. Somewhere in the chaos the 21-year-old died. Nobody knew when across the four days, or how, and for his family it was another example of false hope gradually ebbing away.

A rifleman, Kane, who was close to Harry MacNaghten as he was shot in the legs, bayoneted the German who was wielding the machine gun. Harry's company then fell back behind the ridge where it was consolidated by a surviving officer who arranged a second charge at the Germans. He was very severely wounded almost as soon as he gave the order but carried on until he fell. Then Harry's surviving sergeant rallied the men and went again. Almost every single officer of the 12th Irish Rifles was a casualty and they eventually had to fall back on their own trenches. The fate of wounded men on the battlefield was harrowing. One of Guy Cholmeley's fellow officers was found in no-man's-land a full three days later with a severe wound to the head. Rendered blind he had crawled pitifully about, feeling his way along and trying to find the British lines.

Whether a similar fate had befallen young Harry MacNaghten was never established. After being shot in the legs he was lost in the chaos and listed simply as 'missing believed killed'. For all of its initial success in jumping into the German front lines, the Ulster Division too had failed in its endeavours. The importance of the assault on the Thiepval area was not lost on the men in command as they ordered their troops forward again and again. Every available man they could find was collected and assembled; forty-six out of an entire battalion, commanded by NCOs. With so few men the Royal Irish Rifles were then pulled back to consolidate their position instead.

At Fricourt with the West Yorkshire Regiment, James Knott fell less than a year after his brother. The German gunners had been knocked out prior to the attack but casualties were still horrific.[3] The only part of the line that achieved anything approaching success was the southernmost sector of the

British line. Here British troops achieved what they set out to and demolished the front German system, albeit in the face of much less artillery. They did not, however, make it to the second system of trenches.

The cost of the opening day of the Somme campaign was horrendous. Over 19,000 men died and nearly 60,000 were put out of action on a single day. Of fifteen OEs known to have died on 1 July half were wiped out with no trace. It was the blackest day ever to befall the British Army. The bombardment had not lived up to expectations, no matter how loud and threatening it had seemed. The front was too long and the complexity and depth of the German objectives too deep to be swept aside.

At the end of 1 July there was utter confusion across the British front. If the men commanding the battalions could not adequately assess the situation then Henry Rawlinson did not have a hope when he was relying on their information to plan the subsequent days of his offensive. Yet still, he would be required with Haig to decide what to do next to press the advance on.

Notes
1. Second Lieutenant Richard Willingdon Somers-Smith is buried at Bedford House Cemetery.
2. Major Cedric Charles Dickens would not survive the campaign on the Somme. He was killed during preparations for another major assault near Ginchy on 9 September at the age of 27. His body was never recovered and he too is commemorated on the Thiepval Memorial.
3. The Knott family saw to it that their boys were buried together James's body was labriously transferred north, resting as circumstances dictated in cemeteries and crypts along the way until he could be laid beside henry in Ypres Town Cemetery – an unusual occurrence for one killed on the Somme on 1 July.

13

'The Metal Is Gold and Tried in the Fire'

So what next for the British Army? The sheer logistical effort of deploying the attack on the Somme, and political ramifications with France and Russia, meant that this front could never be abandoned. The offensive had been planned for months and was *the* allied offensive of 1916 aimed at winning the war.

Gains had been made in the south, but Rawlinson was faced with utter failure in the north, which was the worst-case scenario in terms of moving forward. No full-scale advance could be made without first taking Thiepval and other important tactical features. So perhaps Rawlinson should even out the progress before he considered the full advance? In this instance they would eventually be able to make a larger assault on the German second-line system. Haig did not think so. He wanted to continue the gains already made in the south, pushing with the French who had success of their own on the other side of the River Somme on 1 July.

Whilst men crawled about and bled to death in no-man's-land, the British plan was laid. There would now be an attack in the southern part of the British sector to try to gain a favourable position for a main thrust on the second system of German trenches at the ridge running between Longueval and Bazentin-le-Petit. Additionally, there would be a diversionary attack at Thiepval as soon as 3 July.

This diversion failed. Thus began a series of scrappy assaults in the centre of the British Somme front that would attempt to both keep the Germans on their toes and to gain local advantages ready for a larger assault. Control began to drain away from Rawlinson, who was losing his grip on the situation.

Power was passing into the hands of his subordinates just as the weather took a turn for the worse on the Somme.

More troops coming into the area meant more Old Etonians being fed on to the battlefield and amongst them was yet another who had made the transition from schoolboy to soldier in the midst of the war. Marc Anthony Patrick Noble had left school at 17 to do his bit. Born in 1897, Marc was tall, 6ft, with dark hair and dark eyes. At Eton he was not one of those who worshipped the playing fields. He was bright, with a vivid imagination and was passionate about his many interests, which included astronomy, English poetry, playing chess via correspondence with his brother Humphrey, history, music, painting, old books, shooting, farming and politics.

In the nursery he and his sister Marjorie invented sagas 'the length each of a thousand *Arabian Nights*' or prepared lectures for their parents, properly presented (with a blackboard and a jug of water at hand) after dinner. One evening she spoke on Francois I and Marc on Napoleon. As they got older they began producing a newspaper for a favourite aunt called the *En Avant*, the motto of their Brunel relatives. Photography came hand in hand with this new venture and Marc was often out taking pictures of locations such as Windsor Castle and St George's Chapel for their 'historical home' column.

Marc held 'an almost ascetic contempt' for dancing or anything that devoted time to 'playing about with girls.' He was utterly satisfied with his own company. His sister remembered looking for him at their Broome Park home and finding him at the end of a lofty corridor whilst everybody else revelled downstairs. 'The scents of a summer night drifted in through an open window.' She found Marc with his telescope, 'silhouetted against a great Northumbria sky of stars'.

Eton, where he arrived in 1910, tried Marc's patience on occasion. 'One can never forget one is at school. No sooner has one settled down to read than that awful clock booms out that it is quarter past something, and all the illusion is spoiled.' He was, however, fully invested in school life; like Cedric Dickens he was a cellist and as well as his personal interests he was a member of the Shakespeare, debating and essay societies. Marc spent his five Eton years in Samuel Lubbock's house, a fabled abode of notable personages that would include Prince Henry, where the spread on the dinner table was enviously talked over by the boys in other houses.

Marc was a thoughtful boy at the best of times and war had him pondering the grand scheme of things at school. 'I was thinking this evening about my life,' he wrote. 'It is mysterious just to think of the future and what it holds in store for us … I have passed fifteen times the day I am going to die …'

Like William Winterton, Robin Blacker and Yvo Charteris, Marc was another of those who grew to consider their position at Eton untenable as 1915 dawned. By February he had convinced his housemaster that this was the case and was working on his father towards the idea of a commission in the artillery. It was the only choice as far as allegiance was concerned. Marc's grandfather, Sir Andrew Noble, had spent a lifetime fighting with the artillery and in the pursuit of the advancement of gunnery. It seemed only fitting that in this war, so dominated by his craft, his grandson should follow in his footsteps.

Sir Andrew Noble had joined the Royal Artillery in 1849 and within eleven years was Assistant Inspector of Artillery and a member of the Ordnance Select Committee. At about this time he was encouraged by Sir William Armstrong, the hydraulic engineer who produced guns for both the Army and the Navy, to take up a post in the private sector. More importantly he wanted him to take a job with him in Elswick where 60,000 people were employed at his burgeoning armaments factory. Sir Andrew's career rocketed in this forward-thinking environment and he was pivotal in the advancement of every facet of gunnery, be it smokeless powder, a chronoscope for the measurement of tiny amounts of time, or fired gunpowder. By 1877 Armstrong and his team were finally able to begin wrenching antiquated muzzle loaded guns out of the government's stubborn hands.

There was further motivation behind Marc's decision to join the Royal Field Artillery. He had begun to think that he would like to forge a post-war career at Elswick. At the beginning of 1915 he wrote from Eton to his father, who was a director at the factory, attempting to explain:

> I do hope, that in all this matter I have not caused you deep pain … I know that you would have preferred me to stay on at Eton, but … it is not as if I had rushed into it … and I should like to thank you especially for being so considerate about it all … After all, the object of education is to teach us all to be men. I think Woolwich with its stern discipline, its hard work, will do me more good as a keen cadet than staying at Eton [as] a fellow who is looked on as not having done all he might, and feels it too.

The family had always thought that if any grandson of Sir Andrew was to end up at Elswick it would be Marc's elder brother Humphrey. Their uncle even thought that the career might be beneath a boy as bright as Marc, but now Marc himself was resolved and, more importantly, resolved not to do it in a He's-a-Noble-so-there's-a-berth-in-Elswick-for-him-manner. He wanted to enter the place after the war as a competent artillery officer in his own right. 'I do *not* want to go into Elswick through being the grandson of the Chairman and the son of a Director.'

Marc left Eton in April 1915 and proceeded straight to Woolwich, where he revelled in the outdoor lifestyle and in the scientific side of his artillery training, which engaged his quick mind. There was nothing that could be done to change his ambitions. 'It seems a little sad that when the family has helped to create a thing like that, none of the rising generation should help to continue the work … Even if Grandpapa had founded a large business for making sausages or cheap braces … I think it would have been the duty of one of the grandsons to continue it.' For now though, his career was a moot point. Elswick would go on, 'unless the country is smashed up, in which case we won't care about considering our own careers', but for now the war was the priority.

By the time Rawlinson's troops launched their assault on the Somme on 1 July 1916 Marc's grandfather had been dead for eight months, passing away on the very day that his grandson was commissioned into the artillery. Now a subaltern in the 121st Brigade of the Royal Field Artillery, which was attached to the 38th (Welsh) Division, Marc moved off that night from well behind the lines in the direction of the fighting. Arriving near Fricourt in the early hours of 7 July, they immediately began laying out lines of fire. Their target, behind Fricourt itself, was Mametz Wood.

The wood, or what was left of it, had been designated as one of those necessary tactical objectives that would ease the burden of a future full-scale assault in the area and after July 1916 it was to become an unlikely location resonating through Welsh consciousness. The attack was due to be launched just a few hours after Marc and his guns arrived on the scene. Pushing from the ironically named 'Happy Valley' the Welsh Division was to advance towards Mametz Wood over a worryingly wide bit of open ground.

Marc and his gunners began laying out a preliminary bombardment as soon as possible. It was hoped that they would be able to raise their barrage to create a shield of sorts for when the infantry went over the top. Unfortunately though, the infantry ran headlong into a veil of machine-gun fire and the attack faltered. Underinformed and disappointed, Haig threw his toys out of the pram and laid the blame with the Welsh troops, dismissing their commanding officer.

The following day Marc's battery continued pounding away at the north-west corner of Mametz Wood amidst rumours that the Germans were advancing towards Mametz itself. Another exhausting day followed and they fired on the wood throughout the night too until, on 10 July, the Welshmen were ordered to attack. The advance through a smoke screen at dawn was chaotic, but the troops this time managed to infiltrate the splintered, tangled remains of the wood. Marc's battery rolled their guns forward until they were within range of enemy rifles among the trees and kept rapid fire up to try to support the advance. 'I especially admired him,' a senior officer wrote of Marc, '[in] his first taste of real war. He was evidently shaken by the unpleasant things that were happening, as was only natural, but he did his job most gallantly smiling all the time.'

All through 11 July the battle raged as the Germans were pushed right to the edge of Mametz Wood. The scene was one of total destruction. In the confusion German and British shells, no doubt some of them Marc's, crashed indiscriminately into the Welshmen. The following day the battered Welsh Division finally secured the wood at massive cost. Marc bombarded the German front line all day in conjunction with a battery of howitzers. The gain hardly justified the cost, for nearly half of the Welsh troops had vanished, been wounded or blasted out of existence. Meanwhile, Rawlinson was busy planning the continuation of the campaign on the Somme and, as he did so, yet more OEs were marching into the fray.

Fathers in the Great War did not generally share the battlefield with their sons, but one Etonian exception saw William La Touche Congreve fighting in the southernmost sector of the British front on the Somme under his father's command.

Although he sent his son to Eton, General Sir Walter Norris Congreve VC had been educated at Harrow. After going up to Oxford he left early to go to Sandhurst, joined the Rifle Brigade and was awarded a Victoria Cross in the same action as Lord Roberts' fallen son Freddy. After commanding a brigade on the Aisne in 1914, 'Billy's' father was promoted to divisional commander before the influx of new units at the front gave him a corps: tens of thousands of men under his command by the end of 1915. Billy watched, full of pride and 'almost reduced to tears' as his father left his division to take up this exalted post with hundreds and hundreds of men cheering him on his way. 'I think he really wept – if Lieutenant-Generals can weep.'

As for Billy himself, all 6ft 5in of him, he had been born in Cheshire in 1891, Walter's eldest son. He spent his early childhood in India and in Surrey and then went to Summer Fields in Oxford, where he was when he heard of his father's Victoria Cross. An energetic little boy he was devoted to horse riding and could climb like a monkey. In 1904 Billy was sent to Eton and Hugh MacNaghten's house. Not slow, he was however quite lazy and prone to teenage mood swings, although he was a good oar. Perhaps inevitably given his father's occupation, he went to Sandhurst in 1909 and joined Walter's regiment at Tipperary in 1911.

Billy was not long with the Rifle Brigade on the Western Front, taking up his post as a divisional aide. It was a job that ground him down by making him feel that he was not contributing. He had picked up a Military Cross at Hooge and was then awarded the DSO for single handedly forcing the surrender of a substantial body of Germans, although he was modest about how it came about. 'Imagine my surprise and horror when I saw a whole crowd of armed Boches ... I stood there for a moment feeling a bit sort of shy, and then I levelled my revolver at the nearest Boche and shouted "hands up, all the lot of you!" A few went up at once, then a few more and then the lot; and I felt the proudest fellow in the world as I cursed them!'

By the time the Battle of the Somme began Billy had changed position. Tired of being an aide, in December 1915 he was appointed brigade major in 76th Brigade which would fall under his father's command that summer. Dick Durnford had summed the role up rather succinctly the year before. 'Brigade Major is a plum job and they do not give it to fools. It is like being adjutant to a Brigadier, you do all his dirty work for him.' Billy worked long and strenuous hours but loved it. 'Of all the jobs ... this ... is the most dear to my heart,' he said. 'I am more or less my own master ... there is unending work to do [and] there is heaps that's definite to show for it.'

Helping Billy along in his duties was his faithful, if trying, Scottish servant Cameron. Theirs was a love borne out of aggravating each other and they bickered like a married couple. Billy was in the bath one evening and Cameron thought it an opportune moment to tell him that all women were 'terrible ... creatures'. Billy gleefully suggested that he must be referring to Scottish women, whom he thought were 'a poor type'. He got his intended reaction when Cameron raged at him and told him that a good Scottish woman might fix him and 'his extravagant careless ways'. 'This was a counter-attack,' Billy recalled. 'So I told him I was already married, but he didn't believe me.'

Sometimes Cameron found ways to get back at him. Once, he decorated Billy's hut so that it looked partially like a tart's boudoir, with looted carpet and furniture and prints of Sir John French and General Joffre on the walls. Given that looting was prohibited, Billy worried what would happen if the authorities caught sight of his net curtains or his chest of drawers. 'However Cameron would probably rise to the occasion and produce receipts!'

One of their plum arguments was about earwigs. Cameron was adamant that they were dangerous, 'crawling into one's brain and dying'. He claimed he knew of several cases. Billy informed him that he was a fool and a liar 'but he waxed indignant and is as obstinate as a mule. Silly old ass … I say one thing and he contradicts me *flat* and I say, "Damn you Cameron, you don't know what you're talking about." and he says, "Ah well, I know I am right." He very seldom is. The Scotch are a wicked race … they and their earwigs!'

Walter Congreve's XIII Corps had been transferred to his old friend 'Rawly's' Fourth Army in spring 1916 and it was to prove an added challenge as his sector comprised the point where the British lines joined with the French to the south. Added to this, asthma sometimes confined him to his sickbed and he was obliged to conduct proceedings whilst flat on his back. As a commander, Billy's father was hands on and consequently popular. 'Never content to command from the map,' he was keen to get forward and see the men in the line for himself. He cared how they were living as well as fighting. Neither was he guilty of being a yes man or of 'blind obedience'.

Billy and his brigade were not present when his father enjoyed his comparative success on 1 July. In fact, as summer began Billy's thoughts could not have been further from the war. He had gone home on leave and married the daughter of two actors, Pamela Maude, on 1 June. The Bishop of London, whose youngest son had been killed at Hooge with Billy Grenfell and Dick Durnford, presided over the service and they seized the opportunity for a brief honeymoon at Beaulieu. Within days Billy was on his way back to the front. By 1 July he had returned and was at St Omer with the rest of the brigade when they were ordered to entrain for the Somme to join his father.

From Doullens, Billy and his men continued their march south in blistering weather. Three days later he was about to be placed under his father's command and he accompanied his brigadier to a conference at Walter's headquarters. Then, having travelled ahead of the men, they left his father and went to reconnoitre the area around Montauban where they were to take up residence.

The men arrived and began to settle in Walter Congreve's sector where Billy's priority remained getting to know the lay of the land. As Marc Noble arrived and began bombarding Mametz Wood further north, Billy took twenty of the brigade's officers and men up towards Caterpillar Valley in a lorry in the pouring rain where they remained until the early hours. On 8 July the 76th Brigade, which comprised one battalion each of the Suffolk, Royal Welsh Fusiliers, King's Own Lancaster and Gordon Highlanders regiments, began occupying the trenches in front of Montauban, whilst Billy and the rest of the brigade staff took up residence at Bronfray Farm nearby. The Germans continually shelled the 2nd Suffolks in the trenches with gas shells, but as for actual fighting there was more going on to either side of them in Mametz Wood and at Trônes Wood than in the brigade sector.

This appeared to be about to change when 76th Brigade received orders to the effect that they were to be part of an attack on the important ridge behind Longueval on an as yet unspecified date. They began preparing in earnest. As it turned out, all the work they put in creating ammunition dumps, reconnoitring wire defences, practising and carrying stores under increasingly heavy shell fire was to pave the way for different troops when the brigade was pulled from the line and put in reserve. On 14 July the replacements attacked the German second line at Bazentin-le-Grand and Bazentin-le-Petit whilst the battalions under Billy's jurisdiction remained digging to the rear. Their replacements sent a thank you for all the hard work undertaken by 76th Brigade when they enjoyed relatively smooth progress.

Rawlinson's army had in fact scored broader success on 14 July but a decisive breakthrough was very much still out of reach and any hope of one was diminishing. German reserves began to arrive on the scene. Rawlinson put a veto on any more random, localised attacks that would decimate manpower before a proper, large-scale assault could be launched over which he could exercise proper control, but the slaughter carried on regardless of his instructions.

Delville Wood summed up the state of affairs after 14 July. Behind Longueval, which was also coveted, it was a death trap that troops had nicknamed 'Devil's Wood'. Attempts to grab it commenced in force on 15 July. Wave after wave of men were sent into an inferno of shells. The South African Brigade was battered out of all recognition. They came out with less than 800 men of 3,200. On 17 July Billy Congreve's brigade received short-notice orders to follow their expensive example and assault the village of Longueval and the north-west corner of the wood the following morning. The 1st Gordon Highlanders were selected to undertake the task with the Lancasters in support. Officers were rushed up to look at the ground that they were to be attacking in just a few hours and brigade headquarters quickly shifted forward to a quarry just north of Montauban. Overnight any hopes of a calm before the storm were obliterated by constant gas shelling by the enemy and at 2 a.m. the Highlanders moved forwards to get ready for the attack.

They were to move around the north of Longueval, clear the orchards about the north end of the village, clear the houses in the village south of the road that connected Longueval with High Wood, and also to push patrols through the north-west corner of Delville Wood to gain touch with more British troops.

The artillery had tried to quieten the Germans in front of them as much as possible given the lack of notice. There had been a steady bombardment of the position for one hour previous to the assault, then one or two intense bursts lasting five mintutes. Before the Highlanders went off they threw a last fierce flurry of shells at their objectives.

The attack moved off at 3.45 a.m. The north of the village was behind too much uncut barbed wire and it was too well shielded by enemy rifles and machine guns to make a proper advance. The orchards too were 'veritable quagmires' from the recent rain. Germans were found to be entrenched in the village itself, again shielded by uncut wire. The Highlanders were pushed back. They suffered very heavy casualties and some of the King's Own Lancasters were quickly pushed through the village to help consolidate their positions.

By 9.A.m. all movement to the north of the village was impossible because of machine-gun fire. The Germans then began shelling Delville Wood and the village. With no major advance on a broad front to keep them busy, the enemy was able to direct all of their artillery attentions on this one position and they flung shells at Billy's brigade with 'unparalleled intensity' for nearly five hours. At 4.30 p.m. they launched a counter-attack. The northern half of the village was by now completely untenable and when the Germans came on in four waves the British troops withdrew to the south. The 2nd Suffolks began to arrive as reinforcements and together the combined elements of Billy's brigade managed to strengthen their positions and began digging in.

The following day things did not go well at all. General Haldane, commanding the division to which they belonged, travelled through the ruined village of Montauban into the very south of Longueval where he found brigade headquarters ensconced in the quarry. They were under a heavy artillery barrage and Billy had just returned from a dangerous visit about the village to assess the situation. He looked tired, but Haldane said nothing. 'I knew that if I said he was overworking he would scorn the idea.' Billy had worked himself into a state of exhaustion. Cameron was snapping at his heels, urging him to calm down but Billy characteristically told him to shut up.

The brigade was shelled very heavily until dawn on 19 July. Brigade headquarters was hit repeatedly with gas shells and they all had to evacuate. Billy was pulling casualties out of harm's way with a medical officer despite having been exposed to the gas himself; not the only instance of him attempting to help treat wounded men under heavy shellfire. That evening orders arrived for them to attack again the following morning. At 10.30 p.m. Billy arrived at the 2nd Suffolks to inform the battalion of their task. He spoke to all officers and platoon commanders and explained that they were to push off east, clear Longueval and sweep north-east along a road running through the splintered remains of Delville Wood to gain touch with the 10th Royal Welsh Fusiliers. They were then to consolidate the entire area together.

Having explained the plan, Billy then went out to superintend arrangements for the attack. The Suffolks were in place by 3 a.m. but the Royal Welsh Fusiliers had a much harder time getting to their jumping off point thanks to lost guides and shoddy intelligence and had already had to repulse two German attacks whilst they were trying to get ready. It was mayhem and a testament to their resolve. The brigade had been told that 'Princes Street', running east through the centre of the wood, was in British hands but this statement appeared to be rubbish and they could not get more than 150 yards further into the wood from the southern edge. To make matters worse, the leading company of Welshmen was being shot at by their own side because the commander of the nearby 11th Essex Battalion had not been told that friendly troops would be moving about on his front, or even that there was to be an attack.

The Suffolks went off at 3.35 a.m. and the Royal Welsh Fusiliers, despite all that they had thus far endured, ten minutes later. The Welsh were hit hard and because they were unable to co-operate with each other, the attack folded and they had to be withdrawn. They fell back to where the baffled Essex battalion was situated with a contingent of Berkshire men and dug in, changing tack from offensive to defensive.

Reports coming back to the brigade from wounded men and prisoners initially had seemed to indicate that everything was going well. Nothing else came back though and worry began to seep in. Patrols were sent out but could not make any contact with the two companies that had gone out. It was feared that the men of the 76th Brigade had been wiped out entirely.

Billy had been on the move all day trying to establish just what was actually going on. Standing on a road leading to Longueval from the west, he was attempting to get the 2nd Suffolks to secure their position. He had just about decided that he had gathered all the information that he could and was looking to the higher ground in front when from inside the cornfield he was observing a German sniper fired a single bullet. It struck just below the breastbone and 25-year-old Billy Congreve was dead soon after he hit the ground.

His father was still attempting to command the battle. Word reached a member of his staff early in the afternoon via telephone. Events at Delville Wood had reached a critical juncture and Walter was about to send his men forward again in 'a very important and very daring operation'. General Congreve had to be informed, but his keeping his head was absolutely essential for XIII Corps. A staff officer entered the room and gently informed the general that his eldest son had fallen.

'He was absolutely calm to all outward appearance, and after a few seconds of silence said quite calmly, "He was a good soldier." That is all he allowed to appear; and he continued dealing with everything as it came along in the same imperturbable and quietly decisive way as usual.' But the member of his staff was not at all fooled. 'You know perhaps better than I,' he wrote to a friend, 'what the loss of that son meant to him.'

Cameron was utterly heartbroken but fiercely determined to go up under fire and bring Billy's body back. As he was carried to safety the men of the Gordon Highlanders were following with wild poppies and cornflowers to lay upon him. Eight of their officers carried him into Carnoy and he lay there overnight with Cameron keeping unceasing vigil beside him. In accordance with Walter Congreve's wishes two of Haldane's aides, his chauffeur and his servant, the latter who was 'devoted' to Billy, took him to Corbie where he was laid to rest.

Billy had excelled himself on the Somme. In the build up to the attack he had personally reconnoitred the enemy and taken out patrols over 1,000 yards in front of the British lines. He also escorted one of the brigade's battalions to their jumping-off point to make sure they got it right and then remained in the line of fire to get an accurate assessment of how the fighting had played out. For his example he was posthumously awarded the Victoria Cross and at 25 became the first infantry officer in the Great War to be awarded all three gallantry medals available to him[1].

Old Etonians were still marching south to be thrown into the carnage as July progressed on the Somme. 'The Three Generations' were a group of gentlemen well known in Dumfries. Resident at Spottes Hall, the eldest; the bearded kindly grandfather, Alexander Young-Herries, was 89 years old when war commenced and a widower of some forty years. His son, William, was a Cambridge man who had devoted many years to the militia and then the territorial battalion of the King's Own Scottish Borderers. William had married in 1891 but mourned his young wife almost immediately in 1892 as she died after giving birth to their son, the third of the generations, Alexander Dobree, or 'Alick', Young-Herries. 'Scarcely may his father have borne it' had it not been for the little bundle that she left behind.

Alick's temperament was not darkened by this early tragedy. He was a 'bright and happy little creature' not only doted on by his father and his grandfather but by his beloved Nana, who would wheel him about Edinburgh in his perambulator. As a child Alick's days were regimented by prayers and reading at

Spottes. Conversation on religion was encouraged greatly in his pious house-hold and resulted in a passion for scripture. His faith would carry him through his experiences at the front. 'His trust in Jesus Christ never wavered, even amid the darkness and the horror of the war.' Alick was educated at home until he was eleven under his father's supervision and with as much flexibility as possible 'to ensure that the acquisition of knowledge became a pleasure rather than a chore'. In addition to lessons he would study insects, birds and shells with his father or retreat to the shed with his grandfather for woodwork or to develop photographs.

After a stint at prep school Alick arrived at Eton in 1906 and eventually, after the unfortunate demise of his housemaster, ended up with Mr Conybeare. He claimed that this confident, hardworking, helpful young man never gave him a moment's trouble. Never a classicist, Alick specialised eventually in science and excelled, not surprisingly, in divinity.

At Eton Alick forged a friendship that would last throughout school, uni-versity and then into the abyss of the Great War. Francis Ellicott was the grand-son of a bishop and they were 'thrown together' from the first at school. They studied together, sang together in the musical society, rowed together and even sparred together in the boxing ring. In 1911 they went up to Cambridge together and were at Trinity when war came.

Like his father Alick had ties as a Terrier with the King's Own Scottish Borderers and he was hesitant about returning to Cambridge following the summer holidays in 1914. He believed strongly that it was necessary to resist German arrogance and aggression, and was incensed by the invasion of Belgium. His father let him decide for himself what he should do and so it was that he offered himself for service overseas within days of the declaration of war.

Alick was amongst the first officers to be sent to the front and arrived on the Aisne in September 1914. It was hard for him to marry his religious beliefs with the idea of fighting a war:

> I do feel most strongly that Britain is fighting for her own life. We are not only out as avengers of poor little Belgium, which is quite enough to justify our being here – but we are fighting in defence of our friends and our homes, who will most certainly suffer a worse fate than Belgium if those Germans aren't squashed now. Yet I cannot help thinking war is not Christian.

On 31 October 1914 Alick was sent into Messines on board a bus when the 9th Lancers clung onto it for dear life and then returned home in time for Christmas quite broken down. His worried grandfather hovered over him day and night at Portland where his father was with the reserve battalion of the Borderers. Whilst he was there Ellicott arrived, Alick having secured a commission in the regiment for his friend. On 24 April Frank was married to a sweetheart from their Cambridge days with a reception at the Royal Hotel in Weymouth. The couple were keen to be married before he was sent to war and Alick acted, naturally, as his best man.

A few nights after the wedding Alick was sitting down at dinner with the rest of the Three Generations when an urgent message arrived ordering him back to the front. Acting nonchalantly he put together his belongings and set off towards Boulogne and then into the Ypres area where he found his men at Vlamertinghe. He took up command of his precious B Company, which he found had been whittled down to half strength on the salient. Trench warfare took its toll mentally on Alick. He arrived home on leave with two bullet holes in his tunic but refused to talk about them or how they got there. He was Alick 'but he appeared older, graver but still gentle and humorous'.

It was becoming apparent that, as summer approached, momentous events were in the offing. All leave was stopped, training escalated and twice orders to attack a position at Wailly had been cancelled when they were all but ready to go. It was therefore no surprise when, on 2 July, the battalion was pulled from the lines and put on notice to be ready to march immediately.

Less than two weeks later, unaware that Frank Ellicott had been killed elsewhere on the battlefield, Alick and the 2nd King's Own Scottish Borderers began to move southwards. They marched furiously, carried gratefully part of the way by buses, and arrived south-east of Albert on 17 July. Here they found themselves amongst a huge mass of troops that had been gathered for Rawlinson's big push, now due to take place on 23 July.

Two days later Alick's battalion was on parade when orders came. They were told to make their way up to the lines immediately. Marching past Fricourt and Mametz they made their way towards High Wood, another battered collection of trees and shell holes that lay to the north of Longueval. Their guides, when they finally turned up, began taking them through the darkness to the front lines. All around, the guns raged. 'The far flung duel increased in fury as the night advanced, filling the air with a deafening clamour and lighting up the landscape with lurid flames.' They groped their way along in the dark for nearly 3 miles, past Montauban and across a valley to a front-line trench that lay in between Bazentin-le-Grand and Longueval whilst they were 'nearly shelled to death'.

At 1 a.m. on 20 July Alick made his way down the trench giving his platoon officers their instructions. High Wood lay 1,200 yards ahead in German hands.

That night another brigade was to try to take it. As they did so the Borderers were to attack a road junction that ran away from the site. Alick's would be one of three companies going over the top, across gentle rising slope. When they reached the road they were to dig like mad and establish a trench that could be used as a jumping-off point for the battle that was to follow on the 23rd.

At 3.30 a.m. the signal was given, the barrage lifted and Alick led his men over the top. Their task was a daunting one. They climbed steadily, Alick at the front, whilst the German gunners took potshots at them. They reached the road in the face of intermittent rifle fire and began to dig frantically to establish some form of cover. Alick urged them on. 'His bravery went straight to the hearts of the men.' Grimly they held on to their makeshift trenches till midnight. Alick was prominent in keeping the men going, especially when his company sergeant major was badly hit. Before the gravely injured man was carried to a nearby dressing station, Alick clambered up on to the parapet and made a dash to him to be able to hold his hand and wish him well. At the end of the day he managed to scribble a note off to his father. 'Just a line to report all well. It is most interesting (though pretty energetic) here.'

The time had finally come for Henry Rawlinson's large-scale assault. While it commenced on 23 July, for Alick and his men zero hour would come a few hours earlier. The assault between Delville Wood and High Wood would begin first at 10 p.m. on 22 July so that there would be time to take care of 'Wood Trench', an inconvenient landmark that lay in their way.

At noon on 22 July Alick and his men were told to get ready. As night approached the preliminary bombardment commenced. Alick was to go over in the second wave through a cacophony of noise and darkness, the way intermittently lit by flares and flames. His company ran headlong into heavy shell and machine-gun fire and the assault ultimately ground to a halt as the leading companies of the battalion ran into the back of some Royal Warwickshires in front who had turned on their heels after being exposed and their ranks raked by machine guns. Alick soon arrived on the scene. There were men everywhere. All they could do in the confusion of darkness was drop into a trench and cling on. It appeared that the attack was caving in. Disorganisation was rife. One battalion was not even aware that there was a trench in its way. The bombardment, for which, bear in mind, the gunners had not been given instructions until it began getting dark, had not been effective. The men simply couldn't get forward. As dawn broke orders arrived to fall back to their original front line.

Alick and his men, scattered as they were, for now remained forward. He managed to get a hasty report back to his commanding officer and then waited until he received a message telling him to fall back to a trench 300 yards behind which afforded better cover. Just as dawn was breaking on 23 July they got up to move. Concerned that he might not be taking all his men with him, Alick climbed cautiously out of the congested trench and began heading away from High Wood. He edged along a sunken road that ran close to the firing line, stopping every now and again to drop on to the back edge of the trench to look in and enquire if any B Company men were about. 'It is becoming too clear to be moving about,' he told them. 'We must be getting back.' He rounded up six or so men operating under a Sergeant Evans, all of whom climbed out of the trench and began following him.

Some 120 yards on Alick leaned down again and had just turned his head to be back on his way when a shell exploded level with his waist. Alick fell forward towards the trench with his head resting on the parapet whilst Evans sprinted to him. The men in the trench had begun pulling at his arms and shoulders to get him inside and under cover but Alick was already gone. His bottom half had been blown away.

Mortified the men lowered him into their trench and for the whole of that stifling summer day they covered him with a waterproof sheet and sat watching over his remains. As soon as dusk came they carried him for 2 miles under shellfire in the direction of Mametz. When they arrived, men of the battalion that had slipped away from their duties came out to meet the stretcher bearers. Alick was laid to rest at Dantzig Alley, a cemetery which had recently been started near Mametz, 3 miles from his best friend and fellow OE, Frank Ellicott.

His commanding officer and men were distraught. A few days before Alick's death another officer had remarked that he 'looked after his subalterns like a father, even though some of them look twice his age'. The same man wrote to Alick's father to tell him that his son's display had been faultless, proof 'that the metal is gold and tried in the fire'.

The tenderness and care that he had lavished on those he was responsible for remained with them for the duration. 'My last memory of Alick,' wrote one colleague who had been maimed back in 1915, 'will be a very characteristic one, of the loving care with which he bandaged me and helped me out of the trench when I was wounded.'

By the end of the war, only one of the three generations remained, for Alick's grandfather died in March 1918. Alick's was just one of the lives wasted on 23 July in more badly orchestrated attacks that gained nothing. He was 24 years old, a fraction older than the age his mother had been when she died bringing him into the world.

Notes

1. Walter and Billy Congreve are one of only three sets of fathers and sons to have been awarded the Victoria Cross. Johnnie Gough and his father were another (his uncle also won the award, meaning that their family has won it more times than any other) and the third pair to have the distinction are Field Marshal Lord Roberts and his son Frederick. Thus four of the six men concerned are Old Etonians.

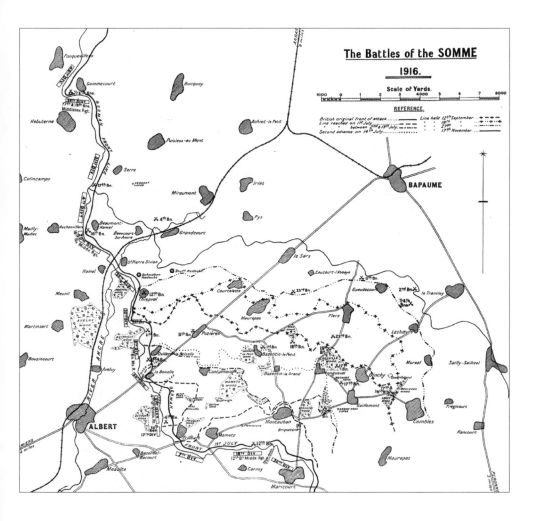

14

'The Gambler's Throw'

By the summer of 1916, the Guards Division in particular was overflowing with OEs who had little experience outside of school. Straight from Eton, they delivered themselves to barracks ready, but not necessarily willing, to fight. Hundreds of boys who had left Eton *since* 1914 were serving in or had already died in the armed services. Hugh MacNaghten was one housemaster finding this incredibly difficult to comprehend. He had seen William Gladstone, grandson of the four-time prime minister of the same name, hovering by the river on leave. He had rowed with the VIII as late as 1916 and with his baby face 'he seemed never to have left at all'.[1]

Another such boy was Henry Lancaster Nevill Dundas. He was 17 when the war began and had always stood out in a crowd. Born in Edinburgh in 1897, his passion was reserved for three aspects of his life: Eton, Scotland and, once he had joined the army, the Guards Division. 'About these things,' he wrote, 'I have no sense of humour.'

He was from the outset a vibrant personality, one of a kind. At two years old, during the Boer War, he would entertain adults by singing 'Rule Britannia' in full (or 'The Absent Minded Beggar' for light relief). Henry liked to shock. One kindly old clerk at Kirkcudbright once asked him how old he was and 4-year-old Henry piped up in the broadest Scotch accent he could muster, 'I'm 65 and drunk every night!' He became a well-known face in Edinburgh. Once he failed to turn up for a French lesson with a tutor and was caught instead joyriding on a milk cart about the streets and shouting instructions to two street urchins doing the driving. On another occasion he wandered away from his guardian and they found him turning the handle of a barrel organ whilst the old man who owned it collected the money. He was a fantastic mimic and his father was utterly baffled one day to pass underneath a window at the family home of Redhall and hear a deep baritone pontificating in a sing-song manner. He found his five-year-old son standing on a table in the nursery, wearing his nurse's nightgown and 'declaiming to an admiring congregation of the servants a sermon in the manner of a parish minister'.

Henry was sent to Horris Hill Preparatory School in Berkshire. His father had loose family ties to Etonian scientific brains such as Jack Haldane and Henry was undoubtedly bright enough to follow them into College at Eton. Indeed he succeeded in making the list of King's Scholars but his parents thought that an Oppidan house, without such a fierce focus on academic achievement, would give their son a broader experience of school life.

Thus in September 1910 Henry entered Hugh Marsden's house. His first years, not unusually, were a trying experience. The elder boys in the house gained some amusement from having Henry sing Harry Lauder songs on demand but Henry had a tendency to mask his self-consciousness by 'forcing himself into the centre of the picture'. He could come off as tactless and on occasion full of himself. 'Exhausting' was a word that one boy used to describe him and several others remarked that he was perfectly likeable, in small doses. His wit and his kindness, though, balanced out his over-exuberant character. Dick Durnford was his classical tutor and a perfect fit. Good natured and patient, he recognised Henry's immense promise beyond his hyperactive nature and lavished much time on him.

As Henry moved through the school and matured into a young man, one school report labelled him as 'exceedingly sharp, almost too sharp for the peace of mind of his Divisional Master (doing the writing), whom he bombards with volleys of incisive and often awkward questions!' The mass exodus caused by the outbreak of war in 1914 pushed Henry to the forefront of the school. He was a competent enough sportsman, representing Eton's fledgling rugby team, and was a member of Pop and an editor of the *Eton College Chronicle*. This he endeavoured to liven up with some sensationalism and sports reports mimicking the cheap press, much to the distress of the Colleger working alongside him. Not a classical scholar in the strictest sense, there was never any doubt, given the influence of his house master, that Henry would choose to specialise in history.

As his departure loomed, Henry knew that he would go to war, although at this point it was just about still a choice rather than a compulsion. He refused to let it cast a shadow on his life at Eton and immersed himself in every facet of school life. Mondays were given over to the meetings of the Scientific Society and on Tuesdays the Shakespeare Society met, his favourite. Thursdays were the Essay Society, Fridays were for Pop debates and Saturday perhaps a lecture from a guest. He was amongst those who created their own magazine, *The Jolly Roger.* 'Of this a master had to be the censor,' scribbling out the quips that went too far with a blue pencil.

In the summer of 1915 Henry's happy existence at Eton was brought to a premature end as he set out for war, putting on hold a history scholarship at Christ Church. 'Well, well, the last letter from the old boy's club,' he wrote at the end of July. 'Tomorrow I tool up to London, dressed as an Old Etonian. Eton never looked more delightful than she does tonight after a week's continuous downpour ... I hope I shall never show myself forgetful of the debt I owe you, darling daddy and mummy for letting me come here ... I can say no more [than] thank you, from the very bottom of my heart.'

There was no military affiliation in Henry's immediate family but he specifically wanted a Guards regiment, for the familiarity of Eton friends, and a Scottish affiliation, so that left one choice; the Scots Guards. It was easy to arrange from school. Since the Guards had been mauled at Loos, the average age of their subalterns had dropped dramatically. For the boys filing out of Eton, the Guards proved to be the most popular destination. It lessened the blow of being wrenched from school. Such were their numbers within the regiments that it became almost a continuation of Eton; the same familiar faces, the same social groups day in and day out. But when they finally made it into battle it was going to be a recipe for heartbreak and tragedy.

Henry joined his regiment at Wellington Barracks in September 1915 at the age of 18½. The thought of going to war did not appal him but he was, in his words, 'rather less enthusiastic about it than I ought to have been'. He began his training in earnest. He spent the winter, thanks to his aptitude for bombing, doing a short course as an instructor at Southfields near Wimbledon and from there he was able to spend much time not only back at Eton but indulging his passion for Gilbert and Sullivan by trawling London suburbs looking for productions and visiting theatres at Wimbledon, Kennington and Hammersmith. He turned 19 in February and was offered a choice of whether he wanted to go out to France immediately or 'wait for warmer weather'. He chose the latter but Henry's reprieve was brief. By Easter he could evade the front no more. It was not until this point, in spring 1916, that he actually underwent any training with the men at Corsham.

There was 'little buoyancy' about his mood when he realised that he was finally 'for it'. At the end of May Henry departed Waterloo Station with a handful of fellow OEs. The young subalterns on their way to the Guards Division were clueless as to what lay in wait for them. The division, they would discover, was extremely introverted. A young Guards officer fresh out of Eton and newly arrived on the front would have next to no contact with any non-Guardsmen. The Guards were inspired by a powerful *esprit de corps* that would not be diluted by the founding of numerous additional battalions as the war progressed. This would help Henry settle in, but for now, even their own formation was a mystery to him and his companions. Henry knew who was in charge of the division, and who commanded the two Scots Guards battalions, but as for brigadiers or which battalions would be operating near him, the whole thing was a 'sealed book'.

At the end of June 1916 the 1st Scots Guards were at Hooge, relieving elements of Canadian units that had been slaughtered in Sanctuary Wood. When the Guards began taking casualties of their own Henry was abruptly summoned to help replace them. Travelling on a night train to Abbeville he cleaned his teeth at Calais, had lunch at Hazebrouck, plodded the last leg to Poperinghe and then 'started off along what is now probably the most famous road in the world'. Henry found Miles Barne, an older OE in temporary charge of the battalion, and joined B Company fresh out of the line.

When Henry joined his battalion the whole Guards Division had just come back from practising for an attack north of Ypres but the stalemate on the Somme meant that everything elsewhere was shelved. Henry found his first experiences of the trenches rather thrilling; the constant shelling especially left its mark on him. 'You are absolutely helpless, as to go into a dugout is merely to exchange burial alive for disintegration and burial dead.' But the biggest impression left on him was the difference between the reality of life at the front and the 'ludicrous optimism' of people in England. This optimism was painted on to 'our lads in the trenches' by the press. He had seen very little of it himself. The mood was not necessarily depressed, but large swathes of men foresaw no end in sight.

Eton remained, thanks to the presence of so many contemporaries in the immediate vicinity, at the forefront of Henry's mind as the Guards were sent back to rest. As the the Battle of the Somme began, to the north he reported perfect blue skies. It all reminded him of summer at school. 'Any water – even a canal – reminds me of the river and any trees – even shell-torn – of Upper Club[1]'. A particular friend, Christopher Barclay, had joined the Coldstream Guards and Henry found plenty of time to pop along and see him. Talking 'Eton shop' on long walks was their favourite pastime and at the end of the month they even had a party, courtesy of brigade headquarters, complete with a band. When they played the 'Boating Song' Henry nearly wept. They danced till midnight, the guns booming away to the south, 'flares stabbing the night all around'; and yet the officers of four of the Guard's battalions could forget everything, even the possibility of being summoned to join in the show 'and revel as at a children's party'.

August saw yet more misery for Haig, Rawlinson and the men on the Somme. On 27 July Delville Wood and Longueval were finally secured thanks in part to an obscenely concentrated artillery bombardment. Rawlinson was making negligible progress. Control by seemed to have devolved completely out of his hands, resulting in a series of messy, disjointed attacks directed by his subordinates that were costing Britain dearly. Douglas Haig was determined that this had to stop, but this did not prevent him putting unrealistic expectations on his generals in terms of what he expected them to achieve whilst they pulled back on the obscene wastage of manpower.

By September, seventy-six Old Etonians were already dead on the Somme but the bloodshed was far from over. It had been resolved that High Wood, Ginchy, just to the south-east of Delville Wood, and Guillemont, a little to the south-west of that, would all have to be taken before an all-out offensive could be made on what had originally been the German third line. Since mid August, at Haig's behest, the Fourth Army commander had been planning the attack. Haig was still demanding a decisive breakthrough. He wanted the ridge behind Les Boeufs seized then, as soon as the gap was opened, a mass of cavalry would flood into it. Yet again, as on 1 July, Haig was pressing Rawlinson to take multiple lines in one hit. Guillemont fell at the beginning of the month and Rawlinson ordered a number of attacks on the Ginchy area to prepare for his big push.

The Guards were transferred to Rawlinson's army and began moving on 19 August towards Albert. The train carrying the 1st Scots Guards crawled south. 'To give added piquancy' they were supposed to be on a special tactical train described in Henry's handbooks as being used for rushing troops from one part of the country to another. Their move was not a surprise. Ever since the 'biff' on the Somme had begun the Guards were certain that they would be destined for it at some stage. 'The atmosphere,' Henry wrote, 'is rather like that in a music hall when the star turn is just coming on … some fun I should imagine.' Evelyn Fryer, another OE serving with the Grenadier Guards after originally enlisting as a private in the Honourable Artillery Company, was sorely disappointed that thus far the Guards had played no part in the big event to the south. Enthusiasm would be too strong a word but the Guards were honestly pleased to get away from the dreaded Salient.

The situation on the Somme at the beginning of September was vague for the troops being fed into the battle, not only as to what they would face but in terms of where they physically stood themselves. They arrived with map references for trenches to guide them but they were often futile. 'The almost entire absence of landmarks caused them to be meaningless.' Battalions were turning up to what they thought was the correct location, only to find that they were hundreds of yards from where they were supposed to be. The scrappy nature of the attempts to take German positions meant that nobody was ever really sure of the overall situation, which caused problems for artillery and for staff trying to manage the troops; doubly so when the troops themselves could not point to their location on a map.

Communications were dire. Messages went awry, for it could take a runner an hour to reach brigade HQ in one sector and many became casualties in the shellfire that swept the whole area. It was not as if they could pick up a telephone either, for the cables were being continually destroyed by artillery. These difficulties and the conflicting reports received by the staff 'were responsible for the vague and often inaccurate instructions which were given to the infantry during this difficult period'.

Troops continued to accumulate in the area behind Ginchy in large numbers for this push. It was, as Henry put it, a last ditch attempt, 'the gambler's throw' as far as the Somme campaign was concerned. Another young Guards subaltern arriving at Happy Valley was a future prime minister, Maurice 'Harold' MacMillan, and he thought that the most extraordinary thing about modern war was the desolation and emptiness of it all. 'One can look for miles and miles and see no human being.' But burrowed into the ground like rats there were hundreds of thousands of men. Harold was 21 when he first left for France. The son of a publisher he was another Colleger who had arrived at Eton from Summer Fields. Rubbish at games, he was sharp enough but struggled at school until his mother finally withdrew him in 1909 after three years. Having gone up to Oxford, Harold was suffering from appendicitis when war broke out and he had to wait until the end of 1914 to be able to gain a commission in the King's Royal Rifle Corps. His eyesight was a worry but he found a medical officer that was sufficiently lenient. Like Yvo Charteris he orchestrated a swap into the Grenadier Guards. This did embarrass him but 'was it so very reprehensible?' He asked years later, 'The only privilege I and many others like me sought was that of getting ourselves killed and wounded as soon as possible'

At Loos, in the action that cost Robin Blacker his life, Harold received a gunshot wound to the hand and was sent home. When he returned to the front in April 1916 it was to join the 2nd Battalion of the regiment. He was wounded again at the height of summer whilst out on patrol when the Germans spotted him and began chucking bombs in his direction. One blew off his spectacles. 'I thought of you all in the second that the bomb exploded in my face,' he told his family. The following morning he felt as if he had the mother of all hangovers but he refused to be sent home and re-joined his battalion in time for the September advance.

Pip Blacker arrived in the area with the 4th Battalion of the Coldstream Guards, a unit of 'Pioneers' who, rather than being a fighting unit, took care of all manner of battlefield duties to make life easier for the other battalions. He found himself in Happy Valley. 'Why Happy? We wondered when we got there.' He only realised just how many troops were present when night fell. 'The slope opposite was covered with men ... They lay on their waterproof sheets, or huddled around fires. At first there was a medley of voices but they fell into choruses and finally into unison and that wide valley resounded with song ... The tempo was slow, the prevailing mood of nostalgic melancholy.' Pip sat and wondered how many of the voices would still be alive the same time next week.

The area itself was filthy; buried under a blanket of flies. It resembled a moonscape. 'You can't imagine anything like it,' remarked Henry Dundas. The entire vicinity was a mass of shell holes 'literally merging one into the other'. Guillemont, he reported, had just simply ceased to exist 'except as a scarred wound'. Ginchy was no better and 'My hat!' he exclaimed. 'The sights ... there ought to be photographs taken of these battlefields and shown in every town or every country in the world and then could the world go to war? I doubt it.' Harold MacMillan was disgusted by the smell of dead bodies lying in piles about the place but there was military junk everywhere too. All around were dumps of material and ammunition, mostly derelict. 'The wastage must be appalling,' remarked Henry, his eye ever on the political side of things. 'But after all, they don't often get a chance to spend £5,000,000 a day in Whitehall.'

In preparing for the upcoming push, Pip's route carried him along a sunken road that had been a site of fierce resistance by the Germans. The fallen defenders still lay there. As he walked past the bloated corpses Pip could hear intermittent buzzing noises. He was baffled until he saw flies emerge through their open mouths. 'A good thing,' he remarked, 'that the poor devils are well and truly dead and cannot see themselves.' When he got to Trônes Wood to assist with tidying up some trenches a literal cloud hung over them. They were unsure of how seriously to take the threat of gas. They were told that the Germans had been releasing phosgene, which apparently had 'a sweetish, somewhat repellent smell'. The air inside the wood made their eyes run. The site was so overrun with mangled foliage and tree stumps that moving about made wearing a gas mask impossible on account of restrictions to vision and movement. 'One did not lightly put on one's gas mask, or give the order that others should do so.' Every time though that Pip passed a dressing station and saw gagging, blue men he was reminded of what would happen if his judgement failed.

By 12 September all the battalions had been issued with bombs, sandbags, rockets, flares, wire cutters and just about every other bit of battlefield paraphernalia that the army could muster. As the day crept ever closer they all visited Carnoy in turn to put their personal belongings in storage. The commander of the Guards called a conference for his brigadiers and senior officers to explain the plans for the advance.

Born in 1893 Oliver Lyttelton was the son of famed cricketer Alfred and the nephew of Edward, headmaster of Eton throughout his time there. Another of Samuel Lubbock's boys, he was bright; 'too clever and too old [for] many average Eton boys'. Raymond Asquith once said of him that his chief defect was 'telling rather long and moderately good stories and laughing hysterically long before he [came] to the point'.

Like Lyttelton men before him, Oliver left Eton and went up to Trinity College, Cambridge. At the outbreak of war he was originally commissioned into the Bedfordshire Regiment where he patrolled the seafront at Dovercourt looking for spies. Along with two Eton friends, including 'Bobbety' Cranbourne, Oliver lasted a month before they all requested a transfer. A period of panic followed until Lord Salisbury, Bobbety's father, raised hell and they were moved to the Grenadier Guards in time for Christmas. Oliver went to France at the beginning of 1915 and eventually became the adjutant of the 3rd Battalion, which was now preparing for a leading role in Rawlinson's last-ditch Somme effort before winter kicked in.

There were four lines detailed on the day's objectives. For the Guards the first, the Green, was 1,000 yards past Ginchy and would require them to swing their line around so that they were facing properly east instead of north-east. Then in stages they would be attempting to advance on towards Brown, Blue and finally the Red line running between Morval and Les Boeufs.

Oliver Lyttelton was to go over first with his battalion and capture the green line. 'Our furthest objectives,' he wryly remarked, 'as marked on our operational maps, were distant, and we cynically supposed that few of us would be alive to reach them.' He had been out reconnoitring the assault trenches from which they were to advance. Zero hour would come at dawn on 15 September.

On 13 September the Guards were still trying to improve their positions but attempts were 'hurriedly and inadequately organised' and ended in failure. Of one company of Irish Guards that went out only thirty returned. Elsewhere Harold MacMillan's battalion attempted to drive the Germans out of orchards to the north of Ginchy, but were forced to concede defeat and just start digging in where they were at the cost of another hundred men.

Whilst one OE was waiting to go into the lines he woke up one morning to see all about them vast looking shapes covered in tarpaulins. The men were completely baffled. It was not until some days later that they learned these were the first tanks, 'mysterious vehicles', Pip Blacker called them. There was a buzz of excitement surrounding them and what they might do.

The day before the big advance was relatively serene. Harold MacMillan was still in the lines, waiting to be relieved whilst the Germans shelled his battalion heavily. One sergeant was mortally wounded, another buried alive and dug out by his colleagues. In the evening the assaulting troops arrived and Harold returned to Ginchy to receive rations and rum. It was a bitterly cold night and all of the men had left their greatcoats in Carnoy. Pip Blacker was stumbling about Bernafray Wood with a platoon of men, 'tidying up' a trench overnight ready for use the next day. Henry Dundas was to miss the show. Ill with a crippling stomach complaint for the two weeks or so leading up to 15 September, he arrived back a fraction too late to take part and found himself kept back from rushing up to join the others. He was going to have to sit and wait. Evelyn Fryer was also one of a number of his battalion kept back. He sat dejectedly at Carnoy listening to rumours of disaster and grew progressively more miserable as the day went on.

The eve of the assault, 14 September, had been a clear but windy day and Oliver Lyttelton had sat and scrawled what he thought might be his last letter to his mother. At about 11 p.m. the 3rd Grenadiers moved off towards their assembly trenches, up a gentle slope where darkness concealed all of the shell holes bleeding into one another. Tensions ran high. The men, weighed down by equipment, were silent. 'There was a sensation that this slowness was prolonging our last night on earth,' Oliver recalled, 'drawing out our last living hours.'

The battalion took up position and proceeded to dig in a little more for safety but there were not enough front-line trenches to accommodate them all. All fires and lights were to be kept down, anything that might betray their position. As dawn approached they were directed by tape and posts laid out by the Royal Engineers. The line they were to attack was a cramped semi-circle. If the units on each side of Oliver's battalion failed, then their flanks would be left wide open to machine-gun fire from another dreaded German strong-point known as the Quadrilateral; or from trenches on the opposite side. At 4 a.m. Oliver and his men were given sandwiches and rum. Some of them tried to sleep. There was little chatter.

Meanwhile the tanks had begun to move up to their jumping-off points and their distant rumbling could be heard by the Grenadiers as they waited for daylight. Three of these new monsters were to advance with the Guards, beginning on their left and crossing over them as they moved on. At 5 a.m. they were seen moving slowly forward on the left flank but apparently aroused no suspicion and did not attract any German fire. In the bitter cold Oliver blew on his fingernails and downed some more rum. Throughout the night the artillery boomed steadily on in readiness for the attack, but the noise was nothing compared to what happened as daylight approached.

At 6 a.m. the heavy guns started, firing forty shells apiece in quick succession. Twenty minutes later it had just begun to get light. Pip was finishing his work in Bernafray Wood when 'the air went taut in a tidal wave of sound'. The noise pressed down on his eardrums and made him feel dizzy. His senses cut out, it felt as if all five of them had been pushed down into a lower plane of consciousness. 'Standing like mutes' they attempted to use some sort of sign language to communicate and waved their arms about in gestures to make themselves understood.

As the wall of the creeping barrage came down, three Coldstream Guards battalions went over in tandem. This was the first time they had attacked together in their history. Oliver Lyttelton watched in the emerging light as they poured over the top. Men sprawled on to the floor instantly. Then it was his turn. The high-pitched scream of a whistle galvanised him into action and with the rest of his battalion Oliver leapt forward. As he and the Grenadiers went over they hunched forward 'like men walking into a strong wind' braving the gust of bullets. As soon as they emerged over the parapet they were met with the rattle of machine guns. Standing less than a yard away from Oliver the commanding officer took a shot to the thigh and buckled. In front of them the Germans had largely survived the artillery barrage. They lurked in shell holes and now they levelled their rifles at the advancing British troops and began to fire. 'With a hoarse blood cry' which stayed with Oliver for years afterwards the Grenadiers rushed forwards and began attacking with their bayonets. They were fierce, unstoppable, like animals. They staggered on as the German fire intensified against them.

Meanwhile, to the north, Harold MacMillan couldn't explain it but he was certain that he was not going to die that day. He had faced the German guns before and the same couldn't be said of some of his fellow subalterns. He recalled one occasion when a young officer found him just before they went over the top. '[He] cried a little – we were only boys and he behaved very bravely … he knew he'd be killed and he was.' Harold and his men were supposed to move off behind the joint Coldstream rush. The Coldstream were to take the Green line, shifting the direction of the attack, and Harold and his men were then to sit in it until the Irish Guards in turn passed through them to seize the next objective. Whilst in place, they were to form a defensive flank to hold the line if the attack started to disintegrate.

In Bernafray Wood, Pip Blacker had literally no idea what was occurring on the battlefield. 'Conflicting rumours percolated' via wounded men who staggered away from it. Daylight had fully come on when he was given a job to do. Pip and his men were ordered to follow the advance, across the pitted, churned route, and somehow mark out a track of sorts through the battlefield for horse-drawn traffic to get to the new front line. Where this track would go, and when it was ready to come into use was all down to Pip. It was not a happy task, for they would be standing fully in the open; target practice for the German gunners as the battle raged on.

The nature of the attack and attempting to shift the direction of their advance as they went forward was causing bewilderment amongst the Guards battalions. On the left of Oliver Lyttelton, one of the Coldstream battalions fell under the British creeping barrage. In the confusion they became lost in the smoke and began swerving north instead of north-east as planned, causing a big swing to the left in the line. The other two Coldstream battalions followed and the whole attack began to veer off track. Oliver Lyttelton's Grenadiers followed in turn and a gap opened just north of the road running from Ginchy to Les Boeufs. With the heavy machine-gun fire scattering the Guardsmen it grew even more chaotic and the units became hopelessly jumbled. Rather than proper platoons there were now smaller groups fighting their way frantically forward and paying little attention to the wider situation.

The most problematic area was a sunken road full of Guards to the north of Ginchy, which accounted for swathes of various Coldstream officers and men. They threatened to fold until John Campbell, the OE commanding the 2nd Battalion, rallied his troops with his hunting horn. It seemed ludicrous to those around him, but he had taken it into battle with the aim of using it for just this purpose in the confusion of the fight. He and his combined force swept forward over the open ground towards the imaginary Green Line and were in position by 7.15 a.m. – albeit too far north along it because of the skewed advance. They had strayed into the area belonging to a division that included Foss Prior and the 8th Rifle Brigade towards Delville Wood.

To the left of the Guards, Foss had returned to the front having finished recuperating from his Hooge wound with lots of time spent at Eton. His battalion was preparing to attack to the east of Delville Wood and with Arthur Sheepshanks he had been out reconnoitring the terrain ready for the attack. They were to advance up a gentle slope and take a line titled 'Switch Trench' at the top of a low rise. Foss had taken one of the battalion's leading companies out over the parapet and charged towards the German lines. Advancing up the hill towards Switch Trench at the head of the battalion the German artillery resistance became heavier and heavier. Jumping into the trench they found that it was still stuffed with Germans. They seized it at bayonet point and moved on. Unfortunately some of the Germans who had surrendered suddenly began attacking Foss' men from behind. Sandwiched in between enemy troops the 7th Rifle Brigade arrived and messy hand-to-hand fighting soon ensued as they tried to even up the score. By 10.30 a.m. the battalion's commanding officer had been wounded by shrapnel and Sheep took over command of the 8th Rifle Brigade. They had reached and taken their first objective but it was costly. Inside Switch Trench, Sheep could only count five fellow officers, a medical officer and about 150 men.

Swept away in the moment, along with the Grenadiers beside him, Oliver Lyttelton was 'fighting mad'. He and his men rushed the summit at the top of the slope they had targeted and paused to take a breath whilst they rounded up prisoners. Looking about, Oliver could see that all of the battalions had become frightfully mixed up. He had some Grenadiers, some Coldstream and some Irish Guardsmen. He could see no other officer so he rounded up about a hundred men close to him and put himself in charge. He organised his ramshackle group. 'Get this parapet straight,' he ordered, 'and dig like hell.' While they were attempting to mop up a powerful enfilading fire was turned on them from the direction of the Quadrilateral, and although they now had some cover two or three of his men quickly became casualties.

At this moment, a German doctor emerged from a nearby dugout, escorted by some of Oliver's men and 'blinking in the sunlight'. Oliver grabbed his opportunity to find out more about their position. 'Do you speak English … where is that fire coming from?' The man pointed to the Red Cross on his arm. 'I am a non-combatant and I do not know.' Oliver pulled out his revolver and absurdly threatened to shoot him. At this the doctor promptly burst out laughing. 'I am quite sure you will do nothing of the kind.' Oliver couldn't help smiling at his own silly threat. 'Get out of here,' he said and watched as the German scrambled up the back of the trench. 'I kicked him not very hard in the behind to restore my self respect.' The doctor merely grinned as he made off. Oliver later learned that he had spent the rest of the day down in the valley under the same heavy fire as Pip Blacker, tending to the wounded with nothing but the stash of field dressings that he had on him. 'A brave man.'

Harold MacMillan by now had gone over the top too. After the first half an hour they had got through the worst of the fierce German artillery barrage. Harold himself had been slightly wounded in the knee but refused point blank to turn back, waiting till there was a halt and then binding it up himself. They halted for a second time at about 8.20 a.m. and found that they were being held up by Germans in a 500-yard stretch of uncleared trench, which they attempted to bomb and rush.

Communications were dire and having despatched pigeons backwards and forwards the fact that the attack in this area managed to retain any kind of clarity was down to an officer named 'Crawley' De Crespigny. Insisting on going about in his forage cap and not a helmet he was to follow Harold MacMillan's battalion, but having found no sign of them he decided that they had already moved on to the next objective and decided to carry out his original orders. He therefore proceeded to the Green Line.

It soon became apparent when they reached it that the area was still rife with isolated Germans, who subjected them to a hail of bullets from a trench and from their open flanks as soon as they began to move forward. They managed, however, to drive back the Germans and rushed the Green Line. When they got there, instead of finding the missing Coldstream Guards, De Crespigny found Germans, lots of Germans shooting at them from all directions. Thinking that they were about to come across their own men they had been in the wrong formation and took heavy casualties. Pushing on though they came into contact with Oliver Lyttelton's battalion and managed to strengthen the right flank of the Guards Division.

Elsewhere, Oliver had noticed that some Coldstream Guards were trying to come up on his side. They appeared to be pinned back by machine guns and so he decided to try to help. He grabbed two sergeants and a few stray men with four light machine guns, Lewis guns. Together they all crawled out of their new line and tried to lay down a covering fire. It proved a thankless task. Never again would he trust a Lewis gun because he could see them having no effect at all. Leaving his little band with plenty of ammunition Oliver crawled back to try to find someone with a proper machine gun.

Pip Blacker meanwhile had made it into no-man's-land and begun work on his track. On their way he and his men found a wounded officer of Henry Dundas' battalion and two quivering, unhurt Germans whose nerves had gone. They appeared to have done all they could to help the Scots Guards officer and so Pip and his orderly stopped to share some ration biscuits with them 'which they ate like starving animals'.

They moved off and a short time later had begun marking out their track with the help of another Old Etonian, Dormer Treffry, a 39-year-old Cornish subaltern. Together they were putting out pickets when the German artillery began potting at them. The first shells hit at a harmless distance some 100 yards away, the second lot screamed over their heads and burst at less than half that distance. The next flurry was right on target.

Pip had been standing some 20 yards from Treffry and as he threw himself on to the floor he looked up just in time to see a shell burst right under the elder man's feet. Treffry was flipped into the air 'like a shot rabbit' and Pip watched his legs spin as if he were doing a cartwheel. Before he had properly registered in his own mind what had happened he was on his feet and running towards him. He had a sick feeling in his stomach and all that he could think was, 'What am I going to see in the next ten seconds?'

Poor Treffry was lying on his back. One of his legs had been almost severed, his femur protruding into the air, and the other was bent back at an awkward angle. Worst of all, his abdomen had been torn open and his intestines had spilled out. Pip saw immediately that there was no hope, but his fellow officer was still conscious. In his head a plan was forming: pick him up, get him over the ridge to help. But then another thought occurred to him. Would it not be kinder to just put him out of his misery?

As they tried to lift him Treffry was trying to speak to them. Pip leaned over and 'in an almost inaudible voice' Treffry croaked, 'Get them out of it. Get out of it yourself. Leave me here.' More shells exploded around them, one just a few feet over their heads. The corporal kneeling beside Pip told him later that if he hadn't been leaning down to hear his fellow OE's words then it would have taken his head from his shoulders.

Together the two of them managed to get the mortally wounded Treffry on to a stretcher and they began to carry him. Pip took the head end because it meant he could face away and he wouldn't have to look at his mutilated body. He had completely forgotten about the artillery bombardment until they began walking. One shell hit a few yards away, plunging into the soil before it detonated and sending up a column of earth high above them. Mud rained down on them and on Treffry. They lowered him for a few moments and Pip sincerely hoped that the wounded man had lost consciousness, but as the last bit of earth splattered on to him Pip saw Treffry shift his head and heard him muttering.

Oliver Lyttelton was still in search of that machine gun when he wandered along a trench and into another OE, Lieutenant Colonel Guy Baring, commanding the 1st Coldstream Guards and looking forlornly for his battalion. 'I've just been trying to give them some covering fire,' Oliver told him. Baring was adamant that he was going to go to join them and began trying to climb out of the trench. 'Not that way, sir,' Oliver pleaded. 'Go round a little, you will get hit there.' He continued to plead but to no avail. Baring clambered up on to the parapet where Oliver heard a bullet strike him and he caught his body as Baring fell back dead in his arms.

Immediately afterwards Oliver, still in his quest for an elusive machine gun, came across a Brigadier John Campbell sitting in another shell hole. This modest abode was the site of his headquarters and there he sat, still with his hunting horn, blowing on it intermittently to Oliver's astonishment. He was overflowing with enthusiasm. He beckoned Oliver over to him and at once they commenced arguing about where they were. Campbell was sure that they had reached the third objective and now occupied the Blue Line on their maps. Oliver was certain they still hadn't progressed past the first, the Green. It was not surprising that the officers were baffled. The maps they carried had been issued a day or so before the battle and they were hugely. inaccurate Eventually Oliver managed to convince Campbell that he was right and that the brigadier was nowhere near as far forward as he had anticipated. Campbell was defiant and recognised that to stop here meant imminent failure. 'Those bastards in that redoubt are holding us up,' he barked. Then came his orders. 'Go and get a few men and bomb them out.'

Having bound up his wounded leg, Harold MacMillan had now acquired a Lewis gun and was on his way to find a use for it when he felt a bullet pierce his left thigh. He threw himself into a shell hole, shouted to an NCO to take over, and that was that. He lay there for the rest of the morning, 'doggo' in the summer weather. Another bullet had drained his water bottle and so, with a dry throat, he read a copy of Aeschylus' *Prometheus Unbound* in Greek that he'd stuffed in his pocket. Doubtless the lead character, a champion of humanity and civilisation, would have been appalled at the man-made carnage going on around Harold. The battle continued to rage and men ran backwards and forwards past him. He played dead whenever Germans appeared. By lunchtime his hole had been blown in twice by shells a few yards off and the pain in his leg had become much more severe. He took half a grain of morphia and there on the battlefield he took a two-hour nap until some fellow Grenadiers came by and helped him to safety.

Oliver Lyttelton was no idiot. The task assigned to him by Brigadier General Campbell was suicidal. 'But needs must when you get an order' and so off he went to collect a dozen or so men with a supply of bombs and they commenced chucking them down the trench in question to try to flush out the enemy. They progressed some 40 yards before he heard a mass of footsteps stampeding towards him. He shouted an order to mount their Lewis gun. The first German to rush round the corner was shot down at point-blank range despite throwing his arms in the air. Suddenly eighty or ninety more arrived, all with their hands up, seemingly oblivious to the fact that they outnumbered Oliver and his men more than seven to one. In less than an hour Oliver, despite his impossible task, had reported back to Campbell in his shell hole. 'The redoubt is cleared, sir, and I have captured about a hundred prisoners.' 'By God!' Campbell exclaimed, 'that's the best thing I've seen done in this war. Damn me if I don't get you a VC for that!' Oliver informed him that the Germans had all had their hands up already. 'My VC vanished.' Nonetheless, the Guards had in part reached the Brown Line, their second objective, and now they began to consolidate their position.

Looking about for something further to do, Oliver decided to try to attack the next objective with the hundred men that he had originally put together. Despite the fact that the timed British barrage had long since crept out of contact, there seemed to be great confusion amongst the Germans and Oliver thought he might be able to 'pick something up cheap'. He discovered a communication trench leading away from the line to the east and took his men along it. Chancing on a practically undefended position they had made it to within sight of the enigmatic Red Line; the last of the four objectives for the day. Les Boeufs lay ahead, within reach, but with only one hundred men and no support on either side he began fashioning a defensive position and sent a message back for help. Relinquishing command to a major who arrived on the scene, Oliver hoped that with a battalion they might take the village.

An hour passed whilst the sun beat down on them. Oliver was distraught. It seemed to him that they had the chance to take the initiative. He watched through a telescope as the German gunners calmly packed up and left. He watched bodies of infantry retiring. 'I was sure that if we had even a brigade handy, we could go for a mile or two without a casualty.' Another hour passed. Then another and another. Unknown to Oliver, a further attack was 'out of the question'. All the Guards battalions active that day had been heavily engaged. Three quarters of their officers were down and two thirds of the men. Finally the Germans re-took the initiative and several hundred of them rushed his mixed body of Guardsmen and jumped into the trench.

Oliver fired all the ammunition from his revolver straight at them. It was utter confusion. One German knelt down and levelled a rifle at him from 5 yards away. Oliver pathetically threw his revolver at the man's head. Luckily the man thought it was a bomb, dropped his rifle and covered his head with his arms. The situation was now hopeless as far as proceeding with the attack was concerned. All hopes of glory and the Red Line were gone. His men being 'hopelessly outnumbered', Oliver scrambled out of the back of the trench and began blowing his whistle to signal a retreat.

For all Oliver's best efforts, little progress had been made on the flanks and he and the other surviving officers were ordered to stand fast and put their lines into a good state of defence. He was sent back to find John Ponsonby to report on what he had seen. Oliver found the brigadier at his headquarters; an old trench with some camouflage thrown over it. He made his report and downed a glass of port whilst Ponsonby joked about a bullet in the seat of Oliver's trousers. He himself had not even noticed it. 'He asked me which way I was facing when I got it.' Joking aside, Ponsonby told him to take a nap for a couple of hours under the table in his dugout. Oliver fell asleep instantly.

The men of the Guards Division, according to Henry Dundas, were 'simply gun fodder'. He would not forget Guillemont, Ginchy in a hurry. He claimed bitterly that 'the dear ones at home in England', preoccupied by Zeppelins over Hertfordshire,[3] would forget those names in a heartbeat. There were bodies absolutely everywhere, 'awful, grinning, greenish black faces with their staring sightless eyes and yellow teeth ... [with the] awful mottled wax-like pallor of the newly fallen corpse'. Harold MacMillan was similarly disgusted. The act of death on a battlefield might, he thought, be a noble and glorious one 'but the actual symptoms are, in these terrible circumstances, revolting only and horrid'.

That night Pip Blacker could not sleep. They had managed to get Treffry to a young medical officer who took one look at him and said it was hopeless. There was nothing to do but put him to sleep and wait for the end. 'I begged him to pump in all the morphia that he could spare.' But Treffry had a tough constitution and did not die till nightfall. Pip heard that as the Cornishman had marched out of Bernafray Wood on 15 September he had told a sergeant that he was convinced that he would die. Pip tossed and turned throughout the night following that awful September morning. 'I could not banish the persistent images ... there he was ... happy, then his broken body.' It was as if he were looking at a photograph album of him. The middle-aged volunteer who had 'lost his sparkle' at Ypres and his life on the Somme wouldn't leave Pip alone.

Henry erroneously believed that the Guards Division was ready for their curtain call as far as the Somme was concerned. 'The Great Biff is over,' he wrote home. His battalion of the Scots Guards had gone in about 750 strong and came out with just 142 men. 'To intensify the general jolliness of the situation', the weather then turned on them completely.

Harold MacMillan was carried by fellow Grenadiers to a doctor who sent him off for further treatment with another officer. The route was being shelled so they dispensed with the stretcher bearers so as not to put them at risk and decided to try to walk. They got separated and Harold found his way out of danger. 'Then I was safe, but alone and absolutely terrified because there was no need to show off anymore, no need to pretend ... then I was very frightened ... I do remember the sudden feeling – you went through a whole battle for two days ... suddenly there was nobody there ... you could cry if you wanted to.' He collapsed into a ditch and lay there until some Seaforth Highlanders found him and moved him on again.

'Having all one's friends killed makes one rather bitter', Henry raged in the aftermath of his introduction to war. 'And then one sees 180,000 are employed in the air defences of Great Britain. Stout fellows. One Zeppelin [taken down] in two years ... Jolly good ... and the filthy press and the damned people go on as if it were the biggest thing in the whole war.' Henry had seen whole swathes of his friends and fellow OEs fall in a single day. In fact, 15 September 1916 was the costliest day of the war for Eton College, with twenty-one former pupils wiped out in less than twenty-four hours. It was 'perfectly heart-rending.' 'I should like to have it pointed out to me where all the honour and glory lies,' Henry raged. 'It is curiously elusive.'

In the 2nd Coldstream Guards only two officers were unhit and it was the same in the 3rd Battalion. In the 2nd Irish Guards ten officers were out of action and in Oliver Lyttelton's battalion, the figure was even higher. Seventeen officers were killed, wounded or missing. The high concentration of Etonians amongst the Guards battalions meant that Henry could reel off whole lists of those he knew. He had counted amongst his friends at Eton Robin Blacker and now Willie Edmonstone, another of their friends and the boy who had suggested that Robin transfer to the Guards, was also dead. Very tall, shy and reserved, 'young as he was when war broke out, he wanted to go at once.' He was killed leading his company when a shell burst in between him and one of his sergeants. He was still 19.

The worst reminder of the loss befell the likes of Henry and his fellow survivors when they were sent out on to the battlefield to lay to rest those bloated, grinning corpses, their friends. He helped miserably to bury the body of the 2nd Coldstream Guards' adjutant and eight men who lay strewn nearby. 'Not very jolly.' Evelyn Fryer was sent out for a day to inter as many as he could find in front of Ginchy. The weather had been hot and the bodies were almost jet black. They buried some 200 men, the Germans outnumbering their own fallen friends. Henry stood and watched in the pouring rain as the body of Guy Baring was buried at Fricourt, 'a melancholy spectacle'.[2] They had also found the body of one of their own, a Scots Guards OE, and had set about making a cross for him. 'Poor old Tim and Willie and Bunny Pease and Lionel Neame and a hundred others.'

Etonian sorrow was not limited to the Guards Division by any means. During the 8th Rifle Brigade's advance Foss Prior had fallen wounded. He was in the process of being patched up when he was hit again, this time fatally. Although he had had to assume command of the battalion, Arthur Sheepshanks was utterly determined that his fellow Eton master would not lie exposed on the battlefield or end up in an unmarked grave. He rounded up some volunteers and he and these men scoured the area under fire until they found him. Foss was saved from anonymity and thanks to his brave friend and Eton colleague, one of the last of the original officers of the 8th Rifle Brigade lies in Bernafray Wood Cemetery.

'Every successive minute' of his war had been an increasing burden on this young man who never believed that he belonged in uniform. Nonetheless he had volunteered to fight alongside his fellow Eton masters. They realised just how much of a sacrifice his participation demanded of him when he took a commission in 1914. Another reluctant schoolmaster and OE had gone with him, Shrewsbury's Evelyn Southwell. Both had followed George Fletcher's example in going to war, no matter how unsuited they thought they were, and in a little over a year both had shared his fate.

Over 160 Etonians now lay dead on the Somme; thirty-eight of them without a grave and destined to be commemorated on the Thiepval Memorial. Seventeen OEs had been buried in Guards Cemetery, Les Boeufs alone. That is to say nothing of the likes of Guy Cholmeley, who had been shipped maimed to England with the threat of death still hanging over them. Attempts to force the German Army into submission on the Western Front in 1916 had now absolutely failed. Winter was about to intervene. Attacks continued until mid November when large-scale assaults were shelved. As had been apparent to Henry Dundas from the moment he arrived in Flanders and to those at the front with him, this was no place for blind optimism. The war was not over. They had not yet even suffered the worst that it could throw at them. The whole sorry mess was now set to continue at least into 1917, pulling more and more of his young schoolmates into action with him.

Notes

1. William Herbert Gladstone was killed with the Coldstream Guards in 1918 at 20 years old. He was buried at Sanders Keep Military cemetery near Havrincourt.
2. The name of one of the playing fields at Eton.
3. The newspapers at home were much preoccupied with the downing of a Zeppelin at Cuffley, Hertfordshire, on 2 September.
4. Lieutenant Colonel the Hon. Guy Victor Baring is buried at Citadel New Military Cemetery, Fricourt.
5. 2nd Lieutenant Evelyn Southwell was also killed on 15 September with the 9th Rifle Brigade. He is commemorated on the Thiepval Memorial.

15

'The Abomination of Desolation'

At the end of 1916 Europe was tired of war; the home front as well as the fighting men. Everyone was feeling the strain. But the decisive break had not come and an increasing number of nations faced another year at arms.

Henry Dundas' mind was still on fallen friends and colleagues. As the cold set in one day he went for a wander through the cemetery at Corbie. He took note of the graves of two OEs including Billy Congreve. 'What a record! VC, DSO, MC … and within an ace of becoming a Brigadier at 25. Incredible!' Impressed as he was by Billy's contribution to the war effort, Henry was most drawn to a desolate little patch where a handful of Germans who had died in British hands had been hastily buried. 'Poor Fritz Kolner of the 2nd Grenadier Regiment. I can pity him almost as much as John MacDonald of the [artillery] who lies a few ft off.' The fact that he was German did not bother Henry in the slightest. 'It is impossible to blame the individual for the sins of the nation … Those at the top make [wars] and profit by them, but the rank and file who bear the burden of it all – what do they get? Nothing.' Pip Blacker was still having nightmares about Treffry and his last mumbled words. His parents too had had about as much as they could stand. With Robin gone and Pip in danger they could not face going home to Vane Tower and had settled in Brittany while the war lasted. 'This war is *not* going to end this year,' Pip assured them at the end of 1916. 'Next spring or summer we will have more big offensives and more colossal losses. *It is useless to hope.*'

Although the Battle of the Somme ended officially in mid November, Douglas Haig wanted pressure sustained on the enemy. For the Allies, as always, the emphasis was on driving the Germans back from the territory they had occupied and over their own borders. Haig still coveted his Flanders offensive, and this was being planned for the summer, but General Nivelle, now commanding the French, had very different ideas. He began planning for a massive push down on the Aisne and the Chemin des Dames in April. For Haig this was happily removed from the usual French determination to ask for more and greater British attacks. However, Nivelle would need the British to take over some of his own trenches to free the men in them for his attack and he wanted a diversionary attack in the British sector. It may have been planned as a diversion, but the Battle of Arras would be a huge undertaking for the British Army.

The Germans by no means intended to be idle. They dreaded the wasteful attrition that had characterised 1916 on the Western Front. They began putting their heart and soul into developing defensive doctrine, coming up with the idea of a more flexible front line that would not require the sort of manpower to cling desperately to it that had cost them dearly during the past year.

Richard William Byrd Levett did not have the kind of constitution as a boy that would have convinced anyone at Eton that he was cut out for life as a soldier. Born in 1897, when he went up to Eton it was to join his cousin Jacinth, who was like a brother to him. He arrived in January 1911 but his inability to get involved on the playing fields did not impact on his happiness at school. He was fit enough throughout his time at Eton to involve himself in the OTC and he developed a burgeoning interest in photography, getting special permission to photograph the chapel and other restricted areas. History was a passion too and the Vice Provost gave him leave to rummage about in College Library. 'Dick' was ecstatic when he found copies of two letters that Charles I wrote mentioning a distant ancestor, William Levett, a page who had ultimately stood on the scaffold next to the condemned king.

Dick was yet another Etonian who was at Mytchett Farm in July 1914. He was 17 and contemplated leaving Eton at Christmas although he acknowledged he was on the young side. He had been to a doctor to see whether he was likely to get through a medical but evidently the answer was negative. '*Everyone*' was departing, so he said and he was dreading 1915 when he would be quite lonely without all his friends. Not having found his way into a regiment Dick went up to Magdalen, Oxford, in March 1915 and found the place bare. There was only one other freshman, an American, and so Dick amused himself with frequent return visits to Eton. As casualty lists mounted he became more and more depressed. 'In yesterday's list I knew four killed and one missing … and three killed the day before.'

He was becoming more and more restless and exploring innovative ways to contribute to the war effort. Perhaps he could find a place in the Army Service Corps? He had also made enquiries about employment in a group that attempted to trace the missing on the battlefields by interviewing wounded men in hospitals. By June 1915 though, none of Dick's plans had come to fruition and, wearing his Eton OTC uniform, he packed his things and went off to the front to drive cars for the Red Cross in the French sector. After awful delays and endless stops to provide papers, as well as letting every train carrying troops or stores past, Dick finally reached Tours, which was a culture shock for the teenager. His minimal lodgings he could adjust to, but the food was another thing. There was simply too much of it and his welcoming hosts looked at him oddly when he failed to eat more than two meat courses at the same sitting. He 'very nearly broke down' when the old man of the house he was billeted in began sucking on a fish head.

The people of the town seemed to him to be largely apathetic, to have given up all hope of a decisive end to the war. Dick was given a 40-horse-power Napier motorcycle, a beast with a dodgy set of brakes and bad handling. Coming down steep hills he was required to turn off the engine as 'the only means of controlling the brute'. At one point he nearly ran into a funeral procession and knocked over a tram. When the locals were enraged he simply pretended that he couldn't speak any French and hurried away. ('It saves a lot of trouble.') His OTC uniform attracted plenty of attention. '*Everyone* stares,' he claimed and the locals would grab him and try to shake the khaki-clad boy's hand.

By November a proper uniform had arrived and Dick returned to England and delivered himself to Sandhurst or, as he referred to it, that 'place of bitter torment'. They were denied fires in the midst of winter and it was so crowded that he slept on the floor. He desperately wanted the King's Royal Rifles. He was morbidly confident that he would get his wish. 'Many people must be killed before it is my turn to leave here¹.' He proved to be right.

By mid December Dick's turn had come and he found himself on a wretched little ferry that had been plucked from its plodding existence going backwards and forwards across the Irish Sea and pressed into war service. Destined for the 1st Battalion, Dick journeyed via Abbeville in the company of two more OEs and on Christmas Eve 1916 he began his advance towards the lines. Taking a group of strangers, new and returning gunners, under his wing he bought them all cakes on the trip. 'This certainly hasn't been an ideal Christmas,' he wrote sarcastically,' but it is one I shall never forget and I shall laugh about it afterwards.'

When he arrived the teenager found that he was assuming command of an entire company as their captain had been offed by a prematurely exploding bomb. He was immediately glum about his surroundings. 'I don't know if you have ever been in this part of France,' he told his father as the rain came down in torrents, '[but] it is the most desolate, poverty stricken place I have ever been in.' It got worse, for Dick was also witnessing the most shocking weather of the war so far.

It began before Christmas with endless rain. One OE general, Hubert Gough, 'to use a mild colloquialism' described the onset of winter as 'beastly'. There was mud everywhere. 'Mud on boots, clothes, hands, rifles and everything one touched.' Henry Dundas' men were suffering just as badly. When the young officers could get around to see them, which wasn't often, they found that they had simply fashioned holes in the mud and now stood in them whilst the rain came down. Materials could not be brought up so men were pulling waterproof sheets over the trenches and squatting beneath them. They got so bogged down doing the tortuous 6½-mile journey to get to the lines that some had to be physically pulled out of the mire. Henry yanked half a dozen out himself. 'We found one man of the 2nd Battalion – his identity disc showed – buried up to the neck in a shell hole and quite dead.' There were many more like him. 'The poor brutes haven't got a chance of getting properly dry. And my hat! They are fed up. No wonder.' Henry was fuming. 'They, the infantry who bear the brunt of the whole thing, get nothing done for them, get paid a pittance compared to anyone else, and then get butchered in droves when the fine weather comes.' The worst of his anger was reserved for the press at home. He had seen a large photo of a battalion struggling through the mud on the way to some trenches and titled 'Merry Mud Larks on the Somme'. 'My God!!' Henry exclaimed.

Dick Levett had found himself billeted at the most vile-looking farm one could imagine, sitting under 3ft of manure. The occupants did nothing to enhance his opinion of the place. 'Three dotty village idiots as farm hands … the farmer and his wife, I think, are dotty too.' His experience of that awful winter got no better. Dick happened to be sitting in the mess alone one night when an adjutant walked in, seized him and had him seconded to an obscure little outlet up in the lines which was to fit men with gumboots. He made a dignified entrance by falling down the stairs into a previously German dugout and received a gruesome introduction to the trenches. He began heading his letters as having come from 'The Abomination of Desolation'. It appeared to be the phrase of choice that winter because numerous OEs were using this biblical quote to summarise their experiences. If he needed to find the dugout again, Dick was told, he need only look for the three decomposing Germans outside the entrance. The thought did nothing to cheer him up. He was then redirected to his own hideaway where he and his servant began bailing out the water with a kerosene tin. Together they suspended two stretchers and tried to sleep. 'Tonight was the worst night I ever remember,' he wrote down when they had finished. 'Sleet and rain and freezing.' Worse, he was within range of the guns for the first time, so he lay there cold, wet and scared of the noise.

Dick, however, was luckier than most. Once passed out, the German shells had no chance of rousing him. One morning a fellow officer came bursting in and remarked, 'Well that wasn't too bad was it!' It turned out that Dick had slept through the devil of an artillery duel that had gone on all night. One of the offending guns had even been parked outside his own dugout. 'He doesn't know what I am like in the mornings,' Dick commented wryly. It became a standing joke amongst his colleagues, who ragged him mercilessly about his ability to sleep through the war. Woe betide anyone that tried to get him up against his will. One night 'some wretched officer', after vigorously shaking him to get him to wake up, demanded that Dick find boots for sixty poor homeless Tommies and somewhere for them to sleep. Dick had neither boots nor accommodation and sat up in bed, ordering the superior officer out of his hole with such force that nobody ever saw or heard from him again. 'The funny part is that this morning I haven't any recollection of it at all but that is what they tell me happened. My deep slumbers amuse everyone.'

The one thing that did get Dick to move were the rats. '*Enormous* things.' They ripped up his magazines and trampled all over his bed with no shame at all. He and his servant had had an adopted mutt that disappeared and one rat was so large that his servant mistook it for 'Poz'. He put his hand out and began stroking it in the dark only to get his hand savaged. 'We couldn't find the matches and there was an awful scuffle and the bed upset.' Dick could reach the other end of a trench within seconds when one appeared and was not in the least bit ashamed. He ended up convulsing with laughter after the pests had been chased off. He had a boyish tendency to see the funny side of absolutely everything and he was bemused by the whole affair. 'A sense of humour saves one here.'

There was no fraternisation, no merriment at Christmas that year with the Germans. Neither side had the energy or the inclination any more. Dick spent New Year's Eve at a Divisional Gas School learning about a new type of helmet that was about to be issued. It was not an improvement at all to his mind, with a nose clip and a mouth piece like a baby's bottle 'which makes one slobber dreadfully'. A battalion of Highlanders were nearby and they raised hell as midnight approached, marching up and down with bagpipes. 'I think the whole battalion was drunk.' Dick himself sat up to see in 1917 in a dirty barn listening to a foreign legionnaire's yarns, 'which he invented with the greatest consistency'. He had also come across another OE, a doctor, and they had become quite friendly. Dick had him to thank for some quite embarrassing and unsolicited advice about avoiding a certain brothel which disturbed his naive young mind quite greatly. He and his companions greeted the new year with cheap champagne. 'Well,' Dick reflected, 'I suppose it will be the most important year of our lives that we shall ever have.'

Shortly afterwards he was moved on again and found himself shouldered with a substantial amount of responsibility for a teenage subaltern. A divisional general had come along and put him in charge of a set of huts that were to be used for resting troops coming out of the lines. They were, in principle, to house a brigade at a time and this would have been challenging enough in itself but when he arrived Dick found that they were in no fit state to be inhabited. They were surrounded by knee-deep mud and he was given 480 men to instal drains, duckboards, even roads to get in and out. This new occupation was thankless from the beginning and Dick found himself the centre of numerous rows which tested his problem solving abilities to the utmost when troops started to arrive. He found that the only thing for it was to stick to the very letter of his instructions; which made him a fair number of enemies amongst the exhausted men traipsing up, but meant that his conscience could rest easy.

At the turn of the year the rain had stopped, but 1917 brought with it an appalling cold snap, 'The hardest winter I ever remember,' Dick claimed. The skies, Pip Blacker wrote, were like pewter. Snow, frost and biting winds combined to make conditions on the Western Front unbearable. It proved tortuous for the men living exposed in the trenches. Birds dropped dead of the cold, ink froze in the pot and rivers iced over. Hubert Gough had never seen more bitter weather in Europe. Stocks of firewood began to run out and men began to suffer the smoky effects of trying to burn damp wood in cramped dugouts and cellars to keep warm. Dick's fingers were suffering but the risk of frostbite was far worse in the trenches, where, he heard rumours, men's ears were turning black. The ground hardened so much that shells exploded without penetrating to any depth. Pip watched the fragments spray out at unusually low angles and wounds in the legs became far more common.

With the hardening of the ground the continuation of the fighting began to creep back into the minds of commanders up and down the front.

Training for new campaigns began in earnest. Although Dick Levett remained for the moment with his huts, Hubert Gough's Fifth Army, including his battalion of the King's Royal Rifle Corps, was to resume harassing the enemy forcefully. Douglas Haig was determined that they would not remain unmolested in the winter months. Gough was to push forward, seizing key positions to make life easier during the forthcoming large-scale offensives. In accordance with this, the Old Etonian wanted to advance his line forward towards a place called Loupart Wood; carrying out a number of minor operations aimed primarily at putting the artillery on a good footing for the spring. Gough managed to press forward bit by bit early in the year and gain a number of advantages as his men attempted to inch across the valley of the Ancre, ejecting the enemy from villages on either side of the river.

Dick had been told that he was not allowed to return to his battalion as it was proving difficult to replace him. But the 1st King's Royal Rifles, and his Eton friend, 'Derrick' Eley, their gas and intelligence officer, would have to take part in one of Gough's key attacks to flush the Germans out of the high ground above the village of Miraumont. Taking it would give the British an invaluable view of the German artillery positions over towards Serre. With a simultaneous action on the north side of the river led by the Royal Naval Division the enemy should evacuate Miraumont itself resulting in serious strategic consequences as far as the salient they were on was concerned.

On 10 February they marched off. It was an exceptionally dark night and the going was hard. Unfortunately for the battalion, a rapid thaw had set in the day before the attack. The ground was slippery and men slipped and skidded on the greasy surface.

Zero hour was 5.45 a.m. on 17 February but it might as well have been a night attack it was so overcast and miserable. The wire in front had not been adequately cut and to add to the battalion's woes they took fire very heavily on both sides. Fortunately a lot of it went high but in the murk they began to lose direction as the division next door began to veer off track. In their confusion these men had also begun throwing smoke bombs about, all of which made it harder for the King's Royal Rifles to stay on track. The artillery's protective barrage was far too thin and moved too fast, for the men were not advancing over frozen ground as expected but thick, sticky mud. The first objective fell to them but confusion was rife. The men had become hopelessly mixed. One company was lost altogether and had every one of its officers killed with almost all of its NCOs. The British were counter-attacked and pushed back.

By 8 a.m. battalion HQ had become edgy. Baffled company commanders had failed to get information to them because they were clueless themselves.

Derrick Eley was sent out to try to find out what had happened and why the attack did not seem to be progressing. He found all manner of troops wandering about and managed to rally them and get them on. Then he went off down the confused ranks trying to place the King's Royal Rifle Companies.

The enemy sniped the British troops heavily and sprayed them with machine-gun fire too. The Germans then resorted to a bombing counterattack to try to drive them back. The battalion aid post was in an open trench and was hit by a shell, killing thirteen including Royal Army Medical Corps personnel. A few of the King's Royal Rifles made it as far as the trench south of Miraumont as planned but they were far too widely dispersed and, under heavy fire, were compelled to fall back. Posts were pushed out as far as possible and they spent the rest of the day consolidating. They had taken some ground, but had failed to reach their ultimate destination and had suffered horrible casualties.

Back at the camp Dick was fretting over their fate. All he received were 'wild rumours'. He feared the worst for his friends and heard that the battalion had been badly cut up, but he was hoping that reports had been exaggerated. 'Naturally we are all anxious and fidgety,' he wrote. As wounded men and prisoners streamed down he seized them, desperately searching for information. The camp itself was now under fire from German artillery as Dick frantically waited for the 1st King's Royal Rifles to be relieved from the lines.

Two days later he had managed to get to the survivors. They had been dribbling in all night and all day in a bedraggled state, wading through the mud as the thaw continued. 'You would hardly know they were human beings.' Worst of all, news came that Derrick had been killed and it threw him into a state of shock. They had been at Eton together, joined the battalion at almost the same time and Dick had seen him but forty-eight hours ago, setting off cheerfully on his way to battle; he had waved him off. The thought that struck with him was that Derrick, like him, was an only son. Dick's platoon sergeant had been killed as well, while leading the platoon in Dick's absence. The guilt was harrowing[2].

The 2nd Division, to which Dick's battalion belonged, had lost a staggering forty-nine officers, roughly two battalions worth, and almost a thousand men in one day. The depletion facilitated Dick's return. Word was that the battalion would be sent back to rest and revive itself, but hopes were in vain. The 1st King's Royal Rifles were to be sent back into action almost immediately.

Dick re-joined his platoon in a nearby rest camp where they were squashed into cold huts. Having shed most of his possessions he was sorry now to have relinquished his stationary job. His servant Farndon was furious with him,

primarily because he had been out since August 1914 and had no inclination to do any more fighting. Dick felt hugely guilty and asked his parents to
fashion a box of treats for him as he'd been 'just like an elder brother'. Perhaps
they could send him some cocoa, biscuits, socks or anything they could spare.
'He would appreciate them and I know he deserves them.'

Any plans for rest and recuperation had been shot to pieces shortly after the
engagement at Miraumont. Suddenly Dick and his battalion were ordered to
stand to because the Germans began retreating from the battlefield. Operation
Alberich, as it was known to those carrying it out, began on a small scale in
late February. As baffled as the British were, there was method, rather than
madness or capitulation, in the enemy's actions. Ever since September 1916,
the German Army (and prisoners of) had been constructing a brand new,
brutal system of defence behind the lines that they had been fiercely clinging
to. Known as the 'Siegfriedstellung' or the 'Hindenburg Line' to the Allies,
the Royal Flying Corps had observed this activity as far back as October the
previous year. This new defensive system stretched from in front of the Third
Army near Arras, all the way along the front of the Fifth, which included Dick,
down past Rawlinson's Fourth Army into the French sector where Nivelle
was planning his assault on the Aisne. After the horrific losses on the Somme,
withdrawing to this strong position would give the Germans a shorter line to
man against any forthcoming Allied offensives.

Instead of filling the trenches in the Hindenburg Line so that they overflowed
with defenders they were loosely held and behind them efforts were put into
strategic strongpoints. Concrete block-houses had sprung up; known as pillboxes. Filled with machine guns which covered the spaces in between they were
halfway impervious to artillery. Further back still was another complex collection of pill-boxes, surrounded by earth, and some were even mocked up to look
like houses with pretend chimneys. Surrounded by copious amounts of barbed
wire, the system relied on letting the British advance and then launching fierce
counter-attacks. There were machine-gun nests and troops ready to pounce on
any invaders who flooded unknowingly over the foremost part of their lines.

On 4 February orders were sent out to get ready for the staged withdrawal.
It would take several weeks and on 22 February, in front of the King's Royal
Rifle Corps in the Ancre Valley, the preliminary stages began. Dick heard a
horrid rumour that they were to shoot forward after the Germans and move
under canvas, but Gough was adamant that his army were not going to barrel
after the enemy at undue risk. Caution and diligence was key. 'Great news of
the Boche retiring,' Dick gloated, although the overriding feeling amongst
Etonians watching events transpire was one of suspicious confusion.

By 1 March Dick reported that he had moved forwards. Despite setbacks such as Miraumont, Gough's army was approaching his intended destination: Loupart Wood. A final push was required to seize his favoured position and the 1st King's Royal Rifles were about to become extremely well acquainted with a nearby objective called Grevillers Trench around a village named Irles. Their objective would be to push towards the edge of a ravine known as 'the Lady's Leg'.

The artillery began to bombard the area and it was blown to pieces, leaving 'tumbled and shapeless masses of earth'. Nerves were frayed as the Germans retaliated and one of Dick's fellow officers flipped completely. In the middle of the night he spied seven Germans in no-man's-land attempting to mend the wire cut by the British artillery. 'This was too much for him,' Dick wrote. 'He rushed around telling everyone an attack was coming and we all stood to. At this moment our people put a terrific barrage over ... Fritz got the wind up, thinking an attack was coming and puts all his artillery on us ... Terrific din ensues.'

At the same time someone let off a whole host of multi-coloured very lights. The poor officer who had started it all was by now out of the trench and ended up flat on his belly when the Germans turned a machine gun on him. Dick's reaction was typical of his youthful reaction to imminent danger. 'It was quite like a show at the Crystal Palace,' he joked. Miraculously nobody came to any harm and as usual he ended up in fits of hysterical laughter at the thought of the elder man hopping frantically around.

On 9 March they rested up as a blizzard blew into their sector but at midnight it was time to leave. Efforts had been made to make Dick look as much like a private soldier as possible. He carried a rifle with a fixed bayonet, sandbags were tied over his knee high boots so that German snipers would leave him alone. 'Boche snipers are very fond of picking off our officers,' his servant claimed. Shivering in their assembly trenches together they were issued soup and then there was nothing to do but wait.

At 5.15 a.m. it began. The artillery barrage blazed to life. Howitzers pummelled the Lady's Leg and Dick jumped on to the parapet, urging his men to follow him. It was still dark and a mist hung in the air. The artillery had done its job; the wire was cut to pieces. As for the German machine guns, one sharp sergeant with a steady hand took out the main offenders with his rifle. They were so eager to get at the Germans that Dick and his men almost outran their own artillery barrage. They lay down in front of the enemy's wire and waited for the shells to subside, Dick checking to see that Farndon was fit and well.

As soon as the British barrage lifted they jumped forwards. The whole of Grevillers Trench was taken and outposts were flung up in one strike. Farndon, though was stuck on the shattered wire. Frantically trying to unhook himself under fire he lost sight of his 'Mr Richard' as Dick ran on. The mist confused him. The men had bunched in areas so try as he might, once everybody started jumping into the trench he couldn't get his bearings or find his officer.

Ordered to dig in, Farndon began frantically helping to consolidate their position. As he burrowed frantically he kept checking about him, convinced that Dick would show up at any moment. The Germans had increased the ferocity of their fire on the trench. Farndon was clearing the entrance to a mineshaft when his company commander came along. There was a rumour going about that Dick had been killed. Had he seen it for himself? He hadn't. A rapidly panicking Farndon requested permission to go and see for himself, but it was refused. He was just planning to do it anyway with a sergeant major when a corporal came running along and said that he had seen an officer who looked exactly like Dick being helped back to safety. Relief washed over Farndon. Finally his captain gave him permission to go off and establish facts for himself. He went running off to the dressing station to find Dick.

The action, it was claimed by the battalion's commander, was 'a notable example of the methods then recently adopted for an attack of limited scope, in which the artillery left the least possible burden on the infantry's shoulders'. It was important that, in this instance, the infantry kept as close to their own artillery barrage as possible, 'even at the risk of a few casualties'. He pronounced the casualty rate of the battalion as 'very light'. They had only lost one officer, which was to be admired. He wrote a very different letter to Dick's parents, as that one officer was their 19-year-old only son, and he had been killed by a British shell.

Farndon found the teenager's body in between the German wire and Grevillers Trench. Dick had been killed by a shard of shell that had struck him in the head. His men picked up his body and carried it to safety. At Albert the Pioneers made him a coffin and he was laid to rest in an extension to the town cemetery.

'It will be a lifelong sore to me that I was not actually by his side when he fell,' wrote Farndon. 'His eagerness, the misty weather and bad luck were the cause.' This veteran of the entire war who had been in it since the beginning was finally broken. 'His loss has given me … one of the hardest knocks of this terrible war.' Dick's parents received a stream of letters from people that had been acquainted with their son that painted a picture of a thoughtful, sweet-natured boy. The maid at his house at Eton even wrote to tell them that she had never forgotten that he would never light his fire on a Saturday, just to try and save her a bit of work. Perhaps the most heart-breaking letter that they received was in their son's own hand. Back in 1916 he had hidden it where they might find it if he were killed:

> I am writing this in case I don't come back. I know how much you will feel it if I go under ... Thanks to you both my life has been an extraordinarily happy one ... I particularly want everything at [home] to go on as if I was coming back one day. You know how fond of the place I was and I should hate to think that [it] was suffering ... So please do everything as if I was away for a time only, and in every way keep the family traditions going. That is the saddest thing of this war, the way so many traditions have lapsed. I don't want mourning or anything ... Your loss of an only son ... is very great but carry on and God Bless You, my dearest parents.

Their teenage boy had survived less than three months at the front.

Notes
1. Just as he passed out in summer 1916 news arrived that his cousin 2nd Lieutenant Jacinth Wilmot-Sitwell was one of them. Serving with the Coldstream Guards, on 9 July he was wounded by a trench-mortar shell and died shortly afterwards at the age of 21. He is buried at Essex Farm Cemetery.
2. 2nd Lieutenant William Arthur Derrick Eley was buried at Regina Trench Cemetery, Grandcourt. He had only left Eton in April 1916 and was 19 years old when he was killed.

16

'I Long to Fly'

The Great War was the first major conflict where all combatants fully embraced flight as a means to contribute to victory. What had been an expensive hobby for gentlemen became an essential part of warfare and an exciting prospect for scores of Old Etonians preparing to join the war effort.

The Honourable Eric Fox Pitt Lubbock was born in May 1893. In the words of his mother, Lady Avebury, he was 'merry, abounding in vitality and high spirits from the earliest days'. He was always an adventurer. 'He has to my knowledge,' claimed one friend of the family dramatically in talking about his resilience when he was a child, 'had seven nasty accidents this week, which would have killed most children but from all of which he has got through with nothing but smiles.' Eric went to Eton at the age of 11, for his parents were determined that he should begin whilst his brother was still at Mr Goodhart's house with him.

Perhaps because of his young age he suffered acutely from homesickness and it was coupled with a dislike for his schoolwork. 'I Eric Lubbock,' he wrote, 'am interested in most branches of natural history, and can [take] no pleasure at all from Latin and Greek … What on earth can be the good of stuffing one's head with languages long ceased to be spoken and all books of which are translated?' Eric was of a generation of schoolboys who watched the birth of the aeroplane. He saw one fly over the school in 1910. 'Today I saw the sight of my life,' he wrote home. 'It was an aeroplane. It looked like a huge bird gliding softly along in the air … I long to fly … all I could think was *I long to fly*.'

The Royal Flying Corps was formed in the spring of 1912 whilst Eric was at Oxford. The first squadron to be fully up and running at Larkhill was No. 3 and a number of Etonians were connected with it. The adjutant was Major Basil Barrington-Kennett, or 'BK', and he vowed that the new RFC should combine the smartness of a Guards regiment such as his own with the efficiency of the Royal Engineers from which they had been born[1]. Another OE was present from the beginning and instrumental in the development of this embryonic outfit. The creative spirit of the Royal Engineers was imperative in fostering this exciting new technology but it was a former Rifle Brigade man who could argue that few in the RFC had done more than he to develop the military potential of the aeroplane.

Reginald Cholmondeley was the son of an army man from Oxfordshire. He had left Eton in 1907 to go into the army, transferred into the Royal Flying Corps as soon as he could, and got his pilot's license in August 1912. He became the first RFC pilot to attempt a night flight the following year. Early in 1914, 3 Squadron was engaged in such diverse pursuits as perfecting forced landings, communications between air and ground, firing guns from aeroplanes, range finding using signalling lamps and using flares to relay artillery observations. Reginald took off on 10 March 1914 again on a night flight. At the time, with no proper lighting in the cockpit and none on the ground to guide him home, it was a perilous mission. Helped along by a full moon at 2,000ft he could see the lights of Andover and Salisbury but he had lost sight of home and had he not been fully aware of his surroundings then he would have found it very difficult to find his way back.

By midnight on 5 August 1914 Reginald's squadron had been mobilised with its twelve war-worthy machines and a week later they departed to the front. Once in France they painted Union Jacks on the underside of the wings. This early in the war they were fired at indiscriminately by overexcited men on the ground, whether friend or foe. The Fletcher brothers saw their machines differently. As an artillery officer, Regie had reason to hate them, and he passed time on the Aisne trying to exact revenge for the hostile shells that the German machines directed on to him. 'Spent rather a pleasant afternoon sniping stray aeroplanes with a rifle,' he wrote in his diary. 'Blazed about 40 rounds at one, but with no visible effect.' He was finally stopped by an order from the major who insisted that he give up. In the trenches George was simply enchanted by them. 'They come out just like butterflies on a fine day, and the air is full of the humming of their engines.'

In the early war of movement, the RFC's objective was reconnaissance, acting like airborne cavalry. No. 3 Squadron spied large numbers of German troops converging on Mons before the retreat put an incredible strain on the Royal Flying Corps. They were forced to pack up and move several times. The aeroplanes suffered from being left out in the open. Transports sped away numerous times, leaving the machines with overworked mechanics who had insufficient tools and equipment to look after them properly. At night they would have to guard the aeroplanes, sleeping under the wings in deteriorating weather as the Germans approached.

It stood to reason that the German Army would not want the Allied machines to fulfil their reconnaissance objectives and vice versa. Both sides began to look at arming their machines. Early attempts were comical. Pilots stuffed revolvers in their pockets; they took grenades up with them with the intention of dropping them over the sides. In October 1914 came one of the first instances of aerial combat. Then on 12 October Reginald Cholmondeley took off from St Omer in a Sopwith Scout, one of the best machines available, and took on an enemy machine. He had had a rifle fitted to one side of his cockpit so that he could try to fly and shoot at the same time, and a carbine on the other, both pointing upwards to avoid his propeller. Not surprisingly he failed to put his opponent out of the sky.

Experimenting with armaments would prove to be Reginald's downfall. On March 12 1915 he was bombing railways during the battle of Neuve Chapelle. Reginald was sitting in his machine whilst it was being loaded with six volatile, converted French shells. One of the bombs exploded, setting off another, and the aeroplane went up in flames. Reginald Cholmondeley never stood a chance of getting out alive. The 25-year-old was buried at Chocques Military Cemetery with the other victims of the accident.

Eric Lubbock had never expressed an interest in anything military, but the instant that war was declared he was eager to play his part. He had been interested in motoring since 1910 and on 6 August 1914 he delivered himself to the Royal Automobile Club in London to volunteer for foreign service. His sister's husband, an officer in the Black Watch, urged him not to enlist. England, he said, would be crying out for young officers soon enough and he was concerned about the experience Eric might have of serving in the ranks. Eric went up to Oxford but as he was not a member of the OTC they could not help him at that stage. Frustrated, he joined a long queue of men waiting to enlist. He was not at all impressed with the doctor who saw him. 'He looked stupid, threw a tape measure around my collar bone and said I was unfit.' Eric was furious. 'Nonsense, said I. I rowed in Trial Eights, surely I'm fit enough.' His chest was apparently too small by 1in.

He remained unperturbed. He had spied an advertisement by the Wolesley Motor Co. and now wanted to drive ambulances. They didn't seem to be overly concerned about the size of his chest but they shared his brother-in-law's concern about him serving in the ranks, 'that it would mean living with the roughest of men and that he could never stand it'. Eventually a form was produced; an application to drive a lorry. Eric did not want to drive a transport lorry. The recruiters at their offices told him that it was the same thing. 'No spider has ever ensnared a fly more successfully than they caught me there,' he said wryly later. Thus he joined the Army Service Corps.

Eric Lubbock was one of only a handful of Etonians who served in the ranks at some point in the war. Despite everybody else's reservations he didn't have any particular problems amongst his fellow soldiers, although it was a culture shock for someone who had experienced such a privileged upbringing. On the crossing he was crammed into the hull of a transport and it was the only time he ever regretted enlisting and envied the officers. He had a terrible headache and the smell was nauseating. He felt so weak when they disembarked that he claimed he could have quite happily drowned himself at the quay. Once in France the 22 year old shared a tent with thirty other men and discovered how limited his vocabulary was, even if he wasn't inclined to follow his fellow soldiers' colourful lead.

His service in the Army Service Corps was only to last for a few months. Eric had always been great friends with Eric Powell, one of the two masters that ran off to war with George Fletcher. He had by now abandoned his intelligence role and joined the Royal Flying Corps as an observer. Eric Lubbock ran into him at the front and by December wrote home to tell his worried mother that he wanted a commission in the RFC himself. It took him a further six months to send another letter home telling her that he was about to be attached to the flying services. 'I am most awfully excited,' he told her. He was, however, constantly mindful of the anguish that his service caused her and fully aware that the idea of his feet leaving the ground would not help her to relax at all.

Nonetheless his RFC career began on 25 July 1915 when he was sent along to headquarters, 'an odd place with apparently lots of doors leading to nowhere'. Lost, Eric was pondering his next move when an officer looked out of a window with some sarcastic advice. 'If you can't find a door come in by a window.' Eric was bemused. 'It seemed quite the thing for a budding airman to do so I did it.'

His record of interesting recruitment experiences continued. He had submitted two recommendations, one from Sir John French who allegedly claimed that Eric had a nose like a pelican and therefore would be good at flying. He also had a similar one from Kitchener apparently saying that he had big feet like a bird, which again showed promise. But it was his motoring background that saw him through. Any sporting prowess, horsemanship or mechanical know-how was jumped on by the flying authorities. Was his eyesight good? 'Good enough to see through you,' he responded. How much did he weigh? 'Ten stone before breakfast.'

His interview concluded, Eric joined a lengthy waiting list to become an observer in the RFC. His mother was resigned to it. She remembered how he had fallen in love with aeroplanes at Eton several years earlier and didn't see what good it was trying to stop him from becoming airborne himself. It didn't stop him from feeling guilty. His father had sadly passed away in 1913 and she bore her anxiety as a lone parent. 'Mum bears it all so well but I cannot imagine what she suffers. She doesn't sleep well and somehow it is too awful to think of her suffering. I owe her so much more than I can ever give and yet I give her pain.'

Eric finally received a summons to join the RFC at the beginning of September 1915 and reported to 5 Squadron near Poperinghe as an observer. He was bombarded with things to learn and it was perhaps a blessing that bad weather denied him his first trip in the air and gave him time to settle down to learning things like Morse and aircraft recognition. There were two other Etonians learning with him, both of them rowers, and so he was feeling quite at home. He finally got up in the air for his maiden flight on 4 September. Cruising over Poperinghe, Vlamertinghe and towards Ypres and back again, he began counting trains, observing troop movements, even sketching trench lines. But methods of communication with the ground were his overriding concern. 'I can send messages by Morse now fairly accurately though very slowly, but can't read yet … My head was never made for dots and dashes!' Aerial photography had really shown its worth at the battle of Neuve Chapelle in March and he was introduced to large box cameras. Pilots and observers had captured the whole ground in front of the 1st Army and then carefully traced the trenches on to skeleton maps. Some 1,500 copies had been produced, which turned out to be massively useful.

Lewis guns had begun arriving for fitting on to machines but whilst arming aeroplanes was being rapidly developed so were methods for destroying them outright from the ground. Nicknamed 'Archie,' Archibald James, another young Etonian in the RFC, shared a nickname with this anti-aircraft fire but it didn't help him get used to it any quicker. He jumped every time a shell went off; 'a nasty big bang and crack'. He was flying a sensitive scout at the time and every time his hand jogged the plane lurched about. Slowly he got over this nervousness and managed to fly normally whilst being harassed.

Thomas McKenny Hughes had left Mr Impey's house at Eton in 1902 where he had been a contemporary of Ego Charteris. Having transferred to the RFC to become an observer he was with 1 Squadron operating out of Bailleul; where the aerodrome was overlooked by the local lunatic asylum. He was constantly harassed when going about his work by a 'beastly hooligan' of an anti-aircraft gun living in between Lille and Roubaix. It was, he said, 'very difficult to give one's undivided attention when in the middle of an elaborate calculation of the number of trains one had a terrific explosion apparently a few yards away and that horrid whistling "ping" of the bits passing.' On another occasion he spoke of trying to count trains under fire. A piece of shell flew into the petrol tank and fuel started pouring out. 'I made a few ineffectual and tardy attempts to stop it with my fingers ... the Huns did not stop shooting at us. What a terrible thing it must be to be a pheasant.' The pilot was adamant that they were doomed but the engine miraculously jumped back to life and took them home.

Flying was certainly not for the faint-hearted. Eric had already been present when his pilot suffered a crashed. They were 40ft from the ground when the engine stopped. 'I thought we were going to land,' he wrote. 'Then she back-fired, and the nose went absolutely straight down. I thought, "we're going to crash." I had no time to think more. I felt myself being hurled down on to that ploughed field for destruction.'

It would not please his mother, as she was simultaneously lamenting the departure of his brother for the Dardanelles, but Eric had solemnly promised to tell her everything. He had felt something strike his head. 'I was thrown clear as we hit the ground and should not have been touched only the front sight of the machine gun just cut my leg ... Loraine the pilot was not hurt ... but our lovely machine was in pieces! The gun stuck in the ground and the camera flew about 50 yards.' Eric finally got up some 30 yards away from the wrecked machine, collected the camera and plates and walked back. 'I must have looked very funny as I landed perfectly upside down in a very soft plough and got up with my head covered and my mouth and nose absolutely full of earth!'

Accidents and mechanical failures were a common feature of life as an airman and few Etonians escaped a smash at one time or another. Henry 'Deighton' Simpson was born in New York State in January 1896. Having been sent to school in England with his younger brother, he left Le Neve Foster's house at Eton in the summer of 1914, hopping aboard the RMS *Olympic* with his family the day after war was declared. His parents wanted him home and he was to fulfil their ambitions for him to go to Harvard, thus being kept far away from the conflict in Europe. 'But his heart was with his schoolfellows' and in November 1914, travelling steerage on SS *Campania*, the 18 year old ran away to enlist in the British Army.

Henry wrote to his parents from the ship declaring his intentions. His father was flustered but confident that his son could be dragged back across the Atlantic. He was more concerned about the future of Henry's education and wrote to Harvard to gain some assurance that when they got Deighton home he would be able to continue his studies. 'He is an exceedingly sensitive young man,' he explained to the authorities. 'Long residence at Eton College has made him quite the Englishman with all the bitter prejudice against the Germans ... The whole thing is really laughable, a tempest in a tea pot.'

His father might have made less of a joke of the situation if he had known just how serious his son was. Deighton's mother chased him across an ocean and located him at Eton staying with a former house master. She found him utterly resolved and could achieve nothing more than a promise that he would wait to receive a commission and not go barrelling into the ranks. He was fully devoted to both England and Eton and she couldn't hold him back. She consented for him to become a British citizen to facilitate his wishes, and at the beginning of November 1914 stood by him at Windsor as he swore allegiance to George V and joined the cavalry.

Deighton transferred to the RFC and was soon at the Western Front until, like many pilots, he suffered a breakdown of sorts. Stationed at Joyce Green in Kent he was grounded and bored and managed to convince the Vickers factory at Brooklands to let him fly their experimental aircraft outside his military duties. On 20 December 1916 he was doing just this when the machine that he was in fell apart in mid air; sadly not a rare occurrence in aeroplanes of the period. Deighton was buried at Crayford in Kent. When it came to settling his army affairs his mother insisted that she was not interested in the pay owed to her son. 'A devoted old Etonian whose happiest recollections and memories of life were always of his old school,' she wanted all outstanding sums paid to the Eton Memorial Fund[3].

Experimenting with munitions and developments in aerial warfare also continued to result in tragedy amongst OEs in the flying services long after the death of Reginald Cholmondeley. Fatalities were often random and inexplicable. Arthur Newton was a young Etonian from Dublin and a pre-war pilot who had transferred to the RFC from the Shropshire Light Infantry. He was an exact contemporary of Archibald James at school and they were serving together in 5 Squadron. On 20 October 1915 he had just taken off and was passing over the wireless hut when he gave a standard tap on his wireless key to make sure all was all right. The machine promptly blew up and killed Arthur and his observer, littering the aerodrome with debris. The authorities exhausted themselves trying to ascertain the cause of this freak accident and eventually surmised that perhaps a petrol leak had created a scenario where the spark from the key could have caused the accident. Archibald was still baffled years later. 'Such a combustible mixture could not have been produced. And if it had been produced, it couldn't have been set off by the spark. But the fact is it did happen, and they were both killed.'

With the many and varied ways that pilots and observers were killed, and the random nature of death, it was unsurprising that many developed a fatalistic attitude or became partly immune to the losses around them. One simply had to move on or go mad. Archibald James was on leave in London and at lunch with two elderly gentlemen when the subject of the 16th Lancers came up. Four Etonian officers had been killed by a single shell on the Western Front. Archibald mentioned it casually in conversation as if it was nothing but was astonished when his hosts became visibly upset before his eyes[4].

In Britain the population was fully aware of the air war because they were witnessing it first-hand. Henry Dundas had yet to be posted to the front in September 1915 when he first saw one of the Kaiser's dreaded Zeppelins in London. The idea that Britain, secure in her island status and the protection of the Royal Navy for centuries, should now be exposed to attack from the air was staggering, earth shattering. Henry had been in London when three of the ghostly invaders glided over the city following the line of the Thames. The anti-aircraft defences, involving huge naval guns at Marble Arch, boomed into action. The first two shells almost hit one and slowly the Zeppelin turned, pursuing a line, as far as Henry could tell, up behind St Paul's and Tottenham Court Road. It began dropping various bombs (mostly incendiary) and caused several fires, a particularly large one just behind St Paul's.

Henry himself was standing outside Tottenham Court Road tube station when it glided overhead. Everyone had thought that people would flock underground at the hint of an attack but Londoners stopped and gaped at the monster overhead. 'It could be seen at an immense height … A vague blurred sausage shape – indefinably sinister – and the car lit up like a train.' All around the sound of the guns was deafening. The theatres began turning out in a panic. Henry made his way along Oxford Street, packed with more spectators, towards Embankment. Across the Thames, off to his right, he could see a huge fire on the opposite bank and 'a most wonderful sight, all the sky lit up a lurid red, and the river molten & shining crimson'. Twenty-five years before the Blitz it was an unbelievable display. 'The great dome of St Pauls silhouetted against the whole. It looked just as if the Cathedral itself were on fire.'

Dick Levett once watched from the steps of the adjutant's hut at Sheerness as an airman managed finally to bring one of these notorious killers down:

> I was just watching that very piece of sky. There was first of all a glowing spot in the sky and then it got larger and larger ... and became a great blazing mass ... floating down quite, quite slowly ... we could see the sky light up when the Zeppelin bumped on the ground ... All the men cheered and then there were scenes of great joy – but what a death! I couldn't help thinking of the wretched men inside as the envelope became more and more in flames.

Whilst the opportunity to claim a victory over the enemy was limited over home ground, with developments in aerial warfare on the Western Front it had become far more common. Eric Lubbock was one of the first British airmen to begin his tally. He was aloft with Robert Loraine, a famous actor, in October 1915 when they were set upon by an enemy machine. Eric was in a panic. All he could focus on was trying to get his gun working. 'I heard Loraine give a great shout but felt neither fear nor triumph. Then our machine turned downwards ... we were diving. I was standing almost on the front of the body.' The German airman attacked again. 'Loraine went all out to climb and attack while I put my stiff and aching hands in my mouth, praying for sufficient life to come back to them.'

Finally they succeeded in driving their opponent to the ground inside British lines. The pilot had been shot in the stomach and died before they got him away but the observer was just a boy of 17. He was a nervous wreck, shaking and crying, 'no wonder, poor thing'. Only a handful of enemy machines had been destroyed or captured at this point and both Eric and Loraine were awarded the Military Cross for their efforts. Their fight had also happened above the trenches which meant that excited troops had watched it unfold. Although they hadn't heard the cheers Eric found that he and his pilot were the talk of the town.

British airmen were not having it all their own way by any means though. With the winter of 1915–16, what became known as the Fokker Scourge arrived to blight the fortunes of the Allied airmen. Archibald James, now a pilot, was commanding part of 2 Squadron. They flew lumbering BE2cs, two-seaters used extensively for reconnaissance and artillery spotting or photography but not designed with aerial combat in mind. They were no match for the single-seater Fokkers. Archibald described their extraordinary rate of climb, which allowed them to get up above their prey and dive down on to them. When they attacked they fired a revolutionary fixed, forward machine gun that sprayed bullets through the centre of the propeller with an interrupter gear that stopped it from shooting the blades off. German pilots merely had to aim the machine in the direction that they wanted to shoot and close in on their target. Lone BE2cs out ranging guns or taking photographs had become sitting ducks.

Thomas Hughes was an enigma in that he actually wanted to remain an observer. He claimed that he would only learn to fly himself if the army gave him the ultimatum of training or a return to the infantry. 'They can't make a pilot out of me; it would be interesting to see how they would deal with a case of studied incompetence.' Eric Lubbock bypassed the worst of the Fokker menace though because he took the opposite view and began training as a pilot.

He arrived back at the front in mid October 1916 as a flight commander with the brand new 45 Squadron. They were hit very badly in their first weeks. Six men were missing in action and another severely wounded in one day. Two days later another pilot died accidentally and then Eric was struck off the strength of the squadron sick. More men had actually been sent home because they were not of sufficient flying standard and by the end of October it became apparent that flinging them into action as soon as they had arrived at the front had been too much. They were withdrawn further back to regroup and undertake a significant amount of training so that they might be better prepared when they were put back into battle

By the beginning of December they had moved forward again. The authorities had learned from their mistakes and now Eric, as B Flight commander, was forbidden to cross the enemy lines with his men until they became familiar with their surroundings. Eric defied the order on Christmas Eve when he went in pursuit of a pair of German aircraft between Ypres and Bailleul:

I got almost directly below the Hun ... Austin, my observer, was able to fire continually while the Hun never got a shot at us. We fired 300 rounds of which far more than half hit his machine and yet he lived. In the end we were some ten miles from our lines so I turned for home ... we all came home very pleased with life in time for lunch.

A senior officer turned up on Boxing Day, however, and Eric dubbed him the 'President of the Society for Prevention of Cruelty to Huns'. He was told that he would be sent home in disgrace if he did it again, which seemed rather ridiculous.

The beginning of the year was frustrating. Activity was quite low, but as the weather improved suddenly 45 Squadron was overwhelmed. Eric was their most experienced aviator and had become something of an expert on aerial photography. At home his mother was frantic. In her diary she noted that on 6 March 1917 the newspaper reported '36 Aeroplanes Down!' That evening Eric had taken his flight out. On their way home they were approached by what he assumed to be three Nieuport scouts. They turned out to be German machines, which promptly started shooting at them. Two of the 45 Squadron machines were downed quickly and the Germans set upon Eric and the other; diving on them from above and behind. He eventually managed to put down near the aerodrome with a spluttering engine, but it had been a close call.

Two days later Eric's mother noted another headline: '56 machines down in two days.' She hadn't heard from him for nearly a week and he was due home on leave. On 11 March she scribbled off a letter, 'When are you coming home … I love you my own so very, very much.' It was returned.

That day, 11 March, was an extremely busy day as far as German aircraft were concerned, with nearly one hundred of them being sighted through the day. The retreat to the Hindenburg Line had commenced and up and down the entire Western Front the Allies were just as active, observing 102 separate targets. Three of 45 Squadron's machines set off on a photographic mission in the morning, including Eric's. One dropped out with mechanical failure but Eric continued on with his remaining companion. Shortly after 11 a.m. they were attacked by two Albatros scouts in full sight of the British trenches. Eric's two-seater machine was no match for this foe and both he and the other British aeroplane were shot down and fell just behind the British lines. All four men were killed, Eric's observer, Thompson, reportedly falling out of the plane on the way down.

Eric had first pondered the possibility of his own death when he got up from his smash with Robert Loraine with a face full of dirt. He was adamant that it did not scare him, whatever it turned out to entail. His mother had his attempt to console her in the form of a letter he had left behind. 'At its very worst it is … absolute blank and therefore why fear it?' It would be, he told her, 'just like going to sleep and dreaming nothing'. He also penned a note to his younger brother, Maurice. 'Help mum and look after her. Do not let her grieve too much, try and keep her interested. I hope you will never see this letter.' Within a month it would be unheard of for 45 Squadron to let any less than half-a-dozen machines fly together for additional protection when crossing the lines. It was a lesson learned too late to save 23-year-old Eric Lubbock, the young Etonian who had looked out on the bank holiday crowds at Ramsgate the day after war was declared.[5]

Notes

1. BK gave up his appointment with the RFC because he thought it his duty to go back to the 2nd Grenadier Guards. He was killed in May 1915 at the age of 30 and laid to rest at Le Touret Military Cemetery. His younger brother Victor travelled in the opposite direction, joining the RFC from the Grenadiers. He was killed (accidentally) nine months after Basil at the age of 28. Their youngest brother, Aubrey, educated at Radley rather than Eton, had already been killed in September 1914 at the age of 24 with the Oxfordshire & Buckinghamshire Light Infantry.

2. Deighton's younger brother John also took to the air, serving as an ensign with the United States Navy's flying services.

3. The incident occurred on 21 February 1915. Major Arundell Neave, 39, Captain Edward Radcliffe Nash, 26, and Lieutenants Nathaniel Walter Ryder King, 27, and Rowland Auriol James Beech, 26, are buried in a row at Ypres Town Cemetery.

4. Captain Eric Fox Pitt Lubbock was buried at Lijssenthoek Military Cemetery. A year later Thomas Hughes joined him. The cemetery now contains fourteen Old Etonians, four of whom served with the RFC. The other two are Arthur Victor Newton and Alwyne Travers Loyd.

17

'Am I Going to Die?'

The air war was becoming completely unrecognisable to the pre-war pilots who had survived long enough to see it into its latter stages. Arthur Rhys Davids KS was still at Eton, and captain of the school, in the summer of 1916. He epitomised those boys, now young men, that had witnessed first-hand the birth of the aeroplane and since 1914 there had been much coverage of airborne conflict in the national press. The thought of becoming a pilot, one of these chivalrous knights of the air, waging war above the battlefields, was tantalising for ambitious young Etonians just leaving school. When, at 19, Arthur got his wings and was sent to join his squadron with famed pilots such as Albert Ball he declared that he was in 'the land of the Gods' before his feet had even left the ground.

As well as cavalrymen Douglas and Lennie Harvey, Mr Byrne's house was to produce two notable pilots. Both had been in the house during Douglas Harvey's tenure as captain. 'Jack' Hay Caldwell was from Invernesshire, the wild countryside bordering Loch Morar, and arrived first in 1907. The second of the boys, Ian Patrick Robert Napier arrived some two years later but he and Jack were similar in age and became great friends, not only at Eton but at home in Scotland during the holidays. Ian was the younger son of Henry Melvill Napier, a Clyde shipbuilder and one half of Messrs Napier & Miller at Old Kilpatrick. Born near Dumbarton in 1895, Ian went up to Eton in 1909 and was a successful rower. A member of the VIII for three consecutive years as well as captain of the boats he rowed alongside the likes of Ronnie Backus until departing school just before the outbreak of war.

Whilst his father's firm began turning out minesweepers and assembling aircraft for the war effort, Ian joined a new army battalion of the Argyll & Sutherland Highlanders almost immediately and served as a personal aide-de-camp in the summer of 1915. Ian was stationed at Ripon with a reserve battalion and went in April 1916 to see a cousin of his mother who was commanding a wing of the RFC. Ian managed to get him to sponsor an application. Orders eventually came through for him to report to No. 1 School of Military Aeronautics at Reading and his training was swift. 'After 1hr 20mins dual with Capt. O'Malley – I flew by myself!!'

Nicknamed 'Naps' or 'Old Naps' by his fellow officers, Ian was rather understated and loathed showing off, but he could not resist one stunt that resulted in a small measure of fame before he left for the Front. It served to advertise the dash and exciting appeal of a life in the air when he glided to a halt on one of the playing fields at Eton and was surrounded by excited observers in the summer of 1916.

Ian arrived on the Western Front in March 1917, a fortnight before Rhys Davids. Both young men had been singled out as having promise and were selected to join scout squadrons. The Great War was witnessing the birth of the fighter pilot. If the BE2cs and other reconnaissance and observation machines couldn't protect themselves whilst going about their work then action needed to be taken. Rather than allocating one superior aircraft to a squadron they were now bunched together in units of their own. Populated by bright young pilots they went out in formation without photographs to take or guns to range. Their mission was to escort the slower two-seaters or fighting as a group to expel the enemy from the sky before the Germans could attempt to bring the working machines down.

Number 40 Squadron, for which Ian was destined, had formed at the beginning of 1916 at Gosport in Hampshire. Robert Loraine, Eric Lubbock's former pilot, had initially been put in charge of the fledgling outfit and eventually they flew off to France in FE8 'pushers', so called because the engine sat behind the pilot and 'pushed' them along. By the time Ian arrived the squadron was under the command of another OE, Leonard Tilney, another of Mr Brinton's boys. He had left the cavalry and qualified to fly as early as March 1915 and was himself barely 21 years old, having left school as recently as 1914. They had moved into single-seat Nieuport scouts, which, although they were second hand in this case, were some of the best-designed aircraft available to the Allies.

Ian's new squadron had been patrolling from Armentières down to Arras some 30 miles south-east of the aerodrome. They had suffered as badly as Eric

Lubbock's squadron in the opening days of March 1917. On 9 March more than half a dozen of their machines were set upon by a group of German scouts from the unit of Manfred von Richthofen, the Red Baron. The flight lasted half an hour during which they dropped out alarmingly. Four machines were shot down and the other four were badly shot about. Number 29 Squadron came rushing to their aid and got one man shot down by von Richthofen, Germany's most prolific pilot during the Great War, for its trouble.

Ian flew his first sorties at the end of the month. No. 40 Squadron were part of a huge effort preparing for the Battle of Arras. With the German retreat, plans had been thrown into disarray, and it became even more crucial to watch what the enemy was up to. Photography and artillery observation were therefore imperative in the run up to the battle and Ian and his fellow pilots were busily engaged in escorting two-seater squadrons over the lines.

Men continued to arrive to replenish those lost as the squadron struggled to retain its full strength. One of them was an older pilot who arrived at the beginning of April. Edward 'Mick' Mannock was suspected of being a bit of a coward when he first appeared. He was 29 years old and had nearly died in captivity at the beginning of the war when he was interred as a civilian whilst working in Turkey. He had since been repatriated in appalling health but had recovered sufficiently to join the Royal Engineers and subsequently transfer to the Royal Flying Corps.

The Battle of Arras began on Easter Monday, 9 April, when the British and Canadians launched attacks eastward. The first morning was successful. The Hindenburg Line was broken and nearly 6,000 German prisoners taken. Almost the entire front-line system was overrun in under an hour and the second within two. By the end of the day some of the third line had been breached and the Canadians had seized Vimy Ridge under the control of an Etonian general.

Five days later, as British troops on the ground pushed on, Ian shared his first aerial victory on an afternoon patrol when he and a fellow officer accounted for a German Albatros. He was having much more luck than Mannock, who just couldn't get going. His flight commander described him as 'like a highly strung pedigree horse at the starting post'. It wasn't for want of enthusiasm. Mannock hated the Germans, said a fellow pilot. There was 'absolutely no chivalry about him; the only good Hun was a dead one'. Mick came from a working-class background and in the evenings he cut a solitary figure in the mess, smoking his pipe and reading. Youthful gossip aggravated him and a 'Hamlet like gloom' hung over him. 'It's all very well for you fellows,' he once snapped. 'You were born with a silver spoon. I had an iron shovel.'

On 29 April the Red Baron accounted for another member of 40 Squadron. A week later every single Nieuport involved in one of 40 Squadron's patrols came back damaged and a Captain Nixon, trying to protect his pilots, was shot down by von Richthofen's younger brother. It had been a trying induction to aerial warfare for Ian Napier.

The offensive persisted for six bloody weeks. On 23 April it was renewed again. Nivelle had failed spectacularly on the Aisne, triggering mutiny among the French, and the British were attempting to relieve the pressure on them. Casualties were horrific. Allenby asked Haig to stop but he persisted. Allenby supposedly warned Haig that the troops being sent in barely knew how to fire their rifles. They were lost all over the battlefield. However, the Germans had been pushed back 2–5 miles along a 20-mile front . These were the biggest advances since static warfare had kicked in at the end of 1914.

The Guards did not play a leading role in the Battle of Arras. Henry Dundas had by now turned 20, and he was not happy about it. 'The kudos out here of being "only 19" is not inconsiderable,' he said and it was sad to think that soon he was no longer able to 'bask in its genial rays'.

More and more young Etonians were arriving to compensate for those lost during the back end of 1916. With the arrival of increasing numbers of school contemporaries, Henry's social circle at the front had begun expanding greatly in the lull since the Somme. Sometimes new friends came from unexpected directions too and he had struck up friendships with some older OEs. On the way back from leave at the end of 1916, Henry met another Old Etonian who had been out with the Irish Guards since 1914. The eldest son of an Irish army officer and nobleman, Eric Beresford Greer, a talented athlete, had been at Mr Impey's house until 1910 when he had gone to Sandhurst. Eric had left for France immediately with the BEF and had survived Villers-Cotterêts, the Aisne and Ypres by the end of 1914. Wounded early in 1915, he spent a considerable amount of time recovering and found time to fall in love and marry Pamela Fitzgerald, the daughter of another Irish aristocrat, before rejoining the 2nd Irish Guards in time for the Somme. That battle had put paid to any optimism that he might have had for struggling towards victory. Eric was becoming more and more cynical as the war progressed. Henry had taken just a fraction of the time to form the same opinions: that the General Staff and politicians were clueless idiots, hell bent on flinging the youth of Britain bodily against the Germans until there was nobody left. Sitting in their train carriage, he and Eric hit it off right away. They shared an artistic bent and soon began an enterprise in that vein. Henry would pen satirical poems about the war and Eric would illustrate them with amusing pen-and-ink sketches. It started off as a 'sort of book' but the latter had a mind to direct their work towards publication in one of the national pictorials.

At the beginning of 1917, Eric's younger brother and fellow OE, 23-year-old Frank was killed.[1] He had been acting as the brigade bombing instructor when a charge went off accidentally. Someone was needed to replace him and Henry, with his bombing experience, was summoned. Life at brigade headquarters was to prove quite jovial for him, all things considered. As well as Oliver Lyttelton, four years his senior, Henry was spoilt by the company of yet another OE. Sir John Swinnerton-Dyer, like Eric Greer, was a regular officer, having joined the Scots Guards in 1910. John and Henry hit it off over dinner one night when they began an in-depth conversation about religion, priests and their role in the war. He immediately became another of Henry's cronies and he duly raved about his sense of humour ('this in spite of being a regular soldier') and his good-natured manner.

Henry was in awe of their commanding officer. To say that Brigadier General John Ponsonby was a character was an understatement. This was the same Ponsonby that had rolled about on the Aisne back in 1914 trying to avoid the intense German shellfire and the same man who had attempted to get the attack at Loos that killed Robin Blacker postponed. Henry was not the only one of his subordinates who adored him. He suffered with a cleft palate, but once officers had learned to understand his style of speech they found him 'wildly individualistic and charming'. He benefitted from complete devotion not only because of his obvious competence, but because he was affectionate and treated his men like human beings.

'General John' was a proud OE. He kept a typed list of all of the Etonian officers in his brigade with their years at school, their houses and details of colours and awards. 'Never,' wrote Henry, 'have I met a better raconteur. His stories of Eton 1880–1885 are perfect. Yet the same period in the hands of another might be a nightmare of tedium.' Ponsonby was famous for his pipe, which nobody ever saw lit, and for his horses. Any man that criticised them, despite the fact that they never once stood still even on the most solemn of occasions, was ordered to stand on a chair in the naughty corner. This punishment served as a frequent one for all sorts of indiscretions. Oliver had had his hands rapped lightly on many an occasion for pointing out that the brigadier had signed forms in the wrong places. 'Any papers which want signing must be brought to me by 2.30 p.m.', were General John's instructions. Anyone bringing any after that allotted time would be forced to stand on a chair in the corner for ten minutes after tea.

The list of transgressions for which one could end up being ordered to stand on the chair was many and varied. No one suffered quite so much as the hapless brigade signalling officer. He had a narrow escape when General John asked him to find a barber to give him a haircut. He had returned with a soldier servant who had never cut a man's hair in his life, but had much experience in clipping horses. He was let off then because the results turned out to be not so bad, but he had a unique aptitude for blurting out precisely the wrong thing in front of General John at the wrong moment. On one occasion the brigadier had been out scouring Poperinghe for an alarm clock. Smugly he had returned with his prize and given it pride of place on the mantelpiece. The signalling officer had been napping on the sofa and he promptly woke up, scowled at it and exclaimed, 'What on earth made you buy that shoddy thing?' He was immediately sentenced to the chair 'for casting aspersions on the Brigadier's taste in hardware'. One morning General John was feeling a little under the weather and although he was up and about decided he was not fit to visit the trenches that day. 'Quite, sir, quite,' the signalling officer agreed. 'You're just like the man who used to say "I eats all right, I drinks all night, I sleeps all right, but when I seek a job of work … I comes all of a tremble".' Up he went on the chair again for his indiscretion.

Of the Etonians, poor John Dyer spent much time hovering upon the brigadier's chair. Before dinner one night in Ypres he jointly announced with another man that they were the 'working members' of the brigade staff, 'thereby lacking in respect due to the Brigadier' and implying that he was idle. One lunchtime at the end of June he was asked by the brigade major how he intended to get back over to brigade HQ and he impertinently scoffed 'ride of course, how do you suppose?' He began to explain that he was not one of those officers whose bodily comfort required the service of a luxuriously appointed motor car to convey their velvet limbs to the trenches. Unfortunately he appeared to have forgotten that General John and the brigade major were about to get in a car and travel up to the lines, so his punishment was considered most just. He even managed to exact upon himself a special stint as far as the chair was concerned. John once called up the commanding officer of the Scots Guards, who had finally got to sleep after days of hard work, only to blankly look at the receiver and admit, 'For the life of me I can't remember what I wanted to say, sir.' For this display of 'gross inefficiency and callous carelessness' General John ordered him to go down to the battalion in person and stand on a chair in their own dugout.

After the initial enthusiasm at the outbreak of war, recruiting figures slumped drastically in 1915. The need for more men, though, was relentless.

Debates began to rage about the idea of a compulsion to serve. On 28 December 1915 the Cabinet accepted the notion of conscripting young men into the armed forces. The bill received royal assent on 27 January 1916 and the Military Service Act was introduced. From now on all men aged 18–41 who were single or widowed without children or dependents and not engaged upon war work, who were not physically unfit or approved conscientious objectors, were required to serve their country in uniform. This put young Etonians leaving school at the very forefront of those being summoned to join the war effort.

Outside his immediate surroundings at brigade headquarters there was an Etonian arrival in the Coldstream Guards that Henry Dundas had been looking forward to. It was to turn out to be the most important one to him by the time his war was over. From his arrival in France, Ralph Dominic Gamble had no enthusiasm for the war. He was adamant that nothing, nothing, was worth the misery that the war had thus far inflicted.

The Gamble family was no stranger to war and disorder. Elements of Ralph's family had fled revolution in France and settled in Ireland. In turn his grandfather was a rather severe-looking officer who braved the Crimean War with the 4th Regiment of Foot before acting as chief of staff to General Duncan in New Zealand against the Maoris. Steering away from the military life he was born into, Ralph's father was forging a successful career in the financial department of the Indian Civil Service when he married a widow, with a young daughter. Their own little girl, Kathleen, was born in 1893 in Calcutta before, in 1897 (by which time Reginald had risen to the role of an accountant-general), Ralph – probably pronounced 'Rafe' – was born at the hill station of Simla.

Ralph Gamble's upbringing was typical of an Anglo–Indian child at the turn of the twentieth century. After spending his early years in the Punjab he was sent to Summer Fields in 1906. From here on out he would be lucky if he saw his parents once a year. When school was dispersed the little boy would be despatched to his grandmother until her death, then an aunt, or other relatives in Tonbridge or Hove to await the resumption of his studies.

Football was taken very seriously at Summer Fields and Ralph was very good at it. On a 'perfect day, sunny and windless' in November 1909 he and his team mates made the short journey over to Horris Hill. Summer Fields won 4–2, with Yvo Charteris scoring one of the goals. It was perhaps cruelly stated that the Horris Hill team was a tad 'over-weighted', but in defence that day, Ralph found running up against him a dark-haired little boy with a wide face who was an exception to that criticism. A tenacious little Scotsman, fond of talking too much, at the end of the game Ralph shook hands with Henry Dundas and the two little strangers went their separate ways. They were, however, on a collision course. In 1912 Ralph joined yet another triumphant flock of boys from Summer Fields on the list of King's Scholars at Eton. Ralph and Henry would pass through the school parallel to each other, well acquainted but not particular friends.

Ralph Gamble, sometimes known as 'Freddy', gave off an aura of one so laid-back that it was an accomplishment that he managed to stay on his feet. This belied his obvious intellect and his steady progress up the school as well as his full involvement in the school's social and sporting life. No boy made it into the revered sixth form by being lazy, nor did he survive in the competitive environment amongst the Collegers by doing nothing, but Ralph continued to maintain his charade. He also continued to play football and at a shade over 6ft was 'an absolute "Dreadnought" of British bulldog courage and endurance'. He was also a talented batsman and had inherited, to a degree, his father's notable talent for tennis.

Everyone who wrote about Ralph prefaced their remarks with 'handsome' or 'very good looking' and one schoolmate even likened him to something from a Grecian vase. A fellow Guards officer who would serve in the Coldstream with him said that he was 'an exceptional youth ... of some brilliance with considerable good looks' and Oliver Lyttelton thought that he was both the most charming and the most handsome individual he ever met. 'You could not imagine that he would ever say or do a mean thing.' All of these enviable qualities might have been tiresome, but for the fact that he was 'nobody's angel' and went through life with a casual air of disinterest and a good amount of cheek that appealed to his friends.

His favourite sparring partner was a Mr Luxmoore. A retired housemaster, Luxmoore was something of an institution, still living on the premises after some seventy years at Eton man and boy. The elderly man frequently entertained boys with teas and debate and it was seen as something of a pastime amongst them to 'quarrel' with him. Ralph took it to entirely new levels for two-and-a-half years and amused himself immensely, although it must be said that Luxmoore appeared to revel in these mock rows with the boys, seeing it as a way of challenging them. When his schoolmates were solemnly writing out their achievements at school in their house books, Ralph was mocking the tradition. Rather than sports colours, clubs and academic achievements he listed himself as Eton's chief Zeppelin agent, claimed that he had only made it to breakfast twice, that he had got away with attending just one Pop debate and seldom retired to bed before 2 a.m. He styled himself as a 'Gentleman of Leisure 1913–1916'.

Ralph could not take himself seriously even in the presence of the head-master, who acted as division master to the sixth form. The 'Brown Man', as the boys referred to Edward Lyttelton on account of his outdoors complex-ion, fared no better at reining in Ralph than he had with his nephew Oliver.

One sweaty summer morning Ralph turned up for lessons clad in a great-coat and a thick, purple cricket scarf. Lyttelton was known to have a preoc-cupation with the boys' hygiene and he was immediately ruffled. 'Take that coat off!' he barked.

Ralph stood his ground. 'I'm feeling rather chilly this morning, I'd rather ...'

Lyttelton was having none of it. 'OANH!' he exclaimed. (This was a grunt that he had a habit of prefacing remarks with). 'TAKE IT OFF!'

Ralph complied. He was naked from the waist up, having neglected to find a clean shirt.

'Oanh. Put it back on.'

Evidently the headmaster forgave Ralph, because in the summer of 1915 Lyttelton took him to picturesque La Panne, just along the coast from Dunkirk, where the Belgian Royal Family had relocated. Prince Leopold, the heir to the throne, was to go to Eton, where thirty or so Belgian boys from well-to-do families had been given refuge in various houses since 1914. He would be put in Lubbock's house with Prince Henry, and Ralph was to act as a private tutor for the summer in preparation.

By Easter 1916, Ralph was about to turn 19, the time had come for him to play his own part in the war. He began his journey to the front with a short trip to Windsor and promptly received a commission in the Coldstream Guards. He was just about ready for the front in October and travelled out to join the 1st battalion. Henry Dundas claimed the Coldstream had been harder hit that any of the other Guards battalions on the Somme and the 1st Coldstream was a shadow of itself when Ralph arrived to help replenish their losses of September 1916.

Ralph had been at the front some six months when, in spring 1917, another officer of special importance to him arrived at the front. When he had just begun at Eton, Ralph had been allocated one of the school's sporting greats as a fagmaster in the shape of Logie Colin Leggatt. Logie was yet another member of the 1912 cricketing XI that had played at Lord's with the likes of George Llewelyn Davies. The eldest surviving son of William Leggatt, another member of the Indian Civil Service, Logie had been born in Bangalore in 1894. At the end of 1912, Ralph's first winter at Eton, Logie also led a famed College Wall team that put paid to Oppidan hopes on St Andrew's Day.[2] As if that were not enough, he played again at Lord's in 1913, was Keeper of the Wall,[3] editor of the *Eton College Chronicle*, helped to run the Shakespeare Society and made the Newcastle Select.

Reginald Gamble, as was part of his irregular routine, returned to England on leave as many summers as possible so to play at the Lawn Tennis Championships at Wimbledon. On this particular occasion, his parents had then sailed east again and young Ralph had been left feeling rather glum. Logie noticed that the younger boy was homesick and it saddened him. As one who knew only too well the pain of having parents far away in India, he was resolved to try to help. As school dispersed for leave Logie penned him a heartfelt note:

> I expect you must have been very upset by your people's departure to India. I wonder if I could do anything to help you? You have plenty of backbone, and what is better plenty of religion, and you will nearly always be able to fight your own battles, but you may be rather hard hit this time and perhaps you would like to apply to someone older than yourself. If so Ralph, I just want to tell you ... that there is one friend of yours who would be overjoyed if he could help you.

He didn't want to be forceful about it ('correspondence at once becomes impossible if one party moves unwillingly to the ink pot') but Ralph was left in no doubt that if he wished to discuss his sadness with someone confidentially, then this hallowed figure of the school was ready to listen. They became firm friends. Ralph's response, if he ever wrote one, does not survive but when Logie left for war 'next to the family' he rated Ralph as dearest to him and the latter was duly supplying him with letters from Eton and keeping him informed about everything that was going on in his absence.

In 1913 Logie had left school, the scene of so much happiness for him. He went up to Cambridge where he remained but a short time before the Kaiser and his army intervened. He volunteered swiftly for the Rifle Brigade at the outbreak of war and before he knew it was put in the 13th Battalion and sent off for training as part of Kitchener's new army.

When Logie departed for war in July 1915 with another Colleger named Charles Rowlatt, he was more concerned for his family than he was for himself. 'I have never disguised to yourself the fact that in these next months you who stay at home have got to suffer very much more than we who go abroad.' It was, he believed, a good experience for him. He argued that he had many failings, and whether he believed it deeply or not, that some of them may be atoned for by 'a little hardship and self-sacrifice'. After all he was young, and as such would it not be an adventure from which he could learn valuable lessons?

Logie related everything back to his life's passion, cricket. He wanted to play the best of all his matches 'and if I do get bowled out – well what a life I've had: the most wonderful family, home life, College at Eton and always a sufficiency of very dear friends. Here I stand,' he told his father, 'what you and [mother] and Eton have made me and God bless you both for all you have done for me.'

School was constantly on his mind at the front. Logie had photos of his three fags in his dugout, including Ralph and the sparkling Reggie Colquhoun, later a house master, who wrote him eight-page letters full of the minutiae of school life. Ralph kept up correspondence firstly from Eton and then from La Panne, which he seemed to be enjoying immensely. Logie and Charles wrote back to school appealing for footballs, boots and equipment for their men and were bombarded with gifts. Then leave came and Logie rejoiced in spending as much of it as Eton as he could. 'Jack' Rowlatt, Charles' younger brother, even organised a scratch game of football in his honour and Logie spent his brief spell at home with his family, Ralph and the others.

Whilst he was gaining plenty of experience in the rigours of trench war-fare, battles were a thing left to the imagination. At the advent of 1916 Logie and Charles had decided that they would rather like to try and get into the Guards, but they agreed that it would be bad form to abandon their battalion of the Rifle Brigade until it had at least seen a fight. 'After that all of us who survive are certain to apply for transfers!'

Suddenly in April 1916 all leave was stopped and Logie was thrust into suc-cessive bombing, gas and bayonetting courses as the British Army prepared for the Battle of the Somme. But then disaster befell him, a disaster that would have struck his worried parents as an enormous piece of luck. Logie was a big, solid young man but on 30 June 1916 he was playing rugby when a tiny little fellow landed on his ankle and snapped it. It rendered him 'a less heroic casu-alty than one might have wished' and saw him removed from the battalion. His only consolation was that it appeared that the 13th Rifle Brigade was not earmarked for a substantial role in the upcoming show. He was still disap-pointed and ended up in an Oxford hospital, resigned to his fate. 'London is apparently full up and as I only just escaped Manchester or Leeds by the skin of my teeth I suppose I ought to be grateful.'

It took months for Logie's ankle to heal, but by the spring of 1917 he had managed to affect his regimental move and now proudly wore the badge of the Coldstream Guards. He was in his element in barracks at Windsor, inviting half of College to tea and revelling in the shared Etonian heritage of his fellow offi-cers. By 1 March Logie had arrived in France with a small draft of Guardsmen and was waiting to be sent up to a battalion. His first mission at the front was to catch up with Ralph. It appeared that the Guards Division, with its huge popu-lation of OEs and familiar faces, was going to fully live up to his expectations. Whilst languishing at the depot he happened to run into another OE, Colonel 'Gilly' Follett, in command of the 2nd Coldstream Guards. Follett had heard that Logie was in the regiment and had intended to try to get him so Logie laid it on as thick as he could. 'I told him I wanted very much to get to one of the fighting battalions and I hope I may be able to get to him.' It worked. Logie arrived at the 2nd Coldstream Guards a week later.

Everywhere that Logie turned in his battalion, to his joy, there was Eton. Of the four officers in his company, three were OEs and one of those had been in Pop his first half. He had caught up with Henry Dundas and Charles Hambro of the 3rd Coldstream, a slightly younger cricketer. He had even spied his French master, Mr de Satge, passing him in his capacity as interpreter to the Welsh Guards.

Whilst the Guards eked out their last few weeks on the Somme there was plenty of time for the Etonian population to socialise. Oliver Lyttelton and Henry went for walks before breakfast. On the way back they would pretend they were still at school. They told themselves that the river was Boveney Weir[4] and had mock conversations about colours, 'You will be second choice for Sixpenny,'[5] and about masters, 'I hope to be up to Broader[6] next half.' So it went on all the way back to headquarters. On one occasion Ralph went off to meet Logie for a picnic. They borrowed bicycles and went off to a wood that still had Germans lurking at the other end to laze about and talk Eton shop whilst on another day Ralph and Henry hitched a lift in a lorry to a nearby village and gorged themselves on omelettes and coffee at the house of an old French dame.

The 3rd Grenadier Guards had fashioned a little show for the entertain-ment of the rest of the division. Henry thought it was wonderful when they put it on for the 2nd Guards Brigade:

> It is an amazing tribute to the Brigade that one can have an officer kissing
> an officer's servant (doing Cinderella) and the Sergeant Major – the greatest
> man in any battalion probably – flirting with a junior Corporal (an ugly
> sister) without the smallest diminishing of discipline. Magnificent really.

There were quieter ways to pass the time too. Henry had been reading a newly published memorial volume about Charles Lister and, largely due to

General John, the brigade staff had begun producing a small newspaper enti-tled *The Daily Dump*. It carried, on his instructions, poems and such trench proverbs as 'Many a muddle makes a medal', and amusing anecdotes about Guards characters. 'Colonel Greer has returned from his visit to Boulogne where he went to consult a famous dental specialist,' it reported one morning. 'In his hurry to get the thing done, he apparently went to the wrong dentist who extracted the wrong tooth. The Colonel we are glad to say looks none the worse for his trip.' Work also continued on Eric Greer and Henry's own newspaper project, although Henry proved rather lazy, claiming that the mud addled his brain. Their poems and sketches were about to come to fruition, however and appeared with regularity in the *Daily Graphic*.

Henry returned from leave in May 1917 to find the brigade preparing to move imminently. Summoned to see General John he was given rather a peculiar job. He was to find out the details of all of the Old Etonians in the brigade with their projected destination once the Guards moved from the Somme. Henry could not fathom what an earth for, but they would all find out soon enough.

Ralph too went on his first leave after almost nine months at the front. He came back refreshed, bringing everyone good tidings from Eton and with his mood much improved, but it was not to last. He went over to dinner with Logie a couple of days later and reported sulkily that he had been taken from his battalion. To his utter disgust he had been summoned on to the personal staff of General Feilding, commanding the division.

Whilst Ralph was furious, everyone else was unanimous in their approval. Having declared that 'of course the whole ADC system was one long period of snobbery and intrigue and petticoats', Henry now did a complete U-turn when it meant his friend being removed from danger. Logie agreed. 'I can't say what a relief it is for me to know that he is out of harm's way for the pres-ent.' In fact, he wished they would just send him home for the duration.

Although the Battle of Arras was over, the resumption of serious hostilities appeared to be creeping ever nearer. The Guards began their move north by way of a stop at Wardrecques near St Omer. On arrival they bivouacked in a pretty little field, but more importantly it was flat. Logie could almost see the wicket in place. Even more happily, it transpired that he was now within reach of his Aunt Muriel.

Muriel Thompson was quite a lady. With her brothers she shared some of the credit for founding the automobile racing club at Brooklands before the war and won the first women's race there in 1908 in her car 'Pobble'. She wanted to follow one of Logie's uncles to war as an ambulance driver but as a woman she was unwelcome, so she had joined the First Aid Nursing Yeomanry. After driving for the French and Belgians, in 1916 she became one of the first women to drive for the British Army, as women were finally permitted to participate in this aspect of the war effort. By 1917 she had risen to second in command of the Calais Convoy and was now conveniently placed to spend time with her beloved nephew when he could get away.

Of course, with a formation so heavily weighted towards Eton, 4 June could not pass unnoticed. Logie's thoughts were entirely with the school on this hallowed day. It was a warm sunny day. 'Oh but it ought to be spent on Upper Club under the trees,' he lamented. 'Can't you hear the pigeons in school yard; lunch at m'tutor's: mayonnaise, cutlets ... wonderfully creamy pudding; more cricket, tea, absences, procession of boats ... fireworks ... Will it ever come again?' He could almost reach out and touch it, but France was a far cry from the banks of the Thames. 'You know the longing ... which hurts?' he wrote. 'I sometimes feel it when I sit and think of the days when I could write KS after my name.'

General John's odd request for a catalogue of Etonians fell into place when a large contingent of OEs converged on St Omer on that breezy evening for a dinner to mark the special date. These 4 June dinners had become frequent the length and breadth of all fronts since 1915, with gatherings of Etonians getting together however they could, toasting the occasion and sending back a telegram to school; but this was by far the largest and most memorable meal during the war.

The band of the Coldstream Guards had set up at one end of the dining hall, which was dominated by a large chandelier decorated with ribbons of light Eton blue. Such exalted personages as Gough, the army commander, and the Earl of Cavan, commanding the corps beneath him that contained the Guards, sat at the top table. After the food there was a sing-song with typed prompts in Latin as well as a rousing rendition of 'God Save the King'. Cavan shushed everyone down after the 'National Anthem' and called Absence as if they were at school. No less than 206 Etonians answered their names, with 116 of them members of the Guards Division.

The singing took up again and the congregation gave a rousing rendition of the 'Eton Boating Song', by which time some of those assembled had taken to standing on tables at the back. They were beginning to creak and groan. Cavan was determined to try to make a speech but naturally could not be heard by anyone that wasn't standing right under his nose. 'This, however, did not prevent everyone from howling with applause whenever he seemed to get to the end of a sentence.'

At some point, someone, 'probably an ex-Tug', wrote out the obligatory tele-gram to be sent back to the headmaster at Eton. He did it in Latin. One of the battalion commanders was called up to construe in front of the crowd. He failed dismally and was given a yellow ticket made out especially for the occa-sion. Gough, no less, was then called up and proved just as incapable and, as this was considered a far worse transgression, he was issued with a white slip[7].

The official proceedings were wrapped up by a rendition of 'The Vale'[8], at which point the first table collapsed. 'Pandemonium reigned.' Cavan tried to opt for a swift exit and sent a polite enquiry to Hubert Gough asking him if he was ready to take his leave. Gough sent an indignant reply back to say that he was busy. At that point the army commander was at the bottom of a scrum on the floor. 'Whenever a group of people were seen a ram[9] was spontane-ously formed by others, and then at once became a vortex of legs and arms.' Logie watched Gough being hoisted around the room by a seething mass of brigadiers and junior ensigns. 'Not very bad,' he remarked. One attendee said that the most vivid memory he had was of what he thought was a brigadier holding another man down by the throat and squeezing an orange into his victim's eye.

Henry managed to contain himself, sitting next to Ralph and opposite Logie. He wasn't one for drinking to excess anyway. They had bumped into a few contemporaries from other units but nobody that he was particularly des-perate to see so he stuck to the usual crowd. He was disappointed with the lack of reverence shown for the occasion by some, the idea that Eton was nothing more than an excuse for an annual orgy, but he got over it. 'Why shouldn't one enjoy oneself as one likes.' Gough and Cavan ran away soon after the mayhem began. General John and most of the brigadiers were hoisted before they too managed to scramble out, after which a mock battle began, the strongpoint being where the band had been until they too scarpered.

Pip Blacker had arrived late and sitting amongst strangers he enjoyed it less than the others. By midnight the room looked more like Ginchy than a dining room and the party began to wind down. He never could figure out whether or not the authorities were apathetic about the rowdy nature of the officers present or whether they looked at it and sympathised with 200 young men 'most of whom had seen hell in the last twelve months' and let them get on with it.

The Daily Dump reported that Captain Smith of the Coldstream Guards had arrived at Wardrecques in a motor car on 8 June. 'His appearance was the signal for all Old Etonians to retire to their dugouts as it was confidently expected that the Captain was on his way round to collect a large sum of money for the damages incurred.' Happily though it transpired that he was merely there to report that there was a huge amount in the event's kitty that more than covered a complete renovation of the dining room. There was even a significant sum left over and this was to be sent to the Eton Memorial Fund. General John relaxed, promptly invited him to tea 'and the room was still filled with a merry and enthusiastic party'.

Three days after the 4 June dinner at St Omer the summer, militarily speaking, started with a bang. The Germans had been holding on to Messines and the surrounding high ground ever since the 9th Lancers had been forced out of it in 1914. Now an Etonian general was leading the charge to take it back. Herbert Plumer was a practical man, popular amongst his men. He had planned for his army to make a limited, concentrated attack to capture the front of the Messines Ridge, but Haig had characteristically doubled his intentions by adding the back side of the ridge and a further advance that took them 3,000 yards from their starting point.

At 3.10 a.m. on 7 June the earth heaved and nineteen mines fulfilled their task, ripping the Belgian countryside apart in the largest man-made explosion yet seen. At the same time the artillery barrage roared into action. The infantry burst forward towards the traumatised Germans. The first objectives fell, including Messines itself. The enemy were in no frame of mind to repel Plumer's men. Just after 3 p.m. the British launched an assault on what had been deemed the final objectives of the day and by nightfall this had been seized from the Germans too. By 14 June they had cleaned up and completed their task in its entirety.

Plumer's assault on Messines was well planned and well executed but more importantly it was a testament to what could be achieved with a limited set of objectives, as opposed to flinging men at the enemy and trying to smash through the Germans. The Guards had remained at Wardrecques, lest they be required to help exploit the situation at Messines, but when it transpired that this would not be the case they began entraining for the Salient in mid June. The news was not received with any joy, for the Guards knew as well as any other regiment the miseries that that awful spot had to offer.

Their new home revolved around what had become the poisonous little village of Boesinghe where the whole area was low-lying and in part dissected by the Yser canal. Aside from the village, one of the other preferred targets of the German gunners was the chateau at Elverdinghe and its grounds. It just so happened that Henry and the rest of the brigade staff were about to follow numerous British units before them and make the building their home. The chateau looked sturdy enough from a distance, but in fact it had been much knocked about by shellfire. Sandbags were stacked up at the doors. Rain dripped through shell holes in the roof and the windows had been shattered. From the empty frames Henry and Oliver could see Pilckem Ridge in the distance, when torn-up sacks did not hang as shields to the elements. They took a bedroom on the first floor to share but almost immediately had to move downstairs where it was safer in the brigade office. Heavy artillery was wheeled amid the splintered trees behind the gardens, where men were ensconced under the walls and in makeshift dugouts, and it started firing from under their noses. The Germans paid them back with such ferocity that Oliver Lyttelton claimed that their teeth rattled in their heads.

On their right the Guards Division met Marc Noble's Welsh Division across the railway. Marc had been resident at Elverdinghe himself in the previous months but he and his outfit were now concentrating down into a smaller space to accommodate troops arriving for the summer offensive.

After the harrowing effect of Mametz Wood on the Somme, Marc's artillery brigade had been pulled out of the lines with the devastated Welsh infantry whom they supported so that they might all restore themselves before they were required to go back into action. It was a long process and they took part in no major offensives, aside from Marc and his guns providing support at Messines. The intervening twelve months had had a significant effect on him though, and although he had just turned 20, emotionally Marc had aged considerably.

He returned home twice on leave before the summer of 1917 and his sister Marjorie noticed that he'd changed. He ordinarily wouldn't speak about 'the unpleasant part' of the war but she could tell by his manner that it had taken its toll. Marc was still there, but he was solemn. Every now and again he would refer to isolated incidents or scenes. A German aeroplane crashing to the ground, the pilot tumbling down in flames whilst Tommies on the ground cheered. At a ruined farm near his guns Marc wandered through a sprinkling of officers' graves, dotted about the weed strewn and unkempt fields. 'It somehow looked so indescribably lonely. Out here one is always as gay as possible, but I think this made me feel quite sad.' Marc spoke to her of removing an identity disc from a man who had been dead and unburied for a long time. 'But you soon have to readjust your point of view,' he reasoned. 'And you simply have to give up associating death with everything beautiful and reverent like you do at home.' As he walked about at night on his own Marc, passionate about poetry, was haunted by the words of Coleridge:

> Like one that on a lonesome road
> Doth walk in fear and dread,

And having once turned round walks on,
And turns no more his head;
Because he knows, a frightful fiend
Doth close behind him tread.

The garden in which Marc's guns were parked reminded him of a post-apocalyptic version of his family home in Norfolk. The field guns sat in rose beds where the flowers still grew out of 'a wilderness of weeds'; the shattered greenhouse was covered in straggling vines. There was no glass left in the frames and the metal was twisted and bent into fantastic shapes by shellfire.

Over 3,000 guns were being assembled in Flanders. Gradually their rate of fire increased as they worked towards a horrific preliminary bombardment, bigger than that on the Somme. On 1 July Marc's entire neighbourhood had been under sustained heavy fire when frantic news arrived at about 8 p.m. that a howitzer battery further along had suffered a direct hit from the Germans countering their fire. The battery's commander was a fellow OE and a friend of Marc's, Jack Bligh, and Marc was determined to go to see if he could help them. Running off with a South African doctor who was attached to the artillery, Marc grabbed a Red Cross car from the nearby field ambulance and drove off to see if they could find any survivors in the mangled dugout. They drove up as far as they could over the pock-marked ground and then got out to walk the rest of the way. They were less than 100 yards off Marc's haunting rose garden when a high-explosive shell came whizzing in and exploded almost on top of them, wounding both men seriously.

At 9 p.m. the car returned, carrying Marc and his South African companion, driven by two men of the Hampshire Regiment who had found them and were returning Marc and Dr Cohen to the field ambulance. The doctor had been struck in the head and across his body, but was conscious and able to tell them what had happened. He was severely wounded but the medical attendant thought that he had a fighting chance and so he was sent down the line[10]. As for Marc, he was deemed a lost cause. He was unconscious from the shock of his injuries and he barely had a pulse. His right foot had been blown off and as well as substantial injuries to his other foot he had a nasty wound to his arm and significant burns. He had lost a vast amount of blood.

By chance one of the medical personnel present knew him. A Corporal Daldry had been a clerk in the estate office at Marc's home prior to the war. He helped to dress the young Etonian's wound and put his arm in a sling. Then there was nothing to do but make him comfortable. They covered him in hot-water bottles and gave him a little brandy, at which point he began to regain consciousness. Marc was largely coherent, clear enough to give his name and other personal details. They were surprised to find out that he was adjutant of his brigade at only 20. When they asked him his religion though, he became upset. 'Why do you ask that? Am I going to die?' Daldry lied to him and told him it was purely for administrative purposes.

Marc was in a substantial amount of pain. At 10 p.m. they gave him a large dose of morphia. He spoke a little, on and off about his guns, his battery, signals. He passed away just before midnight, still lying on a stretcher propped up on trestles with a screen around him and a single acetylene lamp burning by his head. Sewn up in an army blanket under the watchful eye of Daldry he was buried, still wearing his uniform and his arm still in a sling, in the grave near the fellow OE he had been hoping to help. Jack Bligh, 24, and Marc Noble, 20, lie two graves apart in Ferme Olivier Cemetery. The latter had been killed by the very instrument of warfare that his father and grandfather had devoted their lives to developing. Death, the 'frightful fiend' stalking Marc down lonely Flanders roads, had caught up with him on the eve of the next great offensive in Flanders.

Notes
1. Francis St Leger Greer was killed on 1 February 1917 and buried at Heilly Station Cemetery.
2. Every year in November the Oppidans take on the Collegers at the Wall Game. In 1912, with Logie at the helm, College scored an emphatic victory.
3. An Etonian term for Captain.
4. A spot on the Thames at Eton used for rowing.
5. A reference to cricket colours.
6. Mr Broadbent.
7. These tickets were a form of punishment at Eton at the time. The white slip entailed a trip to the headmaster and was considerably worse.
8. A traditional Eton song sung at the end of the summer when boys leave the school.
9. A formation from the Field Game, another form of Etonian football played at the time.
10. Dr Benjamin Cohen subsequently died of his injuries on 3 July and was buried at Mendinghem Military Cemetery.

18

Setting the Tone

For most of the time that Marc Noble had known the area around Elverdinghe it had been a quiet sector. But it was now obvious to the Germans perched on the Pilckem Ridge watching Allied activity that events were pending. They upped their game accordingly.

Brigade by brigade the Guards travelled to the rear, to the town of Herzeele, to undergo intensive training in ten-day stints. General Feilding, commanding the division, sought to verse his men fully in attack methods. Near the village trenches had been dug in an open stretch of ground and the Guards practised assaulting them. Much emphasis was put on working with aeroplanes, signal communications and the medical arrangements. Close to divisional headquarters a sand model had been erected projecting the whole of Lord Cavan's corps sector. Evelyn Fryer and his NCOs studied and studied it to learn all the features of the landscape that they were about to assault. On 6 July even the king himself was present with the Prince of Wales to watch rehearsals with Hubert Gough. When they were not physically practising their attack there was no respite for the Guardsmen. There were conferences, map and aeroplane studies.

In the weeks running up to the move Logie Leggatt had been on all manner of courses on topics such as bombing and bayonet fighting. Pip Blacker had been on the latter course. It was made clear to the pupils that they were not fighting by Queensberry Rules. In addition to sticking your opponent with the bayonet the men were told to smash him in the face with their rifle butt, as well as attempting to knee him or kick him in his crotch. They were told to kick, stamp, claw, gouge and bite whenever they got the chance.

When work was completed for the day the 'Eton Ramblers'[1] atmosphere prevailed. Henry Dundas was the star of the mess. He would intersperse his singing of a vast repertoire of Harry Lauder and Gilbert and Sullivan songs with the mock Scotch sermons that he had been perfecting since he was five. 'The most elaborate and ridiculous perorations came rolling off his tongue enriched by absurd parables, painted by the most characteristic quotations, and driven home with the unctuous insistence and bucolic pedantries of the original.' Henry's buoyant attitude benefited those around him. Oliver Lyttleton claimed that, at least outwardly, he didn't care two straws for the daily and nightly doses of shellfire. 'His nonchalance was remarkable.'

Hugh Ross, an Etonian major in the Scots Guards, had been in a dugout along the garden wall at Elverdinghe for some time and had been intensely shelled day and night. Several of his men had been buried alive and they had had to dig them out. Hugh, at this time, was a shadow of a man and probably should have been nowhere near the line of duty. He arrived at brigade headquarters for dinner one evening covered in brick dust, exhausted and 'nearly through'. Henry was in tremendous form and by the time he finished his routine, despite the fact that outside shells were dropping in the grounds, Hugh was singing along with him. Eventually they both collapsed on to the floor laughing and, for a time at least, Hugh felt a little better.

Their dinners were a primary source of entertainment. Logie was a frequent visitor, Eric Greer rarely absent – 'a brilliant and amusing talker and a great theorist on the war'. They would debate long into the night, cigars in mouth, as they discoursed on life and death. Just four days after the 4 June dinner at St Omer there was another 'Pan-Etonian' gathering, this time just a handful of officers, overseen by General John with Viscount Holmesdale and Ralph present. Two days later Ralph and Henry escaped again. 'We talk pure Eton the whole time,' Henry reported, but 'bitter criticism of the higher command' was another prevalent topic.

Occasionally, on an evening walk, Henry and Oliver Lyttleton would play a four-hole round of imaginary golf. There were pretend clubs, carried by the brigadier and John Dyer. Logie Leggatt was fortunate enough to get over to see his aunt more than once. He was spoiled by the ladies present with two good meals and even a set of tennis before a sing-song.

In the middle of July though, Logie picked up a minor injury that again threatened to remove him from duty right before a major offensive. The offending foot became infected but he was determined that he would be 'skipping about quite happily' by the time the Coldstream Guards attempted to cross the Yser Canal at the end of the month. Gilly Follett had organised for him to be treated at headquarters to ensure that Logie wouldn't be removed from the battalion's strength and whisked off to a hospital somewhere.

Whilst laid up, Logie had time to contemplate what was about to occur. For some months his mother had been urging him to keep a diary. Now, with nothing else to do but mark time whilst his foot was repeatedly bathed in iodine, he decided to give it a go. 'Perhaps it may be interesting to chronicle, as far as possible, my feelings during the next few days.'

The plan for the big push was ambitious indeed. The man-made earthquakes at Messines had opened a lock on the Western Front so to speak. Now, if the situation was to be exploited, Haig needed to kick the door down. The offensive east of Ypres was to be the main thrust aimed at ending the war as far as British contingents were concerned in 1917. Following the abject failure of Nivelle's attempts on the Aisne and the mutinous consequences of his disastrous campaign, there was no longer going to be French co-operation on the scale originally intended. Any thoughts of abandoning the attack were out of the question. If the Germans caught wind of the seditious atmosphere in the French Army and chose to capitalise on it, there could be disastrous consequences.

Whilst political wrangling went on, military preparations continued. Gough had handed over all of his men in the Arras area and was given a new collection of troops with the same title of Fifth Army that would be based further north and included the Guards Division. Generals Plumer and Rawlinson had come up with an initial outline for the offensive but Haig decided that it wasn't aggressive enough and amended it to incorporate a colossal 5,000-yard advance, beyond the range of friendly artillery towards Passchendaele.

It might not have been the first battle in the area, but this would be the first major British offensive. It would also be the first time that the Guards had done all the preparation for a major offensive and then taken part in the initial assault, having been held in reserve at Loos and on the Somme. The sector they had been given was not ideal, primarily because of the presence of the Yser Canal. Up to 70ft wide it was shallow but composed of soft mud 'into which a man sank like a stone'. It provided a sufficient obstacle for both sides to have let it be thus far in the war, content to look at each other from opposite banks. Now, in order to advance towards Pilckem Ridge, the Guards would have to cross it in the midst of battle. The Royal Engineers had constructed an imitation of it near Herzeele for practice, but it was still likely to cause heavy, heavy casualties.

Plans were also being made for the all-important artillery bombardment that would precede the battle. More than 3,000 guns had now been drawn into action and positioned almost wheel to wheel, ready to blaze away at the Germans along the entire front. In the run up to the big day the country-side would be gradually pounded out of all recognition as the Allied artillery attempted to weaken the German position.

Yet again progress across the battlefield was to be marked by a series of coloured lines. The first, the Blue, constituted the German front line and the Gheluvelt Plateau. Gough's men would then move on to the Black Line, the second enemy position on the reverse side of the Pilckem Ridge. Further south it would take in more of the Gheluvelt Plateau. Advancing on to the Green Line the Fifth Army would move across the Steenbeck, a stream that became a flooded nuisance in bad weather. The fourth objective, the ambitious Red Line, was way off towards Langemarck.

Logie Leggatt was jotting down his thoughts on his sickbed and had put them into categories including courage, friends, memories and death. He decided to expand on some of his themes. 'Of myself I expect I am the most hopeless coward,' he wrote. 'I am imaginative, absurdly soft-hearted and cut a contemptible figure at the dentist.' He had been chatting with a fellow OE and Colleger in the artillery at Poperinghe a few weeks beforehand and he had remarked to Logie that it must be very difficult to be gutless if you were in the Guards. 'I appreciate what he means,' Logie wrote. 'If one is at all impressionable – and I am very – the discipline, the whole atmosphere begins to grip one as soon as one joins the Division.' As a sportsman he had never shied away from a good struggle and this, he hoped, was an indication that he would do himself justice in the coming fight.

He thought of his friends constantly. 'Ralph, whom I love next to the family … praise be that Ralph is or should be safe.' Almost without exception the others that he listed were also Etonians. His other fags, masters, then Edward Lyttelton and old Luxmoore. 'It is … easy to see why Eton is to me such a vivid personality. Eton is simply the cumulative charms of my friends.' Logie's memories were also dominated by school. 'My visit to Eton when I heard I was going to get in, my various matches and exams.' Sights and smells jogged his recollections. 'The smell of wall mud, the sound of the doves in school yard, or Lupton's tower clock, or a fives ball [rebounding off a wall].' He could go on and on and it was beginning to sadden him.

Logie did not contemplate the idea of his own death, but the memories of his contemporaries in College that had left him haunted his sleep. Like Regie Fletcher, Logie couldn't believe that one could cease to exist; he refused to believe it. 'The utter annihilation of such characters is quite impossible; they must all be very much alive – somewhere.' He sought to put it into some coherent form for his family. 'Death is simply a jumping-off trench to another and far greater objective.' This gave him no small amount of comfort. 'That being so, if I am to be scuppered in this push, I realise I go in the best possible company, and with hopes of speedily meeting my old friends again.'

Whilst Logie was laid up with his sore foot, preparations for the offensive continued apace. Practice runs crossing the canal at Poperinghe got larger and larger in scale until 500 men at a time slopped across the shallow waterway. The junior officers were still unaware on which date they would be attacking, but dumps had to be created and filled. They and their men carried out continual fatigues to and from the front line as they stockpiled equipment and stores as far forward as possible.

German animosity increased accordingly and as the Guards and the Royal Engineers trekked backwards and forwards they were subjected to heavy shellfire. Evelyn Fryer was terrified, especially when working in the dark. Boesinghe, 'which in ordinary times was no bed of roses', now became an inferno. He remembered one trip in particular. He took ninety men to move heavy trench-mortar bombs to a gun position and they were shelled all the way there and all the way back, shells skimming off the top of the trenches as they moved along. Weary men stacked their loads at the end of their perilous slog, 'praying that the next salvo would not send them all sky high'. One Guardsman referred to it as 'house-moving in Hell'.

The preliminary artillery bombardment began on 16 July. With no built-up areas to aim for in the Guards' sector and a large space until any network of German trenches, the heavy artillery concentrated on woods, farms and any known pillboxes, whilst the field guns kept up a sustained fire on known defences and tried to cut the wire. Nearly twenty trench mortars also bashed away at the enemy's front line whilst machine gunners fired high to harass them with a hail of bullets.

It was a harrowing experience for the enemy troops manning their lines but in return the Germans showered the Guards with gas shells. It was especially bad every morning at dawn when the enemy pummelled them lest this be the day of the attack. When daylight came the repair work would have to start so that when men came out of the trenches at Boesinghe they were physically and mentally exhausted by their work and by the strain of constant alarms and prolonged stints wearing their gas helmets.

By 22 July Logie had managed to get a boot on and was hobbling about in the bright summer sunshine. Twenty-four hours previously his participation in the advance had hung by a thread. As he put it, it was a race between GHQ and his foot. Two days later he reported a stifling hot day as he returned to his battalion. The attack was to be delayed by almost a week. As it transpired, zero day would now be 31 July 1917 because the French had requested longer to prepare. General Feilding immediately organised his men so as to give the two attacking brigades as much rest as possible.

Logie arrived just in time to take part in the last dress rehearsal for the big show. 'It is extraordinary to think how elaborately we've sapped up our lesson when the poor old 13th Rifle Brigade were flung at half-an-hour's notice against trenches they knew nothing about. One does feel that nothing has been left to chance.' The following day, to his delight but not, he guessed, to that of general headquarters, the weather broke and the rain came pouring down. It took the edge off the heat. Nervous anxiety was building. 'The second bell has gone; the crowd is clearing, I'm anxious for the umpires to get out!²'

The 3rd Coldstream Guards were manning the front line as anxiety built in anticipation of the grand offensive. Then suddenly the Germans carried out a manoeuvre that played right into their hands. In the early hours of 27 July two wounded men of the Welsh division next door were seen jumping up and down on the opposite bank of the canal. Charlie Hambro, who had been Captain of the XI as late as 1915, went out to fetch them. When they all came back it was with the news that the enemy trenches on the other side of the canal appeared to have been completely abandoned. Charlie submitted a report that claimed, along with the observations of the wounded men, that there was a conspicuous absence of any Germans all the way back to the Steenbeck, a stream that flowed through what was to be the battlefield.

As it transpired, the Germans had partly run away from the bombardment without orders and partly panicked about the sound of the Royal Engineers tunnelling in the canal banks. This was only to fashion chambers in which to store equipment but it was enough to make them flee. With the Messines mines in mind, General Feilding did not need any more encouragement. Swiftly, he decided to have his men cross the canal that day without any artillery support to seize the opposite bank, thereby removing an extremely dangerous and potentially costly obstacle from the path of his men just days before they were due to attack.

Having been caught out the Germans began firing on the new British positions ferociously and when Charlie Hambro's battalion was withdrawn forty-eight hours later he was one of four officers who had to be removed from duty owing to shell shock. The brigade, commanded by Ma Jeffreys, had however pulled off an impressive feat. The Guards Division would now have control of the canal. The only amendments necessary on the day would be slight adjustments to the timing of the artillery planned to protect them and a short delay to zero hour to allow the troops on their right to come up level with them.

The Guards had made it to the eve of Haig's Flanders offensive, but not without cost. General Feilding himself was almost killed along with Ralph Gamble on 4 July when a stray shell whizzed right by them and exploded nearby. General John went on a walkabout the day before the battle and came back in a depressed mood. 'One meets nothing but wounded men, and one is obliged to keep stepping over dead bodies.' Eric Greer noted in mid July that the 2nd Irish Guards were down to ten fighting officers and two in reserve. Two more, including a company commander, were put out of action forty-eight hours before the battalion went into action. Evelyn Fryer inherited a company of Grenadiers on the eve of battle because his own commanding officer was wounded. He remembered with particular sadness one of the men. He had been designated to attack on the far right on zero day and he joked proudly that he was the right-hand man of the Guards Division. A shell put paid to his ambition a week before the offensive commenced.

Perhaps the most crushing loss from a military point of view came on 20 July. 'Byng' Hopwood, another OE and commanding officer of Ralph's battalion, was walking down a communications trench with his second in command when both were hit by a shell. He was the fourth colonel that the 1st Coldstream Guards had lost during the war. Ralph had been 'devoted' to him and was understandably devastated. The battalion had lost sixty men and six officers, all of them invaluable so close to an attack. Just behind the division was a cemetery named Canada Farm. When the division arrived in mid June it was a mere scattering of graves. By 30 July it was full of Guardsmen killed preparing for the attack on Pilckem Ridge.

From his bed at headquarters Logie had had plenty of time to contemplate the big day in the notes he had been making for his family. 'Sometime in the next fortnight I shall be requested to pop the parapet, cross the ... Yser Canal, and step lightly out in the direction of Pilckem Ridge.' It didn't matter how he was supposed to cover the ground, or why. The fact was that it seemed likely that many of them would not return. So how did he face this? He didn't feel ready, but he was not in control of events as they spiralled towards the attack so what could he do other than try to overcome this doubt and perform as expected? In the run up to the battle his overriding concern was for his family, his parents, his brother and his young sister.

It was with some trepidation that Evelyn Fryer set off for the assembly trenches south-west of Boesinghe. That position had been shelled mercilessly with gas every morning at dawn and they expected no different on 31 July. He moved off in 'a state of pent up excitement, trying to appear calm, but inwardly seething.' Almost without exception the Guards Division was in position by 10 p.m. that night.

Eric Greer was ensconced in a German dugout that now acted as his battalion headquarters. Although only 27, as commanding officer, he was determined to have his battalion of Irish Guards adequately prepared and he went to great lengths to see to everything. He even issued his company commanders with postcard-sized notes that had a map of their sector on the reverse. Once in battle, Eric wanted them to mark their position on the map with an 'X', scribble a note and send it back with a runner. Before setting off Logie quickly penned a note to his parents. 'Well old things, tomorrow it happens ... There's a deuce of a noise going on ... But I'm feeling very fit and keen and calm; far less excited than [at] Lord's ... I feel it is out of my hands now and I pray merely for guidance and courage. Needless to say I'm wearing my Wall scarf, symbol of victory ... So goodbye and thank you once again.'

The initial attack would be made by the 2nd and 3rd Guards Brigades as planned; half of them advancing to the first and second lines (Blue then Black) before the remainder of the troops passed through on their way to the third objective, the Green Line. Finally, elements from the 1st Guards Brigade would pass through the whole lot on their way across the Steenbeck, swinging up to join with the French on their way to the final, Red Line. If, by some chance, the Germans completely folded, tentative plans existed to move towards Langemarck itself.

Arthur Gibbs, a young subaltern in the Welsh Guards, had left Eton at the same time as Logie Leggatt and gone up to Brasenose College, Oxford. He had heard the guns on the Somme but the barrage that began at 3.50 a.m. on 31 July 1917 was a chastening experience. 'I should like some of our munitions workers to come over and see the results of their efforts at home. I have just been thinking of the millions of people who have been working day and night for months for a victory like this.' Evelyn Fryer was listening in his assembly trench when the 3rd Battle for Ypres commenced. 'Hell was let loose ... Hell had been let loose many times before, but I doubt she got quite so much off the chain as on this memorable morning.' The noise was terrific; shells and machine-gun fire from behind them all adding to the din. In the Guards sector as the barrage went off two special companies began loosing off flaming oil drums, setting fire to everything they touched as they span towards the enemy.

When dawn came it hardly looked like summer. The threat of rain hung in a dull overcast sky. As the rest of Gough's army moved off in pursuit of their objectives the Guards stood their ground, waiting for the troops beside them to come up level with their position after the unexpected advance across the canal four days previously. At 4.25 a.m. the barrage lifted and Eric Greer's battalion moved off into desultory shellfire. Twelve minutes later, with unexpected ease, they had reached the Blue Line. Next to no opposition had stood in their way; in fact they had seen precisely one dead German by the time they began consolidating their position.

Half an hour later, Evelyn Fryer had reached the Yser Canal, coming up behind the forward troops ready for when his company would be expected to push forward. 'A false step would have pitched one into a filthy morass.' Through mud and slime they made it across and pushed on.

Meanwhile Eric Greer and his men were ready to move on to the second objective, 600 yards in front of them. On their left their fellow Guardsmen again met little resistance, but the 2nd Irish Guards were enfiladed by a machine gun from amongst the remains of a nearby wood. They would eventually push through to the Black Line by 6 a.m. with four captured machine guns and two trench mortars in tow, but it came at a tragic cost. As they had been about to move on some British guns put a stationary barrage on them, mainly shrapnel. Eric was standing in the mouth of his dugout shortly before half past five when he was hit by flying shards or a bullet, nobody could say. Before he could see how well his efforts would pay off, he was gone. He was the only Guards battalion commander to fall on 31 July.

Evelyn Fryer had studied the ground that he was to advance over relentlessly but it proved to be pointless. As soon as he took his company forward he found that all of the landmarks that he had memorised had been pulverised out of existence by artillery. At 7.15 a.m. they passed through the likes of Eric's Irish Guards to take the Green Line, but they found the way blocked by Scots Guards who had been held up in the initial advance by a machine gun in Artillery Wood. Helping them to stabilise the situation, Evelyn reached his position and awaited the next phase of the artillery bombardment that would signal that it was his turn to go forward.

Everything appeared to be going largely to plan and the Guards even saw Germans retiring in front of them. As Evelyn advanced though, they began to be harassed by a number of hidden machine guns stashed in pillboxes along the Ypres–Staden railway line. Evelyn made for them straight away and his men began firing on a fortified farmhouse. Soon enough a white flag popped up and fifty men came out with their hands up 'crying for mercy'. Evelyn couldn't find any sympathy in his heart for them. 'No one could have blamed us if we had butchered the lot.' These men had fired on them from long range, tearing into his ranks of Grenadiers, and now they wanted mercy. His company rounded them up and led them off as prisoners. 'One offered me some of his coffee as a peace offering. I declined the kind offer and showed him the road to captivity.'

By 8.A.m. Evelyn had led his company to its objective. The remnants of the road were hard to spot but once they had fixed their location they began digging in under heavy rifle fire. Oliver Lyttelton had been waiting for men of his own battalion to reach their destination, but he was not impressed by the task he had then been given. He was to lead a string of mules loaded with ammunition, wire and other stores up to Evelyn and was not looking forward to it at all. 'Mules are allergic to shellfire and if anything burst close to them, they are apt to behave in a most un-Guardsmanlike manner.' He would at least feel more useful than Henry. He felt absolutely awful, 'like a worm', sitting in a deep dugout fashioned by the engineers. He was to do 'a sort of liaison officer job' with the French next door but all he could think about was his battalion advancing in line with Eric's Irish Guards whilst he did seemingly nothing.

There remained but one objective to be taken that day. Logie had sat smoking a pipe as the artillery whipped up a metal storm at dawn, wrapped in his College Wall scarf and waiting to pass through the likes of Evelyn on the way to the Steenbeck and beyond. He was in a jovial mood, determined to go into battle 'as if it were the greatest game in the world and he was playing for Eton'. He and the rest of the 2nd Coldstream Guards crossed the canal at 6.20 a.m. and had a relatively easy time getting up to join the foremost point of the advance, picking up one single casualty.

At this point however, German resistance was beginning to harden. Out of the scattered farmhouses and pillboxes poured heavy rifle and machine-gun fire. On Logie and his men pushed, towards the Steenbeck. The troops on their left became held up and the creeping barrage left them behind. Logie and his men threw out a defensive flank whilst they waited, then together they moved off into ever-increasing artillery fire punctuated by the rattle of machine guns. Whilst their fellow men were frantically digging in the Coldstreamers performed a difficult wheel towards the French line. By 9.30 a.m. they had reached the fourth and final objective for the day after a highly successful innings and, as planned, the stumps were ready to be drawn. The Germans had quite clearly determined to hold fast at Langemarck and it was considered that to push further on was too risky.

Consolidation began and Logie, or 'Elsie' as he was known to his fellow officers, was preparing to move his men into position. He was walking up and down on top of the parapet 'as cheerful as ever' when a bullet struck the 22-year-old down. The Guards may have tasted success on this day, and casualties may have been 'light', but this was one that would hurt his friends and fellow officers immensely. Logie's commanding officer penned an epitaph of which he would have been proud. 'He was an Etonian and a Coldstreamer to the soul.' Logie was the final member of the Eton cricketing side of 1912 to fall in the Great War. Including their twelfth man, the XI of that year served on seven different fronts, was awarded three DSOs, had one of their number taken prisoner and mourned five of their side. They had battled their way to victory in the heat of that July weekend at Lord's in 1912 as a precursor to leaving their schooldays behind and embarking on their adult lives, but the match had turned out to be a glorious last hurrah before the war claimed them.

Not everyone achieved the same results as the Guards along the British front. They had been fortunate and immediately to their right troops made good inroads to take St Julien. But the southern end of the main advance was problematic. Gheluvelt Plateau was an objective and Haig believed that this was absolutely imperative in order for the offensive to succeed. A vast number of men were thrown at it but they had a torrid time and struggled greatly. The front German positions were taken but, in line with their new doctrine of defending the front lines lightly, they had fresh troops ready and waiting to counter-attack Gough's men as they advanced out of the range of their artillery support. The Germans began to push the British back to the Steenbeck and intial gains were lost.

Overall two lines of German trenches and both the Pilckem and Bellewaarde ridges were in British hands. Blue and Black lines could be ticked off, but Green and Red had proved a leap too far. By biting off more than they could chew, the British had suffered under German attempts to repulse the attack and fallen right into their hands. It amounted to some 1,500 yards of enemy territory gained.

As he bedded down and tried to sleep that night in a captured pillbox, Evelyn Fryer considered that for a full-scale offensive his company had got off lightly. Some 117 men had marched out and at the end of the day he counted forty-two, although more would trickle in later. Henry Dundas' battalion had suffered worse, thanks to concealed machine guns on their second advance. Approximately 470 men went in and of those 320 were missing, wounded or killed.

There was more agony for Henry. John Dyer was killed by a chance shell, several miles behind the advance. 'If ever a person deserved all that life could give it was John. The sweetest nature that any man ever had, he hadn't a single enemy in the world.' He bitterly mourned the death of Eric Greer too. It was another cruel, cruel blow to their circle of friends. Statistics about ground gained versus casualties suffered meant absolutely nothing to those left behind.

Henry had been tentatively inquiring about a return to his men and to the fighting line. Now he was completely resolved to return. 'In what capacity I don't care,' he claimed. He wasn't doing it for any love of fighting. 'Doubtless existence in the battalion would be even more idle. None the less, I could laze with a clear conscience – which I can't do here.' As soon as the battalion came out of the lines, Hugh Ross began applying to get him back. A clear plan had evolved. Of their group of pals, an Etonian company commander named Ivan Cobbold had picked up a nasty facial injury, with a broken jaw and several teeth knocked out. Henry wanted to take over from him until he could return.

The rain which had been threatening all day began to fall in torrents soon after dark and the ground became disgusting, un-traversable. It was a suitable reflection of the mood at brigade headquarters. Sadly it was just the onset of weeks of horrific, wet conditions. Oliver was firm in his conviction that the artillery bombardment had caused the unending storm to come down on them.

In what proved to be her last letter to her son, Logie Leggatt's mother wrote that his father, ever the optimist, had slowly ceased to talk of what they might all do after the war. As for her, she said that the three years of waiting had given her a chance to get used to the idea that he might not return. They were firm in their conviction that Logie would do his best; he had never let them down and all her life, if she lived to be a 100 and he didn't live to 23, she would have the memory of the best and dearest boy ever a mother had. She would see him always in her mind, turning halfway down the stairs as he left, saluting her.

Had Logie spent more than a few months at Cambridge then his perspective might have been different. Likewise had Henry or Ralph not walked straight out of Eton College and into the war, then their school might not have figured so prominently in their minds. As it was, there had been no time for their schooldays to recede into the past; they were everything. Eton College to them was a life without death and without the day-to-day hardships of the front or the stresses of battle and it was almost the only life experience that they knew away from their present misery, so they would cling to it fiercely.

In 1915 Logie had written home of his motivations for going to war, and given that his friends, new and old, were becoming ever more cynical about the conflict, his sentiments were apt to appeal to them. 'What am I fighting for? Not at all England with its follies and conceits, simply for about a hundred friends ... for red-brick buildings and a grey chapel ... and above all for the most tremendous tradition I shall ever know.' His love for Eton was infectious. An American colleague, a Harvard man, had been entirely caught up by this group of OEs and the manner in which they represented their old school with passion and pride. 'Does anyone wonder, Sir,' he wrote to Logie's father, 'when such nobleness and strength, gentleness, sweetness and purity is in the hearts of those she sends forth?'

One acquaintance of Logie's put it succinctly when he said that his fallen friend had helped to set the current tone amongst the Collegers. Logie knew that he was not perfect, but his high standards were inspiring fellow Etonians to look up to him as an example when the time came to leave for war. Those that followed him aspired to emulate more than his sporting achievements. Logie conducted himself in such a way that he embodied a school spirit that meant a lot to the large numbers of very young men on their way to the front with limited experience of life outside their boarding houses.

If anyone had been exposed to Logie's example it was his former fag, Ralph. In turn, the likes of Henry had come to know and love him during the war. The eldest members of their coterie had now been struck down: Logie, John, Eric. They had left little more than adolescents behind. The war, however, would carry on. The example of Ralph and Henry's lost friends had set the tone. Now it would be up to the youngest of them as the killing went on and the Flanders offensive began to look as if it might take on the same wasteful, relentless momentum as the campaign on the Somme the year before.

Notes
1. A cricket club comprising Old Etonians.
2. At lunchtime at Lord's the crowd was allowed to promenade on the pitch. They were warned of the resumption of play by a series of bells. The stragglers would then be shooed away by policemen and the match would begin again.

19

'HELL'

At the end of the first week of August Henry Dundas got his way and assumed command of Ivan Cobbold's company. 'I am more pleased than I can say,' he assured his parents. 'I shall be able to keep it warm for him till he comes back. I only hope I shan't be inadequate.'

He settled in quickly, but it was not a difficult task, for the entire company had been wiped out in the opening phases of the summer offensive and he was starting afresh. He was thrilled to be amongst Scotsmen. He could discourse on Hearts and Hibs with them. He didn't think his NCOs were loud or violent enough but he was over the moon when he heard a corporal charged with the Lewis gun marching along humming Gilbert and Sullivan 'and the less common bits, such as "see how he fares", "For he is a pirate king" etc … I must speak with him on the subject.'

To bolster his conviction that he had been right to go back to the battalion he had a letter from General John thanking him for his work on his staff and wishing him well. 'I should have done the same, I am sure.' He was, however, apparently mindful of Henry's youth. 'Your reputation for bravery is so high that it will probably lead you astray!' He imparted some wisdom that he hoped would keep him safe. 'Don't go and charge the Boche by yourself or stick your head over the top so that they can get a pot at you. Remember you are a Company Commander, so you are precious.'

It was sensible advice from his beloved general. At the age of 19 Henry would now have responsibility for over 200 men and the rank of captain when his company came up to strength. The average age of the four company

commanders in the 1st Scots Guards at this juncture of the war was 20 years
and 3 months. They had assumed a rank and position that took some ten years
to achieve in peacetime. 'And to this,' Henry recalled joyfully of he and his
predecessor, 'Ivan and I were thrown out of the ECOTC proficiency in 1915
for Idleness. Ha! Ha!!'

He still managed to find shades of school life everywhere. Dundas was
eagerly awaiting the arrival of Tommy Goff as a subaltern in his own company. 'It will be nice having someone who was at Eton in those Halcyon
days.' Ralph was of course nearby, having been given his old job at brigade
headquarters, regardless of the anger he had expressed at being taken from his
battalion to join Feilding's personal staff. Henry couldn't give a damn if he
was disappointed, he thought it 'delightful.

He went to Canada Farm to visit the graves of John Dyer and Eric Greer.
Henry was slightly consoled to see that they were buried almost next to each
other. In his own regiment they had said a sad goodbye to little Esmond Elliot,
cox of the VIII in 1913, who had died of wounds in the aftermath of Pilckem
Ridge. And an Eton contemporary had been awarded the Victoria Cross for
protecting an NCO of the Royal Engineers as he tried to cut enemy wire. He
was hurt but refused to abandon him and died of his wounds as a result. 'It is a
queer war,' Henry wrote. 'Dunville … was with me at Eton and did not seem
to have the makings of a hero, and now look at what he has done.'

Death was everywhere he turned. In fact it was to be an overriding, miserable theme as the rest of 1917 played out and continued to mercilessly
hack away at Henry's friends and acquaintances. Despite the success of the
Guards' endeavours at Pilckem Ridge, overall the grand strategy attached to
the Ypres offensive had overreached, learning nothing from events on the
Somme the previous summer. Attempts to follow up the opening day were
destroyed by shocking weather. It rained solidly. In fact it would only stop on
three days during the entire month of August, leaving the battlefield a scene
of unimaginable horror.

On 10 August the downpours had eased off just long enough for Hubert
Gough to order another assault. Not enough concentration was placed on the
crucial Gheluvelt Plateau and it failed miserably, with matters hampered by the
appalling conditions. Gough, though, appeared to be oblivious to unfolding
events. He ordered another attack on 16 August, again not placing proper attention on the plateau. Tanks detailed to take part were useless on account of the
mud, and the fighting was desperate. In the grand scheme of things it mattered
little that Langemarck itself had been taken, for it had cost 15,000 casualties that
Britain could ill afford. Up and down the line there were shattered formations

that could no longer function properly, and seventeen more Etonians died in the mud of Flanders because of the inept operations in August, nine of whom had only left school since the summer of 1914.

Patience was not a virtue associated with Hubert Gough, but his cavalier nature had been partly what singled him out to Haig above his fellow OEs, Rawlinson and Plumer, when Haig had appointed him to head his summer offensive. As August played out, though, the commander-in-chief failed to check his subordinate when he began to lose control of the situation. Neither did the government intervene as Gough continued to throw men forward. Gough would later point the finger at Haig, but whichever was responsible for the continued failure, it could not go on. The British line had been improved, but at horrific cost.

At the end of the month, Haig, his force having suffered nearly 70,000 casualties, was forced to take action. He no longer had faith in Gough's aggressive approach and so he called on the ailing General's fellow Old Etonian, Plumer. The victor of Messines had achieved success by biting off small objectives and holding on to them properly before repeating the process. It was slower and more methodical but it was far less costly.

The first of his measured steps came on 20 September in the Battle of the Menin Road. The Germans counter-attacked furiously but Plumer had not overstretched and for the first time the enemy's system of sending up specific divisions to hit back after a British attack failed miserably as they yielded some 1,000 yards in places. The next step came on 26 September at Polygon Wood. The Germans suffered a second defeat and, more importantly, they began regressing to tactics reminiscent of the Somme, packing out their front lines to try to stem the khaki tide.

On 4 October the British pushed for Broodseinde, their eye on Passchendaele and the high ground beyond. Overall the attack was another success, but these tactical achievements were far from cheap in terms of casualties. OEs continued to fall, and not all of them on the field of battle. Perhaps one of the school's most pointless and cruel losses of the war came at the end of September.

Ronnie Backus, who had travelled out with the 8th Rifle Brigade in 1915, had dug himself out after being buried alive, had been shot on the salient, and shot again on the Somme, only to suffer one the cruellest deaths on the Western Front. In the early hours of 23 September a gunner was making his way along the road to Steenwerck with a horse and cart when a flash of light drew his attention. He followed it and found a man lying face down in a ditch. The glint of Ronnie Backus' wristwatch had caught his eye.

A crumpled bicycle lay nearby. Gunner Deane of the 46th Royal Field Artillery cradled Ronnie's head on his lap as he raced him back to his battalion on his cart, but he died shortly afterwards. Having dined with a nearby battalion he had been riding his bicycle home when he was hit by a blacked-out lorry. The driver didn't notice and carried on trundling along.

Despite only having superficial bruising, a post mortem revealed that Ronnie, having survived everything the war had thrown at him, had suffered massive internal inuries. As well as massive haemorrhaging into his stomach and a lacerated kidney, his left leg had almost been severed from his pelvis. The 23 year old was buried at Westhof Farm Cemetery.

Plumer's tactics were proving effective but they were also time consuming and winter was closing in. Strategically speaking these small advances were not going to make any kind of decisive breakthrough. If the ridge on which Passchendaele itself was perched could be seized before operations shut down for the winter then the Allies would be on a strong footing till spring. Thus another assault was planned, this time on Poelcappelle and the surrounding area.

Ralph Babington was another OE to have come from Mr Le Neve Foster's house. Like Robin Blacker he arrived at Eton late; in 1914, after a planned naval career evaporated due to illness. Like Simpson he was completely irrepressible when it came to the idea of fighting the Germans. He left school at Easter 1916 and arrived on the Western Front to join the 3rd Coldstream Guards the following spring. 'In that small body there was a giant heart,' a contemporary wrote. But it was a young heart, and a naive heart. Ralph was characterised by his obsession with getting out to the front before the war ended. Once there it was all his more mature fellow officers could do to get him to keep his head down, he was so keen to see what was going on across no-man's-land.

Unfortunately the rain returned just after the Battle of Broodseinde. On 8 October Ralph Babington began leading his platoon up towards their assembly position as the rain cascaded down. A German shell plunged through the darkness and into their ranks, killing Ralph and several of his men before they reached the battle. He was 19 years old.[1]

The 2nd Coldstream Guards waded across the Broembeek towards Poelcappelle before dawn the following morning, waist deep in water and clinging to fallen trees and floating German debris. The Germans either ran away or came hurrying out to surrender, surprise etched on their faces. The thick mud meant that guns could not be wheeled into their optimum positions, and when the British artillery fired them it was on an unstable footing.

The resulting barrage was far from consistent. The Guards were luckier than most. Whilst they and the French on their left enjoyed relative success, the same could not be said of the rest of the line. A few small advances were made towards Passchendaele, but they were pushed back. Even the Guards' progress had merely brought them closer to Houthulst Forest. They had not dealt with the German defensive horrors that lay within.

In all, seven more OEs would die in the assault on Poelcappelle on 9 October. Nobody put the brakes on the offensive despite increasingly atrocious conditions. Just three days later, abandoning Plumer's cautious approach, they went again, spurred on by Haig's ill-placed optimism. There was no measured attack this time. At the First Battle of Passchendaele on 12 October men were going to be flung against the supposedly teetering Germans in the hope that they would topple over.

Victor Alexander Cazalet, 'Teenie' on account of his diminutive size, had left Eton in 1915. He shared his hatred of the war with his elder brother Edward, also an OE, and with one of his school cronies, Henry Dundas. But war was an inevitability in Victor's future when he left school and he too joined the army.

In September 1916 a Household Battalion was formed in London, drawing in men from reserve units of the Blues and Royals to serve as infantry. By this point Cazalet's extraordinarily close family was already suffering the loss of Edward. He had been killed with the Welsh Guards on the Somme in September 1916 as part of a nonsensical relief that took place mid battle and cost the fledgling battalion a large perecentage of its officers. A year later, having witnessed first hand the horrors of Arras, Victor had reached the rank of captain and got his own company.

He had been on leave, but arrived back at Poperinghe on 5 October in yet another rainstorm to find that his battalion had been providing support for the assault on Broodseinde. The men were traipsing about exhausted, wet and coated in mud. He appeared to have missed the show and was not sorry. He would much rather have had his bed, his fire and his copy of *Mansfield Park* than shells, mud and Germans. Victor's joy was short-lived when he was told that he would have to go up into the line with the battalion almost immediately as another officer was ill. 'My heart sank so I could hardly speak,' he admitted. 'I am not really a coward, but the sudden contrast was a little trying.'

Plumer and Haig had decided to push again for the high ground around Passchendaele. Victor's division would be pushing on the left of Poelcappelle itself. The march up into the line was absolutely miserable. They trudged over duckboards that sank further and further into the slime under their feet whilst the downpour continued. Victor tried to put his mind somewhere else and as he trudged along mile after mile he was pondering government policy reform on old age pensions and tax reductions amongst other political issues.

They were joined by a guide who was to escort them across the shell-torn, wire-strewn, waterlogged landscape to their starting spot. He dumped them in the middle of a field where they were given a few waterproof sheets to put up. In the wind and pouring rain Victor couldn't figure out what on earth to do with his, so he stuck a rifle and a bayonet in the ground to prop it up, pinned the sides down with rum jars and tried to get some sleep.

'Lord, what a noise' was all he could say about the barrage that signified the beginning of the assault on Poelcappelle on 9 October. The shells were falling rather close. He sat up next to his pathetic tent and watched them with a backdrop of a beautiful autumn sunrise. 'The whole world seemed to be lit up, and the sky was bright with German SOS signals and the flashes of guns. Gradually the morning broke, but the noise went on … The most lovely sunrise made us feel there were other things in the world except war.' They sat in that awful field all day until they were ordered back to the camp they had started from in pitch darkness. 'So we bundled the men out of shell holes, all half asleep and very hard to wake and find, and still more difficult to make them put their equipment on and get a move on.'

Victor and his men were entitled to hope that their ordeal was over but the following afternoon they were told to go and relieve an Essex battalion. They would soon be required to make an attack. 'Imagine this on tired men. It was Wednesday, no one had slept since Sunday.' Loading themselves up with bombs and shovels they met more guides and began trudging back towards the front line. 'We three officers dug little niches in a hole and tried to settle ourselves for the night, but the cold again kept us from getting much slumber.' After freezing in their shell hole all night it transpired that still no orders had arrived for their attack and so they sat and waited. 'Then the shelling began, and it was dreadful just to sit there helpless and get shelled.'

Finally their orders arrived. 'Twenty-four items to be read, digested and explained to the men before dark and no-one allowed to stand up, only run from one hole to another.' Shellfire was taking its toll on Victor's company whilst he was called to a conference in a mud-smothered pillbox crammed with a dozen or so officers. Their objective, they were told, was a cluster of German defences known as Requette Farm. They rounded off affairs and then came uncomfortable, wooden partings. 'Good luck old chap.' 'Take care of yourself.' 'The very best of luck.' As cheerful as they tried to be, they knew they would never again stand in the same room as a complete group.

'Then began the most awful night I ever remember,' Victor recalled. 'It was pitch dark, impossible to distinguish any landmark and no one knew the ground. And such ground. It is quite impossible to describe, the shell holes, craters and such being beyond belief – dreadful.' He was deeply religious and throughout this nightmare spell he sat and prayed, trying to calm himself into acceptance and to find some meaning in what was going on around him.

The journey to the assembly point was a disaster. The Householders were struggling along in a downpour when a shell landed right in the middle of them and wounded nearly a dozen, including stretcher-bearers:

> It seemed that the acme of hell on earth had come. No stretcher-bearers, ten wounded men in the wet groaning for help. The company all mixed up ... Oh the rain! ... We tried to dish the rum and water out to all these frozen, soaked, tired men. Meanwhile I was trying to get some men to carry the worst of the wounded who could not walk. One poor man, I remember, kept yelling for help, and I could not do anything until the stretchers came back ... It was doubtful they ever would.

The first battle of Passchendaele began before dawn on 12 October. As soon as the British barrage opened the Germans responded furiously. One shell landed in the middle of the Household Battalion. 'It blew us all over,' Victor wrote. He heard a fellow officer say, 'It's got me.' 'I feared it had, [a fragment] had gone right through his steel helmet and reached his skull ... I waited a few minutes by his side trying to get him to speak, but I saw that he was breathing his last, so I left him to his servant and went on with the battle.'

The battalion was under heavy fire from Poelcappelle itself. Victor formed a defensive flank out of scattered Householders and waited for the barrage to lift. Up and down the battlefield men were being sucked to their deaths in the unforgiving mud and drowning in shell holes. Mud clogged up the rifles and put them out of action. Even some trench mortars and machine guns had to stop firing because the ammunition was so filthy and wet.

Finally Victor and his exhausted collection of survivors managed to storm Requette Farm. They found four enemy machines guns in a pillbox and twenty-five men that they seized as prisoners. They fell on leftover rations of German black bread like animals. As the day wore on the Householders clung on until they were almost completely surrounded and forced to fall back. Their machine guns were smashed and they had run out of food, water and ammunition. As evening approached, the last thing Victor would have wanted to see was another order to attack, but along it came. He was being sent two platoons of the Rifle Brigade for support and he was to retake the farm. It was physically impossible. The Householders could do little more than expend the last of their energy trying to repel a German counter-attack and the idea was abandoned.

The attack on Passchendaele had failed. It had cost the British Army 13,000 men. Some 80 per cent of the Householders were casualties and of fifteen officers, only Victor and one other were still in one piece. In return they had gained a few hundred yards, and then lost it again. For five days Victor had been scratching a living with his dwindling company in the most despicable setting and they had gone some sixty hours without sleep. Across half the days of that week in his diary he simply scratched angrily one word: 'HELL'.[2]

After the first battle of Passchendaele operations were scaled back dramatically, but the Ypres offensive was tragically pressed on across a much shorter front in horrific conditions. Some 12,000 men perished in a second assault on Passchendaele itself and four days later British and Canadian troops were thrown forward again. The village finally fell on 6 November but it was hardly significant against what it had cost in human life. All the strategic objectives that had made it so important now seemed to have been forgotten.

The Third Battle for Ypres finally ceased in mid November. The battle would become symbolic of the horrors of industrialised warfare and the carnage of the Great War. No fewer than sixty-five Old Etonians had died on the Western Front since July and a third of them had still been pupils at Eton in the summer war was declared. Only two of those that fell would be commemorated on the Menin Gate. The loss of life had now become so staggering that William Butcher, a Colleger who left Eton in 1910 and died with the London Regiment on 16 August 1917, would be one of the very last of the tens of thousands of names marked down for it. The men who fell in Flanders after this date and were lost on the battlefields overflow on to the memorial at Tyne Cot. No less than 34,952 of them are commemorated on the panels that border the cemetery, overlooked by a cross of sacrifice mounted on top of a pillbox. Nine of them are OEs who fell during the fighting on the Salient in the summer and autumn of 1917.

For all the suffering on the Western Front, the trials of those that had survived were far from over as far as 1917 was concerned. Part of the reason that Haig had persisted for so long on the Salient in the face of deteriorating weather was to mask a highly secretive attack being planned. Some 60 miles to the south, an Old Etonian General had an eye on breaking through the Hindenburg Line.

The Hon. Sir Julian Byng had arrived at Eton in 1874 and gone through Mr Mozley's house with his two brothers. To avoid confusion in a world where everybody referred to each other by their surnames they were known as 'Byngo', 'Bango' and, in Julian's case, 'Bungo'. (To make things even more confusing he would one day take up the banjo.) He described himself once as the worst scug in the school and his reverence for his studies was indeed evident when he traded a Latin book for two ferrets and a pineapple. He came from a large family and as a seventh son had had to pay his way through the army by trading polo ponies. It had been worth it, for in April 1917 he proved his capabilities by commanding the Canadian Corps through their triumphant seizure of Vimy Ridge on the opening day of the Battle of Arras.

Byng's reward was promotion to command of his own army that summer. His Third Army was resident in a sleepy part of the line to the north of the Somme. In fact it was so calm that the Germans had been sending their exhausted men there to recover and had dubbed it 'the Sanatorium of the West'. What if, the orchestrators of this new plan thought, they could surprise the enemy and smash through the Hindenburg Line between the Canal de l'Escaut and the Canal du Nord?

Manpower was an issue and so the plan put in front of Haig in mid September called for a revolutionary new type of attack. Unlike the low-lying, saturated terrain about Ypres, the ground was perfect for the use of tanks and so hundreds of them would be employed. Instead of a lengthy and loud bombardment that would alert the enemy, tanks would be used to smash through the wire, absorb enemy fire and forge a path for the infantry following behind. The Germans could be overrun before they realised what was happening to them. When it transpired that victory was not imminent in Belgium, Haig approved Byng's attack and preparation began in earnest at the end of October. Brigade commanders were informed early on, but at battalion level silence prevailed.

John 'Marcus' de Paravicini was said to be the youngest major in the British Army. He was one of those who was to be kept in the dark until the assault towards Cambrai was imminent. Born in 1895, just a stone's throw from Eton at Datchet, he was descended from Robert Walpole, the first British prime minister. The middle son of a renowned sportsman, who was an FA Cup winner with three England caps and an outstanding cricketer, Marcus had gone straight into a banking career with Barclay's on leaving Eton in 1913. He volunteered as soon as the war began but having rushed himself on to a waiting list of young men wanting to be officers in the King's Royal Rifle Corps, he dashed off a letter to the War Office a fortnight later. He had learned just how many men were waiting for commissions and asked them to re-route his application to one of Kitchener's battalions. As a result he was sent to the 11th King's Royal Rifles and by the age of 21 had risen to second-in-command of the battalion. Marcus had served on the Somme and pursued the Germans to the Hindenburg Line, as well as taking part in operations at Langemarck for Gough and in Plumer's subsequent operations.

Had he not been wounded, Marcus' brother Percy would have been present with the battalion, but it was Marcus alone who arrived in the Cambrai sector in mid October with the battalion and settled near Fins. Their division, the 20th, occupied a complicated part of the lines that undulated up and down various valleys and spurs. The attack was to begin on 20 November, although Marcus would not be told until a week before. The King's Royal Rifles were not stupid, though. They were withdrawn to the rear to undergo training in conjunction with tanks and new ammunition dumps were springing up all around them. Not only was something clearly afoot, it appeared to be something big.

Byng's caution bore fruit. Under a thick veil of mist nearly 500 tanks were pulled together, the noise of their movement masked by the sound of British airmen buzzing overhead in the days leading up to the battle. As much as 137 miles of armoured cable was being run out in front of Marcus' division for communication, and for four nights guns were wheeled up, camouflaged and then quietly left in position. On the night of 19 November, intermittent bursts of machine-gun fire masked the rumbling of the tanks as they formed up ready for battle.

The following morning they rumbled from the mist into the battle, the infantry proceeding in long queues behind them. Marcus' division attacked north-east across the Hindenburg Line towards Cambrai, their objectives La Vacquerie and beyond that the high ground known as Welsh Ridge. Marcus and his men were to stay in reserve until this had been accomplished and then seize the crossings of the St Quentin Canal in between Marcoing and Masnières further on with the aid of sixteen tanks.

Up and down the line Byng's men advanced as many as 4 miles in a few hours. The Germans had been on alert but the surprise was a success. When Marcus' brigade went into Masnières the population had no idea what was going on. The men were surprised to see such normality. Women had been wheeling perambulators in the streets before German artillery fire came crashing towards them and the brigade interpreter ran back and forth attempting to get civilians evacuated.

But for all of the Third Army's success, key objectives still sat in German hands. That night the 11th King's Royal Rifles were ordered up to push on and take Crèvecoeur, further along the canal, with twelve tanks. Their lonely attack commenced in the middle of the following afternoon. Marcus and his men were enfiladed from Rumilly to the north-west and from the high ground north of the canal, so that in spite of several efforts to force a passage during the day, little progress was made. Byng had tried to push on but continued attempts failed. Late on 21 November a halt was ordered and consolidation began. Marcus had to settle for digging in to the south of Crèvecoeur.

Haig was insistent that the attack be followed up but of course the element of surprise was gone. The Germans had now had time to regroup and organise. To the north of Marcus and his battalion, Byng's men had failed to take the hugely significant ridge in front of Cambrai itself, on which Bourlon Wood sat. Haig had warned Byng about seizing it swiftly but he had not taken heed and now it was to become fiercely contested.

Shortly after he had penned his thoughtful letter to Henry Dundas, General John had left the 2nd Guards Brigade. Promoted, Ponsonby had taken over 40th Division who were now suddenly called upon to throw themselves into the fray for General Byng by relieving the battered 62nd Division who had been having a torrid time in the environs of Bourlon Wood.

General John's men struggled towards the imposing heights that included the wood, fighting their way through traffic. Arriving after dark on 22 November they had no chance to properly reconnoitre their objective and Ponsonby was forced to hurriedly cobble together a plan of attack to take Bourlon itself and the wood. The petrol for their accompanying tanks only just arrived in time and smoke shells that were to have masked their assault were lost somewhere on the deteriorating roads to the rear when the men burst forwards.

In truth 40th Division had little to no idea what they had launched themselves at, especially as far as the wood was concerned. Artillery shells sent oaks and firs splintering in all directions. The noise was deafening and men struggled to clamber over aspens and hazel. Thankfully enemy resistance was much less determined than expected. They got to the northern edge of the trees but had to dig in because the advance on either side had not kept pace. As for the village, some battalions had been all but destroyed. General John's men were scattered throughout the area, some of them isolated inside Bourlon itself. The position that night was shaky.

Under the circumstances, his men were acquitting themselves well, but the general was ordered to push on and wrench the village out of German hands. In addition, he ordered the wood consolidated, as there were numerous enemy troops hiding amongst the ruins of the trees. Communications were beginning to break down in the chaos. General John had actually managed to get the assault on Bourlon delayed until more tank support could arrive, but his new orders could not get through because German shells had smashed crucial wires and one of his brigadiers commenced the attack on 24 November as planned. Ponsonby was not even aware that his men had got into Bourlon and been forced back to the southern outskirts of the village until 8 p.m. that night, at which point he hurriedly made reserves available to the units concerned.

Inside the wood a bitter, relentless struggle had been going on all day. General John's exhausted men beat off numerous counter-attacks as they gallantly tried to hold on to the ground they had taken. Trees continued to crash down around their ears and amongst the wrecked greenery gas lingered ominously. They were rapidly losing their lines of communication back to Ponsonby and in the early evening they had sent out a distress call. One determined counter-attack from the enemy and they would most likely be flung from Bourlon Wood altogether.

Five more Etonians had already fallen in General Byng's localised offensive at Cambrai, but now Ponsonby's former men and the rest of the Guards Division had been ordered south, indicating that the number of OE casualties was about to increase drastically.

The Guards had been resting for three weeks after their exertions at Poelcappelle when orders suddenly arrived on 9 November for them to move south. It was an arduous journey and Henry Dundas, heading towards his first experience of battle as a company commander, was amongst those starting to feel the physical strain.

They had no idea where they were going or what for. Whilst Marcus de Paravicini fought for Crèvecoeur the Guards were being ferried painfully slowly towards the front in buses. Henry sat throughout 22 November to the south-west of Cambrai, struggling to recuperate from the journey in appalling weather with little shelter, cheered only by an unexpected reunion with one of his Eton friends waiting with the cavalry to exploit a break in the German line.

Whilst General John threw his men at Bourlon and the wood on 23 November, in command of the Guards, General Feilding was told that it was extremely unlikely that his men would have to relieve any division presently in the line. His staff ran back and forth, baffled by contradictory orders. Then came the inevitable: an order to relieve 51st Division in the line fighting immediately next to General John's men. Once his staff officers had spent much of the day running about looking for them, the Guards struggled up to the front in the dark, without a clue as to their surroundings. The 51st Division had pushed forward towards a village by the name of Fontaine-Notre-Dame, which sat to the south-east of Bourlon Wood, but much like Bourlon it had become bitterly contested and had changed hands several times. When the Guards arrived the troops there had no clue that they were to be relieved and were completely unready.

On 25 November, Feilding was informed that his men would attack at the earliest opportunity. He was livid. This would require attacking from a salient into another salient towards a village as yet untouched by artillery fire; it was tantamount to suicide. He demanded a conference with the corps commander and outlined his objections. He was told they would have to wait for General Byng to arrive and give his verdict.

Byng told him, in effect, to get on with it. On 27 November the Guards Division would attack Fontaine-Notre-Dame and try to prise it from German hands. Feilding went racing back to his headquarters with less than twenty-four hours to mastermind his attack. The only complete brigade he had that was fresh and unused was the 2nd, including Henry Dundas and the 1st Scots Guards, and he hurriedly sent out his orders.

The men had been lying out in the open as the snow fell the previous night and were wet through as they struggled forward. They were finally in place at 1 a.m., just a few hours before the attack was to commence. The front held by the Guards Division was some 5,000 yards, more than twice as long as that which they had successfully attacked at Pilckem Ridge, and they had less men available. It was not a testament to the leadership of the British Army. Desperate to obtain the high ground they did not realise that, having failed to seize these objectives when bolstered by the element of surprise, they were now attempting to achieve the same result with a small attack by hurried troops when the Germans, freshly reinforced, were fully aware that they would be coming.

Battalions of Grenadiers and Coldstream Guards were to assault Fontaine itself, but Henry and his Scotsmen were to take up a place on a sunken road leading south away from the village in order to provide protection for them. The Grenadiers ran straight into heavy machine-gun fire and saw their officers cut down in droves. Likewise the Coldstream were being decimated but by 7.15 a.m. the village was largely in British hands.

A company of Scots Guards was meanwhile attempting to come up to meet them along the sunken road in a miserable drizzle. Two OEs, Colonel MacKenzie and Arthur Kinnaird, whose father had lifted the FA Cup as part of the same side as Marcus de Paravicinis, had edged up in a snowstorm the night before to try to get some understanding of the situation. Unfortunately the road proved not to be quite so 'sunken' as they thought in some places and sloped uphill, giving the Germans in Fontaine a clear field of fire to scythe them down as they attempted to approach the village.

As they crawled towards Fontaine, Kinnaird's men were subjected to murderous machine-gun fire. Arthur was hit in the leg. As he attempted to turn around on the floor to try to escape he was hit again, this time in the back. One of his sergeants, a Glasgow policeman named Thomas McAulay, dragged him 400 yards to safety, fighting off two enemy soldiers as he went and clambering back up after being floored twice by concussion from nearby bursting shells. Attempts to get up to Fontaine cost his company all its officers and half its men. Only McAulay was left to lead them in beating off a German counter-attack. For his actions that day MacKenzie nominated Thomas McAulay for the Victoria Cross, which he was duly awarded. Despite McAulay's efforts, Arthur Kennard could not be saved and died in a nearby dugout. He was 32 years old.[3]

Henry Dundas would consistently refer to the affair as the 'Fontaine Massacre'. For all their efforts, the Guards were doomed to fail, just as Feilding had predicted. They simply did not have enough men to hold the village and, in the face of mounting counter-attacks, they were overrun and forced to withdraw to their starting line. By 29 November, when the division was withdrawn, they had chalked up over 1,000 casualties, including nearly forty officers. Waiting for them to the rear was a thank-you note from General John for their efforts. His own division had been battered before they too were finally pulled out of Bourlon Wood and the nearby village.

To all intents and purposes, the British attack on this sector was now over. They were expecting some sort of counter-attack in return, but little did they know that the Germans were planning a brutal, large-scale assault, battering both sides of the British salient that had formed in an attempt to cut it off.

As darkness fell on 29 November Marcus de Paravicini and the 11th King's Royal Rifles trudged up to relieve another battalion in the line near La Vacquerie. At 7 a.m. a magnificent din opened up to their right as the enemy came barrelling towards the British positions further south. The German counter-attack rolled like a breaking wave towards the battalion. The division next to them had been broken and men streamed back towards Gonnelieu. Marcus and his men were next. The artillery arrived first, cascading down all over the British front and severing communication lines. The Germans used high explosive, gas and smoke to screen their advance. Then came dozens of aeroplanes, almost skimming the ground they flew so low, unleashing torrents of machine-gun fire into panicking troops. Emerging out of the smoke at

8 a.m. came the infantry, breaking into the battalion's ranks from in front and behind, rifles trained on the fleeing British soldiers.

Marcus fled his battalion headquarters on his hands and knees with nothing but a revolver for protection. One of his riflemen followed close behind. They had made it some 20 yards when a low-flying enemy aeroplane came bearing down on them and opened fire. The rifleman screamed out in pain as he was hit in the leg. He looked up just in time to see Marcus' revolver shot out of his hand. He watched as the young major scrambled on a few more yards and threw himself into a shellhole. The King's Royal Rifles had been overrun. They had no choice but to fall back as lines and lines of German infantry descended upon them. Men with machine guns perched up on Welsh Ridge attempted to pin the enemy down but they too were overwhelmed. They removed parts from their guns and abandoned them.

Rifleman Field languished on the ground until the Germans rounded him up with other prisoners. Rumours abounded as to the fate of the young major. Field never saw him again and the only other account was from an unknown rifleman who claimed he had seen Marcus de Paravicini running from a support trench when he was shot down by a low-flying aeroplane. Marcus' family were still hounding everyone from the War Office to the Netherlands Legation in 1919, but the 22-year-old was never seen or heard from again[4].

The situation at the end of the day was critical. Marcus' division was without reserves or any artillery support. The German attack had advanced as far as 3 miles in places. Men of the Sherwood Foresters had been sent to help plug gaps and the 11th King's Royal Rifles cowered in the Hindenburg Line. It was imperative that men be found from somewhere to try to counter-attack. Eyes began to turn to the exhausted Guards Division, still catching their breath after their 'massacre' at Fontaine-Notre-Dame.

Even before the Germans had launched their infantry assault on Marcus de Paravicini and his battalion, a telegram arrived at Guards Division HQ to say that the Germans were assaulting with great force and that they ought to be ready to move at a moment's notice. They had barely finished breakfast. They couldn't believe it was possible. It wasn't until the isolated khaki figures appearing, running over the hill, turned into a mob that the gravity of the situation began to sink in. Shells started to drop closer and closer to the camp.

Two hours later three brigades of Guards were stumbling about the front amidst conflicting orders whilst men streamed the other way, fleeing the onslaught. The 3rd Guards Brigade had been ordered to take back Gonnelieu. They advanced across the open ground and flung themselves bodily at the German defenders. Along with the arrival of tanks, the Guards action at

Gonnelieu was instrumental in grinding the impetus out of the German counter-attack.

No less than twenty-four Etonians fell during the operations around Cambrai in the closing months of 1917. For OEs the year had seen mounting casualties, with name after name being read out in the chapel at school. Nobody understood this better than Patrick Shaw-Stewart.

He arrived home from Gallipoli completely spent. During 1915 he had lost Julian Grenfell and his brother Billy, as well as Charles Lister. His loneliness was compounded by being sent to Salonika to act as a liaison officer with the French Army. He was not at all impressed with the lack of activity on this front, especially when his own battalion, the Hood, had been sent into the thick of things on the Western Front. It gave him plenty of time to mourn his ever-decreasing circle of friends.

Having stuck at it for several months, Patrick became determined to escape Salonika and made more than one attempt. Sadly, as an intelligence officer he proved too intelligent and they didn't want to let him go. There he sat on his quiet front pushing pins into maps and stewing about his wasted energy. 'Nothing,' he told Julian and Billy Grenfell's mother, 'can conceal from me the fact that I am superfluous here.'

The best promise he could extract was that he could join a battalion in the east, not his own in France. 'Being killed in France ... in the Hood with my old friends is one thing: being killed chillily on the Struma after being pitch-forked into God knows what Welsh Fusiliers or East Lancashire Regiment is quite another,' he sulked. Finally, having returned home sick at the beginning of 1917, Patrick managed to manipulate his way to France, arriving there in April. He even managed to convince the military authorities that he was fit for service, but not anywhere in the east where the climate would rekindle his supposed health issues.

In the aftermath of Cambrai the whole of the frost-covered Welsh Ridge had been put in the hands of the Royal Naval Division. There was no end in sight. The British Army was exhausted, depleted and depressed as 1917 came to a close. It felt to Patrick like death came daily. 'I wonder if this war has been especially hard on my friends,' he had speculated as early as 1915, as Charles Lister lay dying. 'John Manners ... [George Fletcher], the other Fletcher, Julian and Billy.' The list went on, taking friends and academic rivals. Only acquaintances that he cared little for seemed able to escape the grim reaper.

Many believed that the dead had gone to a better place but Patrick didn't have such faith. He needed evidence and he had seen none. He was lonely and depressed, but he still displayed a doggedness about seeing the war through, albeit with none of the exuberance that had accompanied the first volunteers, him included, as they dived into uniform. 'We had lost most of our old illusions,' wrote his friend Ronald Knox, who shared his pain as far as their Eton and Balliol friends were concerned. 'The time had not yet come when we were to draw our breath and then sigh it out again in relief at the tidings of victory.'

When Raymond Asquith fell on the Somme in 1916 Patrick was crushed:

> It makes me more inclined than anything that has happened yet to take off my boots and go to bed. When people like Julian died, you felt at least that they had enjoyed war, but Raymond! That graceful, elegant cynic, who spent his time before the war pulling Guardsmen's legs, to be killed in action in the Grenadiers, it is so utterly incongruous … that it was seems to make it almost the blackest thing yet – and for me personally there seems to be no man left now whom I care a brass button for, or he for me, except darling Edward.

Then came the final blow. Darling Edward, Edward Horner, fell on 21 November at Cambrai with the 18th Hussars. 'I suppose it's the same for everyone,' Patrick surmised glumly, but it didn't make it any easier. 'Every time I remember that nearly all my friends are dead, I take some form of imaginary morphia, and promise myself work, or love, or letters, or fall back on the comforting reflection that I may soon be dead myself. Wonderfully cheery that.'

By December Patrick had a company of the Hood under his command. In fact, the banker who had had to call on Julian Grenfell to be shown how to operate his Sam Browne belt was briefly in command of the battalion. 'Lord bless my soul,' he exclaimed. Patrick thought some that had gone before him might roll over in their graves, but there was nobody else left. 'It just shows what we are all reduced to nowadays,' he told his sister.

Nothing much had been occurring in their sector in the run up to Christmas, but on 29 December, as darkness fell, the Germans shelled them violently with gas. At dawn the next morning, Patrick was doing his rounds of the lines when the enemy put up a barrage again, smashing in trenches, sending dumps of ammunition sky high and destroying dugouts. Patrick was being accompanied by an artillery liaison officer, who urged him to send up an SOS rocket, but Patrick did not want to. He maintained that it was only a minor raid on another part of the line and that if he sent up an SOS everyone would think he was 'windy'.

In fact, white-clad Germans, camouflaged against the snow, were about to emerge from the mist. Patrick would never see them. As the barrage continued a piece of shrapnel ripped off part of his earlobe. Blood spattered on to his face, ran down his forehead and into his eyes, obscuring his vision. The artillery officer was insistent that he go back and get himself fixed up, but Patrick was determined to finish his rounds. He had barely moved off when another piece of shrapnel flew up towards his face and killed him instantly.

The day before his death he had reiterated how worthless his own life seemed now that all the friends that he had loved were no longer with him. His prediction about joining them had been borne out. Patrick Shaw-Stewart joined Julian and Billy Grenfell, Charles Lister and Edward Horner on the ever-increasing list of casualties at Eton. The penultimate year of war had cost 205 OEs their lives.

The United States of America may have entered the conflict, and the blood shed at Passchendaele might have masked the chaos within the mutinous French ranks, but Russia had finally capitulated, embroiled in revolution. Germany might have looked as if she were staring into the void in 1917, but it was the Kaiser's men who looked to the last year of the war with hope. At the onset of 1918 they were utterly determined to crush Allied resistance and bring the Great War to a close.

Notes
1. Ralph Vivian Babington was laid to rest at Ruisseau Farm Cemetery, Langemarck.
2. Victor had previously declined the offer of a staff job. However, the Household Battalion was disbanded at the beginning of 1918 and so he went willingly to act as an advisor to General Sir Henry Wilson who had just been appointed Chief of the Imperial General Staff and military advisor to the Prime Minister. He never married, but was a godfather to Elizabeth Taylor. He was killed in an air crash in 1943.
3. His brother, Captain The Hon. Douglas Arthur Kinnaird, also an OE, had fallen in October 1914 with the battalion. He is buried at Godezonne Farm Cemetery.
4. John Marcus de Paravicini was commemorated on the Cambrai Memorial along with 7,056 other men who vanished in November and early December 1917. Eleven of his fellow Old Etonians who also disappeared on the battlefield are remembered on the panels with him.

20

'Shaking the Faith'

If the young Etonians on the Western Front thought that they had seen it all before the end of 1917, the final year of the Great War was to eclipse anything that they had yet witnessed. 'The year of Our Lord 1918 was sensational and astonishing,' wrote Pip Blacker. The stagnant trench warfare that he and his fellow officers had survived thus far was about to be replaced by the drama of a war of movement, but as yet he noted an air of 'staleness and apathy'.

As far as the men were concerned, they had done their bit. The French and British had earned the right to take a step back and 'take it easy until 1919 or 1920 when the war was finished, mainly by the Americans'. There was no inkling amongst any of them that this would be the year in which the conflict would draw to a close. 'It is easy today,' Pip wrote in the aftermath, 'to forget how dubious the future looked till just before the end.'

The tail end of 1917 had well and truly taken it out of Henry Dundas. In December the 20-year-old was sent home. As early as November his physical health had become a concern. Henry was pulled out of the line and sent home in time for Christmas, to the joy of his parents, with an ambiguous heart complaint. It seemed that senior officers were determined to give him a rest. He spent his time relaxing at home and at Eton, which he was ecstatic to see again. 'This place is fascinating. Just being here is a joy in itself, strolling about as one used to … ah me!'

In February, back at the front, Henry turned 21 and had a 'marvellous' coming-of-age dinner with the old gang. He spent the evening boozing with Ralph Gamble and Oliver Lyttelton, and deemed it 'well worth the headache the next day!' But nothing could detract from the grinding monotony of war. He and Ralph sat and had a heart to heart about all the friends they had lost thus far. For them, 31 July 1917 was the blackest day of the war. Eric Greer, John Dyer and Logie Leggatt were 'absolutely irreplaceable'. The turnover weighed heavy on them both and they were beginning to feel like old men. 'One feels it all the more so with what is practically a new generation of officers who have never even heard of Eric and John,' lamented Henry. 'What wonderful people they were.'

Although Ralph, Henry and their fellow OEs had had enough, 1918 promised more fighting, more hardships and ever further thinning of the ranks of Old Etonians. In fact it would prove to be the most savage year so far in terms of the scale of the fighting. As spring approached the Germans were planning a monumental offensive. They had no choice but to attempt a push on this scale as the country could not sustain itself for much longer. The burden of fighting and Britain's naval blockade strangling their supply lines were forcing their hand.

The collapse of Russia facilitated German plans. Huge numbers of troops could now be pulled from the Eastern Front and sent into France and Flanders, where they would enjoy numerical superiority over the Allies. But this window of opportunity was destined to slam shut in their faces with the arrival in force of the Americans, and they knew it. As summer approached, there would theoretically be virtually infinite numbers of men arriving from across the Atlantic to fight for the Allied cause. It was clear to the Germans that if they had not won the war by this point, the strain of battling this new foe would tip the scales and doom them to ultimate defeat. The race was on to win the Great War.

The German high command began planning to throw everything it had at the British in the hope that defeating Haig's armies would cause the French to capitulate. Many different plans were concocted but in the third week of January, Ludendorff, controlling the Kaiser's army, made his choice to begin with 'Operation Michael'. The German Army was going to attempt to smash through south of Arras and on the Somme, and then it would turn to roll north-west up the line. A few days later Operation Mars would commence, assaulting Arras. In April, as soon as the ground dried up enough, Operation George would punch through on the River Lys in the Armentières area and push up towards the English Channel. There would be no respite for the British until they had been completely destroyed.

In their planning, German military commanders could proceed safe in the knowledge that nobody at home was going to impede their endeavours.

Douglas Haig did not enjoy the same freedom. He and the prime minister were engaged in a battle of their own that had soured their relations to the point of Lloyd George scheming behind Haig's back with the French. He had now conspired with them to ensure that the British would take over more of the front. From St Quentin down to the River Oise was to come under British control at the beginning of the year.

As if this was not bad enough, Haig would be extending lines south without the reinforcements that he had told the government he needed. Astute as ever, Henry Dundas had already recognised the lay of the land. 'Everything now depends upon Americans and the uselessness or otherwise of their fighting troops, who will be the main source of reserves against the German divisions from the Russian front. In fact they will form about the only reserve, as it doesn't look as if [we have got] any more men and the French certainly haven't.'

Haig had estimated that he needed over 600,000 men to maintain the BEF as it stood. He got 200,000, and many of these were not in optimum condition. In command of the Fifth Army, Hubert Gough was mortified by some of the men he received. Large numbers, he claimed, were returning wounded and he journeyed out one snowy day to inspect a draft that had just come in. Getting out of his car and kicking off the blizzard that had streamed in through the window he found more than half of the men wearing wounded stripes, some two or three. 'It struck me at the time as unjust,' he later recalled. 'While there remained at home many thousands of comparatively young men who had never seen a shot fired.'

Determined not to send men to Haig to be sacrificed as had happened at Passchendaele, the prime minister wanted to keep them at home, where the politicians and not the commander-in-chief could decide when they would be needed. At this crucial juncture of the war, Haig was forced to wholly reorganise the British Army on the Western Front to accommodate his lack of manpower. Brigades were reduced from four battalions to three. Each division shrank significantly. Not only that, but this enforced restructuring destroyed the operational experience gleaned so far. Henry watched sadly as Guards battalions, including the 2nd Irish, were sent to 31st Division. 'They looked magnificent,' he wrote sadly when he thought of Eric Greer and what he would make of it. 'But as I looked at all the things that Eric used to be so fond of – their drums and one or two things like that – I wept quite properly. Poor Eric.'

Gough was understandably mortified with this re-arrangement of his army. His force had been weakened immeasurably and as far as he was concerned, the set-up was not a patch on what it had replaced. But it was done, and done in the knowledge that very soon his men would be required to stand up to a large-scale German offensive. Every attempt, as Gough later put it, should have been made to ensure that when the storm came the army was in the best possible position to resist it. This was simply not the case.

For the British Army, preparing to face a large-scale offensive delivered at them and not the other way around, was a new concept and would require a monumental amount of work. Borrowing heavily from the enemy's defensive developments, the BEF began reorganising to defend in depth. Facing the Germans first would be the Forward Zone. This was not designed to be the strongest held and most fiercely fought over position. This was to be the Battle Zone behind, the most important feature of this new, flexible British system of defence. A little over 1½ miles in depth and taking advantage of all the best features of the landscape in any given area, the Battle Zone was to be where the British Army would hold fast and try to halt the attackers. Much of it would not be permanently occupied. Troops to the rear would be on alert and would rush in to man their posts in the event of an emergency.

Between 4 and 8 miles behind the Battle Zone was a Rear Zone. Here rough defensive lines were marked out, or 'spit-locked' as opposed to being properly dug for now. It all sounded deliberate enough, but unfortunately the planning was not matched by the manpower available and consequently the Battle Zone, and in particular the Rear Zone, were underdeveloped.

Whilst the troops were being schooled in the principle of elastic defences, it was imperative that the RFC remain attack minded so that vital intelligence on German troop movements could be gathered. The Royal Flying Corps went to work. Along with its efforts, trench raids, patrols, the interrogation of prisoners and the knowledge that two successful German generals had been reallocated to a specific part of the front, made it clear, by late January, that the attack would fall upon the Third and Fifth Armies. Both were commanded by OEs, in Generals Byng and Gough, and formed the southern part of the British sector on the Somme and to the south of Arras. Efforts would henceforth be focused on this area as much as possible without neglecting the other end of the Western Front.

What the RFC found was disconcerting. In front of the two OE commanders there was evidence of, among other things, fourteen new aerodromes, large ammunition dumps and constant movements by rail towards the existing front. Throughout February more and more trains were spotted. Airmen daily took scores of photographs of German batteries that would enable the British gunners to work out where to direct their fire. Bombing raids were also increased. Large ammunition dumps, significant concentrations of rolling stock, aerodromes and factories took precedence as targets.

Whilst these machines went about their business, fighter squadrons made as much of a nuisance of themselves as possible. Ian Napier had worked very impressively as a liaison officer with the French on the left of the Guards Division in the summer of 1917. He returned to 40 Squadron from his sojourn, by which time they had undergone a conversion to the SE5a, one of the highest rated scouts at the front.

Work began in earnest with their first real dogfight of 1918 on 6 March. Ian and his fellow pilots took off mid afternoon and found seven enemy scouts hovering about above the lines, attempting to stop the British airmen from carrying out their bombing and reconnaissance tasks. Ian picked one out and went for it. Darting to within 30 yards of it he opened fire with both the gun above his head and the one in front of his cockpit and let off short bursts. The enemy machine appeared to spin off in a funk. Pulling away Ian spotted another German aeroplane. He let off 150 rounds at it and got lucky, the machine dropping out of the sky and coming to ground north-west of Lens. It was a profitable day for the squadron and they claimed four enemy machines destroyed and two forced down out of control. Luck was not with them three days later when they suffered the loss of one of their number. The wings fell off Leonard Tilney's plane at 12,000ft. Aged 22 when he fell to his death, Tilney was the 61st OE to die with the flying services.

On 17 March dark clouds descended on the would-be battlefield. The RFC found itself grounded at just the wrong moment. Rain began to fall and for four days reconnaissance was impossible. It was miserable timing, for although the British airmen could not get into the air, other sources indicated that the offensive was about to begin. A captured German NCO, a pilot and a handful of deserters all confirmed the date: 21 March 1918.

Hubert Gough had been embroiled in a bitter struggle with GHQ over where to place his limited reserves but Haig had the entire front to think about and he refused to divert them all to Gough, however unjust it might have seemed to the army commander who was about to bear the brunt of the German attack.

On 20 March 1918 Etonians in the Oise Valley were changing places in the Forward Zone. Morice Julian St Aubyn came from a Cornish family and on the outbreak of war had entered his father's regiment, the King's Royal Rifle Corps. Like most of the Etonians now manning Gough's army, Morice was no stranger to the front. Many of the tired young men serving in 1918 had racked up multiple wounds since the beginning of the war. He had had to have shrapnel pulled from his back a week before his battalion witnessed horror at Hooge in 1915 and he had been shot in the stomach on the Somme in September 1916.

The 7th King's Royal Rifles, which was part of the 43rd Brigade, also included George Llewelyn Davies' brother Peter. They trudged backwards into support. If, however, an emergency called for it, they would be required to take up position in the Battle Zone, a line of strong points in front of the village of Benay. This was to be their first time engaged in this duty and so that night they planned to man the Battle Zone as a practice session. By the time they set out though, information taken from the prisoners had filtered through. Their practice was upgraded to a precautionary measure. Most of the Riflemen, however, didn't expect an enemy push.

Passing Morice St Aubyn on their way into the Forward Zone were the 6th Somerset Light Infantry. Amongst their number was a former Colleger named Paul Hobhouse. The son of a Somerset gentleman, the 23 year old had gone up to Oxford before volunteering to join his local battalion. Wounded in the shoulder by shrapnel at Hooge and having survived huge blood loss, Paul had also been shot in 1916. That night Gough's front was ominously quiet. The German guns lay silent. Morice St Aubyn's battalion was in position in the Battle Zone by midnight. They sat illuminated by the moon, counting down the hours till they could return to Benay for breakfast. Paul Hobhouse's men were digging saps in front of them. Downing their shovels they settled down to await morning in their posts.

Before dawn the foreboding silence was broken by the fiercest bombardment the war had yet seen. Gaspard Ridout had still been at Eton in October 1916. He was an exceptionally shy boy but bright, the only OE to get into Woolwich in his intake and passing out third. The son of a banker, born in Newcastle, he was still a teenager when the Germans began their offensive in March 1918. A great many of the British guns were positioned further back to await organised, strong resistance in the Battle Zone when the enemy appeared on the horizon; but some artillery remained in the Forward Zone to take up targets behind the German lines. Gaspard's battery belonged to the 331st Brigade of the Royal Field Artillery. Stationed towards the southern end of the British Sector they had been at Hargicourt, surrounded by barbed wire to give them some semblance of protection, since the beginning of the month. For the past week they had been attempting to harass German battle preparations as much as possible, but at 4.45 a.m. on Thursday 21 March the enemy targeted the British artillery with every kind of shell imaginable.

At his headquarters, some 30 miles behind the lines, Hubert Gough was awoken by the dull roar of the fierce bombardment occurring in the distance. He jumped out of bed, ran into his office and got straight on the phone to Haig's headquarters. After putting down the receiver he went over to his bedroom window and caught his first sight of the fog that had enveloped his army. He could barely make out the branches of a tree in the garden 40ft from the window. The weather had played right into enemy hands. 'The stars in their courses,' he wrote, 'seemed to be fighting for the Germans.' The bitter irony of the mist was not lost on Henry Dundas either. 'It is really rather uncanny the way the weather favours the Boche. It is the general topic of interest and is shaking the faith even of the padres,' he complained bitterly. 'Think of our pathetic offensives – drowned at birth like so many puppies by deluges of rain.'

To the east, Gaspard Ridout and his battery were under phenomenal strain. The German artillery was to fire 3.5 million shells on that single day, 1.6 million of them in the first five hours. As soon as it began Gaspard and his battery were ordered to put down a barrage in response, but the fog turned a nightmare scenario into a veiled, hellish reality as they flailed around blindly trying to work their guns. Shrapnel and gas came out of the thick mist. All lines of communication had severed. The only way to get word was to send a runner into the fog and hope that he would survive long enough to reach his destination. If he could find it.

Elsewhere in the Forward Zone the infantry was sitting in the fog with no peripheral vision, waiting for the German infantry advance to begin and for the enemy to land on top of them. Their numbers were not high enough to maintain a continuous line and so they were strung out in a series of outposts. Paul Hobhouse's company of the 6th Somerset Light Infantry was huddled in deep dugouts, listening to the crashing of shells outside. Runners were despatched back to take news to the 7th King's Royal Rifles at Bernay. A significant infantry attack was quite clearly about to take place.

Even further behind the King's Royal Rifles, at Brigade HQ, they had no idea what was going on at all. They sent their own runners into the fog towards the Battle Zone to gauge the situation and find out if anyone knew what was happening to the Somerset Light Infantry. Delays made the flow of information irrelevant before it had even found a senior officer. By the time news came back, to say that despite the intense barrage the Somersets had not yet seen any signs of the German infantry, they had been all but wiped out by the enemy troops.

After five hours of horrific shellfire the German infantry began their advance. The enemy was now becoming well versed in stormtrooper tactics.

Firstly would come specially trained, handpicked troops, infiltrating the front line and bypassing strong points. They would rush for the artillery deep in the British lines with grenades, rifles and flame throwers following; attempting to take them by surprise. Attacking troops were now fully supported by aircraft flying low and firing on top of the British troops. The strong points they had ignored would then be hounded by heavily armed troops before finally the standard infantry would come over the top.

The Somerset Light Infantry stood no chance. On the left, A Company withstood the brunt of the initial assault and was brutally attacked from behind before enemy troops pushed swiftly on and decimated C Company in support. Almost immediately Paul Hobhouse and his men were surrounded. Just after nine a young officer came along from the left and popped his head into a dugout with a message to say that the rest of the A company had been overrun and captured by the Germans. Paul appeared, dishevelled without his collar and tie, but in his hurry he had still managed to grab a revolver. He ordered the men inside up and out quickly to go and support whoever might be left.

They moved up to the trench that had been occupied by A Company and found it deserted. There was not so much as a dead body about, which confirmed the young subaltern's claim that they had been taken prisoner. The mist was so thick that they could not see more than 20 yards. They had only just arrived when a sergeant called along the trench and said that there were Germans inside it to their right. They ran back to get Paul who was in company HQ. 'Tell Sgt Irving to block the trench,' he ordered. 'I will be up there in a minute.' He jumped up into the open and made his way across to the platoon, arriving before the messengers themselves returned.

They blocked up the trench with old limbers and other debris that they found and Paul sent men off to get more ammunition. They ran back to say that they couldn't get into their support line to complete the task because there were Germans there too. Together they all scrambled out of the front side of the trench and turned around to fire on the enemy coming up from behind.

Bullets fizzed about their ears. A few Germans approached the Somersets saying 'prisoner' and holding up their hands. A forty-year-old stretcher bearer who had been pressed into action was all for letting the confused-looking men surrender. 'Don't fire sir,' he urged, but Paul was far more suspicious. 'Don't be a fool King, he retorted. 'It's one of their tricks.' They opened fire and the Germans hunched over and ran away. One of the men called out, 'We shall have to surrender,' but Paul wasn't having any of it. 'We must fight to the finish,' he shouted.

Seeing their captain's resolve the men steeled themselves and fell back 30 yards with Paul to take up a better position. The stretcher bearer was well and truly fired up now. He noticed two young men had stopped shooting. 'Keep on firing,' he hollered. Paul turned around and grinned at him. Stray bullets had begun picking off this fierce little band. King was on all fours bandaging one of them up when two more enemy soldiers popped into view. Paul fired at them with his revolver, and threw himself into a nearby shell hole. The stretcher bearer hauled his wounded charge to his feet and they began making their escape too. By noon up and down the front the Germans had decimated the Forward Zone. They were now streaming past the 7th King's Royal Rifle Corps in the Battle Zone and they too were compelled to retire.

Meanwhile Gaspard Ridout, whose belongings had been blown sky high by enemy fire and his brigade of artillery overrun by the enemy, was swamped by men fleeing the Forward Zone, pouring past the guns. By 10 a.m. both A and C battery's anti-tank guns had been captured by the enemy although their officers and gun crews had mostly managed to run away. The same could not be said of Gaspard and his Battery. The Germans were to the front and rear. The guns still in action were firing over open sights at close range when they were ordered to fall back. There was no chance of getting their precious guns out. They began wilfully destroying them in the knowledge that they would have to be abandoned. It was a horrific day for the 331st Brigade and B Battery was particularly badly hit. In all ninety-two men were missing, dead or wounded and of their officers ten were unaccounted for, injured or dead, including 19-year-old Gaspard Ridout[1].

At lunchtime the fog finally lifted and the men of the Royal Flying Corps ran for their aeroplanes. The RFC had been well versed in what to do when the attack came. Their priorities were protecting working machines, attacking troops detraining and ground strafing the German advance. Ian Napier and 40 Squadron belonged to First Army north of the River Scarpe but they were soon seized to help Byng's force to their right. German airmen were out in force, firing machine guns on to the ground and directing artillery fire on to troops. British airmen began sending back details of masses of Germans moving forwards. Roads for 10 to 15 miles behind the lines were packed full of grey-clad men making their way up to the battle.

Similar scenarios to that of 43rd Brigade were being played out all along the Fifth Army front. The Somersets and the King's Royal Rifles had been scattered to the wind. Hubert Gough had been receiving reports since mid morning but they made little sense. He didn't even find out that Byng's army had been hit in force too until late afternoon. All that was certain was that his entire army was under attack and that the Forward Zone was already a write off. Those holding it on 21 March had been largely annihilated. To try to attempt to counter-attack with so few men was tantamount to suicide and the only thing for it, so far as he could see, was to try to hold up the tidal wave of grey German infantry long enough to keep the onslaught from swallowing his army whole. Falling back with a modicum of control beat hands down the idea of wasting lives trying to fight it out. Reserves were going to be scarce. If all went to plan he could expect to have five divisions trickle in over a five-day period. They would have to suffice for a 42-mile front being overrun by hundreds of thousands of enemy troops.

Nearly 40,000 men had been wiped off the strength of the British Army in one day, with hordes of them taken prisoner. Although the Germans had made limited inroads into the Battle Zone and despite the fact that the Third Army was still holding the salient formed by the fighting at Cambrai the previous winter, the enemy advance would continue in force the next day. The situation for Gough was critical. His men would have to fill gaps, guard new flanks as they appeared, attempt to keep in touch with those either side of them in the midst of a violent attack and scrape together any man they could find to do it as the command structure fell apart. To say that the situation looked bleak for the Etonian general and the Allies as a whole was an understatement. For the life of him, Gough could not imagine how they were going to hold it together. The only light at the end of the tunnel was that the only objective of any huge strategic significance was Amiens, which was some 40 miles to the rear. Surely the enemy couldn't push them back that far?

For all their determination and aggression, the Germans were not executing a definitive plan about how to proceed with their offensive. Seeing as they had enjoyed most of their success against the southern end of the Fifth Army and the likes of the 43rd Brigade, they made the fateful decision to press on here instead of rolling up the line towards Arras as originally envisaged. The nature of their offensive had been altered completely.

On 23 March reinforcements finally began to arrive. At dawn, shrouded again in fog, Gough was wondering just how much longer his men could hold out in the face of incredible strain and hardship. His army now resembled a rabble more than a coherent military force as they retreated for dear life. Traffic congestion on the road was unimaginable and holding back the Germans had degenerated into localised, desperate scraps. The previous afternoon much of Gough's force had managed to get across the Somme. Haig issued orders that the river should be held at all costs. It was never viable command. Orders had been given to begin blowing up bridges and any other crossings that would carry the enemy across behind them, but these were not as effective as the retreating British hoped. It was evident that the Rear Zone, never mind the Battle Zone, was not going to hold. To the north Byng had finally given up the gains of Cambrai and pulled his men out of their salient.

The 7th King's Royal Rifle Corps was attempting to pin back the Germans at Jussy across the Crozat Canal. The enemy was rampant. Reinforcements of cavalry had come up to join the battalion, who were also bolstered by stragglers from the Somersets and some non-combatants, but the Germans relentlessly pressed in an attempt to get across. At about 3 a.m. a small number managed to use one of the bridges just north of Jussy which had been half blown up. Morice St Aubyn was in front of them, surrounded by a unlikely band of men he had inherited, remnants from brigade and divisional works details, and he quickly rallied them and attempted to make a stand. This ramshackle group managed to hold off the German advance and push them back over the canal but just as they succeeded in throwing them across Morice was killed. He was 25 years old. Despite his hard work and the sacrifice of his own life the Germans soon began crossing in force. Heavy fighting developed as the enemy had now got across the river on either side of them and dwindling reserves were thrown in.

With 40 Squadron, Ian Napier was engaged in constant aerial activity. On 24 March the situation was critical at the juncture between the Third and Fifth armies where their SE5as had been deployed. It was alien country for them, devoid of the familiar landmarks they had come to rely on to get them safely about the country. Any snobbery about being scout pilots was gone. They spent most of the day flying as low as they could, a high-risk occupation in itself, dropping bombs on the Germans and hammering them with machine guns. After three days of relentless work they were falling asleep in their cockpits. 'One day I got so sleepy,' said one of Ian's fellow pilots, 'I didn't know what the Dickens to do. It was with the greatest difficulty that I could keep my eyes open at all.'

Gough would have been fully aware that he was on a hiding to nothing in trying to hold the Somme. The previous day the remnant of his army had fallen back up to 6 miles in places and the Germans were swarming around Ham. He had practically no reserves, his men were exhausted, starving and were suffering the soul destroying ignominy of retreating back across the Somme battlefields of 1916. All those months of attrition were wiped out in a few hours.

The French were putting men in to the south but as dusk fell on 24 March, what was left of Gough's Fifth Army was still imperilled and being forced back by the German onslaught, whilst Byng's army was being pulled back with them. In his sector Albert had now fallen too. All that the British had fought and died for on the Somme in 1916 was in German hands. The enemy might have been getting further and further from their own supply lines, but as exhausted as they too were, Amiens was now properly under threat.

The following day, the weight of the RFC was thrown at trying to attack the Germans on the ground like never before as the enemy advanced on the junction between the Third and Fifth Armies. Ten squadrons from the First Army were sent down to drop everything they could carry on the enemy. They fired 313,000 machine-gun rounds into the German ranks and dropped 50 tons of bombs.

No. 40 Squadron had gone from having two squadrons at their aerodrome to having five crammed on to it. 'It would make you roar with laughter,' said one of their pilots. 'We only had about three machines which would go the other day and we all three sallied forth on a squadron patrol! All the pilots seem to be new and what aren't new are on leave, so there you are.'

Ian Napier's squadron had come apart since the beginning of the year. He himself had been wounded and as well as the death of his fellow OE, Leonard Tilney, another pilot had had a bullet through the abdomen and more were missing. An unfortunate boy had also gone down in flames in sight of one of his fellow officers, although thankfully he got away with a miraculous slight burning to the face. Ian's flight had become 'a sort of training show of half a dozen new pilots' who had been thrown in to try to rebuild the squadron. They were beginning to feel as if they lived in the air.

Something had to give. On 26 March a conference took place at Doullens at which Douglas Haig, in no position to assume power himself, advocated Foch taking over overall command on the Western Front. By this point the British commander-in-chief's priority was ensuring that the Allies did not fall apart. Back at Fifth Army headquarters, Hubert Gough was not even aware that the meeting had taken place. He had been earmarked as a scapegoat for the tragedy that had befallen his army. The following evening he returned from visiting his commanders to find Douglas Haig's military secretary waiting for him. He asked to see him alone. 'He … told me as nicely as he could that the Chief thought that I and my staff must be very tired, so he had decided to put Rawlinson … [in] to take command.' Beyond saying 'All right,' the only other question that Gough had was when his fellow OE would arrive to assume command. On 28 March Hubert Gough's career as a soldier was effectively over. His fellow Etonian arrived in the early evening. Gough filled Rawlinson in as much as he could, and then made himself scarce to avoid embarrassment for either of them. His command of the now unrecognisable, shrunken Fifth Army was at an end and soon he would be bound for home. 'I left ... not at all sure where I was to get a bed or dinner that night.'

One of Gough's last acts as commander of the Fifth Army was to establish a line to try to hold on to Amiens. Fifteen miles in front of this crucial town, and loosely based on some old French lines from 1915, anyone they could find was thrown into manning it, including non-combatants. They clung on doggedly.

Whilst their push on the Somme was petering out in the face of British and French resistance, the Germans were still intent on ending the war. Operation Mars commenced on 28 March to push the British out of their stronghold at Arras. Having lent their services to the chaos above Byng's army, 40 Squadron's own was being dragged into the fray. The enemy launched a series of attacks but no fog aided them. Ian Napier and his fellow pilots flew over the town and the surrounding area, again engaged on ground targets. At 1.30 p.m. they were up to patrol the main road between Arras and Cambrai and found that it and all the smaller surrounding roads were choked with troops and transports. It was the same around Douai. Going down as low as 300ft they showered them with bullets and bombs in an attempt to slow the German advance and sent the enemy troops stampeding about the countryside.

Ludendorff's latest operation was to be unsuccessful. The impetus of the German offensives was failing across the board by 30 March. British resistance had been stubborn, Amiens had held and the exhausted Germans were getting further and further from their supply lines. The enemy had not finished though. Before the offensive on the Somme had fully petered out there were ominous rumblings to the north in the area around La Bassée. As part of their last ditch, kitchen-sink policy the Kaiser's men were about to make an assault around the River Lys and the high ground near Arras: Operation Georgette.

The RFC was well aware of what was going on. On 31 March, scout planes spotted large concentrations of German troops on the move. One observer counted fifty-five trains moving about Armentières and roads to the German rear were full of men and supplies.

The Royal Air Force was formed on 1 April 1918 by merging the RFC with the Royal Naval Air Service, but for Ian Napier it was the least of his concerns. Number 40 Squadron was back within its own allotted area. They had flown from their hard work on the Somme back up to Flanders for what was to be yet another nightmare. Another of the squadron's number was almost delirious. 'The war was being slowly lost down south, but we had given up watching the show, so what did we care?' All they could do was concentrate on their own fight and they were none too impressed when their own sector came under threat. 'The [blank] Germans started disturbing the peace north of the canal! In no way could this have annoyed us more. We couldn't have the Huns playing any silly little monkey tricks on our little patch.' The powers that be within the Royal Air Force appeared to agree. In addition to returning their borrowed strength to the correct area they had also diverted extra squadrons from Dunkirk towards the Lys.

Number 40 Squadron had resumed its more familiar role of offensive patrols as German preparations on the ground gathered force. On 6 April Ian took off to patrol the area directly east of Arras on what turned out to be a highly fruitful outing. Almost immediately he saw four German machines buzzing west along the line of the Scarpe and he dived on them to attack. They scattered out of his way, all except what he took for an Albatros, which remained in his sights. Ian charged at it, spitting off rounds from his machine gun at close range.

The enemy airman zoomed up and Ian followed, firing another short burst from the Vickers and hitting his prey in the engine. The Albatros glided in front of him and for a panicked few seconds it seemed that they might collide. Ian veered off sharply and managed to get out of the way. The German machine pulled away and drifted off, steam pouring out of it and its propeller motionless.

Looking about for something else to do Ian trundled off at a calmer speed. He had lost significant altitude during the fight and he climbed steadily back up to 10,000ft as he flew north-east towards Douai. Some fifteen minutes later he spotted another enemy aircraft emerging from some cloud cover. Ian was in the mood for another scrap and he pulled up to get over the top of it and hide himself in the sunlight.

He burst down out of the glare and took it on. He got to within 100 yards of it and came from behind, blasting away with his gun. Either his fire was accurate and wounded his opponent or he did not seem to share Ian's enthusiasm. The enemy airman didn't return fire, he simply turned east for home and began diving away. Ian stalked him closely, emptying as much ammunition as he could into it for good measure. He followed it down to 8,000ft then watched as it continued losing height and finally crashed into some houses near Brebieres[2].

Three days later the German offensive on the Lys began and the ground was once again blanketed in thick fog. Cloud remained low all day and by the time the RAF could get into the air Portuguese troops holding the middle of the line had been overrun, leaving the flank of John Ponsonby's division dangerously exposed. The Germans were already crossing the River Lys. It was a very different scenario to that on the Somme, where no hugely significant objective was at risk until Amiens. The northern part of the Western Front was cramped and every bit of ground was critical.

Once again information was essential as was any influence that the airmen could have on slowing the German advance. Ian and his fellow pilots plummeted to low heights to strafe the enemy as they surged forward. The relentless work continued the following day. Mist and rain hampered the squadron until lunchtime but as soon as it cleared the skies were alive with activity. A bulge appeared in the middle of the front and the British line was in danger of coming apart as it stretched further and further. By nightfall German troops were in Nieppe, Merville and, heartbreakingly, Messines, so valiantly won the year before. Douglas Haig recognised the gravity of the situation and would issue his famous rallying call to his troops:

> With our backs to the wall and believing in the justice of our cause each of us must fight on to the end. The safety of our homes and the freedom of mankind … depend upon the conduct of each one of us at this critical moment.

The next day, 12 April, was vital. The British line had to hold long enough for reinforcements, or the tide could turn drastically in favour of the Germans. The outnumbered Allies had already withstood the enemy onslaught for three days. Now the Kaiser's men had their sights set on Hazebrouck and, beyond that, the Channel. It was unthinkable that either should fall into enemy hands.

Whilst troops on the ground desperately tried to close the gap at Merville, 40 Squadron was told to concentrate wholly on enemy advances coming up to the village from Estaires and Neuf Berquin. Ian Napier went up before breakfast and was over Estaires itself at a height of about 8,000ft when his patrol engaged a number of enemy aeroplanes. The scrap he was engaged in broke up and he picked on another Albatros lingering nearby. He fired long bursts from both guns, letting off nearly 300 rounds. The German plane turned and arced away south-east. Then, suddenly, it flipped over on its back in mid air and fell away out of control.

Number 40 Squadron was not done for the day. In the afternoon a special patrol of twelve fighter machines, half of them from Ian's squadron, went looking for German observation balloons. The RAF really did perform with its back to the wall. It was the busiest day of the war thus far for the British fliers. All day long they took off, fought, hounded the Germans on the ground, landed, refuelled, re-armed and went back up again. The Royal Air Force dropped more than 2,500 bombs on the enemy and fired 115,000 rounds of ammunition whilst the working machines took nearly 3,500 photographs of events up and down the front.

On 15 April Ballieul fell but, crucially, Hazebrouck remained in British hands. The Salient had to be evacuated back to Pilckem Ridge, which was painful, but it was done in an orderly fashion. Reserves were arriving from other fronts and stalemate was setting in. Rain now began to hamper the efforts of the RAF to get into the air. 'As far as an unbiased spectator can judge,' quipped one of the pilots of 40 Squadron, 'the War still continues, at least, this is the conclusion I have come to from fairly diligent reading of the *Daily Mail*.' His sarcasm was in the vein of Henry Dundas. 'Apparently we are still "winning" ... We have lost all the guns and most of the men on the front, but as this was fortunately anticipated by Sir Henry Wilson and Lloyd George, we have little to worry about.'

Number 40 Squadron continued to work long, now largely unrewarding, hours in 'beastly' weather. Ian Napier scored another victory before the month was out but also had a narrow escape of his own. He was flying at high altitude one day when he observed an enemy machine some 12,000ft below. To get to it would require a steep dive. He shot down, engine throttle all the way back for some 6,000ft. 'Suddenly the machine gave a terrific vibration ... I pulled out of the dive by winding back a few notches.' He plodded carefully and slowly west and on landing found that on three out of his four wings the spars were splintered badly. Ian's machine had very nearly broken up in mid air.

Ludendorff had been fully aware of what would happen if his country failed to win the war in the spring of 1918, but fail they had. As exhausted as the faltering British and French troops were, they had reinforced themselves with reserves and more contingents of Americans had begun to arrive. The Germans had taken large areas of ground on the Somme, but the gain was negligible when it hadn't set them up strategically for victory. They had also suffered crippling casualties and possessed limited resources to replace them.

As a result of Germany's spring offensives, yet another group of Old Etonians had been swept aside. In fact the British Army had suffered almost a quarter of a million casualties. On 23 March 1918 the school's list of casualties tipped over 1,000. The chaotic nature of the retreat across the Somme meant that many families suffered anguish in trying to establish what had happened to their young men. Leonard Tilney received a fitting burial[3]. Morice St Aubyn's body was lost when his battalion fell away from Jussy. He was eventually commemorated on the Pozieres Memorial. Dedicated to the missing of 1918 on the Somme it names more than 14,000 casualties who vanished without a trace as the German Army surged forward. Also named is Paul Hobhouse, but his case was far from clear. In the aftermath of the battle his mother was told by another officer that he was safe, a captive in German hands. Relief must have washed over her but it was in vain. Weeks later it transpired that this piece of information had come to the officer second hand and was therefore far less reliable. She obstinately, and quite understandably, refused to believe that this literal lifeline could now be taken away. But all of her hopes were futile. It's likely that 23-year-old Paul Edward Hobhouse never made it out of the Forward Zone on 21 March.

Hubert Gough was another sort of casualty altogether. He was far from flawless as a military commander, but to blame him for the fate of the Fifth Army during the German offensive would be wrong. A substantial amount of culpability could be laid at the feet of Lloyd George and the politicians who had been intent on interfering with military affairs. The enemy may have overrun his own force but Gough was adamant that he knew why the Germans had ultimately failed. During the course of the Fifth Army's retirement in March he had learned of a South African contingent massacred. Gough later wrote, defending his conduct and that of his men in March 1918:

> Thinking about all the far-flung elements … fighting alongside Brits the words of the Eton boating song come back to me: 'And nothing on earth shall ever sever the chain that is round us now.' The principal links in that chain seem to me to be a sense of duty and a generous sympathy for each other, wherever we come from. As long as those characteristics mark the people of this Empire, I do not fear its destruction.

He spoke with hindsight, but the sentiment rang true. For the German Army the future now looked ominous indeed.

Notes
1. 2nd Lt Gaspard Alured Evelyn Ridout was laid to rest at Jeancourt Communal Cemetery Extension near St Quentin.
2. Ian Napier's first victory over the Albatros on 6 April was never officially credited. He was certainly not the type to brag or claim an honour he hadn't earned, but he did list it on his own record of his air victories, fully believing he had forced it to ground.
3. Major Leonard Arthur Tilney is buried at Cabaret-Rouge British Cemetery, Souchez.

21

'Every Shot Is Telling'

When RMS *Lusitania* went into service in 1907 she was regarded as the fastest, most beautiful ship afloat. Nearly 800ft long and built like a luxurious floating hotel, she was the last word in transatlantic liners. *Titanic* and her sister *Olympic* outsized her and 'Lusy', as she was affectionately known, saw her own sister ship *Mauretania* go faster, but she was still a favourite on the transatlantic run. Indeed, of the four she was, in spring 1915, the only one still plying this lucrative trade. Although *Lusitania* had been prepared for life as an armed merchant cruiser, when hostilities commenced she was deemed too greedy in terms of coal and so was left to continue her normal work, albeit it under Admiralty supervision.

One of the menaces this ocean liner would have to contend with as she continued to ferry passengers at high speed back and forth across the Atlantic was the submarine. Submarines were not a new concept, nor were they received well in traditional naval circles. Nelson referred to underwater craft as 'bulgarious … sneak dodges down below.' The idea of attacking a ship from beneath the waves was still viewed by many seamen as a type of piracy.

On 18 February 1915 Germany stepped up its underwater activity with a campaign of unrestricted submarine warfare in response to a British blockade of her ports. Since the reign of Henry VIII ships were supposed to stop and search an enemy, then give the passengers and crew time to depart the scene safely before sinking them. this concept did not marry with that of the submarine. Now all gloves were off. The Germans would attack and sink any British ship they could. Almost all the waters surrounding the British Isles were declared a war zone by the enemy.

British ships began resorting to tricky tactics to avoid being attacked by German U-boats. These included running up neutral flags to mask their identity. *Lusitania* herself had been adorned with an American flag at the beginning of the year as she made an eastbound crossing, arguing somewhat feebly that it was to signify that she had neutrals on board. Despite the threat though, the Royal Navy remained largely apathetic. As First Lord of the Admiralty, Churchill didn't think the threat significant and in the first two weeks of the German campaign only seven ships were sunk out of nearly 3,000 arrivals and departures from Britain. Throughout April only seventeen merchant ships had been attacked. Nearly half of them had subsequently got away.

Sir Cecil Spring-Rice, at Eton just before Henry Rawlinson, was the British Ambassador to the United States. On 29 April a proof of a newspaper advertisement with an anonymous note landed on his desk. The advert appeared to be a warning and it was apparently to run in several newspapers on 1 May. It stipulated that neutrals sailed on British ships at their own risk. On this very day *Lusitania* was due to depart New York on the latest of her homeward crossings bound for Liverpool and the warning was construed by some as a direct threat against her.

Spring-Rice had originally dismissed the note as a hoax but when it actually appeared in print he cabled London with details. A few people due to sail transferred off the ship and some cancelled their crossing altogether, but it was reasonable to believe that the submarine menace would not affect the great ship. *Lusitania* could outrun any U-boat easily, was faster than most warships and there was an option to provide her with a naval escort once she reached the designated war zone. Thus, as if nothing had been learned from the tragedy of the *Titanic* disaster, she was still considered 'as unsinkable as a ship can be'.

One passenger who seemed to be unperturbed by the threat of the U-boat menace was Bernard Audley Mervyn Drake. He was 23 years old and had arrived at Eton in 1904, yet another of Mr Brinton's boys. 'Audley' had no time for cricket, unlike John Manners whose room was close by, although he was an enthusiastic footballer. Dry and witty, he took a lively part in the House Debating Society. Once called upon to discuss the new concept of daylight saving time that had been put before Parliament, Audley dismissed it in a tongue-in-cheek manner. It would never catch on, he claimed. 'Many people enjoyed their after dinner bridge and would not miss the evening for worlds.' Not to mention what would happen to the train timetable. 'All clear-minded men in Parliament,' he reminded the room, 'had opposed the Bill as absolutely futile.'

As soon as he could, Audley took up science as his speciaility at Eton and after Cambridge he had travelled to the United States. His father was a highly talented electrical engineer and Audley was to follow him into the family business. He had settled temporarily in Detroit in 1913 to acquire a working knowledge of the electro-chemical industry, possibly in conjunction with some military work for the government. He had been having a very merry time and loved the bubbling 'energy and kindness' of the Americans that he had met.

The time had come though to return home and contribute to the war effort. Originally booked into a spacious cabin on A Deck, Audley switched with his travelling companion, Frederick Lewin, a motor engineer and director of Friswell's who dealt in Peugeots and Renaults and had been visiting New York. Home for Audley for the duration of the crossing was now to be a small but ample first-class cabin on the inside of the ship. D-41 was located just behind the second funnel several decks further down, by the main staircase and passenger lifts servicing the first-class accommodation.

In all, 1,260 passengers, including three stowaways, were aboard *Lusitania* as she sailed into the Hudson River at lunchtime on 1 May. They included munitions and equipment manufacturers, shipping men, convalescent soldiers and men hoping to enlist. The war had slowed trade. Of 540 first-class berths only 290 had been filled and down in third class there were only 367 out of a possible 1,200. There was, though, a noticeably large contingent of children on board. As well as thirty-nine babies there were a further thirty-nine young girls and fifty-one little boys.

There was plenty to keep Audley occupied in first class, including the opulent gold-and-white lounge with its stained-glass ceiling. Right outside his cabin was the outstanding feature of the ship, the double-tier first-class dining room with its elaborate marble columns. The Verandah Café was open all along one side and filled with greenery, hanging baskets and wicker chairs to resemble a pavement café ashore. The ship's orchestra played music before the furniture was unbolted for dancing and for those who wished to remain active out on deck there were games of shuffleboard or medicine ball throughout the day.

Always present though was a worrying undertone of what they might be sailing towards. On 6 May a warning message began to be tapped out at intervals, alerting ships to the fact that a U-boat had been making a nusiance of itself off the southern coast of Ireland. Just before 8 p.m. this warning was received by the wireless operators on board *Lusitania*. A second coded alert then followed detailing submarine activity about Fastnet which was some eighteen hours away.

Captain William Turner had received much advice from the Admiralty on how to keep his ship safe, including avoiding headlands and passing harbours at full speed so as not to dawdle near submarines. At sunset that evening he gave orders for the crew to extinguish all outboard lights, to cover the skylights, draw the curtains in public rooms and darken the portholes.

That night at a concert Turner, who was not a people person and had deigned to join the event despite having once described passengers as 'a lot of bloody monkeys', assured his charges of their safety. Nevertheless some of them slept in the public areas and some sat up in their cabins fully dressed. A number of passengers had formed a little committee to teach their fellow travellers how to put on lifebelts and one group of young men had got together and decided that in the event of an emergency it just wouldn't do to push women and children out of the way to get to their positions in the lifeboat. They would meet up towards the stern and decide amongst themselves what to do next.

At dawn on 7 May a thick fog came down. Concerned about running into shallow water as *Lusitania* sailed into the war zone, Turner was compelled to slow down to 15 knots, the top speed of the very submarine lurking in the water according to the warnings. At 10 a.m. the fog began to lift and the ship's speed picked back up as the spring day grew sunny and clear. Although they were now travelling at 18 knots, the burst of speed the passengers were expecting to carry them into port did not materialise. Some hoped that they might be waiting for an escort.

An hour later another warning came in from Queenstown on the southern coast of Ireland and Turner ordered all the portholes closed and as many of the watertight doors as possible. He doubled the lookouts, had extra men placed on the bridge and ordered the engine room to be ready to make a run for it if necessary. Nothing was being left to chance.

U-20, under the command of 32-year-old Walter Schweiger, had finished unsuccessfully chasing an ageing British warship when she resurfaced at 1.20 p.m. The commander was called to look out on a conspicuously large ship coming into view, 'a forest of masts and stacks'. The crew of the U-boat didn't know it, but 14 miles to the south-west it was the *Lusitania* emerging over the horizon. Possibly unaware of the ship's identity, they submerged immediately and began racing towards her as fast as they could; but at 9 knots when under the surface it couldn't possibly be fast enough to catch her. They got within 2 miles but *Lusitania* was heading away from them. It appeared as though Turner and his ship had been lucky.

Some twenty minutes later *Lusitania* came within sight of the Old Head of Kinsale, blissfully unaware that Schweiger had her in his sights. Owing to the fog Turner had been travelling further towards land as a precaution but he had since reverted to his original course. The ship jolted and began making for the Coninbeg lightship, some four hours north-east off the coast of County Wexford. He had unwittingly played right into *U-20*'s hands. As Schwieger looked through the periscope the *Lusitania* had turned straight for him. 'She could not have steered a more perfect course' if she had been trying to give him a target to fire at. Schwieger was not about to lose his chance. He closed to within half a mile and at 800 yards a single bronze torpedo shot out of the *U-20* and made straight for the passenger liner.

On the starboard side of the *Lusitania* one of the lookouts had just come up on deck when he saw two white lines racing towards her. He grabbed a megaphone and began hollering to the bridge. Captain Turner was nearby and he ran up the stairs to the bridge on hearing the commotion. He arrived just in time to see the torpedo strike his ship in between the second and third funnels on the starboard side, right where Audley Drake's cabin was situated.

Many of Audley's fellow first-class passengers were finishing lunch or out walking on deck. There was a loud bang, a shaking sensation and a column of white water shot up and cascaded down on the deck amongst smoke and fire. A rumbling came from deep inside the ship and almost instantly a second-ary explosion went off. Turner immediately ordered the ship turned towards Kinsale some 10 miles away. The steering had failed and his next inclination was to try to bring her to a stop but steam pressure had plummeted. The *Lusitania* continued to plough helplessly through the calm sea. The main stair-case outside Audley's cabin, leading from the lower portion of the first-class dining room, was already beginning to fill up, overrun with passengers in a state of rising panic attempting to push their way up on deck. The ship had immediately begun to list to starboard. Four minutes after the torpedo struck, whilst many were still dazed and wondering what to do, *Lusitania*'s electrical supply failed completely. Much of the inside of the ship was rendered pitch black in an instant. Terror-stricken passengers felt their way along darkened passages and up staircases to try to get out into the open.

Unlike the *Titanic* disaster, so fresh in people's minds as they ran towards the lifeboats, the *Lusitania* would not take some two hours to sink. She now had about fifteen minutes until she plunged beneath the waves and, as yet, she still had more than 1,200 people on board. Whether or not passengers and crew stood a chance of being saved was a lottery.

A group of butchers jumped inside a food lift to try to reach the upper decks. They became trapped and others who had found a way out were haunted by the sounds of them hammering in the tiny enclosure that would take them to their watery graves. A young mother ran to fetch her baby daughter and suddenly remembered that the woman in the next cabin had a toddler. She burst into the cabin and there he was, having been put down for a nap. She tried to pick him up but the little boy was too heavy and she could not carry both. She had to leave him behind.

The ship's bow was beginning to dip below the surface and the list had now reached some thirty degrees. Thanks to the recommendations following the *Titanic* disaster there were more than enough spaces available for everybody on board in twenty-two boats slung from davits as well as twenty-six more collapsible ones with folding sides stacked about the boat deck. Passengers were swarming up from all classes to make their escape, some of them screaming.

The ship's list was growing worse. People began naturally running to the port side of the ship, which was rising higher and higher away from the water. Launching boats was proving to be futile here though. They clunked against the hull as the crew tried to launch them, spilling frightened passengers into the water some 60ft below. The lack of seamen left one officer shouting for help from male passengers to try to push more than two tons worth of lifeboat away from the ship so it could be launched safely, whilst beating off men trying to jump in. One boat smashed on to the deck and rolled along it, crushing those in its wake. Others that managed to get to the surface crashed on to people who had fallen out as they flailed in the water.

Things were even worse on the starboard side. There was no public address system for communicating with passengers and the shouts of the officers and seamen were drowned out by the screams and anguish of those attempting to pile into the boats. Here the list had caused the boats to swing away from the listing hull and left an 8ft gap. Some jumped it, others consented to be thrown across but many terrified women and children stood rooted to the spot and refused to move. The ship's forward momentum meant that boats hitting the water were dragged into the path of the next and over all of those that had fallen in. A trail of humanity was being left in the *Lusitania*'s wake.

It was still less than fifteen minutes since Schweiger's torpedo had pierced the ship's side. Boats couldn't be detached from their davits in the chaos and were being dragged underwater with their terrified occupants still in them. The angle of the ship meant that the 80ft funnels were now hanging overhead. Children were being handed off into the boats but many had become lost in the panic. One young man returning to Britain to enlist found two abandoned babies on deck, shoved one under each arm and jumped towards a lifeboat. As the end neared passengers began to line the rails and jump into the water to escape being sucked down with the ship, some of them stripping off to give themselves more mobility.

The *Lusitania*'s four bronze propellers were now sticking out of the water, still turning. To those on the starboard side the list had become so pronounced that it looked as if she might roll over on top of them entirely. Icy water was beginning to wash over the top deck and the stricken passengers and crew were running out of places to flee to. As the sea cascaded towards them people were sucked under and washed away. Charles Frohman, the man who had funded J.M. Barrie's *Peter Pan* on both sides of the Atlantic, appeared to have made peace with his fate. He was heard quoting the play in the final seconds. 'Why fear death? It is the most beautiful adventure that life gives us.'

At 2.25 p.m. Walter Schweiger decided that he had seen enough. He had the *U-20* turned around and made off, deciding that it would be too much to launch a second torpedo at his victims. He was not unmoved by the scenes, but consoled himself with the knowledge that they had seen a cruiser nearby and that if he were to try to help, his comparatively tiny submarine could make very little impact on rescuing those condemned to the water.

Lifeboats still swung from the ship and the stern remained packed with people when the *Lusitania* met her end. She was only in 340ft of water and the bow stuck on the seabed, but any momentary hope that that might act as a reprieve for those still aboard was soon snatched away. The beautiful liner pivoted, let out a roar and fell gracelessly to the bottom on her side.

Of nearly fifty lifeboats, only six had been successfully launched. Everyone else who had not already suffered a fatal injury or become trapped inside the ship now thrashed helplessly in the water. Gradually hypothermia and exposure overcame them and they began to die. Distraught women who had been clinging to their dead babies let them go and watched the little bodies float away. One survivor drifting along with the current heard someone singing 'Abide With Me', but gradually the cries died away and a hush descended over the water.

News of the ship's fate was wholly different to that from the front, where death was a likely outcome. Schweiger was dubbed 'The Baby Killer' amidst worldwide public outcry and disgust. No less than 1,201 people died when the *Lusitania* was sunk on 7 May 1915, including Audley Drake, one of eight Etonians to die at sea in the Great War, four of them whilst travelling as passengers[1]. His body was never identified. Audley was 23 years old. His travelling companion was lost too, so piecing together Audley's movements throughout the sinking is impossible. Nobody survived who would have been able to tell his story, but what is certain is that he died in an eighteen-minute window of panic and despair thrust upon over a thousand civilians by Germany's policy of unrestricted submarine warfare.

With Audley went 128 American passengers. There was outrage in the United States, though at this juncture it did not translate into a willingness to go to war as Britain might have hoped. Although Schweiger and his crew were greeted as heroes when they returned home, Germany was soon confronted with the consequences of this single act and was ultimately compelled to put an end to her uncompromising U-boat policy.

When she resumed it two years later though, America joined the Allied cause. Her soldiers marched off to war having seen recruitment posters depicting the sinking of the famed Cunard liner and they did so with cries of 'Remember the *Lusitania*'. She may have failed to get 198 Americans safely into Liverpool, but in 1917 the tragic ship arguably helped to deliver two million of them to Europe to tip the balance of the war in favour of the Allies.

Compared to the army, navy traditions at Eton were extremely limited, even allowing for the difference in the size of the two services. Of some 5,650 Etonians who went into uniform during the Great War, less than 3 per cent of them joined any of the naval services[2]. There were various reasons for this huge weighting towards the land forces. For sixty years or so the structure of recruitment for officers in the Royal Navy had dictated that a boy went to Dartmouth for training at the age of twelve or thirteen. Two years later he would go to sea for a period of three more years. This obviously meant the foregoing of an education at the likes of Eton and explained why so few OEs found their way to the Royal Navy. In 1913 a system of special entry for public school leavers had been established to try to deal with an increasing demand for naval officers. It enabled boys of seventeen or eighteen to choose the navy over the army when leaving school bent on a career in the armed forces, but at the onset of the Great War the scheme had simply not been in existence long enough to have had a significant impact.

A lack of naval tradition amongst Etonian families also explained low numbers of them going to sea during the Great War. Boys were flocking to the army to follow ancestors and living relatives who already had an affiliation with a certain regiment and there was not the same heritage in place to propel them towards the water. Yet Etonians still managed to populate all corners of the Royal Navy. George Lascelles Kirk, a pre-war engineer, was picked out to put his skills to use in submarines, whilst three OEs acted as surgeons and two as chaplains. The son of a housemaster joined the staff of Room 40 in naval intelligence after a wound brought his army career to an end and, at 18, the

9th Earl De Le Warr declared himself a conscientious objector and instead of going to the front he took up work with the Royal Naval Reserve in a trawler section.

Charles Alexander John Fuller-Acland-Hood was one wartime school leaver who took advantage of the public school scheme and opted to join the navy. Despite the fact that his family bore numerous connections to the army, part of his surname indicated a rich naval heritage. Captain Alexander Hood, his great grandfather, had accompanied Captain Cook around the world and was later killed aboard his ship HMS *Mars* in 1798. Wounded whilst battling a much older French ship of the line off the coast of Brittany, he apparently succumbed to a nasty leg wound just as the opposing captain was surrendering his sword into his hands. Another relative was Sir Samuel Hood, mentor to Nelson, a vice-admiral and a hero of the Napoleonic Wars.

'Charlie' had arrived at Eton in 1910, another of Hubert Brinton's boys. Suffering severe growth spurts, he also spent a year recuperating from a nasty double break of his collarbone that hampered any attempts he might have made to have an impact on school life. In 1915 he left Eton to go to Newport Pagnell for intensive cramming to give him a good shot at his navy exams. He was promoted to Midshipman in time for the beginning of 1916 and wasn't at all sorry that he had chosen a different path from his schoolmates. 'I like being in the navy very much,' he wrote. He visited Brinton whenever he could and had tried to promote the Royal Navy as a viable option for those about to leave school and join the war effort. 'It is a grand life and I wish you would crack it up to any members of the house who may be thinking over it. The opportunity of the Public School entry is well worth [it] and I don't think it has been sufficiently advertised at Eton.'

In mid May 1916 Charlie was happily back at school on leave, 'full of glorious spirits and sun' before he rushed back to duty at Rosyth in the Firth of Forth. There too was a cousin of his, Rear Admiral Sir Horace Lambert Alexander Hood. A former naval secretary to Churchill, Hood had his own Eton connection. Having joined the navy at 12 he was not an OE himself, but his elder brother was. Horace had recently married an American widow with at least three children from her first marriage, including one son, George Nickerson. On returning to England after the wedding in 1910 they had decided to send him to Mr Heygate's house where he still resided in 1916.

Horace Hood embodied the proud spirit of the Royal Navy heart and soul and his record read like an adventure yarn. Handsome, bright, enterprising and brave, not to mention still only in his mid 40s he was one of the youngest flag officers of the fleet and had earned a DSO battling hand-to-hand with dervishes alongside the Hampshire Regiment in Somaliland. The daughter of his stepson's housemaster remembered him with great fondness. She was friendly with George's sisters and was mesmerised by the fact that the dashing admiral had two different coloured eyes. 'This hereditary distinction proved so fascinating that I found it hard not to stare at him and lament my own pair that matched.'

In 1915 Hood had assumed command of his own squadron and raised his flag in HMS *Invincible*, the ship to which Charlie Acland-Hood had subsequently been sent as soon as he was ready to go to sea. Their ship was a groundbreaker. Whilst Admiral Fisher was brainstorming the future of naval warfare and sending his German counterparts into a state of panic with his revolutionary battleship HMS *Dreadnought*, he was also masterminding a new type of warship for the Royal Navy.

Not quite battleships, but better than an armoured cruiser, their comparatively light armour was supposed to be offset by top speeds of an impressive 25 knots, which would enable them to outrun destruction at the hands of an enemy ship. HMS *Invincible* was the first example of what were to be dubbed 'battlecruisers'. Launched in 1907, at 567ft she was armed with an impressive array of 12in guns, maxims and five torpedo tubes to complement her speed in what was considered to be an unbeatable naval combination. Elizabeth Heygate had been invited by the admiral with her brother to look over the ship at Portsmouth before the war and was just as mesmerised by it as she was by Hood's eyes. They presented their passes at the dockyard gates. 'Saluting figures sprang to attention' as they followed a rating on to the ship, clattering up and down steel companionways. 'He explained the mysteries of gun turrets and we threaded our way under hammocks strung in unexpected places.' She was amazed at the use of every available bit of space. The name *Invincible* was stamped everywhere like Royal Navy propaganda and she believed in it wholly.

Despite the aggressiveness of the naval arms race and its contribution to the outbreak of hostilities in 1914, all the sea-going firepower that had been accumulating in German and British ports had yet to face each other in battle in the early summer of 1916. The Royal Navy had thus far not been impressed with the cautious endeavours of the German High Seas Fleet. British sailors retained the upper hand, but to their chagrin did so sitting still doing nothing whilst the army was being decimated. A number of plans had been considered for luring the Germans into battle, but ultimately what was the point when by risking very little the Royal Navy was effectively winning the war at sea?

The German High Seas Fleet was loath to emerge and risk a full-on confrontation with the Royal Navy's Grand Fleet. But all of this changed in

1916 when the offensively-minded Vice Admiral Reinhard Scheer took over command of the Kaiser's ships. He was determined to end the British blockade that was crippling Germany. Although he shied away from taking on the whole of the numerically superior Grand Fleet, he thought that he might be able to draw off a smaller portion of it. Then by flinging every facet of naval warfare at them, ships, aeroplanes, submarines, he hoped to chip away at British naval supremacy.

Scheer was in paroxysms of rage when Germany was forced to withdraw her policy of unrestricted submarine warfare in the wake of the sinking of the *Lusitania*. For an advocate of it such as he was it was humiliation on a grand scale; and humiliation aimed at the German Navy. Something had to be done and he resolved to put his fleet to sea.

Almost as soon as Charlie Acland-Hood returned to HMS *Invincible* he was on the move. His ship, HMS *Inflexible* and HMS *Indomitable* formed Horace Hood's 3rd Battlecruiser Squadron, the 'Invincibles', and they were being detached from their counterparts at Rosyth and sent further north to Scapa Flow. There, behind steel submarine nets and minefields, the Grand Fleet sat at anchor under the command of Admiral of the Fleet Sir John Jellicoe. It had been ordained that all three of the Invincibles needed some gunnery practice and they were to spend three weeks in the Orkney Islands with him.

Whilst they were thus engaged, Scheer was planning to make his move. The Germans had constructed battlecruisers of their own to keep pace with the Royal Navy and he had planned to use some of them for a raid on Sunderland. Just near enough to a major British naval centre, he hoped to attract David Beatty's attention and coax him out with the remainder of the British battlecruisers under his command at Rosyth. Submarines would be waiting for them and if they got clear of those, 50 miles away he would be skulking in the North Sea. Scheer intended to dispense with British battlecruisers and then make a run for it before Jellicoe and the Grand Fleet could reach him from Scapa Flow. In this way he would avoid confronting the numerically superior British fleet.

Unfortunately for the German admiral his plan, set for the end of May, was scuppered by bad weather. Rather than abandon it altogether he formulated an alternative scenario based on the same principles. He would apply the initial attack aimed at drawing out Beatty to British shipping in the Skagerrak to the north of Denmark's Jutland peninsula instead of at Sunderland. The British battlecruisers would still have to steam past his submarines and he could still corner the survivors in the absence of Jellicoe and his battleships before making his getaway.

At 1 a.m. on 31 May Scheer's battlecruisers, led by Franz von Hipper, began raising anchor. The main High Seas Fleet followed an hour-and-a-half later, and ninety-nine ships headed towards Horns Reef, just off the westernmost point of Denmark. On the way Scheer received three messages relaying movements of British ships. He brushed them aside. There didn't seem to be any unity to them and they were spread out. Little did he know that the entire Grand Fleet had put to sea and was heading in the same direction as his own ships.

Intelligence had seeped through that seemed to indicate that the High Seas Fleet was getting ready to move. Both at Scapa Flow and Rosyth the Royal Navy began to raise steam on 30 May. At 5.40 p.m. the orders arrived. 'Germans intend some operations commencing tomorrow.' They were to proceed to the east of the Long Forties in between the coasts of Scotland and Norway and be ready for whatever awaited them.

At Scapa Flow the steel submarine nets were pulled aside. Excitement was rippling through the ships at anchor, including Hood's battlecruisers. Two hours before Scheer and Hipper had even sailed, 150 British ships were already moving. On a damp misty night *Invincible* steamed south through the Hoxa Sound and out into the North Sea with Jellicoe's force, carrying 18-year-old Midshipman Charlie Acland-Hood with her. They would have had no idea what was in front of them, for an oversight in Room 40 informed Jellicoe that Scheer was at anchor when in fact the two fleets were on a collision course.

The first shot of the Battle of Jutland was fired at 2.30 p.m. on 31 May 1916 when Beatty and his battlecruisers engaged von Hipper's smaller force. Sailing gung-ho into trouble, Beatty found himself in the midst of the entire High Seas Fleet. The Germans were ecstatic, but what they didn't realise was that Jellicoe was at sea and that Beatty was now in a position to turn and run to the north, luring them into a trap.

On board HMS *Lion*, Beatty sailed towards the Grand Fleet to deliver the pride of the German Navy into its hands. Jellicoe had been steaming south towards him, but he had dispatched Hood and his fast battlecruisers to go to Beatty's aid. *Invincible* sped south. Screened by light cruisers, Hood's squadron, however, couldn't find Beatty and his ships. The weather was deteriorating and the light was becoming dim. An hour later, as Charlie Acland-Hood's ship ploughed through the North Sea looking for their countrymen, Jellicoe sent a communication to the Admiralty. 'Fleet action imminent'.

Half-an-hour later the Invincibles steered into the path of four of Hipper's light cruisers. One of the ships travelling with the squadron, HMS *Chester* came under heavy fire. Hood saw the flashes through the murk, heard the guns and *Invincible* steered towards the stricken ship. He arrived just in time. The crew of the *Chester* was massively relieved to see Hood put his flagship in between her and the enemy. The Germans were taken completely by surprise and fled the British battlecruisers back to their admiral. Hood sent a message over to *Indomitable* congratulating them on their shooting. Spirits were high. They believed that they were indeed 'indomitable' and that their admiral was 'invincible'.

Hipper responded by sending a large contingent to engage *Invincible* and the rest of Hood's force. HMS *Shark* was sunk but the German sailors, although vastly outnumbering the British at this point, panicked at the sight of the Royal Navy ships. Hood turned his squadron back towards the main fleet and continued looking for Beatty.

On board HMS *Iron Duke* Jellicoe had continued sailing south, but with no effective communications from Beatty he had no idea what he was steaming towards. At 6 p.m. he finally came within sight of *Lion*, 5 miles away, going east off his starboard bow. Where was the enemy fleet? He asked Beatty but he had no idea. Jellicoe's position was precarious. It would take time to deploy his ships and if he delayed too long they might sail into danger. He was desperately in need of accurate information. At 6.15 p.m. he gave the order to deploy anyway and the Grand Fleet began swinging into line. It was a crucial decision. In twenty minutes, if he had played his hand right, he could have a 6-mile-long line of ships ready and waiting to open fire and the High Seas Fleet would have sailed right into his range.

After its engagement with Hipper's light cruisers, *Invincible* had sailed west. Off their starboard bow the Grand Fleet loomed into view. Suddenly Beatty appeared on their other side, coming right at them. Hood's Invincibles were supposed to be sailing off *Lion*'s stern but if they attempted to get there they would obstruct the fire of Jellicoe's ships. Hood took the decision to have *Invincible* turn and take up a position in front of Beatty instead.

At about 6.20 p.m. she led the squadron on a turn and they began steaming 2 miles in front of *Lion* on a parallel course with five German battlecruisers some 5 miles off her starboard beam. Beatty had already begun firing on the three to the rear and so Hood ordered his force to do the same on *Derfflinger* and *Lützow*. *Indomitable* watched the flagship from behind. It was 'a glorious sight ... a huge bow wave and white wake, her smoke streaming back and her battle flag flying'. On *Lion*'s bridge excitement built as they watched Hood's flagship steam towards what looked like the decisive moment of battle. The gunnery practice undertaken by the 3rd Battlecruiser Squadron at Scapa Flow paid off. Every time *Invincible* fired a salvo the vessel shuddered and lurched about in the water. As Charlie and the crew ran back and forth through the ship the stench of cordite fumes increased.

Atmospheric conditions meant that although the British ships had a clear field of vision, Hipper's men found themselves masked by cloud in return. In the failing light ships drifted in and out of the mist and low-lying cloud, lit up by flashes from the guns. The Germans were tormented by the Royal Navy's fire when they could not themselves see what they were shooting at. *Invincible* flung shells at *Derfflinger*. In eight minutes she hit *Lützow* numerous times. From the bridge Hood called up to the ship's gunnery officer. 'Keep it up as quickly as you can! Every shot is telling!'

German shells were managing to find her in return though. One salvo hit aft but luckily didn't do any damage. Then suddenly the German battlecruisers emerged from the haze on the starboard beam and caught sight of their opponents. On *Derfflinger* hearts leapt. 'The veil of mist in front of us split like a curtain at the theatre … Clear and sharply silhouetted against the horizon, we saw a powerful ship … on an almost parallel course at top speed. Her guns were trained on us and immediately another salvo crashed out, straddling us completely.'

Still under fire, the Germans were ecstatic. Finally they would be able to see where their shells were landing. They had taken enough punishment from the British warships and now they could fight back. When Hipper's ships trained their guns on Hood's squadron it was terrifying. 'On the starboard bow we had the German Fleet throwing everything they had, including their toothbrushes at us.' They continued firing frantically back at them.

A veil of smoke and flame began to descend over the water. The worst of the shelling began falling upon *Invincible* at the front, targeted by two German battlecruisers. With her light armour she was no match for the shells now being flung at her. The thin armour of the battlecruisers had already been tragically exposed two hours previously, when HMS *Queen Mary* went to the bottom with over 1,200 men onboard. It was a lottery. If a shell hit one vulnerable spot then disaster would strike.

And that is exactly what happened. A salvo rang out from the German battlecruisers and fell amidships. Towering above the deck was a gun turret, 'Q'. A shell plunged through 7in of steel, blowing the roof off and barrelling down towards the ship's magazines, packed with tons of cordite.

At just past 6.30 p.m. a red glow appeared in the middle of *Invincible* as a flash ignited all the way down the turret. There was a terrific flash as two of the ship's magazines blew up and the ship was ripped in half. The whole central section, boiler rooms, coal bunkers and the two gun turrets, was consumed by a huge fireball. An awning from the bridge was tossed skyward, masts collapsed inwards and a huge column of black smoke mushroomed several hundred feet high. Metal rained down and debris engulfed the ship. As soon as the explosion was finished the ship plunged into the sea. In just a few seconds HMS *Invincible* and almost her entire crew had ceased to exist. Boiling hot bits of shrapnel pelted down on top of *Indomitable* nearby. When the smoke cleared she was gone. Cheers rang out from *Derfflinger*. The two pieces of the hull came to a stop sticking out of the shallow water.

When other British ships swept past the scene they thought it was a German wreck and cheered. The awful realisation sank in as they went past the shattered hull and saw *Invincible's* name painted on the side. Men who had survived her instant destruction had been clinging to the stern, but they gradually slipped into the water. They began to drown. The waves were littered with floating kitbags and hammocks. Of just over 1,000 crew, only six men were eventually saved by HMS *Badger*.

Neither Charlie Acland-Hood, the only OE lost at sea with the Royal Navy during the Great War, nor his cousin Admiral Hood were amongst the men saved. Back at Eton, Mr Brinton had seen yet another of his boys go. Mr Heygate was forced to steel himself, knock on George Nickerson's door and tell him that his stepfather was dead. His own daughter Elizabeth was in a state of shock. She remembered her visit to Portsmouth and her tour of Charlie's ship. 'HMS *Invincible* I read under the ... quarter deck, HMS *Invincible* circled the sailors' caps in gilt letters and as we walked away again I saw the name in foot-high letters on the bow.' Now those letters stuck out of the North Sea on her broken hull and everything she and the rest of the country had been led to believe about the infallibility of the Royal Navy was rocked. She had not been invincible at all.

With the sinking of the *Invincible* came the next phase of the battle. Regie and George Fletcher's brother Leslie sailed into action with the rest of Jellicoe's ships aboard HMS *Colossus* as the two fleets engaged. Scheer was suddenly faced with the Grand Fleet deployed for battle when he did not even know they were at sea. After an emergency manoeuvre he eventually fled. Leslie's ship was hit twice throughout the course of the evening but the last surviving son of Charles Fletcher was to be spared at the Battle of Jutland. Scheer managed to slip away and despite scattered fighting through the night, by daybreak on 1 June he was out of sight. The battle, which had ended in a draw of sorts, was over.

Whilst the Battle of Jutland was the only full-scale engagement between the Royal Navy and her German counterpart, this did not mean that Britain's sailors sat idle for the rest of the Great War. Neither did all of their activity revolve around dreadnoughts and large-scale warships. Of 163 OEs serving at sea almost 65 per cent of them had found their way there via the Royal Naval Volunteer Reserve. Founded in 1903, its mandate was to facilitate civilians who did not work at sea, but were enthusiastic sailors, yachtsmen and the like to volunteer for naval service in times of war.

Amongst over a hundred OEs serving with the RNVR was Lieutenant-Commander Geoffrey Heneage Drummond. Born in 1886, he came from a large banking family that would found the Royal Bank of Scotland and was a cousin of Elizabeth Bowes-Lyon, the future queen. The Drummonds were more than doing their bit for the war effort with seven sons and a daughter in various uniforms and one brother was the same 'Bones' Drummond who had been killed at Hooge in July 1915 with the Rifle Brigade.

In childhood Geoffrey had fallen down a stone stairway and dislocated his neck. As a result a bone still pressed on his spine and he suffered from severe headaches. His education at Eton was thus limited to a few terms, as was his time at Christ Church, but Geoffrey, charming and witty, always had an interest in the water. He had spent much time yachting on the south coast and around Europe prior to the outbreak of war.

Desperate to do his bit, even though he once referred to himself as a 'professional invalid', in December 1915 Geoffrey was accepted into the RNVR at the age of 29. Although an expert yachtsman Geoffrey presented himself at Southampton in January 1916 for what was to be extensive training. He was forced to 'pig it with fourteen or so other bravos' ('the scramble for eggs and bacon and steak and kidney pie was hectic') whilst they were all instructed in an array of subjects including seamanship, navigation, gunnery, Morse and semaphore.

He was eventually given command of a motor launch. These little craft were a new concept during the Great War. Some 80ft long, they were designed for anti-submarine activity and harbour defence. By January 1918 Geoffrey was in command of *ML254* at Dunkirk. The flotilla at Zeebrugge was busy with intensive training and he and his crew picked up the slack. At one point he did thirty-two consecutive night patrols along the coast. Then, on the thirty-third patrol, he was suddenly summoned to take part in a daring enterprise.

An initial raid on Ostend and Zeebrugge had taken place at the end of April 1918 to try to block the port of Bruges, which sat some 6 miles inland. Populated by U-boats. The Germans had been developing it since 1914 and used it is a base to launch their U-boat attacks on Allied shipping. The plan was to sink two old cruisers in the mouth of the canal at Ostend and three at Zeebrugge to stop submarines getting out. The raid on Zeebrugge enjoyed limited success, but at Ostend they failed completely.

On the night of 9 May the Royal Navy attempted to resolve that failure. A host of volunteers from the first attempts to cut off Bruges put up their hands again. HMS *Sappho* and HMS *Vindictive* were selected, stripped bare and reinforced with concrete ready to be sacrificed. Admiral Keyes took four monitors along for support with eight destroyers and five motor launches, including *ML254*. They sailed in under a smoke screen, with support from an RAF bombardment and artillery on the water. Once in position the two cruisers would scuttle themselves whilst the monitors and destroyers covered them. Then Geoffrey and the other motor-launch commanders would pull up alongside and take off the volunteers.

The Royal Navy contingent sailed from Dunkirk after dark on 9 May. En route, *Sappho* was hampered by a minor explosion that forced her to turn back after her speed plummeted to six knots. They were down to one cruiser but the operation pressed on. By 1.30 a.m. they had approached Ostend. The fog had thickened considerably and now completely shrouded the water as the aerial attacks and the Royal Marine artillery bombardment began. Two piers marked the entrance to the canal but *Vindictive* was forced to sail back and forth looking for them. The motor launches supporting her had lost sight of their charge. Geoffrey too was flailing but turned inshore and luckily managed to find her again.

'Just as I got there *Vindictive* loomed up going all out.' His launch sped off, but try as they might it was all they could do to keep up with her. At the third attempt she had managed to find the canal. German artillery immediately began showering *Vindictive* with shellfire. One dropped by the side of *ML254* and Geoffrey was blown off his feet. 'The fireworks were amazing and very pretty. The star shells were red, green, blue and yellow.' Then there were the flaming onions being flung in consecutive green strings. 'I got one string along my bridge; it took off the back of my right hand and broke everything there; signal lamps, switches etc. but by the mercy of Providence the compass and its light and the telegraph handles and chains were untouched.' Shells continued to dog the motor launch. One burst right by the mast, killing a crew member and maiming the coxswain and Geoffrey, a copper driving band plunging into the back of his left thigh.

Already damaged from the Zeebrugge raid, one of *Vinidictive*'s propellers was severely hampered. As she attempted to swing sideways to block the harbour entrance, crippled by shellfire, her commander was killed along with most of the occupants of the bridge. His wounded first lieutenant, Victor Crutchley, tried desperately to manoeuvre but the ship would not respond and she drifted into a sandbank and came to a stop, only partly blocking the canal.

Geoffrey, detailed to pick up her crew, approached her. They had just reached the piers at the mouth of the canal when a bullet penetrated his collarbone. In the fog he could barely see what was happening and he ripped open the canvas roof to his bridge. Despite his wounds and the numbness brought on by serious blood loss, Geoffrey hauled himself up to balance on a shelf, his head and shoulders sticking out into the open whilst he worked the telegraphs with his feet.

Crutchley was not going to be able to rectify the situation and so he ordered everyone to evacuate *Vindictive* and for the ship to be scuttled. Whilst the charges were being prepared he staggered around the decks looking for men to shoo on to *ML254*. The plan had been for Geoffrey to approach her on the opposite side to the enemy fire, but things had gone awry when *Vindictive's* steering ceased to function.

Geoffrey was forced to sail his launch alongside in full view of the enemy. Lit up by searchlights, machine-gun bullets raked *ML254*, two lodging in his duffel coat. Men were throwing themselves on to his motor launch, scrambling down ladders whilst being sprayed by machine-gun fire and peppered with shells. Some of them broke their ankles as they jumped down on to the packed deck of the little vessel.

ML254 began to back away with thirty-eight of *Vindictive's* volunteers cowering on her deck. Still hanging on to the wheel despite his wounds, Geoffrey headed out to sea towards Admiral Keyes and HMS *Warwick*. His launch was badly damaged and he flashed out SOS signals on his electric torch. They went dead slow to try to keep her afloat as every wave lapped over the forecastle. Their wardroom was ablaze, perilously close to their petrol supply. Crutchley, who was proving to be 'a tower of strength' in organising men to bail out the drowning launch, now frantically tried to apply a tourniquet on Geoffrey's numb leg as he huddled by the wheel. His trousers and shoes were saturated with blood and it had seeped out on to the deck all around him.

Bleeding heavily and clinging on to consciousness, Geoffrey pulled up alongside HMS *Warwick*. *ML254* was so waterlogged that she was almost unsteerable. Once all the occupants were safely off a charge was set to destroy her. At the last minute one of his engineers seized the ensign and they shredded it and distributed the pieces between the survivors.

Geoffrey, who would almost lose his left leg, might have considered himself lucky to be aboard *Warwick*. But his ordeal was not over yet. He was sitting in the wardroom semi-conscious in an armchair when it suddenly collapsed underneath him. Light bulbs fell all around him as the ship struck a German mine off Ostend. Another officer dragged him up by his shattered arm, which shook Geoffrey to his senses and urged him forward. 'I staggered after him dropping one leg down the ammunition hatch which woke me further and crawled up the ladder on deck.' A destroyer was lashed alongside and they made for Dover.

The raid could hardly be considered a success. HMS *Vindictive* had only partially blocked the approach to Bruges. Nonetheless naval personnel had performed bravely and three Victoria Crosses were handed out, one of them to Geoffrey Drummond and another to Victor Crutchley.

The injuries that Geoffrey Drummond suffered at Ostend did nothing for his existing health problems after the war. However in 1939 he was determined to play his part. Not considered fit for the RNVR, Geoffrey eventually ended up in the Royal Naval Patrol Service as an able seaman. In April 1941 he was carrying a heavy sack of coal aboard HMS *Pembroke* when he took a fall, hitting his head on the deck housing. Lieutenant-Commander Geoffrey Heneage Drummond VC died on 21 April in hospital at the age of 55, a worthy example of the service rendered to their country by the tiny fraction of Old Etonians who chose to make their contribution at sea.

Notes

1. Three more OEs were killed when their troop transports sank. These were Captain David Salomons, Royal Engineers (HMS *Hythe*, 29 October 1915), Lord Kesteven, Lincolnshire Yeomanry, aged 24 (SS *Mercian*, 5 November 1915) and Lt Geoffrey Ashmore, Royal Engineers, aged 42 (SS *Transylvania*, 4 May 1917).
2. This figure does not include the boys who joined the Royal Naval Air Service. When the Eton war list was compiled in the early 1920s E.L. Vaughan included them with the Royal Flying Corps and the Royal Air Force.

22

'The Light that Failed'

Despite the failure of the German Army to barge its way to victory on the Western Front in the spring of 1918, the end of the war seemed anything but a foregone conclusion to the exhausted troops now trying to regroup after their ordeal. 'The possibility that the moral and material resources of the Germans had fallen so low,' wrote Pip Blacker, 'that the war might be won in the autumn did not seriously occur to us till later.' Whilst everything moved north in April the Guards waited, now part of Byng's Third Army, south of Arras.

The weather was miserable at the end of April. It did not look like the Germans were at all interested in an advance, in fact it looked more like they might begin retreating as patrols of Grenadiers found abandoned forward trenches south of Ayette. Some captured Germans seemed to give the impression that rather than contemplating an attack, they were afraid of being overrun themselves. The idea of the Guards advancing slightly to assume a ridge around the village of Moyenville began to take shape, but aside from some desultory artillery fire and the odd enemy raid, it felt as if they were in a lull as far as fighting a war was concerned.

There really was a sense that the British Army was drawing on the last manpower available to it. Ralph Gamble had found himself in command of one of his old masters from Eton, which was a bizarre feeling. Geoffrey Headlam was nearing 40 but had requested a transfer from the OTC, which he had joined on the outset of war. In the 1st Scots Guards, Henry was bemused by the arrival of Hugh Marsham-Townshend. A 40-year-old former militia man whose younger brother Ferdinand had already been killed with the regiment back in 1915, he had a son, John, who had just arrived at Mr Goodhart's house at Eton. Now Henry found him serving as his subordinate. 'He calls me Sir!' he exclaimed.

For Henry though, one person at the front had gained an importance far above any of their fellow officers. He and Ralph Gamble had become utterly inseparable. Hardly more than acquaintances at Eton, they had moved in different social circles and had differing interests. At the front though they shared a loathing of the war along with an intense passion for their old school. The memories of Eton were all, as young men who had gone straight from Eton into the army, that they had to fall back on to try to escape the horror around them. They spent all their spare time together and whenever an invite was extended to one, it was unthinkable that the other should be excluded. Once away from their battalions they took immense pleasure reliving school days, talking about friends and acquaintances, which they called 'Eton Shop.'

One by one Ralph and Henry had seen their friends falling around them, whether dead or sent home wounded, and it had created an unbreakable bond between two young men who found empty spaces nearly everywhere else at the front. Oliver Lyttelton pointed out the extent to which Henry Dundas valued companionship and friends at the front. 'I remember him many times in the winter of 1916–1917 walking five miles along the Somme roads in the rain and five miles back again for the pleasure of exchanging a quip with the brigadier.' Of Ralph and Henry he said that 'their intimacy was so close that it barely escaped sentimentality. [Henry] had more friends than most men and yet besides this one friend all others were as nothing. He would have given anything that he possessed to him, he would have followed him anywhere'.

Jeffrey John Archer Amherst, Viscount Holmesdale, had been a contemporary of both young men at Eton. An officer in Ralph's battalion, he was a fan of both Ralph, with his 'unmistakable quality of innocence', and Henry, with his 'dazzling smile and scintillating sense of humour'. He described their friendship as 'a David and Jonathon relationship without a trace of anything unhappy, difficult or questionable'.

Henry articulated his own views on friendship. He had been reading Kipling's *The Light That Failed*, which championed the close relationship between two young men:

What a wonderful thing friendship is, and how easily misconstrued ... intellectually speaking – into gross homosexuality. It is considered a dreadful thing to say 'I love so and so', yet 'love' is the only word which describes one's feelings to really great friends, and it is only the people who realise this who succeed in the sphere of friendship.

By the end of spring 1918 Henry was back in command of Left Flank Company, living with a French family comprising an elderly couple, two teenage girls who appreciated his gramophone and a small boy whose favourite pastime was swinging a cockroach attached to a piece of string around his head. He had by now proven himself a more than competent commander. McAulay VC had told him that having him in command of them was a source of pride. 'I almost embraced him,' wrote Henry in response. He had himself already been awarded the Military Cross in the Cambrai area in late 1917 for a brave, pitch-dark attack and consolidation and in May 1918 he received this gallantry award a second time.

A patrol of Guardsmen had been sent out under another officer to try to identify the enemy troops opposite and the moon emerged, lighting them up in full view of the enemy. They were caught under heavy fire. Only two men returned unscathed and four men had vanished, including the officer. Henry seized an NCO and off they went in search of their missing friends. Coming under the same fire, Henry was shot in the elbow but his companion, who had a bullet pass through his helmet and miss his skull, managed to help him home. Henry's wound continued to bleed profusely and his servant McIntosh tried to insist that he go with him to an aid post. But Henry would not hear of it. It would have left one single officer with the company and so he swallowed the pain and remained, making out his reports and waiting for his men to stand down the next morning before he would let his servant drag him off to seek treatment. Along the way Henry's only preoccupation was getting food for his companion. 'Can you give my friend ... some food,' he asked, 'as he has not had anything to eat since last night?' 'I have often thought since,' wrote McIntosh, '[how many] officers would have referred to their servant as their friend?'

It was not the first time that Henry had shown an utter disregard for his own personal safety, despite General John's warnings about his role as a company commander and how precious he was. On one occasion, when his men were laying a wooden track at Pilckem Ridge, they came under heavy fire. 'The Captain just kept walking up and down the slip of road as if nothing was happening,' wrote one Guardsman. 'When the men saw the example that [he] was showing ... they very soon all returned and resumed work.' One of the men noticed a hole in the Henry's burberry, made by debris from one of the shells. He did not shout at his men for running away, he simply smiled when he saw them coming back to join him.

On another occasion, in front of Langemarck, Henry crawled 300 yards in broad daylight with an orderly to begin marking an alternative route out for his men in miserable weather to save them from a mile of drudgery and a shower of German shells. The area was void of landmarks and 'a sea of mud'. All he had to mark their route was remnants of tape he had scraped together stuck end to end.

On such missions his sense of humour did not fail him. Henry's reconnaissance reports were a source of entertainment for the brigade staff. 'When his report was presented it was written as likely as not on the back of a private envelope and among a mass of useful information gathered ... and by taking quite unjustifiable risks, there would be one or two deductions intended to be merely farcical.'

Despite his record Henry felt guilty about his elbow wound as it meant he would be sent home for a month. 'I'm afraid I feel rather a scrimshank getting hit just now when things are so uncertain.' It had not escaped him though, that it would be a period of respite for his parents. 'I am awfully pleased for your sakes, you poor darlings. It means a good long spell of freedom from anxiety and we shall have enormous fun.'

He utilised his time at home fully. His sister Anne was pulled away from school and with their mother they spent a few days in London including a day down at Eton, where Henry had spent much of his time. His father was with him to see the Eton and Harrow match. It was a low-key affair played at school rather than the usual grand Lord's affair. Mr Dundas watched proudly as Henry, Ivan Cobbold and another friend went on a recruitment drive trying to talk boys into the idea of joining the Scots Guards when the time came for them to stake a regimental allegiance.

The reality of the war, though, was never far from his mind. Towards the end of June word arrived that a non-OE officer named Holmes, affectionately known as 'Sherlock' by his fellow officers, had been sitting on Henry's bunk in their dugout when he had been killed by a German artillery shell. Shocked, Henry's first inclination was to get back to the front as quickly as possible. By the end of July he had returned to his company and the daily grind had resumed. 'Everyone seems to be very confident that the Germans are very low, and the line seems to be very quiet and comfortable.'

While Henry was away the Guards had undergone a month of training and recuperation. There was a real sense amongst them 'that Hindenburg and Ludendorff had done their worst ... that their bolt was shot' and that when they went back on the offensive the Allies would have the upper hand. They were being thoroughly versed in open warfare for the next phase of the war, incorporating and developing lessons learned during the grand German spring attacks. Different national contingents were pooling their ideas. The New Zealanders sent NCOs along to the Guards to be trained and the Canadians supplied others to give a demonstration in patrolling and raiding in daylight. Feilding was trying very hard to give the men some time for rest and relaxation too. There was a gymkhana organised by one brigade, a horse show by another and the Grenadiers played the Welsh Guards in a 'mass football match', twenty-five men on each side with four balls in what turned out to be a 'Homeric struggle'.

The Guards were also busy instructing American newcomers to the Western Front, ready for their induction into the war proper. Their visitors were from the 80th Division. All of the men appeared to be from a Pennsylvania mining district and 'American' was only a loose description of these troops, who had been born all over the world and communicated in 'a babel of tongues'. Henry found them 'amusing, interesting and rather arduous'. They were 'very apt, very keen and very ignorant'. Britain had had four years to adapt to the industrialised warfare of the Western Front; now their new allies would have to catch up quickly.

Henry could hear his servant McIntosh chatting away to their NCOs in the next room of their dugout and his company sergeant major, Mitchell, was enjoying himself immensely bossing them around. Henry found the Americans' effervescent enthusiasm amusing, 'so full of ardour to get over to the Germans and do them in'. Their commanding officer was remarkably energetic and eager to oblige. He went constantly around the lines, which Henry found wryly amusing. 'Four years hence?' After a period of instruction there were then stints in the line in the company of the Guards. Henry was to act as a consultant of sorts. 'I shall give excellent advice, but avoid exercise as much as possible. The hot weather makes one very lazy and disinclined for active participation in the war.'

On 8 August a British assault was led by General Rawlinson and his Fourth Army that the Germans would refer to as the 'Black Day'. Aimed at pushing the enemy away from Amiens, to which they remained perilously close after Operation Michael in March, in five days the British managed to drive the Germans up to 12 miles back in some places. Although the British were out-numbered significantly they took thousands of prisoners and captured hundreds of guns. The French attacked too and forced the enemy to hurriedly evacuate a large swathe of territory to the south.

As of 13 August though, German resistance began to harden, even if they were still on the defensive. Haig decided at this point to change things. Rather than push an ailing attack forward he switched the focus to another sector. Byng's Third Army now came into play, attempting to surprise the enemy with a strike near Bapaume.

By mid August the Germans had begun pulling back in front of the Guards. They remained in Moyenville and Hamelincourt, but were in no mood for a fight. The Division flung nearly 700 gas drums at them in the former village, which they had now been looking at since April, and the enemy barely reacted. Byng's attack was to take place on 23 August in conjunction with some of the Fourth Army north of the Somme. It was decided though, that two days prior to this it was necessary for some of his men, including the Guards, to launch a limited attack north of the Ancre to take care of a line of fierce German resistance. The 2nd Guards Brigade, including Ralph Gamble's 1st Coldstream Guards and Henry Dundas' 1st Scots Guards, were selected for the job.

The relevant units were pulled from the line and sent back to Saulty on 16 August for training. They were not told what was afoot but Evelyn Fryer, with the last of the brigade's three battalions, the 3rd Grenadier Guards, was suspicious. 'There was much conjecture as to what this meant, the official explanation being given out that the enemy was massing opposite us and a new attack was imminent and therefore it had been decided that each division should have a complete brigade in reserve for counter-attacking purposes.' They swallowed this tale at first, but once the Guardsmen began to practice counter-attacking and their research focus fell on positions such as Moyenville *in front* of their positions he surmised that they would be going forward themselves.

Ralph had missed almost all the final preparations, even though he would be commanding one of the Coldstream companies in battle. He arrived back at the front from leave on 19 August and dined with Henry at Corps HQ; 'very pleasant, with a band playing Pinafore'. Twenty-four hours later Ralph was loading his men into lorries for the journey to their assembly positions. Loaded down with ammunition, sandbags and shovels, they were issued with rations, including lemons, chocolate, tea, rum and cigarettes as they waited for zero hour. Henry would be acting as his battalion's second-in-command and thus not leading his company into battle. That job would fall to Marsham-Townshend. Henry spent a strenuous night with a roll of tape, marking out assembly positions before heading back to battalion headquarters to help oversee the attack.

The attack on 21 August was to take place along a 9-mile stretch from Miraumont to Moyenville to try to turn the line of the old Somme defences from the north. On their front, the 2nd Guards Brigade were to push south-east. In charge of the brigade since the departure of General John was Bertram Sergison-Brooke. Youthful, just as precious to Henry as his predecessor and more commonly known as 'Boy' Brooke, he planned to have Ralph's battalion on the left moving on Moyenville itself and Henry's on the right, with Evelyn Fryer's waiting in a sunken road at Boiry to come up an hour and a half later to push through towards a railway line which comprised his brigade's final objective.

The initial Guards attack was as tactically advanced as was possible. In addition to artillery the men were to co-operate with sixteen tanks, which would pass in front of them at zero hour and mop up any German resistance. Ralph was to have five of them in all and in addition to paving the way for his company, they would cover their consolidation as well as then searching all the ground in front of their final objectives. Whilst all of this was very well thought out, if the tanks got into difficulties the attack had to carry on. 'Opportunites by the action of the tanks must be exploited but the advance is not dependent on the progress of the tanks and will continue without them if necessary,' he had been ordered.

Ralph's battalion was full of Etonians – Collegers, to be exact. Ralph would take charge of No.3 Company, with an old boy of Rugby School, Roderick, as a subaltern. He had as another subaltern young Jack Rowlatt KS, out of Eton just about a year, the younger brother of Charles, Logie Leggatt's good friend. Another of the battalion's subalterns was William Roe, a Colleger and future housemaster who like Jack had only left Eton in 1917. With headquarters for the day was Charles Austin, or 'Charlie' Pittar, a third Colleger who had left in 1917 with Roe and Rowlatt. Although a phenomenally talented athlete and a bright boy, Charlie had trouble with his eyesight and so operated with divisional troops rather than a fighting unit. One of his main responsibilities in the hot weather was getting a sufficient supply of water up to Ralph, his fellow officers and their Guardsmen as they attacked.

After 10.30 p.m. the battalion began moving up in companies. Behind them Evelyn Fryer had pored over his maps and learned everything he could about Moyenville, Hamelincourt and their environs. But he had done that at Boesinghe a year before, and what he had memorised had been gone by the time that he arrived, wiped out by artillery. 'We all knew our objectives on the map; those of us who had taken part in big offensives before were less sanguine of finding them easily on the actual ground.'

The 1st Coldstream were in position by 3 a.m. with Ralph's company on the left of the line. It was a very quiet night for shelling. They fared better than

Henry's battalion, who in his absence were sitting with their gas masks on being pelted with noxious fumes. As the night wore on a thick mist began to envelop them. The tanks, which had set out to rendezvous with them, were fumbling around in the fog somewhere, lost. The terrain was unknown to them and they were unable to find the assembly positions.

As per orders, the infantry attack was not to be influenced by the presence or otherwise of the tanks. Zero hour arrived at 4.35 a.m. By this time the fog was impenetrable. The situation was compounded by a smoke barrage that the 75th Brigade of the Royal Field Artillery had been ordered to lay down across this section of the front. Ralph and his Guardsmen were unable to see 3 yards in front of them. At the head of his company on the left of the line, Ralph anxiously awaited the arrival of the tanks. He gave them ten minutes' grace and then, not wanting to get left behind the rest of the attack, he ordered his Guardsmen forward into the dense pall.

As luck would have it, the tank shortages had little impact on the Guards' advance. The Scots Guards ran into some nests of machine guns but the German shells being flung in their direction were inaccurately aimed and caused few casualties. Despite a total lack of vision, by 6.30 a.m. Ralph and the rest of his battalion had advanced some 1,000 yards in the right direction, taken Moyenville and were rounding up prisoners. Roderick was killed by a chance bullet as they reached their objective but across the Guards' front casualties were markedly light as a result of the Germans' disinterest in engaging them. By 7 a.m. they were all consolidating their ground and, as planned, Evelyn Fryer's battalion of Grenadiers passed through and attacked the railway embankment ahead.

By mid morning the summer sun had burnt off the mist and it was a hot, stifling day. 'A frightfully hot day. Ye Gods, how hot!' remarked Henry. Boy Brooke had been crashing around, dripping with sweat, which amused him no end. Pip Blacker appeared in the evening for a chat, as did his own company sergeant major, with stories of how he 'did in' eight Germans coming out of a dugout which he described to Henry 'with gusto'. Henry's only complaint was the weather. 'The heat is a little trying, but McIntosh is getting the water situation in hand. I must shave, then I shall be more comfortable.'

Across the board the British attack had met with success and they were now lined up ready for the larger advance on 23 August. Henry was surprised at how easy it all seemed in their sector. 'The tanks who were assigned to us were not very helpful; however, the chaps did everything themselves and the casualties are very light.' His precious company, in fact, had suffered just one Guardsman wounded.

That evening the Germans began shelling Moyenneville heavily but made no attempt to counter-attack. As darkness set in Ralph took his company and another, and managed to advance the Guards' line some 500 yards further on into the outskirts of Hamelincourt. In the course of the night Jack Rowlatt was severely wounded, badly enough that the 19 year old would lose a leg. Ralph was now the last officer with No.3 Company.

In spite of fierce German resistance he managed to establish a number of strongpoints that they clung on to until dawn. Shortly afterwards though the German infantry moved up to counter-attack. At 4 a.m. an SOS signal shot up along the Guards' front. The British artillery blasted into life and Lewis and machine gunners took up their weapons. Saxon troops brought up especially to retake the area from the British failed with heavy casualties. As elsewhere on the British front, advances were made to prepare for the main attack the following day, recapturing Albert and advancing between the Somme and the Ancre. The enemy had to be content with skulking backwards raining shells down on the Guardsmen nearby.

The German artillery shelled Ralph and his Coldstream battalion unrelentingly for the rest of the day. Explosives cascaded down on what was left of Moyenville, picking off the men. Ralph managed to grab a brief respite at lunchtime when he retreated to a sunken road to the rear and ate lunch with Henry, but then he was compelled to return to the battered village. Their commanding officer, a fiery OE named Jack Brand, was frustrated. 'The battalion could have taken Hamelincourt without a casualty in the afternoon of 21 August, and further, could have advanced the whole of 22 August (if only the tactical situation had allowed it) with very much fewer casualties than we had sitting still acting as a target to the enemy's guns.'

Young Viscount Holmesdale was going about his business two hours later when a deeply distressed messenger came rushing from No.3 Company. 'Mr Gamble has been killed, sir.' A shell had gone off right next to Ralph, and although spared obliteration, death for the 21-year-old was instantaneous. As he absorbed the news, a darker realisation began to sink in for Jeffrey Holmesdale. Somebody was going to have to go and tell Henry. He walked along to the Scots Guards to do it himself. It was 'a ghastly business'. Henry was staggered, shocked, totally speechless. They remained in silence for some time until he asked Ralph's fellow Coldstreamer if he could get him the regimental badge from Gamble's cap. Holmesdale agreed and left him to his thoughts.

A few hours later Henry sat down with a pencil and some paper and poured his heart out to his parents:

I can only write about myself tonight. Ralph was killed this evening, and nothing is the same. I love Ralph more than anyone in the world except you two. It was only this afternoon that I had lunch with him in his company headquarters and now I shall never see him again in this world ... But writing is no good. God, how I wish I could talk to you about him ... John and Eric and Sherlock – I could remain the same because I had him to talk to: they were his friends as well as mine and now he has gone and I can't be quite the same ... But I can't write anymore. I can't see the paper properly. My friendship with him was perfect and life can't be quite the same, especially out here, where I am alone.

There was no time for Henry to dwell on Ralph's death though, for the Scots Guards were being ordered back into the battle. That evening instructions were given for the battalion to continue the attack the next day. Henry was to help orchestrate proceedings from the Scots Guards' headquarters as they attempted to capture Hamelincourt. They were moving off to their assembly positions four hours after he began writing his letter.

The battalion went forward on Hamelincourt with the aid of three tanks just after dawn and, despite a heavy artillery bombardment, managed to take it. The Coldstream Guards continued the advance. At 5 p.m. orders were received for the 3rd Guards Brigade to relieve them all. It became a miserable, drawn-out process but finally by the following morning Henry was back at Ayette with his battalion where they would now spend time regrouping. But all he cared about was getting to Ralph.

His body was waiting at a casualty clearing station and Henry was insistent that he see him. 'He must have been killed instantaneously, thank God.' That afternoon they buried Ralph at Bac-du-Sud British Cemetery on the road from Arras to Doullens. Henry was desolate. 'Life without him will be almost unbearable.' In his grief Henry found solace in Tennyson's *In Memoriam.*' Written by the poet over a number of years in honour of his beloved friend who had died suddenly of a brain haemorrhage when the pair were much the same age as Ralph and Henry, it felt startlingly relevant. 'You can't realise what it is and to what extent the war binds people together out here,' he told his parents. 'I try to think that it is only seeing him off on a long journey, at the end of which we shall meet again as we used to do – but it's terribly hard. I suppose, like John Dyer he was too good for this filthy world. He was so marvelously brave and so wonderful with the men. Because war and soldiering were no more his aim than they were mine.' Suddenly Henry began making constant references to the idea of the afterlife. It became a theme in his letters:

'Deep folly! yet that this could be –
That I could wing my will with might
To leap the grades of life and light,
And flash at once, my friend, to thee.

'I thought I had forgotten to cry,' he wrote in anguish. 'Now there are times when I just can't stop … God has taken him now, and I'm left with the memory of him in all the phases and chances of the last unforgettable two years. And so one must just go on, never doubting that the time will come when I shall see him again. I wish you'd known him better, but you will some day.'

Having come out of the line the Coldstream were next door to the Scots Guards and Henry went to see Ralph's servant. He still couldn't believe that his friend was gone and the loneliness he felt was painful. 'What a meeting we should have had after the battle. He would have dined here and I should have lunched there, and this afternoon we should have gone and had tea with the brigade. But what's the use of saying all this?' Henry invited Jeffrey Holmesdale for a drink after dinner, but once he arrived he couldn't find it in himself to talk. 'Again he said almost nothing, but asked if I would go for a short walk with him. We went out and we sat down. One of his Scots Guards Pipers came up and he asked him if he would please play his pipes a little, perhaps a hundred yards or so away.' Henry had become attached to a particular piece of music, but sitting in the moonlight Holmesdale found it agonising to have to sit and listen to it. 'The Piper marched up and down playing that desperate lament "The Flowers of the Forest" … Emotionally it was almost unbearable. After a little while I got up to walk back to my unit leaving Henry sitting there, the Piper still playing. We had spoken no word.'

Whilst the Guards reorganised and underwent training at Ayette, Henry visited Ralph's grave whenever he could. He was keeping a cursory eye on the war's progress. 'The battle goes well. These marvellous Canadians captured Monchy Le Preux today. All the eagles are gathered together for the stroke which is to break the Hindenburg Line forever.' Always though he came back to his grief. 'How he would have loved it. We would have discussed it and gone over all the old ground again – Ribecourt, Flesquieres, Bourlon Wood.' On 27 August there was a renewed attack on a brilliant summer's day and then the Scots Guards were again relieved from the line.

The fact that he still had his company to concentrate on was helping Henry to hold it together, just. Numbers were dwindling in left flank too but he had another young OE subaltern left. 'I can talk to him so easily about

Ralph. It does me such a lot of good going over these last two years. How wonderful they've been. John and Eric and Sherlock and old Logie Leggatt and I shall see them all some day.' As September approached and the advance continued, Henry was faced with having to go over ground from 1917 that was simply full of old associations and reminders. 'Even looking at a map now is perfectly grim:'

> I climb the hill: from end to end
> Of all the landscape underneath,
> I find no place that does not breathe
> Some gracious memory of my friend.'

'Just a week ago today I was sitting with him in the sunken road the other side of Moyenville ... Old Scott has got *The Mikado* out here. The gramophone is a great comfort. All the tunes he liked, and we used to play at Arras, I expect he can hear them now:'

> He is not here; but far away
> The noise of life begins again,
> And ghastly thro' the drizzling rain
> On the bald street breaks the blank day.

'The Coldstream are in reserve this time, and I should be writing to him via Brigade to tell him what was happening.' Everything that wasn't related to death and destruction at the front for Henry had been connected to his best friend. 'All that Cambrai time – I always used to find the Brigade or he would come along to the Battalion. Every day at Gouzeaucourt he and the Brigadier used to come up – and then when we came out of the line what meetings and arrangements; and most of the time I find myself thinking it was all unchanged – and then the truth comes back and hits one a great blow.' Jack Brand had recommended Ralph for a gallantry award and he was posthumously awarded the Military Cross. The Colonel gave Henry a copy of the recommendation. 'It says as much as any words can say. But nothing can describe what he was.'

On 29 August the Germans evacuated Bapaume and two days later Australian troops crossed the River Somme. The following day they seized back Peronne. As Henry and the rest of the Guards remained in reserve, the rest of Third Army helped to push the enemy back right across the battle-fields of 1916. By the beginning of September the Germans were falling back 'in haste and obvious disorder' to positions covering the Hindenburg Line and the Canal du Nord north of Havrincourt. It was now the turn of the Guards to resume fighting and they would assume the responsibility for pushing towards the canal.

They commenced their attack on 3 September and it was surprisingly easy to advance. The Germans put up almost no fight. 'So strange and novel, indeed, was the sensation caused amongst officers and men by the unwanted absence of hostile machine-gun fire and the comparative silence of the enemy's guns, that the troops first advanced with an unnecessary caution, suspecting some cleverly concealed trap.' In front of Henry's men there was little save for a lot of dead horses, a few corpses and the inevitable flies. 'The advance became a route march, a Sunday walk-out, edged with tense suspicion … Twice or thrice they halted and began to dig in for fear of attack.' Cautiously they approached the old British front line to the north-west of Lagnicourt.

It was here, on the banks of the Canal du Nord, that the Germans had elected to defend in force. The Guards got to within 5 miles of it, but the approaches to the west bank were held in strength and the impetus of the Guards' advance slowed. They were now faced with machine guns and heavy artillery bombardments as well as gas shells being pelted on their rear positions.

The Germans had dropped their front line just in front of the Hindenburg Line and before an attempt could be made on this formidable defensive system, these covering positions had to be dealt with. This task would occupy the British for much of September. On 4 September Henry reported that he was back by Bourlon Wood, with all its memories of 1917. 'The Germans are retreating … and we are just walking after them to see what happens. The sight of Bourlon Wood brings Ralph back so tremendously. All these places do.' Attempts to continue to push the Germans back towards the canal continued, but to no effect.

By the middle of the month it had become clear to the higher authorities that the enemy could not be dislodged from their positions along the canal to the north of Havrincourt and south down to Ephey without a properly organised attack. These outworks of the Hindenburg Line had to be taken in this way before a final attack could be made on the canal and the main defensive system behind, and the general advance could continue.

The Guards took a passive role on 12 September when the Battle of Havrincourt began. Other units managed to take Trescault and Havrincourt itself, whilst to the north 57th Division took Moeuvres. The weather began to turn and Henry and his men had to contend with thunderstorms. Cautiously, because of the rising intensity of the German artillery, they had also been setting themselves out to defend in the face of a counter-attack if necessary. Probing across the canal in their sector was proving frustrating. The 'in-and-out skirmishing' in the nearby trenches reminded all who had survived it of the Hohenzollern Redoubt in 1915. 'The fighting was well nigh as intricate and, to those who were actually concerned in it, it appeared to be equally unprofitable.'

Preparations were underway for a major offensive to be launched on 27 September that would require the Guards to cross the canal. By 15 September, despite incessant artillery harassment, they were close enough to the canal to start reconnaissance of the obstacle. The main point, one of which they were already well aware, was that there was no water in it. The Canal du Nord was under construction in 1914 when the war began and, unsurprisingly, work had been curtailed by four years of conflict. Getting across it though was not going to be easy. The canal varied in width but the walls were almost perpendicular and smooth. Aside from where shells had taken chunks out of them and created footholds, it would be impossible to climb without using portable ladders. On the opposite bank the ground sloped uphill toward the enemy trench systems and so the first battalions across could expect to be met by fierce fire.

The German artillery continued to pick away at Henry's company, in particular the officers. 'We are frightfully short ... now,' he reported. 'We want about twelve junior officers at once, but, I don't suppose we shall get any ... the companies aren't much above 90 rifles in the line.' At times he was struggling to concentrate on the job at hand. Henry Dundas' father had noticed a marked change in his boy. Something of the inherent vivacity that everybody so loved about him, had gone. 'Four weeks ago today,' he wrote, 'and just about now, 6 o'clock in the evening:'

> Whatever way my days decline,
> I felt and feel, tho' left alone,
> His being working in mine own,
> The footsteps of his life in mine.

On 20 September he spent some more time sitting by Ralph's grave. 'It is a wonderful thing that *In Memoriam*. I just sat there and read it, with its almost uncanny power of being applied to one's own particular case.' On the way back Henry managed to stop at a clearing station to see Christopher Barclay, another of Ralph's fellow officers in the 1st Coldstream. He had been shot in the stomach and had to have the bullet extracted through his back. The journey took

Henry via the Arras–Bapaume road which he hadn't seen since he had passed along it with Ralph. 'What a golden memory.'

Plans for 27 September had now been finalised. Broadly speaking the First and Third armies were to attack on a 13-mile front opposite Gouzeaucourt with the Guards Division on the left of the line. Once again the 2nd Guards Brigade was to carry out the attack. They were to cross the canal, take the Hindenburg Line's support system, and then advance along a spur of high ground running north and east of Flesquières. Once the brigade had taken the first objectives, the 1st Guards Brigade would pass through them and advance towards the final point, an imaginary line going from Marcoing down to Cantaing, where they would push out tentative patrols towards the Scheldt river and wait for another division to come through them in turn. It was going to be a crucially important day. If these objectives could be secured and the Hindenburg Line conquered, it could signal the beginning of the end for the German Army.

Henry was to lead his own company this time. They began taking up their positions at 6.30 p.m. on 26 September. Steady rain soaked them but failed to hamper their progress much and everybody got into position across the slippery ground. Then, at 4.30 a.m. on 27 September the preparation of the entire brigade was hit by a hostile bombardment that caused a fair number of casualties amongst the Scots Guards. Luckily it was only short and it wasn't followed by an infantry attack. Zero hour came and the battalion punctually went off at 5.20 a.m.

The 1st Scots Guards moved forward under a particularly effective artillery barrage. Henry and his men had little difficulty crossing the canal, having been supplied with light ladders crafted by the Royal Engineers. Getting across might have proved easier than they expected, but the Germans put up stout resistance in the trenches on the other side, in particular with machine guns. They were assaulting an intricate network of trenches but the attack continued and the battalion had reached its objective by 7 a.m. Shortly afterwards the 1st Guards Brigade passed through them and continued the advance.

Until mid afternoon, by which time the British attack from the north had begun to make some headway, the Scots Guards were exposed to a galling machine-gun fire from the direction of Graincourt as they attempted to consolidate their new positions. As they went about their work a particular machine gun nearby continued to exact casualties from the still-advancing troops. Henry climbed out of the trench to reconnoitre where it was for himself. He had only gone a few yards when he was hit, probably by a waiting sniper.

Men who tried to rush to his aid were hit too. Then two of his company dropped their rifles and tried again. They were not fired on, presumably because the Germans thought that they were stretcher-bearers, and they managed to carry him to safety. He lived for a few minutes and did not speak. As Henry's chest ceased to rise and fall, another of Eton's lights burned out on the Western Front. All that was left was the hope that in his final moments, he was comforted by the anticipation of setting out on the journey he had come to believe in so profoundly: to find his way back to Ralph, and the rest of his fellow Etonians that he mourned so deeply.

The Guards Division was relieved that night. When the Scots Guards crossed back over the canal and retired to Boursies they carried Henry's body with them. McIntosh, devoted to him, escorted him the 6 miles as Henry was carried by German prisoners. He rounded up Henry's precious blackthorn walking stick, given to him by the daughter of an Edinburgh judge, and his book of poetry so that they might be sent home to Redhall. The following day Henry was laid to rest at Boursies. The whole of his company was present with a vast array of his friends. The pipers played 'The Flowers of the Forest' for him one last time.

At home his parents received hundreds of letters of condolence. Boy Brooke said that Henry's death and that of Ralph Gamble 'were the two greatest losses the Brigade had had'. It was high praise from the brigadier who had made Henry glow with pride every time he referred to him by his first name. His colonel was similarly upset. 'Henry was the life and soul of the battalion, and was loved by us all. As a soldier he was magnificent, so wonderfully capable, gallant and cheerful. He was adored by his company who would have followed him anywhere.'

Perhaps the most heartfelt notes though came from his men. 'I can hardly yet realise that he is gone from amongst us,' mourned McIntosh, 'and that we shall never hear his cheery voice again.' His company sergeant major wrote on behalf of the whole company:

> I cannot tell you how much he is missed by us all as we had been in many tight corners together and we always knew when we had your son leading us we would get through if there was a way through at all ... I am sure we shall never get another like him ... Captain Dundas led his men to the very last and was the same as he always was – a hero.

There was a sense amongst those that had known him that in Henry the world had lost a young man of real promise. 'Guido' Salisbury-Jones, leading a company of Ralph's battalion, described his friend as "an outstanding per-sonality' and credited him with an ability to lift those around him. 'There was so much that I owed to Henry's invigorating influence. He had a capacity to bring out any latent talent that I possessed. I had never regarded myself as a wit, but in his company I found myself capable of repartee which astonished me. It was Henry who at Eton one day decided to substitute "Guido" for my real name "Guy". That was thirty-five years ago. The Italian version has remained to this day as a heritage from that immortal friend of my youth … Poor Henry,' he mused. '[Gifted above average] he might have been a future Prime Minister.' J.M. Barrie knew him and had noticed his potential too. 'I thought so much of your boy that though you don't know me you will per-haps allow me to say how deeply I sympathise with you … He seemed to me … to be marked for notable things.'

Henry had survived Ralph Gamble by five short weeks and together they had almost reached the end of the war, only to fall in its final weeks. 'To see them together was to see youth at its best,' wrote Oliver Lyttelton, 'and the charm of their presence, the freshness and gaiety in their companionship are beyond my powers of description. The memory of them is the most poi-gnant left to me of all the tragedies of the war.' Of 21-year-old Henry Dundas he wrote: 'Age, disillusion, decay, never touched him. Like a bright flame he burnt and is suddenly extinguished. To his friends the world is darker.'

23

'Folded in the Dark Cloud of Death'

As October dawned and the Allies continued in pursuit of the Germans, the realisation dawned that the war might be won. In the preceeding weeks the idea that the Allies were advancing towards victory had taken hold. Pip Blacker had first begun to feel it in late August, but now the feeling had gained momentum:

> In an initial darkness, this hope first flickered intermittently like a will o' the wisp, and then steadied, first to an uncertain glow, and then to a continuous illumination which quickly intensified and culminated in a victory so total that at first it did not seem real.

Ludendorff had reached the end of his endurance and offered his resignation at the end of October. Bulgaria had already capitulated on 30 September, a month later Turkey followed and then, on 3 November, Austria–Hungary surrendered on the Italian Front.

The final Allied offensives on the Western Front began the following day in wet, miserable weather. The Germans had been pushed back on part of their front to Mons. In just over four years, the Great War had come full circle. Shortly before dawn on 11 November 1918, in Foch's personal train in the forest of Compiègne, a desperate German delegation signed the armistice. Oliver Lyttelton was by now brigade-major for the 2nd Guards Brigade. In the early hours he was awoken by a memo telling him that the war was to end at 11 a.m. that morning. He fell asleep again. When he joined Boy Brooke at breakfast it wasn't until the brigadier asked if there was any news that Oliver remembered the order and said, 'Yes, sir, this: the war is over.'

Pip Blacker was in the Bavay area, a place of scattered border towns where the 9th Lancers had taken refuge after their ridiculous charge long ago in 1914. 'News about the armistice ran round like fire … Faces radiating joy emerged from blankets and everyone struggled to their feet. Pandemonium!'

That night, he and another officer walked to the eastern edge of town and stood looking out on the countryside. For four years the eastern horizon had been intermittently lit up by gun flashes and flares. Now it lay silent.

Back at Eton, as the bell in the courtyard struck 11 o'clock on 11 November 1918, the boys went barrelling out of their classrooms, shouting, cheering and celebrating the end of the war in scenes of unparalleled joy. A small group of slightly more reserved Collegers walked into Eton and spied Charles Fletcher across the High Street. Excitedly they ran over to him to celebrate the news with the elderly man. None of them knew what to do. Tears stained the old man's cheeks. After more than four years of a seemingly interminable war that had robbed him of two sons, a stream of acquaintances and countless pupils, it was finally over. The boys watched uncomfortably as the old man broke down in front of them and sobbed at the side of the road.

After the initial jubilation that greeted the news at the front, perhaps surprisingly an air of gloom set in. 'I ought, I realised,' wrote Pip Blacker, 'to be feeling exultant. But I did not … I wondered what my father and mother were doing at that precise moment.' He was overwhelmed by misgivings about what was going to happen to the world now that it was all over. More importantly, the war might be over, but Robin was still dead.

Oliver Lyttelton and Boy Brooke rode about the troops:

> Everywhere the reaction was the same, flat, dullness and depression … we had some scores to pay off, and now they would never be paid. We began to wonder what England would be like, whether we should have enough to live on … what our account at Cox's might be. This readjustment to peacetime anxieties is depressing, and we all felt flat and dispirited.

Counting the cost of the Great War was harrowing. There were some ten million dead, perhaps more than double that figure wounded. Patrick Shaw-Stewart had been truly heartbroken when he wrote of the continual loss as early as 1915. 'The fact is that this generation of mine is suffering in their twenties what most men get in their seventies, the gradual thinning out of their contemporaries … Nowadays we who are alive have the sense of being old, old, survivors.'

This book has told of 128 Old Etonians who fell during the Great War but this represents only 10 per cent of the school's casualty list. The Western Front had seen the bulk of the school's losses, but Etonians who died during the Great War are buried in nearly thirty different countries, including two who fell in Northern Russia after the armistice was signed, thirty-one who fell after the engagement at Qatiya in April 1916 on the march toward Jerusalem that followed and six who were killed in East Africa, half of them serving in the ranks as the Germans attempted to divert Allied resources from the Western Front.

Eton's losses ranged from those, such as Robin Blacker who had barely passed their eighteenth birthday, to Field Marshal Lord Roberts, who died at the age of 82 at St Omer after inspecting Indian Troops in November 1914.

Each and every loss was mourned but some had a wider impact on the world. A talented scientist, Henry Gwyn Jeffreys Moseley was a contemporary of Einstein and his research altered scientific understanding of atomic structure, allowed the proper placement of elements in the periodic table, enabled identification of solid samples without destroying them and pinpointed three missing elements. It was widely believed that he was on course to a Nobel Prize.

When he was killed serving as a lieutenant with the Royal Engineers at Gallipoli, the German scientific community mourned him as much as the British, who flogged the War Office with the consequences of not having heeded their requests to remove Harry Moseley from danger. Now the most promising British physicist of his generation was dead. Paperwork had gone forward to facilitate his extraction from the front, but not in time. Ernest Rutherford was livid. He declared that 'to use such a man as a subaltern [was] economically equivalent to using the *Lusitania* to carry a pound of butter from Ramsgate to Margate'.

The press carried headlines like 'Death of a Genius' and 'Too Valuable to Die'. There could be very little doubt that Moseley's death helped Rutherford and the scientific community to convince the public that certain brains, 'being a national and even a military asset', should be protected during the war. It had, however, mattered little to Moseley himself. Henry had not only displayed a relentless determination to become a subaltern and put himself in harm's way, but had already refused numerous job offers connected with the war effort that did not require getting shot at.

In addition to the 1,168 known to have died, of the five and half thousand OEs who served some 1,500 more were wounded and 130 taken prisoner. In the course of their service, Old Etonians amassed almost 2,000 honours and awards, including thirteen Victoria Crosses and 548 Distinguished Service Orders, forty-four of them with a bar and four with two bars. There were some 750 Military Crosses, including thirty-seven men who were awarded the medal twice, like Henry Dundas, and four who received three citations. Neither did this figure include almost 600 more decorations awarded by foreign armies, such as the *Légion d'Honeur* conferred upon Ian Napier for his work as a liaison officer with the French during the summer of 1917.

The survivors had to try to build a life in the aftermath of a conflict that had entirely reshaped their consciousness and in many cases brought an abrupt end to a sheltered childhood. Victor Cazalet was one of a multitude of young men who now matriculated late at Oxford and Cambridge. It was a muted atmosphere, but they were all in it together. The nature of university life seemed trivial, juvenile and irrelevant given all that they had seen.

The feeling of uncertainty remained unsettling for those who had to return to work. The whole life experience for many young Etonians returning home was waging war. Oliver Lyttelton wanted to marry the daughter of a duke. 'I had a few hundred a year and my pay and nothing else. I looked likely to revert to being in second-in-command of a company.' Promotion looked distant. 'You could hardly get into the Guards' Club for officers.' He would embark on a political career and with Harold MacMillan would serve in Winston Churchill's cabinet during the Second World War. In 1957 the latter would become prime minister himself.

Aubrey Herbert ended the war operating as a liaison with the Italian army in Albania. He lost his sight completely not long after the conflict ended and was advised that having all his teeth extracted would help to cure his blindness. The operation resulted in blood poisoning and he died in 1923. He left a widow and four children. He was 43 years old.

When the war ended Ian Napier had flown some 200 hours, shot down one enemy aircraft in flames, put seven more on the ground, forced two to land on his side of the lines and shot down three out of control. He returned home and joined the family business in the first of many business ventures. He was twice married and fathered three sons. He died an old man, two months short of his eighty-second birthday in 1977.

Aside from those who fell at the front many Old Etonians had been maimed. Night flying in particular caused a constant stream of deaths but it was essential for the air defence of London from German raids. Philip Babington and Eustace Ralli were exact contemporaries at Eton and in May 1918 were practicing flying by night with the aid of a searchlight. The pair were involved in a tragic smash. Babington suffered 'serious injuries' but, in the passenger seat,

Ralli's back was broken. He spent over a year in hospital before he ultimately succumbed to his injuries at the RAF Hospital in October 1919. He was 21 years old.

Perhaps one of the saddest victims of all was David Stuart Barclay. Barclay served in Henry Dundas' battalion, arriving in 1916. A quiet boy, he was five days younger than Henry. His life was shattered on 15 September 1916 when he was struck in the face by a bullet as this final stage of the Battle of the Somme raged. His injuries were horrific. 'Poor David Barclay is wounded very badly,' Henry told his parents. 'Shot in the face somewhere he is blind in both eyes and his hand is very badly shattered … what a wicked thing this damned war is.' David survived, blinded and mutilated, for seven months before he finally weakened and slipped away at his home in Norfolk in April 1917. He was 20 years old.

But in many, the wounds were not visible: a generation of young men emotionally scarred and tormented by the horror that they had witnessed. Some Old Etonians would never come to terms with what the conflict had done to them. Reginald Mendel was just 18 when he left Eton in 1915 for the Royal Field Artillery. His family situation was complicated as far as the war was concerned. His father was a director of Harrods but of part-German descent. His mother was visibly distressed by the stigma of this Germanic connection. 'Rex' as he was known, was at the front when his father died at the beginning of 1917. On 3 May he was wounded whilst walking through Arras when a shell burst nearby and threw up some paving stones. Rex was thrown to the ground, dazed and his lower abdomen and the top of his legs suffered crush injuries. He suffered in silence for a week before he delivered himself up as sick and during his recovery was working at the War Office. One morning at home, he got out his revolver, put it to his head and pulled the trigger.

His heartbroken mother wrote a frantic letter to the War Office, lest they think her boy was a coward. 'Fear, through ill health of not getting back on active service preyed on his mind, with results as per certificate.' Rex's colonel seemed of a mind to try and ease her distress. 'No one was keener to fight for his country than he was, and he did splendidly during the nine months he was out with me here – With such a brilliant career before him – I mourn his loss more deeply than I can possibly tell you in words, and feel as if I had lost a very dear and brave son.' The truth was though, that 20-year-old Rex could not bear the thought of going back to war.

One of his contemporaries in College, Charlie Pittar, had survived the last rush of the Guards towards Germany following Moyenville, including being gassed, and witnessed the armistice after his exploits of August 1918.

Following his demobilisation he gained a nomination to follow his father into the Indian Civil Service and for two years he worked as a probationer at Queen's College, Oxford, whilst helping to teach classics and mark papers locally at the Dragon School, his old prep school. He was preparing to go off to India to begin his career but the war had robbed him of his ability to take part in sport, whether it be the effects of being gassed or the emotional strain brought on by shell shock and the loss of his friends, which manifested itself with persistent headaches, insomnia, dark moods and fits of depression.

One Sunday night in August 1921 Charlie bid his parents goodnight and went off to his room after supper. His mother popped up to see him. He was working and she asked him if he was busy. He waved her away. 'Yes, I'm very busy.' Shortly before 8 a.m. the following morning his father went to his study. On the desk was a note from Charlie warning his father to be careful of gas upstairs. Rushing to his son's room he found that it was full of fumes. His 23-year-old son was dead in his bed, with a tube attached to a gas stove and the supply switched on. His body was cold.

'I cannot ask you to forgive me for what I am going to do,' he had written in a note to his mother. 'And I don't think you will ever realise my general state of mind. There seems to be a sort of cloud which oppresses me. Today I've been throughout in a most extraordinary state – a mixture between deep depression and wild excitement, and always this cloud.'

Eric Greer and Billy Congreve were just two newlywed OEs who died leaving pregnant widows. Both gave birth to baby girls. In 1919 Billy's best man, William Fraser, committed himself to helping to raise his friend's daughter and married Billy's widow. Eric Greer's daughter, Erica, was born at the beginning of 1918. In another tragic twist his young widow, Pam, would not live to see the end of the war. A victim of the influenza epidemic that ravaged Europe in 1918, it fell to Eric's parents to raise their little girl.

Parents who had lost their sons found a myriad of ways to come to terms with the void created by their deaths. Ralph Gamble's heartbroken father gave up his post in the Indian Civil Service, shattered by the loss of his only son. A workaholic, William Garstin, was to commemorate his boy Charlie in the best way that he knew how. He went to work. In 1917, with all of his knowledge of the East and his experience of public works, he was made a founding member of the Imperial War Graves Commission, and with it not only assumed responsibility for honouring Charlie's sacrifice but in part for that of every one of His Majesty's subjects who fell during the war.

At the beginning of 1918 Pip Blacker had spent a good deal of time with the father of one of his best friends at Eton. E.W. Hornung, author of the

Raffles books about a gentleman thief, had lost his only son, Oscar, in 1915 and, as Pip put it, 'reacted in rather a peculiar way'.[1] He felt an overwhelming need to put himself as close to the front as possible, to share his son's experience. He had begun work for the YMCA which provided canteens for soldiers behind the lines.

E.W. based himself in Arras, but instead of establishing his canteen in as safe and comfortable place as he could find, as was the norm, he opened his 'tea-totallers bar' close to the front line. This humble little abode was in fact a hole dug out of the side of a sunken road, with corrugated iron walls and a makeshift roof. There he dispensed hot, sweet tea in half a dozen battered enamel mugs with biscuits to passing soldiers. Word got around that he was a celebrity and, dressed in basic khaki, as the kettle steamed away he chatted with his beloved 'customers' about their homes.

E.W. was a portly gentleman and he suffered greatly from asthma in the damp, cold conditions. However he appeared to revel in his ordeal. 'The worse the hardship, the more he was pleased; the nearer he felt to Oscar, whose experience he was sharing.' Whenever his path crossed with his friend's father, Pip thought that E.W. appreciated greatly the chance to talk about his son and another of their friends, Bartle Frere, who had been killed in 1916.[2]

E.W. spent a night with them in January 1918 and Pip put him up on the bed of a fellow officer who had gone on leave. 'Before going to sleep we talked about Oscar. Any new thing I could tell him, he said, was like a priceless jewel.' They talked about what they might do if they survived the war but Pip was unconvinced. 'He supposed, he said, that he would go on writing, but I could see that he had misgivings. He had lost zest and seemed to have little to live for.'

For his part, the elder man revelled in every moment spent in their dugout and in the opportunity to talk for a prolonged time with someone who had known his Oscar so well. 'He was now out here in his grave; but which of them was not?' Pip was the last one left and his safety caused E.W. no small amount of anxiety. 'I lay awake listening to his even breathing, and prayed that he at least might survive the holocaust yet to come.' Pip believed that there was something stoic and heroic about the actions of this one grieving father:

> The hardship to which he was subjecting himself during the long hours in his sunken road derived from his bereavment. He was honouring the memory of his son by giving the humblest service to those whose experiences came close to Oscar's.

Henry Dundas' family faced an uphill struggle to come to terms with the death of their precious boy. By the early 1920s his father and his eldest sister, Anne, had journeyed the length and breadth of the Western Front, visiting his grave at Boursies and looking out over the Canal du Nord. When his remains were transferred to Hermies Hill British Cemetery 2 miles away in 1925 his parents visited him every year until the outbreak of the Second World War. The inscription on his headstone matched that upon Ralph Gamble's 30 miles away: 'I thank my God for every remembrance of you'. Seeing the front for himself brought his father some measure of comfort given that his child lay so far away from home. 'I have seen myself hundreds of cemeteries,' he told the assembled crowd at the opening of the Slateford War Memorial. 'From Ypres to Armentières and down to the Vimy Ridge: from Arras all round by Bapaume to Havrincourt and Cambrai: along the Hindenburg Line to St-Quentin, all round the region of the Somme and south as far as the forest of Villers-Cotterêts … where our men fell in the early days of the war. All these cemeteries are well cared for, and, though still uncompleted for the most part … they lie, officers and men side by side, symbolising the comradeship that was theirs.'

Henry's mother never recovered from the loss of her only son and the rest of her life was tinged with a bitterness that she would take to her grave. Her relationship with her daughters was coloured by the admission that, given the choice, she would have elected to keep him with her instead. Her hatred for the Germans never subsided. Every Sunday she attended St Martin's church in between Slateford and the Haymarket in Edinburgh. 'She would frown and cough with disapproval should the rector ever be reckless enough to murmur from the pulpit some pious sentiments about forgiving our enemies.' She trained him to refer to the Germans as 'the Boche' or 'Huns' in his sermons and even claimed to have hit former Prime Minister, Stanley Baldwin over the head with her umbrella in the mid 1930s over his failure to rearm.

When she passed away, some three decades after the battle on the banks of the Canal du Nord, Henry's mother left instructions that in her coffin should be placed a small flag he had made for Left Flank Company HQ on his final leave. Henry had hand-stitched one for each of his battalion's companies, believing that they would be a source of pride for the men.

His sisters idolised him for the rest of their lives. Anne carried in her handbag well into old age her brother's final letter, urging her to behave herself at her seventh boarding school after being expelled or having run away from all the others. She ensured that the annual commemoration for her brother appeared in *The Times* well into the 1990s when she herself died, making it the longest running of all such notices. Her greatest fear as an old lady was that when she passed away, so much time would have elapsed that she would not recognise Henry when she got to heaven.

In the spring of 1919 Eton's hierarchy invited thirty-one OE generals of the rank of major-general and above to visit the school so that they might show their appreciation. 'Nowhere are [your] services more highly honoured and valued than at Eton, to which you are ... and which is proud to number you amongst its sons.' A staggering 165 OEs reached the rank of brigadier-general and could not be accommodated, but eighteen exalted military figures were available and they arrived in late May to cluster together outside the chapel to have their photograph taken and to address their audience.

It fell to General Plumer, as the senior officer present, to give a speech worthy of the occasion. 'We all of us realise that we are not here today as individuals,' he began. 'We are here as representatives of the great army of Etonians who have, during the last four-and-a-half years upheld the honour of their school in the service of their country.'

The thought of Eton had kept many of them going during times of hardship:

As you know, we never lost an opportunity during those four-and-a-half years of assembling on 4 June, or St Andrew's Day ... assembling together to discuss Eton topics and reviving Eton memories. I can assure you that these gatherings were a great tonic to us. The old forgot that they were old and became young – at any rate they behaved as such. All of us forgot that we were tired.

The boys of Eton College, he claimed, had not failed to do their bit:

The British Empire has emerged triumphantly from the greatest ordeal with which she has ever faced, and Eton claims that in that ordeal and in that triumph she has played a part worthy of herself. She does not base that claim on the prowess of achievement of a few individuals who happened to be in a position of authority and influence at the time, but she bases her claim on the large number who gave up much, and the many who gave up all, not prompted by any expectation or even desire for self-advancement; but simply by the wish to do what they knew was their duty.

It was not he, nor the assembled generals, he said, that were responsible for victory, it was the spirit of those who had not returned, including almost 1,300 Old Etonians:

We owe a debt to them, and it is for us to try and pay it … We can pay it by upholding in our lives the honour of our school as they upheld it by their deaths.

Plumer would not have been disappointed, for those that fell have not been forgotten at Eton. Reminders of their sacrifice are around every corner. Their names border the schoolyard on memorial panels and individual plaques circumvent the cloisters with more personal tributes supplied by their families. George Fletcher's prized French flag now hangs in the ante chapel at his father's behest, but perhaps the most poignant salute is the legacy of one single death on the field of battle.

In 2012 the Collegers decided to amend a tradition of over a century so that they might remember one of their forebears. On special occasions they now raise their glasses and toast 'In Piam Memoriam LCL'[1]. Each of them leaves school aware of who Logie Colin Leggatt was and knowing that he laid down his life in Flanders when he was a fraction older than they are. Magnify his sacrifice by well over a thousand and you have some idea of what Eton College, as just one community of many, contributed to the Great War.

Notes
1. Second Lieutenant Arthur 'Oscar' Hornung was killed on 6 July 1915 with the Essex Regiment. His body was never discovered and he is commemorated on the Menin Gate. He was 20 years old.
2. Bartlett Laurie Stuart Frere was killed with the Bedfordshire Regiment on 13 November 1916. He is buried at Knightsbridge Cemetery near Albert.
1. In Pious Memory LCL.

Sources

Personal papers belonging to the following OEs that are in private hands were either consulted or information kindly donated by:

David Barclay
Guy, Harry and Hugh Cholmeley
Bernard 'Audley' Mervyn Drake
Geoffrey Drummond
Henry Dundas
George and Reginald Fletcher
Eric Greer
Francis and Douglas Harvey
John Lee-Steere
Logie Leggatt
The Hon. John Manners
Reginald Mendel
Marc Noble
Ian Napier
Charles Pittar

Also: Diary belonging to Algernon Lamb (with thanks to Clive Morris, 1st The Queen's Dragoon Guards Heritage Trust and 'Firing Line', The Museum of the Welsh Soldier, Cardiff Castle)

Eton College:
Eton College Chronicle 1885–1928
Eton College Registers 1841–1919
House Books 1900–16

House Debating Society Books 1909–17
Papers of John Burdon Sanderson Haldane
Papers of Richard Selby Durnford
Papers of Edward Cazalet
Miscellaneous School Periodicals

Imperial War Museum:
George Schack-Sommer
Major Valentine Fleming
Thomas McKenny Hughes
Archibald James

Royal Air Force Museum:
Papers of Captain Ian Henry David Henderson

National Army Museum:
Papers of Major-General John Ponsonby

National Archives:
WO 95
WO 339/374
AIR 1

Newspapers and Periodicals:
Illustrated War News
The Graphic
Scots Guards Magazine
The Times
Westminster Gazette

Books:

Amherst, Jeffery, *Wandering Abroad* (London: Secker & Warburg, 1976)
Avebury, Baroness, *Eric Fox Pitt Lubbock … A Memoir By His Mother* (London: A.L. Humphreys, 1918)
Bailey, O.F & Hollier, H.M., *'The Kensingtons' 13th London Regiment* (London: Regimental Old Comrades Association, 1936)
Ball, Simon, *The Guardsmen* (London: Harper Perennial, 2004)
Beckett, Ian F.W., *Ypres: The First Battle, 1914* (Harlow: Pearson Education, 2004)
Birkin, Andrew, *J.M Barrie and the Lost Boys* (New Haven and London: Yale University Press, 1979)
Blacker, John, *Have You Forgotten Yet? The First World War Memoirs of C.P Blacker, MC, GM* (Yorkshire: Leo Cooper, 2000)
Bladersburg, John Ross of, *The Coldstream Guards 1914–1918* (Oxford: Humphrey Milford, 1928)
Bruce, Anthony, *The Last Crusade* (London: John Murray, 2002)
Buchan, John, *Francis and Riversdale Grenfell, A Memoir* (London: Thomas Nelson & Sons, Ltd, 1920)

Card, Tim, *Eton Renewed: A History from 1860 to the Present Day* (London: John Murray, 1994)

Chandos, Viscount, *The Memoirs of Lord Chandos* (London: Readers Union, 1964)

Clark, Ronald. J.B.S., *The Life and Work of J.B.S. Haldane* (Gateshead: Nothumberland Press, 1968)

Congreve, Billy, *Armageddon Road, A VC's Diary 1914–1916* (London: William Kimber, 1982)

Cooper, Duff, *Old Men Forget* (London: Rupert Hart-Davis, 1953)

Craster, Micheal, *Fifteen Rounds a Minute* (Barnsley: Pen & Sword, 1976)

Desborough, Lady, *Pages from a Family Journal, 1888–1915* (Eton: Eton College, 1916)

Doyle, Peter, *Loos 1915* (Stroud: Spellmount, 2012)

Dundas, R.N., *Henry Dundas, Scots Guards: A Memoir* (Edinburgh: William Blackwood & Sons, 1921)

Edmonds, Brigadier-General James, *History of the Great War, Based on Official Documents* (London: MacMillan, 1922 etc)

Eton College, *List of Etonians Who Fought in the Great War* (London: Riccardi Press, 1921)

Ewing, John, *The History of the 9th Scottish Division 1914–1919* (London: John Murray, 1921)

Ewing, John, *The Royal Scots, 1914–1918* (Edinburgh: Oliver and Boyd. 1925)

Fawcett, H.W. and G.W.W. Hooper, *The Fighting at Jutland* (London: Macmillan & Co. Ltd,. 1921)

Fitzherbert, Margaret, *The Man Who Was Greenmantle* (Oxford: Oxford University Press, 1983)

Frew, David, *A Young Borderer – A Memoir of Alexander Dobrée Young-Herries* (Edinburgh: William Blackwood & Sons, 1928)

Fox, Frank, *The History of the Royal Gloucestershire Hussars Yeomanry, 1898–1922* (London: Allan & Co., 1923)

Fryer, Evelyn, *Reminiscences of a Grenadier, 1914–1919* (London, Digby, Long & Co., 1921)

Gibb, Harold, *Record of the 4th Royal Irish Dragoon Guards in the Great War, 1914–1918* (London: Saward Baker, 1923)

Gillon, Captain Stair, *The King's Own Scottish Borderers in the Great War* (London, Thomas Nelson & Sons, 1930)

Goodman, Martin, *Suffer and Survive* (London: Pocket Books, 2007)

Gordon, Sir Home Seton Charles Montagu, *Eton v. Harrow at Lords* (London: Williams & Norgate, 1926)

Gough, Hubert, *The Fifth Army* (London: Hodder & New Stoughton, 1931)

Harrington, Peter, *A Family Record. Wemyss, Mary Douglas, Countess of* (London: Curwen Press, 1932)

Hart, Peter, *The Somme* (London: Cassell, 2005)

Hart, Peter, *1918, A Very British Victory* (London: Phoenix, 2008)

Hart, Peter, *Gallipoli* (London: Profile Ltd, 2011)

Hart, Peter & Steel, Nigel, *Passchendaele: The Sacrificial Ground* (London: Cassell, 2000)

Headlam, Cuthbert, *History of the Guards Division in the Great War* (London: Murray, 1924)

Heilbron, J.L., *H.G.T. Moseley, The Letters of an English Physicist 1887–1915* (California and London: University of California Press, 1974)

Herbert, Aubrey, *Mons, Anzac and Kut* (London: Hutchinson & Co., 1930)

Heygate, Elizabeth, *A Girl at Eton* (London: Rupert Hart-Davis, 1965)

Holmes, Richard, *Riding the Retreat* (London: Pimlico, 2007)

Horne, Alistair, *MacMillan, 1894–1956* (London: MacMillan, 1988)

Hough, Richard, *The Great War at Sea, 1914–1918* (Oxford: Oxford University Press, 1983)

Howson, Hugh E.E., *Two Men: A Memoir* (London: Oxford University Press, 1919)

Inglefield, Captain V.E., *20th Light Division History* (London: Nisbet & Co., 1921)

James, Robert Rhodes, *Victor Cazalet: A Portrait* (London: Hamilton, 1976)

Jones, Henry Albert, *The War in the Air,* Vols 1–6 (Oxford: Clarendon, 1935)

Kay-Shuttleworth, Sibell E.M., *Edward Kay-Shuttleworth, Captain 7th Rifle Brigade, Staff-Captain 218th Infantry Brigade, 1897–1917* (London: Chiswick Press 1918)

Kipling, Rudyard, *The Irish Guards in the Great War* (London: Macmillan & Co. Ltd 1923)

Knox, Ronald, *Patrick Shaw Stewart* (London: Collins, 1920)

von Larisch, Oberleutnant Heribert, *Das … Dragoner-Regiment Nr. 18 im Weltkriege 1914–1918* (Berlin: Stalling, 1924)

Levett, Richard Byrd, *Letters of an English Boy. Eton College* (Spottiswoode: Ballantyne & Co. Ltd, 1917)

Lewis, Gwilym H., (Bowyer, Chaz, ed.), *Wings Over The Somme, 1916–1918* (Wrexham: Bridge Books, 1994)

Lloyd, Nick, *Loos 1915* (Stroud: Tempus, 2006)

Lowther, F. Loraine Petre, *Wilfrid Ewart and Sir Cecil. The Scots Guards in The Great War 1914–1918* (London: John Murray, 1925)

MacKenzie, Jeanne, *The Children of the Souls: A Tragedy of the First World War* (London: Chatto & Windus, 1986)

Mannock, Mick, *Mannock VC (*London: Neville Spearman, 1966)

Maurice, Sir. Frederick Barton, *The Life of General Lord Rawlinson of Trent* (London: Cassell & Co., 1926)

Maurice, Sir Frederick Barton, *The London Rifle Brigade 1859–1919* (London: Constable, 1921)

Murland, Jerry, *Aristocrats Go to War* (Barnsley: Pen & Sword, 2010)

Murphy, Charles Cecil Rowe, *The History of the Suffolk Regiment 1914-1927* (London: 1928)

Nicholls, Jonathan, *Cheerful Sacrifice* (Barnsley: Pen & Sword, 2010)

Noble, Marjorie, *Marc Noble. A Memoir* (London: Country Life, 1918)

Oughton, Frederick, *Ace With One Eye. The Story of 'Mick' Mannock VC (*London: Frederick Muller Ltd, 1963)

Ponsonby, Frederick Edward Grey, Baron Sysonby, *The Grenadier guards in the Great War of 1914–1918* (London: Macmillan & Co. Ltd, 1920)

Preston, Diana, *Lusitania, An Epic Tragedy* (New York: Walker Publishing Company Inc., 2002)

Prior, Robin and Wilson, Trevor, *Command on the Western Front. The Military Career of Sir Henry Rawlinson 1914-1918* (Barnsley: Pen & Sword, 2004)

Repington, Mary, *Thanks for the Memory* (London: Constable, 1938)

Ribblesdale, Lord, *Charles Lister, Letters and Memoirs* (London: T. Fisher Unwin Ltd, 1917)

Richards, Frank, *Old Soldiers Never Die* (London, Faber & Faber, 1933)

Roberts, Richard, *Schroders: Merchants and Bankers* (Basingstoke: MacMillan, 1992_

Sackville, Charles, *Lord Worsley* (London: D.E. Dalton, 1924)

Sheppard, E.W., *The 9th Queen's Royal Lancers* (Aldershot: Gale & Polden Ltd, 1939)

Simkins, Peter, *Kitchener's Army* (Barnsley: Pen & Sword, 1988)

Snelling, Stephen: *The Naval VCs* (Stroud: Sutton, 2002)

Spence, Magnus: *Buried in his Uniform* (Unpublished, 2004)

Stone, Norman, *The Eastern Front, 1914–1917* (London: Penguin, 1998)

Thornton, Lt Col and Fraser, Pamela, *The Congreves* (London: John Murray, 1924)

Titchener-Barrett, Robert, *Eton and Harrow at Lord's* (London: Quiller Press, 1996)

Westcott, Arthur: *Life and Letters of Brooke Foss Westcott, Sometime Bishop of Durham* (London: MacMillian, 1905)

Whitton, Lt Col F.E., *History of the 40th Division* (Aldershot: Gale & Polden, 1926)

Wyrall, Everard, *The History of the Second Division, 1914-1918* (London: Thomas Nelson & Sons, 1921)

Wyrall, Everard, *The West Yorkshire Regiment in the War, 1914-1918* (London: John Lane, 1924)

Notes on Sources

The following constitutes the main sources consulted for each chapter. A comprehensive set of notes is available at www.alexandrachurchill.org.

IWM – Imperial War Museum
TNA – The National Archives
RAF – RAF Museum
ETON – Eton College Archives
MAG – Magdalen College, Oxford
HAR – Harvard, Cambridge, Massachusetts
NAM – National Army Museum

Introduction
Eton College Registers 1440–1919
Published lists of Etonians who fought in the Boer War, First World War and Second World War

'The Faces of Souls in Hell'
The papers of 2nd Lt Walter 'George' Fletcher
IWM Marden

'Shrapnel Monday'
Published memoirs of Lady Mary Garstin (later Mary Repington)
IWM Marden
Published memorial volume for Francis and Riversdale Grenfell, John Buchan
TNA War Diaries for 9th Lancers, 18th Hussars

'Our Little Band of Brothers'
Private papers of 2nd Lt The Hon. John Manners
Mons, Anzac and Kut – War memoirs of Aubrey Herbert
Fifteen Rounds Per Minute – Michael Craster

'God Won't Let those Devils Win'
Papers of 2nd Lt Walter 'George' Fletcher
Papers of 2nd Lt Reginald William Fletcher
Memorial volume for Lord Worsley by his father, the Earl of Yarborough
IWM Woodroffe
IWM Fleming

'To Die Would Be an Awfully Big Adventure'
J.M. Barrie and the Lost Boys – Andrew Birkin
Papers of 2nd Lt Walter 'George' Fletcher
RAF – Henderson
ETON – Haldane

'The New Argonauts'
Memorial volume to Lt Cmdr Patrick Shaw-Stewart by Ronald Knox
Memorial volume to The Hon. Charles Lister by his father, Lord Ribblesdale
Mons, Anzac and Kut – Aubrey Herbert
The Man who was Greenmantle – [—] Fitzherbert

'I Feel an Outcast to be Alive'
Family memoirs privately published by Lady Desborough
ETON – Durnford
Memorial volume to Captain Edward Kay-Shuttleworth published by his wife

'Till Berlin'
IWM – Schack-Sommer
Regimental history of the 18th Dragoner Regiment

'Pitifully Humorous In Its Imbecility'
Family memoirs published by the Countess of Wemyss
Memoirs of C.P. Blacker, edited and published by J. Blacker
'We Had Not Been Taught To Surrender'
Family memoirs published by the Countess of Wemyss
TNA – War Diaries of the Royal Gloucestershire Yeomanry Hussars
Regimental histories of the Gloucestershire and Worcestershire Hussars

'To Hugh or Blighty'
MAG – Papers of 2nd Lt Harry Cholmeley
Regimental histories of the Suffolk Regiment, as well as those of the 13th (Kensington)
    Battalion and the London Rifle Brigade
Peter Hart's volume on the Battle of the Somme was also invaluable

'The Metal is Gold and Tried in the Fire'
Private papers and memoir to Lt Marc Noble
Memorial volume to both General W.N. Congreve VC and Major W. La T. Congreve VC
Memorial volume to Captain Alexander D. Young-Herries

'The Gambler's Throw'
Private papers of Captain Henry Lancaster Nevill Dundas and memorial volume
   published by his father
Memoirs of Lord Chandos (Oliver Lyttelton)
Memoirs of C.P. Blacker, edited and published by J. Blacker

'The Abomination of Desolation'
Memorial volume to 2nd Lt Richard William Byrd Levett
Papers of Captain Henry Lancaster Nevill Dundas

'I Long to Fly'
Memorial volume to Captain The Hon. Eric Fox Pitt Lubbock by his mother, Lady
   Avebury
IWM James
IWM Hughes
HAR Papers of 2nd Lt Henry Richard Deighton Simpson

'Am I Going to Die?'
Papers of Captain Henry Lancaster Nevill Dundas and memorial volume published by
   his father
NAM – Ponsonby
Papers of 2nd Lt Logie Colin Leggatt
ETON – *Eton College Chronicle*
Memoirs of Lord Chandos

Setting the Tone
Papers of Captain Henry Lancaster Nevill Dundas and memorial volume published by
   his father
Papers of 2nd Lt Logie Colin Leggatt
Reminiscences of a Grenadier – E. Fryer
Divisional history of the Guards Division

'HELL'
Papers of Captain Henry Lancaster Nevill Dundas and memorial volume published by
   his father
Westminster Gazette, January 1918
Memorial volume to Lt Cmdr Patrick Shaw-Stewart by Ronald Knox
Divisional history of the 20th (Light) Division

'Shaking the Faith'
Papers of Captain Henry Lancaster Nevill Dundas and memorial volume published by
   his father

The Fifth Army General H. Gough
War memoirs of G. Lewis
Peter Hart's volume on 1918 was immensely valuable in understanding this complicated
    juncture of the war
Papers of Captain Ian Napier

'Every Shot is Telling'
Papers of Lt Cmdr G. Drummond
Lusitania – an Epic Tragedy – Diana Preston
The advice of *Lusitania* expert Eric Sauder was also invaluable
A Girl at Eton – Elizabeth Heygate
Castles of Steel – Robert K. Massie
The Naval VCs – Stephen Snelling

'The Light That Failed'
Papers of Captain Henry Lancaster Nevill Dundas and memorial volume published by
    his father
Divisional history of the Guards Division

'Folded in the Dark Cloud of Death'
Papers of Captain Henry Lancaster Nevill Dundas and memorial volume published by
    his father
Interviews with the family of Captain Henry Lancaster Nevill Dundas
Memoirs of Lord Chandos
Interviews with the family of 2nd Lt Reginald Mendel
TNA – Service files of 2nd Lt Reginald Mendel
ETON – *Eton College Chronicle*
Memoirs of C.P. Blacker, edited and published by J. Blacker

Index